WOMAN UNLIBERATED

WOMAN UNLIBERATED
Difficulties and Limitations in Changing Self

C. MARGARET HALL

Georgetown University

HEMISPHERE PUBLISHING CORPORATION
Washington   London

WOMEN UNLIBERATED: Difficulties and Limitations in Changing Self

Copyright © 1979 by Hemisphere Publishing Corporation. All rights reserved. Printed in the United States of America. No part of this publication may be reproduced, stored in a retrieval system, or transmitted, in any form or by any means, electronic, mechanical, photocopying, recording, or otherwise, without the prior written permission of the publisher.

1 2 3 4 5 6 7 8 9 0   L I L I   7 8 3 2 1 0 9 8

Library of Congress Cataloging in Publication Data

Hall, Constance Margaret.
   Woman unliberated.

   Bibliography: p.
   Includes index.
   1. Women—Psychology. 2. Feminism—United States.
3. Political participation. 4. Self-actualization
(Psychology) 5. Social role. I. Title.
HQ1206.H233   301.41'2   78-21874
ISBN 0-89116-097-3

To my mother and grandmothers

Contents

Preface xi

Acknowledgments xiii

---
1 NECESSITY OF POLITICAL ACTION 3

Political Action and Change 5
Political Action and Public Opinion 7
Political Action as Attention Getting 8
Scope of Political Action 11
Political Action, Rights and Responsibilities 13

---
2 WOMAN AS GOAL OF POLITICAL ACTION 17

Woman and Social Goals 18
Woman as Caught in a Dilemma 19
Enlightened Political Action 21
Personal Growth and Political Action 22
Extrapolitical Development of Woman and Political Action 23

3 SELFHOOD AND PERSONHOOD VERSUS MOTHERHOOD, SISTERHOOD, AND WOMANHOOD 29

Woman Is Whole 30
Dependencies 33
Awareness through Crisis 36
Feeling, Thinking, and Acting 38
Resistance from Others 40

4 WOMAN AND FAMILY 47

Family Contact 47
Intergenerational Influences 49
Spouse's Families 52
Immediate Pressures 54
Adaptiveness Hinders Growth 56

5 CHANGING WOMAN IN THE FAMILY 61

Interrelatedness and Change 62
Quality and Quantity of Contacts 64
From Reactivity to Respect 66
Child Development 68
Overresponsibility as Irresponsibility 70

6 ON SELLING SELF AT A SACRIFICE PRICE 75

Compromise as Sacrifice 76
Overresponsibility as Sacrifice 78

Investing in Self   79
Others' Expectations and Sacrifice   81
Just Price   83

7 SELF IS MORE THAN A SUM OF ROLES   89

"I" Transcends and Integrates Roles   90
Activity outside Roles   92
Integration of Personalized Roles   94
Layers of Self   95
Flexibility and Strength   98

8 ECONOMIC INDEPENDENCE AND BEING A SELF   103

Economic Adaptiveness   104
Economic and Emotional Dependence   106
Territoriality   107
Last Will and Testament   109
Material Needs   111

9 WOMAN IN THE HOME AND OUT   115

Family Influences   116
Shared Responsibilities   118
Boundaries of Self   120
Time and Energy   123
Limitations   126

10 AND THEY ALL LIVED HAPPILY EVER AFTER . . .   131

Happiness as Respect   133
Woman and Man   135
Continuous Growth   137
Autonomy and Security   139
From Pain to Fulfillment   141

APPENDIX: THE BOWEN FAMILY THEORY   147

Historical Development   150
Concepts   152
Applications   155
Systems Thinking   158
Implications   160

Bibliography   163

Index   165

Preface

Woman Unliberated is a personal statement as well as a synthesis of my professional research in human behavior and social relations. The ideas presented evolved from experiences, contacts, and readings that have been instrumental in changing my life. Discovering self and acting from my own increasingly integrated inner beliefs have enabled me to perceive myself and others differently. These new-found rich dimensions of my daily life provide a constant flow of new perspectives on reality.

Dr. Murray Bowen and the family systems theory he developed have contributed much toward the growth of my ability to clarify my personal and professional options beyond the usual rather limited traditional expectations for women. My professional effectiveness in working as researcher and therapist with a considerable number of families and women proved itself to be dependent on my ability to change self in relation to those who are emotionally closest to me. These different activities led me to believe that acts that make use of opportunities to be a self are more crucial to increasing the quality of new life and others' lives than liberation as currently defined by the women's movement. Perhaps the discovery of self and the personal fulfillment that results from more integrated activity by self can be meaningfully described as a "prepolitical" phase of liberation.

Although many goals of the women's movement are significant and necessary for effective individual and social change, a more personal awareness of self on the part of both women and men would most probably substantially enhance the success of large-scale political programs. I believe that I can contribute more to those who are emotionally close to me and to others in society by being a strong self than by playing conventional roles and conforming to traditional expectations, including active engagement in political movements.

My need to write this book stems in part from my dissatisfaction with much of the recent literature about women, and with mass media portrayal of women and the women's movement. In my opinion these reflections of public attitudes present a distorted view of human potential and focus on the more dehumanized aspects of personal and social change processes. I do not need to imitate either women or men if I act from self, although I may choose to participate in traditional female or male activities.

Woman Unliberated is also a product of personal and professional reflections, and as such it is biased in many ways. The fact that I choose to address myself to women more frequently and more directly than to men is not meant to suggest that the ideas used do not apply equally to men. The vital human need to develop self knows no sexual boundaries.

C. Margaret Hall

Acknowledgments

My deepest gratitude is for personal inspiration and constant challenges from my English and American families. I could not have conceived a book of this kind without the many glories and trials of an intensely rich family life.

My greatest professional indebtedness is to Murray Bowen, M.D., a Georgetown University colleague, who presented the core ideas of this book to me over the course of several years. I modified some of the propositions of the Bowen theory as they became part of my own life, but most of the concepts I use here are inextricably related to Bowen's contributions to the study of human behavior. I would be unable to appreciate self and others as fully without these particular perspectives.

Other colleagues and students at Georgetown University have encouraged my efforts to write *Woman Unliberated*. Members of the Department of Sociology as well as members of the staff at the Family Center, Department of Psychiatry, Georgetown Medical Center, have given much unwitting guidance to my project. The families and staff I worked with at Frederick Community Mental Health Services in Maryland also provided unfailing sources of ideas and experiences.

A Georgetown colleague, Brenda Broz Eddy, and a writer friend, Pam Ginsbach, played critical parts in launching my manuscript. Pam Ginsbach was particularly adept at translating some of my academic and theoretical terms into more palatable form.

Pat McMahon gave me detailed comments and suggestions on early and late drafts of *Woman Unliberated*. Without her skillful and timely assistance many of my discussion points would be less intelligible. The ideas of Marian Fetter, David Harris, Mary Jane Kubler, Rick Peterson, and Ann Richardson were also most useful in shaping my final manuscript.

Samantha Hawkins and Ellen Dorosh undertook the painstaking work of typing the manuscript, which kept the book alive at all stages of development. William Begell, president of Hemisphere Publishing Corporation, gave constructive encouragement in the later stages of completion of *Woman Unliberated*. It is indeed difficult to express my gratitude adequately for all these contributions and support.

Chapter 1

Necessity of Political Action

Since the breakdown of kinship in ancient Greek society, and throughout the modernization of Western society, daily life has been increasingly influenced by political policies and controls. I am given a political shape that reflects the historical time I live in. Individual political shapes vary considerably from place to place and generation to generation, and they are essentially the product of legislative measures rather than of personal definitions or actions.

Man, woman, and child are given their own particular political shapes. The allocation of these kinds of boundaries may be viewed as a prerequisite for the existence of modern societies. In our present-day society the range of possible political shapes has become a concern of various interest groups and political action agencies. Groups that offer specific political shapes to their members compete with each other over which can offer the most influential or powerful political shape. For example, the American Medical Association can give its members more power and influence in society at large than the American Sociological Association can give.

One assumption frequently made about such contests for advantageous political shapes is that one's political boundary is the most essential characteristic of one's being and actions. Although this description of an individual's life situation may be accurate where extreme measures of coercive political control are exercised, in many Western societies there is sufficient ambiguity or flexibility in existing legal structures to allow an individual to do other than merely conform to political pressures.

Optimally, my available options will allow me to carve out a shape for myself that goes beyond the conventional confines of my delegated political shape. My action is ultimately limited by the laws of the society in which I live, but these laws need not necessarily cramp my daily existence or strongly influence the many decisions I must make. Rather than become a victim of circumstances, I can choose to be an opportunist in planning my activities. Even though my freedom to act is relative and limited by others' rights and responsibilities, I can be effective if I perceive more, not fewer, options than actually exist. Narrowing my horizons is not conducive to imaginative and resourceful activity.

In order to describe and define my human condition objectively, I must examine both my cultural heritage and my evolutionary development. I am so trapped in the subjective aspects of my historical conditioning, however, that it is extremely difficult for me to be objective about my own nature. Seeing myself for what I am may be one of the greatest challenges I can face and one of the most difficult tasks I can undertake. The consequences of my being human may be faced voluntarily or involuntarily, depending on particular problems or circumstances. However uncomfortable this process of confrontation may be, I cannot afford to deny the reality of these issues.

Although I live in and depend on political networks, there are many other significant and influential dimensions of my existence. Political measures are influential in shaping my behavior, but my most intimate emotional dependencies are the essence of my life. I am freer to choose a more or a less meaningful life when meaning is not legislated. I must decide what is meaningful to me. I cannot use others' beliefs without losing self.

POLITICAL ACTION AND CHANGE

Although political action is generally organized explicitly to bring about specific changes in society, most members of society automatically resist innovation, and the status quo is more likely to be maintained than altered by the planned programs. Even though political means are widely recognized as effective channels of social change, in reality even minimal modifications of existing conditions are frequently impossible or extremely difficult to achieve. Most of the roadblocks to effective social and political change may be emotional pressures and resistance, but these influences are usually defined in exclusively political terms.

If political action can become more effective, legal innovations may eventually modify widely held attitudes and values. Changes that are usually viewed as being "within" me may only be possible if they are accompanied by specific conditions in the wider society. A chain of events appears to be set in motion whereby external controls and restraints modify my behavior, and my changed behavior then modifies my beliefs. However, I can modify some of my own beliefs without external conditions being changed. I cannot wait for broad structural changes to precipitate my own inner changes, although inner change will be enhanced by some kinds of external changes.

In contrast to long-term changes in belief, short-term behavior changes are relatively easy to accomplish through the application of political measures. Restrictions on particular kinds of behavior may be effectively enforced for a brief period, but these modifications generally cannot be maintained for long periods of time.

In instances where political action is not able to bring about real change, or where political action has been intentionally organized to inhibit change processes, the lack of movement may become a catalyst in precipitating alternative change processes. From what may be a more objective viewpoint, political action appears to be merely one vehicle of social change. This is not a widely held belief, however, and political action continues to be recognized as the most effective means of social change.

Popular opinion also suggests that political action is the only force sufficiently powerful to modify traditional institutions. Political action is thought of as the primary agent in facilitating changes for woman in society. For example, I am supposed to be able to participate more freely in occupational, educational, economic, and political activities as a consequence of effective political action. When political programs cannot or do not change my legal status and socially recognized position in society, however, I must find alternative ways of accomplishing these essential changes. Although I must live with my political shape, I need not necessarily be bound by it. My political shape need not be the strongest influence in my daily life. There are alternative ways to change self and go beyond my political shape within the legal framework of society.

If I emphasize only the role of political factors in personal and social change, my awareness of the many complex influences underlying these phenomena will be dimmed. I cannot ignore my political status, however. I must know the degree to which my life is controlled and defined by political institutions so that I can sculpt my personal boundaries and go beyond political or legal confinements where my responsibility and integrity demand this.

POLITICAL ACTION AND PUBLIC OPINION

Public opinion about woman cannot be changed in a short period of time. Although political action may eventually play an important part in changing general attitudes, political action alone does not appear to be sufficient to bring about a decisive modification of public opinion. Personal beliefs are influenced by a complex variety of factors that go beyond what we conventionally describe in political terms.

Some critical questions must be considered in relation to modifying public opinion: Whose attitudes will change most readily? Whose attitudes should be changed? How long will it take for a particular opinion change to be accomplished? How can attitudes be changed most productively? What are the consequences of changing specific attitudes and opinions?

When these concerns can be addressed more objectively, political programs may be viewed as a relatively minor part of a sequence of events that culminates in attitude and opinion change in society. Legal changes are merely one phase or aspect of a cycle of broader change processes. My engagement in political action may bring about changes in my own and others' attitudes and opinions, however, even though the particular political goals of my efforts are not accomplished. The experience of political participation, rather than its consequences, may be a decisive influence on such changes.

If I am not dependent on political action to define self,

I need not wait for specific political changes to heighten my awareness of self or modify my functioning position in society. For example, I can change my response to others' punitive sanctions when I choose not to conform to traditional expectations. I cannot afford to wait for particular legislative measures to come into effect before I take this action.

I am encouraged to fight many battles to become politically liberated. The issues I am invited to engage in, however, are frequently not those which will contribute most usefully to my being a person in my own right. If I act as a responsible self instead of engaging in socially defined political action, I will eventually be able to influence others by my action and may precipitate further changes in society. In contrast to self-generated change processes, political action cannot guarantee personal or social change.

A woman or man is primarily a person rather than a member of a particular sex. Personhood is important to an individual and to the whole society. My efforts to be a self may ultimately be more radical or more innovative than are my attempts to become politically liberated. As a liberated woman I may find that I merely duplicate the action of other liberated women or play roles that duplicate male activities. The degree of togetherness necessary for concerted political action frequently brings about a condition where self is annihilated in the process of working toward specific practical goals, however much these goals may be viewed as components of personal growth.

POLITICAL ACTION AS ATTENTION GETTING

To the extent that political action provides me with an opportunity to define self, it is a pragmatic means of facilitating my growth and changing my position in society. A consciousness of the wide range of shared concerns of woman and man must be a prerequisite for effective political, legal, and attitude change, however. Political action directed exclusively to one or the other group may create imbalance in the degree of necessary interdependence between woman and man. The increased togetherness of woman with woman that occurs when woman engages in political activity for self may polarize woman and man and adversely affect the maturation of their interdependence. The effectiveness of motivation and moves to change self do not depend on the political action of others. I endanger self by relying on woman to define my responsibilities.

Within these limitations of political action as an agent of change, political programs may serve a valuable function as attention-getting devices for woman and man. For example, I may take for granted that woman's interests are protected and well represented in society until I am shown that woman is discriminated against in a particular profession. Woman's participation in legislative procedures may also provide me with models of thinking and action responses to restrictive practices in general.

The attention-getting qualities of political action can provide invaluable inspiration. My immediate response to political activity I admire will generally be to imitate or to participate in that action. If I am to sustain an awareness of my own interests throughout the impact of this inspiration, however, I may have to curb my inclination to be drawn into the political activity in order to be sure that I continue to invest my attention and energy in my own responsible goals or objectives. Optimally, I should appreciate political action for its attention-getting capacities and benefit from this dividend without sacrificing my own responsibilities. I cannot give way to my automatic tendencies to deny the existence of my own separate interests and to doggedly follow others without losing self in my political involvement.

Political action may credibly be considered as one of the most potent attention-getting devices in modern mass society. The media report many news items related to the participation of woman in political movements, and this information attracts the attention of both woman and man. For individual or social change to be effective and productive, the interest of both woman and man must be focused on relationship issues.

My political activity may serve as an attention-getting device to members of my family. My genuine interest in specific issues related to woman and my political action for woman may heighten the awareness of my spouse, children, and parents. The heightened awareness of members of my family generally benefits all concerned. An enhanced ability to make objective observations about human interaction can be applied to a variety of circumstances by both woman and man. If my engagement in political action does not prove itself to be useful as an attention-getting device, however, my involvement may have a deleterious effect on my growth and development.

If I reactively invest most of my feelings and energy in political action, I risk denying my dependence on my family and cutting off self from emotionally significant others. I can change self effectively only when I am able to maintain meaningful contact with members of my family. My overinvestment in political activity encourages my denial of needs and responsibilities that go beyond the political activity I am engaged in. One of the most significant outcomes of this situation is that I transfer my emotional dependency from my family to a political group and, predictably, delay my growth and maturation.

Political action is limited in its capacity to change self

and to initiate broad social changes. Its usefulness as an attention-getting device is restricted. Insofar as political action heightens general awareness of dominance and adaptiveness in human relationships, political action is important. Insofar as political action demands and receives an inordinate degree of commitment and involvement, its effects can be harmful for participants in the political action and for those who are emotionally close to the participants.

SCOPE OF POLITICAL ACTION

Political action that is successful in changing the position of woman modifies all other relationships in society. The impact of programs or movements on behalf of woman may not, in fact, be felt most directly by woman. Legislation that prevents occupational discrimination against woman may affect man or child as much as or more than it affects woman, for example. Political action for woman also generally heightens awareness of woman's concerns, rather than awareness of the concerns of man or child. Feelings may easily become polarized when only one group in society achieves heightened awareness of its specific concerns.

Can woman define her interests through political action? Can the interests of groups related to woman be defined through political action? Can political action facilitate the effectiveness of my life planning, growth, and development? Although political action may purport to respond to my basic needs, it cannot be meaningfully sensitive to the complex array of my personal concerns. The content and scope of any political program must necessarily be very general. It is unrealistic to think of political action as an effective means to promote my individuation as a self. Even enlightened political action remains limited in its capacity to respond to my own goals and needs. Furthermore, although political action may set the stage for change, it cannot guarantee that real change will take place. Political measures may be used to structure part of a situation, but they cannot necessarily initiate change processes. They may serve to bring about some modifications in behavior, but political action alone will be insufficient to change attitudes and beliefs.

A political system is pervasive and potentially omnipresent in society. Although a hypothetical legal equality of individuals may be widely recognized and accepted, such a universalistic and general focus may be evidence of a lack of appreciation of the intrinsic uniqueness of individuals. My personal freedom is not merely one of the possible outcomes of a particular political movement. My freedom is perhaps more accurately described as a culmination of complex individuating emotional processes than as a consequence of specific strategic political maneuvers. Can an unliberated woman be more alive and more of a self than is a woman who is liberated? Can an unliberated woman be a mature and more effective member of society than is a liberated woman? Who is liberated? What am I liberated from? What am I before I am liberated? Can liberation be self-defeating?

Political and legal changes may not be significantly instrumental in my broader growth and development. Although political and legal activity related to the woman's movement may create a feasible structure for some aspects of my growth and development, these situational possibilities are insufficient conditions for my more complete and more effective self-actualization. I am responsible for my own choices and I must make an extraordinarily large number of difficult and complicated decisions if I am to grow as a self. Integrated political action cannot account for myriad circumstances and respond effectively to their different combinations. Furthermore, I cannot renege my responsibilities to political authority or influence if I am to strengthen self. I will ultimately be freer if I am not very dependent on a political system for protection and direction. Freedom from political influence improves the quality of my life as does freedom from pressure and expectations related to traditional roles.

POLITICAL ACTION, RIGHTS, AND RESPONSIBILITIES

Although a political system may define and guarantee a certain number of human rights, it cannot give a clear indication of what individual responsibilities are. One characteristic of my social existence, however, is that I have unique responsibilities that are vitally important to both self and society. To some extent my responsibilities are dependent on my awareness of self and on my ability to put my thoughts into action. From a social perspective, the overall development of society may depend more on the combined creative expression of unique individual responsibilities than on combined similarities in behavior. The capacity of political action to promote welfare and progress is limited, as political measures necessarily focus on the most general conditions in society.

Some political and legal action on behalf of woman in society is necessary to create or maintain more egalitarian relationships. Political and legal aspects of my formal position in society are integral parts of my overall performance and level of functioning in relation to others. Freedom is not largely a political or legal aspect of my existence, however. My ability to act more or less freely as a self is a product of many complex emotional processes. When I behave maturely and consider the options available to me, I am able to control some of the dictates of my automatic animal reactions and responses.

Perhaps I will contribute more toward social change if I see myself as a person than if I view self as a political agent. The liberation movements, in spite of their great diversity, frequently overemphasize the importance of political measures for change. This restricted perspective tends to generate more stereotypes of woman and more rigid expectaions for her behavior. My plans for changing self must be self-focused rather than based on others' behavior if they are to be productive for me and for others.

Although political action may protect my individual rights to some extent, political action cannot define my responsibilities without undermining some of my freedom and integrity. I am more responsible for self when I decide on a particular course of action than when I allow others to define my options. It is only through assuming my responsibility for self that I can be free. Even though political action may be necessary for woman's ultimate or general well-being, I must also carve out my freedom in personal ways.

Chapter 2

Woman as Goal of Political Action

In order to evaluate the strengths or weaknesses of political programs, the capacity of society-wide legislative measures to respond effectively to the real interests of individual members of a specific group or members of related groups must be questioned. If woman's interests and needs are a primary focus for political action, the interests and needs of members of other groups may not be met satisfactorily. However, legislative responsiveness to general pervasive interests and needs is necessary for the preservation of society. The survival of the species is more salient for general social well-being than is individual survival.

Although political measures may define an adequate "life-space" for woman, it is not possible to create a "life-pattern" for woman through political means alone. Without being repressive in some ways, political action cannot provide clear directives for living. Most of my personal needs cannot be satisfied by legislation or political action. Only I can be the judge of what I need or want in order to live my life decisively and responsibly. Without losing freedom, I cannot depend on a political system to legislate my responsibilities.

Some of my personal needs can be met by legislation, but political action essentially provides only the groundwork for my creation of self. Although a few effective political measures may be necessary conditions for my personal development, they alone cannot bring about these changes. I must assume responsibility for self. If I delegate this vital need to any form of political machinery, I will lose self.

WOMAN AND SOCIAL GOALS

Political programs inevitably contain irreconcilable contradictions if they try to focus on both social and individual goals. These inconsistencies may impede woman in several vital respects, although the intrinsic inadequacies of political action may not be irreparably detrimental to woman. However, my growth and development appear to be more influenced and conditioned by my position in my family than by my position in a legal-political network. The quality of my participation in political, work, religious, or friendship systems is less significant in my life than is the quality of my participation in my family.

A description of my vital needs in relation to those who are emotionally closest to me produces an alternate view of self to the more conventional legal-political characteristics of status. A family systems perspective suggests that self is a product or meeting point of emotional forces within a relationship network of intimate others. One extension of this definition of self is that the number and nature of personal needs woman or man has is thought to depend on the degree of intensity of emotional interdependencies in the family system.

Political programs cannot usually deal effectively with personal and emotional issues. Those who are in leadership positions in society are themselves emotionally dependent beings, and they are frequently unable to be even minimally objective about their own or others' needs. In some societies, legislation or political action that would directly affect families is forbidden by custom and mores, in order to protect and preserve what is believed to be the moral right of privacy. Family is frequently considered to be an area of privacy for all, regardless of sex or age. In many societies, traditional models of family relationships cannot be modified by political or legislative policies so that privacy may be preserved.

Another limitation of political action presents itself when the ethic of family privacy is considered together with individual and social needs. Emotional needs do not usually fall within the scope of political and legislative action. Emotional interdependency, perhaps the core of relationships of superordination and subordination, is generally not a legitimate subject for governmental concern except where it concerns societal survival. These kinds of issues are generally recognized and dealt with only in small groups, being virtually ignored by large-scale political action and policy. Much of my intimate and everyday life is concealed from political direction and legislation.

WOMAN AS CAUGHT IN A DILEMMA

I am caught in the dilemma of having unmet personal needs that cannot be satisfied by past, present, or future political action. I cannot depend on political measures in order to grow and develop, and yet my growth and development are necessary for my long-term survival. I must recognize my emotional dependence in order to become more independent in my intimate relationships through action. These are the entrapments and freedoms I must deal with.

Many of the characteristics of woman's dilemma are shared by underprivileged and minority groups. Members of these groups, as well as woman, are overly adaptive and are unable to pull up from their dependent functioning. Their habitually subservient and powerless positions in society are maintained by those who have more advantageous functioning positions.

The factors that contribute to the persistence and enhancement of inequalities in society are not solely those we generally describe as political. Several influential predisposing conditions are inherent in the emotional dependencies and patterns of interaction between different groups in society. The most primitive and most deep-seated aspects of human behavior are emotional. Many of the qualities conventionally considered to be components of political pressures may be more accurately thought of as components of emotional fields in human relationships. It is perhaps the very binding nature of emotional forces in any given "political" situation that makes it difficult for members of disadvantaged groups to surface from conditions of overdependency and act for self. Individuals and groups who have impaired functioning positions have been "projected on" or scapegoated by dominant others as a consequence of the conflicts and unresolved emotional issues existing in and among a variety of groups in the same society.

Underfunctioning in an overdependent scapegoated group is not easily altered. Patterns of behavior in the more independent powerful groups must generally be modified before significant change in the scapegoated group is observable. If behavior in this dependent group is modified, however, related groups will predictably demand that the group return to its former dependent position. This sequence of events illustrates that improvement in functioning in a previously underfunctioning group threatens all who are in some way related to that group. Perhaps changing emotional relationships is the greatest challenge human beings face, especially as most behavior is based on or affected by the interplay of emotional networks and processes. I am an emotionally dependent being and actor.

ENLIGHTENED POLITICAL ACTION

When woman can define herself and her goals, enlightened political action may be able to approach these goals. An important responsibility for initiating enlightened political action to meet woman's needs rests with woman herself.

The definition or description of woman's personal goals may include identifying individual needs. Goals and needs are usually thought of in terms of social expectations, rather than in relation to what those concerned really believe their own goals or needs are. Only when actual and realistic objectives are specified, however, can political programs become more effective.

Planned and integrated political action is more enlightened than is an incoherent or disjointed series of legislative moves composed of automatic responses to woman's short-term emotional demands. These kinds of immediate demands are generally manifestations of group process rather than of representative personal goals. Political action that responds to short-term emotional demands and pressures and reinforces existing emotional dependencies will predictably be ineffective. Consistent long-range plans demand much conscious effort, and consequently their effectiveness is not as likely to be neutralized or negated by inner inconsistencies and contradictions as are superficial short-range plans. Political action, although intrinsically limited in its potential for bringing about real change, can be more enlightened and more effective than current short-term legislative measures suggest.

PERSONAL GROWTH AND POLITICAL ACTION

Political action should optimally create conditions conducive to increased self-awareness. Unless political action has the explicit and implicit objectives of creating conditions for my growth and development, inequalities in existing structures will tend to become increasingly institutionalized. Furthermore, the pace of institutionalization may accelerate, and the discrepancies between social and personal goals and responsibilities may increase. Political action that does not create conditions for personal growth and development contributes to alienation by increasing levels of anxiety and dysfunctioning in society at large. Programs designed to control discrimination against woman in particular occupations, for example, may generate more tensions than they create freedom for woman. Liberation can not be legislated.

My personal growth and development is largely a consequence of inner change and motivation, although I am unable to define myself outside a relationship context. Political action at best "sets the stage" for my inner growth and development, and at the same time suggests where I may surpass the confines of a particular program. I am my own responsibility, however, and my growth will be largely prepolitical in its first expression or uninfluenced by political measures.

Political action in the United States is generally directed toward modifying personal and family relationships only when behavior is unacceptable to family members or to the wider community. It is in the context of my family, however, that most of my intimate vital needs are met. Also, my family of origin or extended family is an effective arena for initiating changes of self, by virtue of its being the most interdependent relationship network I participate in. My personal growth will be most challenged in an arena of this kind, just as my personal growth may be most impaired in this context.

In contrast to my family, a political system is markedly ineffective as a setting for my personal growth and development. A political system, like a work system, can easily replace its members and effectively exclude those who attempt to make changes in their positions in the group. Although both political and work systems may be thought of as emotional systems to some extent, these groups present their members with a restricted range of opportunities and challenges for change. Political and work systems also may not last sufficiently long to allow effective change by their members. Dealing with my connectedness with my family is a necessary and perhaps a sufficient condition of my personal growth.

EXTRAPOLITICAL DEVELOPMENT OF WOMAN AND POLITICAL ACTION

Political action may be of secondary or even incidental importance in promoting changes in woman's position in society. Although political action can contribute toward the development of my potential, it cannot guarantee my growth, nor is it the most significant prerequisite for change in self.

Political action may be more effective as an instrument of change when I participate directly in particular programs. Through my involvement I come to rely more on my efforts and perceptions than on the achievements and perceptions of others. My political involvement is inevitably accompanied by "extrapolitical" growth and development if I accomplish a real change of self in this context. One characteristic of my extrapolitical growth is the maturation of self that evolves through diversified contacts with members of my family. Unless this kind of extrapolitical development occurs, there is a possibility that political action that appears to be enlightened could increase my irresponsibility rather than promote my responsibility for self.

The extrapolitical growth and development of man is an integral part of woman's realization of her potential. Although many changes for man will automatically follow the patterns of woman's improved functioning position, an increase in man's self-awareness and planned action for his goals could accelerate and improve the quality of some of woman's changes.

An examination of human relationships indicates that in no way can woman's potential be realized through impinging on others or by manipulating them. Groups directly affected by woman's changing positions include man, child, and the elderly. Woman cannot make effective gains for self at the expense of members of these groups, just as members of these groups cannot make effective changes in self at the expense of woman.

The issues of whether woman is or should be liberated or unliberated provoke many questions. Much debate about the political, cultural, or sexual aspects of these concerns may have an unproductive outcome. Polarization through discussion will not promote inspired mutual growth and development. Perhaps one of the most significant biological processes among human beings is dependency in emotional relationships. This view emphasizes the importance of shared primitive aspects of human behavior for both woman and man rather than physiological differences between woman and man. Woman and man are equally interdependent and equally in need of extrapolitical development of self in the context of intimate relationships.

Chapter 3

Selfhood and Personhood versus Motherhood, Sisterhood, and Womanhood ─────

When I recognize the limited influence of political action on my life, I am more likely to be able to turn to my own resources imaginatively and develop personal strengths. A first step in my inner growth is to go beyond seeing and thinking of myself as a player of roles. *Sisterhood, motherhood,* and *womanhood* describe roles that tend to be segmented and contradictory. If I habitually base my behavior on these relationship models, I will be a complement to others and will be unable to be myself easily or effectively. Tired and trite references to my spouse as my "better half" illustrate the established tradition of perceiving spouses as parts of each other. However, if I allow myself to be half a person, I sacrifice my uniqueness and integrity. Each spouse must act as a complete person in order to contribute to the other and to those outside the marital relationship.

Playing stereotype roles and conforming to others' expectations will deaden my spirit. If I do this I lose self in my own eyes and in the view of family members and those who are emotionally close to me. Relationships founded on traditional norms frequently become predictable to a point of dullness. The relationships rigidify as patterns of behavior are repeated. Each party in these relationships loses credibility as a "real" person. If I am to be an effective mother, I must allow myself to be an approachable and imperfect human being rather than an omnipotent, nurturing caretaker, which some of our cultural images and norms suggest and at times dictate. A mature relationship must be sufficiently flexible to cope with and benefit from deviations from traditionally prescribed behavior.

WOMAN IS WHOLE

Selfhood and *personhood* are used here to describe consistently integrated behavior that goes beyond specific roles and expectations and yet partially incorporates conventional roles and expectations. Selfhood and personhood transcend political definitions of individual rights and responsibilities. Although sensitive to some of my concerns, the woman's movement may disregard a number of my personal needs by typecasting me as a "sister" or, by implication, as a "superwoman." Although I may succeed in shaking off some of the traditional influences on my behavior, I will have a strong inclination merely to exchange one set of restrictive roles for another. I can lose self either if I am overly adaptive as a wife or if I am overly dominant in a work setting. When I move from one role to another or from one functioning position to the reverse functioning position, I do not change self or realize my potential as a person. These shifts merely modify the appearance of my continued adaptiveness.

My political "liberation" may be no more than a transfer of my dependence on my family to the woman's movement. Participation in political action may in fact hinder my development of self. I can be sure that my awareness of self will be heightened and my behavior modified only when I act differently in my family. I value self more and contribute more to others when I refuse to transfer my dependence on my family to other groups or settings. When I act from my own beliefs rather than from particular political ideologies, I develop self. I can only contribute my own values to the wider society if my contribution is to have a constructive impact on others. I cannot imitate or buy into others' beliefs and at the same time make optimal contributions to them.

The opening up of new employment opportunities for woman has resulted in a variety of personal and legislative changes. However, laws that allow discrimination against me in employment or in other social settings may not restrict much of my freedom to be a person. My experience of hiring or on-the-job prejudice against me as a woman may not be the first awareness I have of my limited options. Meeting discrimination of this kind is frequently an integral part of a later stage in my development of self. I cannot begin to make decisions about whether or not to take a job or return to school unless I have some degree of self-awareness and have identified a few personal goals. These initial stages in becoming a self may be thought of as a prepolitical phase of liberation. I behave as a self when I can effectively integrate my day-to-day activities with my own selected long-range goals and beliefs. This complex, continuing process may or may not include employment or confrontation with legal discrimination.

The terms *motherhood* and *sisterhood* define specific relationships. An emphasis on these relationship terms suggests that I cannot be a person without another's response. However, if I restrict my behavior to playing relationship roles for long periods of time, I will eventually corrode my sense of self. I am a self when I decide to accept relationship roles as only part of my life plan. I may decide to conform with many aspects of the role of being a traditional mother and at the same time be an effective mother. If I allow others to impose their expectations for a mother on me, however, I will not be an effective mother. I must selectively determine my behavior as a mother as much as possible. This choice may involve discarding others' more traditional beliefs, as I consider that they would inhibit my actions and development as an integrated self. I must reach beyond stereotype relationships in order to be a self.

When I can delineate others' expectations and stay out of some of the "traps" for self in traditional roles, I will be able to value self more positively than when I allow myself to remain or get caught in these traps. I am not an unfulfilled woman if my sense of joy is uninfluenced by seeing floors sparkle with cleanliness or by smelling freshly laundered clothes. If I take genuine pride in shimmering tiles and spotless laundry, however, I am not less of a woman. I must evaluate responsibly both what society expects of me and what I expect of myself. My perception of each set of expectations is strongly influenced by my beliefs. Before I can act for self, I must be aware of at least some of my own beliefs.

With some effort I can discover a few genuine positive characteristics about myself. If I focus on these attributes, I can gradually substitute some of my strengths for my weaker personal qualities. I need not emphasize limiting my negative tendencies. I can benefit more from discovering what I can do well and concentrating on these activities than from giving my attention to what I do not really choose to do. When I select my own behavior options I become more of a person and, consequently, more of a mother or more of a wife. By acting as a self I add important modifications to the conventional roles of mother or wife.

Sisterhood, motherhood, and womanhood may be important aspects of my being a person. If I think of myself only as sister, mother, or woman, however, I can easily lose contact with my vital wholeness. These relationship-based roles may become all-important, and I may find that I must strain myself to fit into the specific patterns of expectations related to these roles. If conventional models of behavior are not compatible with my beliefs, it is essential that I do not try to imitate them. I can annihilate self with efforts to please others. I must reflect on the range of options available to me and decide who I am and what I want to do. Undue or persistent compromise of self will result in loss of self.

DEPENDENCIES

All human beings must ultimately depend on others for their existence and fulfillment, especially on family members or on intimate relationships that have continued through time and will persist in the future. This need may be as crucial to individual survival as the more recognized and more immediate needs for water, food, and air. Although the consequences of my not recognizing my emotional dependency on others are perhaps not as visible or essential for my physical well-being as the deprivation of food or water, my acknowledgment of my need for emotional relatedness may be a critical component of my existence. I may not be immediately aware of the negative consequences of my not having personally meaningful experiences on a day-to-day basis, but emotional dependencies will gradually prove themselves to be essential to my development as a person. I cannot deny this need for others over a long period of time without impairing self and others.

If selfhood or personhood is to be achieved, personal contacts with family members and emotionally significant others must be increased and diversified rather than decreased and intensified. In recent years there has been a growing estrangement between different generations. One typical pattern of behavior is that young people leave their nuclear family of origin and live a considerable distance from parents and grandparents. This geographical separation often creates or increases emotional distance between family members. The loss of frequent contact and meaningful intimacy between generations appears to threaten the stability and viability of U.S. families more than other trends. The combination of geographical distance and emotional estrangement between family members rigidifies the vitality of this intimate relationship network.

Overindependence is essentially a denial of dependency. Young adults frequently leave or cut off their relationship with their parents and relatives in order to prove, ineffectively, that they are mature individuals. Although I may think I am more self-sufficient if I declare my independence from my family, I deceive myself. If I recognize the necessity of maintaining family ties while at the same time refusing to allow myself to be trapped by them, I have a greater opportunity to be my own self than if I deny the existence or importance of these vital relationships. If I am married, the need for contact with my family of origin may appear to be less important than if I am single. Through my marriage I create a complex network of alternative relationships in which to invest my feelings. The links with my parents and other relatives may be ignored more easily if I am married than if I am not married. My spouse and children generally have more visible emotional demands or needs than my parents, and my intense involvement in my immediate nuclear family may hide my continuing dependence on my parents and siblings. My need for meaningful contact and exchanges with my family of origin may not surface until a crisis in my nuclear family presents itself.

I have been programmed to be very dependent on my

parents and spouse. In order to deal with some of the inevitable consequences of this overdependency, I cannot reactively deny or minimize the intensity of my relationship with them and their pervasive influence on my behavior. I may even marry to please or displease my parents. When I behave in order to please or displease emotionally significant others, I express my overdependency on them. I am more of a self when I am less eager to conform with or rebel against parental expectations.

As a woman my close bond with my mother is often understated or not recognized as a continuing strong influence in my life. Even though I may not wish to acknowledge this influence, my relationship with my mother frequently serves as a model for my relationships with other women. When I am able to act as a self with my mother, I am more able to be a self with others. If I do not allow myself to be dependent on my parents, my spouse, or my children, I may transfer my need for dependency to political, religious, or social groups. My participation in these groups will intensify to the extent that I am emotionally cut off from intimate others. For example, wearing trendy fashions and partying constantly may indicate intense group participation in the social life of singles.

If I am separated or divorced, I may automatically reactivate my dependency on my family of origin as I break away from my spouse. To the extent that my marital relationship was overly burdened with anxiety, expectations, and other feelings, my separation or divorce may have been precipitated by a lack of contact with my family of origin. In spite of physical distance, some of my feelings will continue to be invested in my separated or divorced spouse, and I may find that it is as difficult to have a mature divorce as it is to have a mature marriage.

Distinctive patterns of interaction tend to be repeated

in different generations of my family. The age when my first child is born and the spacing of subsequent births may be identical with or strikingly similar to patterns manifested by other women in several generations of my family, for example. I may prefer to think that I have many choices to make in my life, but it is perhaps not coincidental that I married at the same age that my mother was when she married, had my first child at the same age that my mother was when she had her first child, and gave birth to as many children as my mother's mother. My deep-seated emotional behavior may be much more imitative and repetitive than I would like to believe.

To achieve selfhood and personhood, maintaining relationships with my siblings is not as essential as maintaining contact with my parents. My bonds with each parent and my parents' relationship with each other make up the most vital original triangle of all my relationship systems.

The ties between my parents and myself may become more charged with feelings when I bring potential spouses into my life. My male friends are frequently similar to or markedly different from my father or other important male relatives. The more dependent I am on my father, the more likely I am to select a spouse who is either similar to or markedly different from my father. If I have a large family of origin, the degree of dependency I have on my brothers and sisters may to some extent decrease the intensity of my bond with my father. Contact with my extended family can also reduce the intensity of my nuclear dependencies and contribute toward my selfhood and personhood.

AWARENESS THROUGH CRISIS

Awareness of myself as a person and awareness of the extent of my dependency on members of my family may seem unimportant to me unless I have tried to deal with crises in my life. Stresses in my intimate relationships are usually painful or frightening. My growth and maturation necessitate readjustment in my personal life, which is characterized by discomfort. My growth is neither open-ended nor easy to accomplish.

I will react to a crisis with attempts to neutralize or run away from the pain involved. Even though I may know intellectually that the rewards resulting from growing through the pain will be invaluable, I also soon realize that I will have to endure considerable stress in order to make even the smallest changes in self.

It is extremely difficult to accomplish anything other than superficial changes in the level of my functioning. I can change my job or change my spouse more easily than I can change myself. I cannot become more tolerant in my behavior or more selective in what I choose to do without engaging in exhaustingly painful and demanding inner deliberations. In changing self, the tensions created between self and others are so difficult to cope with that I will probably pay lip service to change and at the same time resist modifying my own biased attitudes and beliefs about self and others. Dramatic reorganizations of my external surroundings or of the composition of my social relationships are easier to accomplish than is acting as a self. I must be persistently courageous if I wish to examine my day-to-day behavior objectively.

A crisis or turning point in my life is a propitious time to initiate or continue efforts to change self. Personal traumas of this kind include the death of a person who is emotionally close to me or the loss of my job, for example. I do more fundamental growing during stress periods than when I remain unchallenged by congenial circumstances. A crisis produces conditions that heighten my realization of the acuteness of my needs for meaningful contact with intimate others. To illustrate this process in a different context, psychotherapy and its subsequent effectiveness are generally precipitated by crisis conditions in a given relationship system. It is only when I can observe and specify which personal dependencies are difficult for me to cope with that I can begin to modify my behavior.

Changing self is not an immediately satisfying experience. The pain associated with the change and the predictably negative reactions of others to my change preclude this possibility. Perhaps some parallels may be tentatively drawn between my changing self and a religious conversion. Religious conversion and changing self both involve sustained deliberation and an eventual shift in inner beliefs. Religious conversion is generally a more final and rigid shift in personal beliefs and values than is change in self, however, which optimally includes maintaining a degree of flexibility in beliefs and values. Unlike change of self, religious conversion does not necessarily entail continued efforts to question and modify beliefs and behavior. Acceptance of a particular dogma may restrict, rather than broaden, my belief system. Although my religious conversion may be a part of my change of self, the depth and scope of my ultimate change of self goes beyond what is conventionally thought of as the domain of religious concerns.

FEELING, THINKING, AND ACTING

An important aspect of my achieving self-awareness is my continuing willingness to identify contradictions and discrepancies in my behavior. I may find, for example, that I respond to others in a variety of disjointed ways, and that some of my responses contradict my most important beliefs. One dimension of this disparity between my beliefs and my behavior is that I will generally act according to expectations that are not my own. This tendency to respond directly to others' demands may gradually become crystallized and increasingly discernible in my attitudes and behavior. When this happens I may realize that I am becoming more and more trapped in stereotype roles such as those of wife and mother. My way out of these impediments is to strengthen my capacity to choose goals and behaviors congruent with my beliefs.

In order to neutralize or reverse my strong tendency to automatically play socially acceptable roles and meet others' approval or expectations, I must ask myself whether I prefer to respond to a particular situation conventionally or in a more unpredictable way that reflects my personal convictions. Would acting from my own beliefs mean that I would behave differently? After I have chosen a specific direction and particular goals for myself, it is easier to be consistent and effective in my expression of self. The cumulative process of aligning self and behavior may be described as a vital integration of purposeful activity. When I can define my own goals and remain aware of them, I operate from a position where I can make action decisions that reflect my beliefs and convictions. For example, if I know that practicing a particular skill has long-range importance and significance for me, I will be more likely to practice that skill if I do not let my chosen long-range goal drift out of awareness.

While I progress in the direction of acting for self, I must remain sufficiently aware of who I am and what I choose to do, so that I will be ready to reconfirm self when others try to pressure me to return to my former roles and behavior. A response I can predict when I am able to change self is resistance from those who are emotionally close to me. The amount and intensity of the resistance I encounter is usually a reliable indicator of the degree of my success in achieving real change in self. If others praise the results of my efforts to differentiate self, there is a greater likelihood that my behavior has been modified at a superficial level only. If I act from an increased awareness of self and changed beliefs and convictions, family members and those I work with will tend to be proportionately critical of me. To the extent that I have been successful in changing self, these people will also try to influence me to change back to my former self. I will be strongly inclined to change back to my original level of functioning in order to keep these significant emotional relationships peaceful and stable. My automatic behavior is toward togetherness rather than toward individuation.

RESISTANCE FROM OTHERS

Resistance from others will present itself in a variety of seemingly disparate forms. If I am married, the most powerful resistance to my change in self generally comes from my spouse, even though my spouse may verbalize appreciation of my newly defined self. My spouse may be able to accept intellectually my changes in self and voice admiration of my efforts and accomplishments, but resistance will eventually surface in complaints about other areas of our relationship or symptomatic behavior. For example, if I decide that I do not want to continue to entertain my spouse's business associates, he may intellectually agree with my position, but at the same time show resistance to my decision and changed behavior. My spouse may disapprove of other of my activities or refuse to come home in the evenings. Such a response is in large part a manifestation of my spouse's emotional need to have me return to my former behavior, so that he can continue to feel comfortable in our established patterns of dependency. If I maintain my changed level of functioning, my husband will gradually adjust his behavior in our relationship and show more integrated respect for these changes. The degree of my spouse's emotional dependency on me will make these adaptations necessary if our twosome is to continue to be viable.

My spouse's resistance to changes I make acts as a powerful pressure on me to go back to my established ways of behaving. I will find it difficult to withstand this resistance. A chain of emotional reactivity has been set in motion. If I am successful at predicting and expecting resistance to my changes, however, I will be less vulnerable to my spouse's pressures to return to my former self than if the resistance takes me by surprise.

My children will also resist my changes in self. Generally my children's responsive behavior is more overt and not as sustained as my spouse's resistance. If I choose to take a job outside my home, my children might compare me negatively with their friends' mothers and declare that I am not a "real" mother as I do not stay home through the day. In spite of their initial resistance, if I can maintain meaningful emotional contact with them they will gradually recognize and appreciate my increased confidence from taking this job and expressing self actively. As I strengthen self they will become more mature. My children's increased autonomy is a consequence of their intense dependence on me. Whereas my spouse may choose subtle or sophisticated means to resist my changes in self, my children have a fairly limited range of modes of resistance. Although my children may become sick or may have a minor accident as a response to my changing self, neither of these reactions will usually persist. My spouse's reaction and resistance, in contrast, is generally more intense or more chronic.

Pressures from my parents and in-laws are also powerful components of the opposition or resistance I must deal with when I choose to act outside the regular confines of traditional roles and expectations for woman. My selfhood and personhood are hard-earned. As I am a woman, my mother and mother-in-law have significant positions in my intimate relationships, especially when I modify my action interpretation of traditional feminine roles and values. The degree of my success in behaving as a self in relation to my mother is perhaps the most stringent test of my new capabilities. My "prepolitical" liberation or freedom to be a self can only be attained through my becoming more objective about the influence my parents continue to have on my behavior and on the major life decisions I make.

One way to withstand the emotional power of negative or positive reactions from significant others is to state my position on a particular issue and behave consistently in accordance with that position. I need not justify my beliefs and actions to others. An explanation of my activities may detract from my effectiveness and make it more difficult for me to assert myself on the immediate and on subsequent occasions. I may choose to discuss my long-term goals and values with others before I make decisions, but I am not obligated to defend my decisions once I have made them. A justification of my behavior will usually serve to weaken rather than strengthen my position and self.

Others' resistance to changes in self cannot be expected to disappear through time. Resistance takes different forms and varies in intensity, but remains a latent force in any given situation. Crisis situations and stress are most likely to precipitate resistance, especially as these are times when I may expressly try to make changes in self by acting differently in relation to those closest to me. If my child is sick, for example, my husband and parents may try to exert influence over me by pointing out that I am expected to be attentive to my child in this situation.

In contrast to the demanding behavior of others in periods of stress, periods of calm may be conducive to others' showing more tolerance of my changed self. I must constantly stay alert for shifts of anxiety in my relationship system, however, so that I can withstand overt and hidden pressures on my behavior. Leading my life as a whole person will enrich my life indescribably more than will perpetuating mechnical role playing or participating in a restricted exchange between a small number of roles. My selfhood and personhood can take me beyond the fairly restricted range of activities generally associated with motherhood, sisisterhood, and womanhood.

Chapter 4

Woman and Family

My necessary dependency on my family need not restrict my activities. I cannot afford to view my family as a negative influence in my life, as it is in this particular relationship system that I can grow and develop self most effectively. When I recognize that my need for my family is my most challenging context in which to change self, I must modify the conventional view that I should break away from my family in order to be liberated or to grow as a person. I must mature within and in relation to my family, as this is perhaps the only arena in which I can consistently become a self. If I cut myself off from my family, I at the same time abandon the optimum setting for attaining real change in self.

FAMILY CONTACT

If I am to change my behavior, I must modify my relationships with those emotionally closest to me, especially with members of my nuclear and extended families. My family is the most influential membership group, due to the members' intense emotional investment in each other. My family has more continuity than most small groups I belong to, and cannot disband overnight. I was born into my family, and will exit only when I die. The dependencies and commitments between members of my family are markedly more binding than those in emotional systems such as religious and political groups. Whereas social or work groups can easily exclude or dismiss me if I make unacceptable changes in my behavior, I have continuing opportunities to work out differences and conflicts with members of my family with little fear of being permanently rejected by them.

With a sufficient degree of awareness, objectivity, and planning, I can begin to reverse some of the programming and conditioning processes in my family that have molded my individual development. Until I am at least intellectually aware of the general extent of my necessary emotional dependence on my family, I cannot make significant changes in self. Woman's need for emotional dependence and the existence of advantageous opportunities to grow in her family have been largely underestimated.

If I experience relationship difficulties with my spouse or children, it is likely that my anxiety is more directly influenced by my relationship with my parents than by my immediate nuclear family relationships. I will tend to be more easily angered by my spouse and children if my father is out of work, for example, than if there is no stress in my family of origin. My latent or manifest anxiety about my father's well-being is one facet of the intensity of my continued dependence on him. My concern for my father may be so pronounced that other intimate relationships will prove to be unusually difficult as long as my anxiety is high.

The roots of my emotional development and intimate relationships run deep. The likelihood of success involved in my working out changes in self solely with my spouse and children is slight. My efforts must be accompanied by frequent and diverse contacts with members of my parental families of origin if I am to be in touch with my most significant and most long-standing emotional relationships. If I am to strengthen self I must be able to recreate the emotional circumstances of my birth and antecdent emotional conditions in my family wherever possible. My most personal and intimate past stretches back over many generations and incorporates some of the past emotional interdependency and influences of these generations.

INTERGENERATIONAL INFLUENCES

The quality of my emotional dependence on my mother and grandmothers is critical in my development of self. I can become more objective and more independent if I have some knowledge of my mother's and grandmothers' patterns of interaction in my family. If I can gather information from relatives about familial expectations for my mother and grandmothers and about my mother's and grandmothers' behavior in relation to these expectations, my awareness of self will be heightened.

One of my most important immediate goals in self-development must be to become more objective about interaction in my family. The patterns of behavior that involve my mother and grandmothers most directly are strong influences on my own behavior. If my maternal grandmother sees herself as an adaptive person, and other family members see her as dominant, I must check other family members' perceptions further in order to become more objective about my maternal grandmother and ultimately about myself. If I experience resistance to my career plans from my mother or grandmothers, for example, I can perhaps discover some of the ways they had to face and deal with similar dilemmas in their lifetimes. These explorations will eventually allow me to become more disengaged from the emotional content of their criticisms of my behavior and the criticisms of other family members. Criticism is itself an expression of emotional dependency.

Although much of my activity consists of imitating or repeating the behavior of those who are emotionally significant to me, it is difficult for me to delineate precisely where these imitations and repetitions occur and to observe their frequency in my own behavior. I may like to think that my life is fundamentally distinct from my parents' lives, but in actual fact I tend to act in ways either similar to or diametrically opposite from their behavior. Ideally, I should be able to modify these patterns or models for myself. I am overly dependent on my parents when I repeat their established behavior patterns in my own life, or when I act only in ways that radically reverse their patterns.

It is easy for me to believe that I am completely different from my mother. If I manage to convince myself that I am quite unlike her, however, I deceive myself. Although my mother may not have a career outside her home, and I may be unmarried with a career, we are more alike than is superficially apparent and than we admit to ourselves or to teach other. When I closely examine my own behavior together with my mother's actions, I find many strategic similarities in how we both behave. My mother and I are equally intense in the degree to which we become emotionally involved with those close to us, and we are both perfectionists in the diverse kinds of work and activities we undertake. We may do different things and interact with different intimate others, but the intensity of our investment in high priority activities and the connectedness we establish with intimate others is markedly similar.

Although I may intellectually agree that it is crucial for

my well-being to make and maintain meaningful contacts with my family of origin, I will not necessarily want to do this or be able to do it easily and effectively. I will resist many changes in this relationship system as they will appear to be overwhelmingly difficult to accomplish. An additional complicating factor is that if I make a geographical move away from my parents, the physical separation between us can encourage the development of emotional estrangement between my nuclear and extended families.

As well as having to adjust to the "normal" conditions of social mobility in our society, I am vulnerable to other stresses and strains. I will absorb some of the contagious anxiety society manifests due to the threat of nuclear war, the population explosion, and increased pollution of the environment. The impact of these combined sources of tension will serve to generate further increases in my tendency to withdraw from contacts with parent and grandparent members of my family. The imminent death of my oldest relatives will precipitate additional anxiety, especially if family dependencies are activated in the course of my efforts to differentiate self.

Loss of contact and pervasive emotional cut-offs between members of different generations in my family weaken and close that relationship system. Unless I recognize my continued emotional dependency on my parents and make efforts to keep these contacts open and viable, my children will gradually cut off their relationships with me. The increased frequency of emotional divorces in families will ultimately weaken most families and society at large. My survival is largely contingent upon the survival of my family.

If I come from a large family, I may have a more clearly defined self than if I come from a small family.

Large families frequently have a less intense and more open network of emotional dependencies. The proportions of female and male members of my family are other important influences on the degree of autonomy of my behavior. If I am a female and come from a family that has a large number of female members, I may be more likely to be an achiever than if I am female and come from a family where there are many males or equal proportions of females and males. I may not be programmed with unfavorable comparisons betwen females and males if I come from a predominantly female relationship system.

My functioning position in my family also depends on the nature of seniority and ranking in my family. Who has the strongest influence on members of my family? When I am aware of the variety of subtle but powerful influences my parents and grandparents have on my behavior, I can begin to free myself from their emotional dominance and pressure on my life. I am a small part of an intergenerational system of influences. I can benefit most immediately from examining my mother's, grandmothers', and great-grandmothers' experiences, and from delineating their influences on me. The maternal intergenerational line is the most powerful continuum of dependence and influence for woman.

SPOUSE'S FAMILIES

Initiating and maintaining relationships with my spouse's families of origin is less significant for my effective development as a self than is the quality of the contacts I establish with my own parents and their families. However, I cannot constructively ignore or deny my dependence on my in-law families. Contact with different members of my spouse's families can generally be renewed and kept sufficiently alive through meetings for special occasions rather than through the kind of continuous efforts I must make to maintain emotional contact with my own families. I need to interact with my in-laws in many different personal ways, and to see them and be viewed by them as a person. My in-law family system can reject and exclude me from its network more effectively than my own family can, however, and I cannot count on this group as a stable and continuing emotional context for my growth in self.

My perception of different members of my husband's family can be strongly influenced by my spouse without my being aware of the extent of his influence. I may conduct most of the relationships I have with members of my spouse's family "through" my spouse. I easily accept his perceptions of his family members as my own, and depend on his participation in order to communicate with his family. I bring my spouse into my relationships with members of his family instead of building up my own personal contacts with them. I must create and maintain direct and intimate two-person relationships with my in-laws if I am to stregthen self.

The ways in which my in-laws see me depend very much on how they see my spouse and my spouse's place in their feeling system. If my spouse is very emotionally significant in his own family, for example, I may be correspondingly less emotionally significant in my spouse's family, or I may be viewed negatively by my in-laws. If my in-laws perceive my spouse negatively, however, I may be viewed positively. This complementarity in feelings and perceptions may also occur between my parents and my spouse: My parents' perception of my spouse is strongly influenced by the emotional tone of their perception of me.

An interesting additional observation about the influence of my spouse's family on my behavior is that

I am able to interact with my mother maturely, I will be able to get along with my mother-in-law fairly well. Mature exchanges with my mother-in-law are in large part contingent upon the success of my efforts to interact maturely with my mother. This complementarity of influence will tend to occur even though my mother and mother-in-law may seem completely different from each other in how they think, believe, and interact with others. The intensity of my past and continuing dependency on my mother makes it more difficult for me to relate personally and meaningfully to her than to my mother-in-law, a more recent relationship. This observation challenges the popular belief that suggests I will find it more difficult to get along with my mother-in-law than with my mother.

IMMEDIATE PRESSURES

Although both my nuclear family and my extended family are emotionally significant to me, the quality of my interaction with my family of origin is more significant for my success in changing self than are my contacts with my nuclear family. It is easier for me to be objective about my family of origin than about my nuclear family in that the system of relationships with my family of origin is generally further removed, spatially and in some respects temporally, from my day-to-day activities and concerns. The challenges I confront in my family of origin also tend to be more deep-seated than the "pseudo" emotional issues that surface in my nuclear family.

One of the greatest difficulties I face in relating to my parents is that I must grapple with long-standing ingrained behavior patterns that have satisfied my parents' emotional needs over the years. My parents sustain an uncannily powerful capacity to prompt a successful regression in my behavior within a short period of our establishing contact. I can enter my parents' home with specific attitudes and intentions, and within a couple of hours behave in ways that negate my plans and merely extend my past programming. My parents' continued dependence on me is evident when they criticize me harshly for rather trivial improprieties in my behavior. In these respects my parents perpetuate their behavior as caretakers or disciplinarians, and I allow them to do so. Our interdependent ongoing behavior tends to be based on shared past performances and past occurrences rather than on present realities.

However difficult it may be to break out of established patterns of behavior in my family of origin, it is less possible to modify patterns of dependency in my nuclear family. When my spouse goes out of town on business, I am usually more able to achieve a manageable degree of emotional distance from him than if I interact with him continuously. The degree of relief I feel from this temporary separation reflects the extent of my emotional bondedness with my spouse. I may use opportunities of this kind to take a more objective look at myself and at my relationships with my spouse and my children. When my spouse is away from home, I may also be able to make some decisions that would be more problematic in his presence. Behavior of this kind indicates that I may tend to function less efficiently and less effectively when my spouse is home than when he is away. When my spouse is home, I relinquish decision making to him or avoid making decisions.

It is difficult not to be at least partially trapped in the intensity of my emotional dependence on my spouse. However, I would not necessarily be able to maintain my improved level of functioning throughout a prolonged period of separation from my spouse. It is more likely that

I would accumulate dependency needs during this time and find alternative ways to transfer my dependence to others. Sooner or later I would repeat my former tendencies to delegate or avoid decision making in the new relationships I created in the transfer of my dependence on my spouse to others.

ADAPTIVENESS HINDERS GROWTH

Traditional stereotypes emphasize the expectation that adaptive behavior is appropriate for woman and dominant behavior suitable for man. Adaptiveness and compromise can hinder emotional maturation as much as dominance can. A mere reversal of roles and expectations between woman and man will not increase the freedom of either sex. The enhancement of self-awareness and the capacity to behave consistently as a self are more significant aspects of increased freedom for both woman and man.

Compromise endangers my well-being in that sacrificing my own judgements for others' decisions can contribute toward an eventual loss of my own self-awareness. I will be in a more advantageous and meaningful position when I stand by my beliefs and risk making mistakes than when I compromise, especially in matters of great concern and importance to me. I cannot afford to be immaturely rigid in my views and actions, but I need to make day-to-day decisions with my chosen long-term goals in mind. Many subjects do not concern me directly, and I can compromise with integrity in these areas more easily than in areas that have significance for me. When I habitually adapt to others' demands or needs, I relinquish my functioning position as a self. In order to strengthen self, I must stand my ground on issues that are important to me. The related challenge is to be flexible in my behavior without compromising self. I must deal with the pain of displeasing others when I decide to maintain an unpopular stand.

I can have a constructive influence on my family when I engage in a variety of nontraditional and traditional activities to express my individuality. I will generally find my family life more meaningful if I pursue a career or other activities outside my home, than if I relate more exclusively to my spouse and children. My communication of the quality of my job experience may be one of the most positive contributions I can make to the lives of my spouse and children.

The existence of sufficient numbers of creatively adaptive families in society may ultimately depend on whether woman and man can change their expectations of each other and of their parents. There is a great probability that I will be a mature spouse or a mature parent if I can see self and others more objectively. I must allow self and others to act without imposing my praise or blame. At a point in history when the roles of spouse and parent have become crystallized or dysfunctional, a breakthrough in shared expectations may improve the quality of human life and freedom. I can successfully discard some of the unworkable parts of conventional models of behavior and become more producitve through my expression of self. Although this transition is not an easy one to make, when I live my own life I will not be a victim of circumstances, nor will I be trapped in my family. My creative adaptiveness will not hinder my growth.

Chapter 5

Changing Woman in the Family

Although the media have publicized many different kinds of changes in woman's roles in the family and in society at large in recent years, a picture of woman as a whole person has not been clearly presented. Piecemeal and fragmented illustrations of a variety of lifestyles of woman have tended to obfuscate the possibility of seeing woman as a vital self.

Contemporary literature on woman suggests that behavior oriented away from family responsibilities is more "enlightened" or more liberated than behavior that is oriented toward family interaction. This extrafamilial or centrifugal thrust of personal activity is perhaps not as conducive to effective change in woman's or man's positions in society as is behavior oriented more directly toward responsible family involvement and interaction. It is largely through the manifest and latent intensity of my closest intimate personal relationships that I can discover self, grow, and develop most productively. My family is the most impassioned feeling system I belong to, whether or not I am willing to recognize that fact.

As well as being the context for my most deep-seated emotional behavior, my family is my most predictable relationship system. Evidence of my involvement in my family includes my difficulty in maintaining an awareness of even a small proportion of the visible repeated behavior patterns in this group. Even though I may not see these repetitions clearly, I realize that when patterns of interaction in my family are upset or disrupted, a range of reactions from those most affected by the interruption is more predictable than it would be in a similar situation in other groups. If I am the one who upsets, disrupts, or interrupts my own family processes, I can expect negative reactions to be focused on me, especially from those who are emotionally closest to me.

It is easier for me to change self if I plan to play a different part in my family emotional system than if I respond to anxieties of the moment and make occasional moves to modify my functioning. It is easier for me to maintain my changed self when I know that if I am able to withstand the impact of immediate criticisms of my changes, others will eventually change self and have increased respect and tolerance for my contributions to our shared relationship system. I need my family interrelatedness in order to be a whole person, even though I can be most easily annihilated by my family togetherness.

INTERRELATEDNESS AND CHANGE

My family is an emotional unit, and it may or may not have pervasive boundaries in relation to other groups. Overlapping dependencies in my family are so complex and intricate that a shift or dislocation of any one part will lead to changes in related parts, and gradually to a modification of the functioning level of the whole system. Although there is a perpetual drive toward increased fusion and togetherness in my family and toward the maintenance of emotional equilibrium, if there is a sufficient degree of change in the functioning levels of self and other in my family, the quality of interaction throughout the system in my behavior, my whole family may eventually become more differentiated and show increased maturity and flexibility in the ways members relate to each other.

Changes in my position in my family are predictably accompanied by changes in the responses and positions of those closest to me. All members of my family are emotionally entwined with me and each other, although there is generally no expressed acknowledgement of the extent to which this close interrelatedness and interdependence of feelings and needs exists. Even though family jokes or stories may highlight members' resemblance to each other in physical appearance and behavior, these similarities are not perceived as possible challenges to the well-being of the individuals concerned. My position as a woman in my family and in society at large is essentially a consequence of my position in the intimate emotional interrelatedness of my family. It is only when I can change the nature of my participation and the responsibilities I assume in this family involvement that I will be able to behave more effectively and more responsibly in the wider society.

A chain of events perhaps captures the thrust of these related changes and illustrates the influence of family dependency on my behavior in other social groups. Change in self and in my position in my family is followed by a shift in the level of my functioning in the wider society. If these changes in self are maintained in the context of my family, and if I am at the same time able to stay in touch with the family emotional system, other family members will gradually change their levels of functioning and behave more maturely.

QUALITY AND QUANTITY OF CONTACTS

My nuclear family is the most intense emotional system I participate in within my entire family network. The multigenerational span of any family contains many different nuclear families. My relationships in my nuclear family are highly charged and frequently overloaded with feelings. The tendency toward emotional tightness or a high level of anxiety in my nuclear family is due in part to its restricted membership. To the extent that this small group interacts as a self-contained unit, anxiety in the nuclear family will easily be heightened. When my most intimate personal relationships are overloaded with emotion, my interaction with members of this group and their interaction with me become reactive and predictable. These behavior patterns may rapidly become repeated stereotypes or ingrained rigid habits. I cannot easily change my part in such crystallized transactions.

When the emotional climate of my nuclear family is anxious, I am more likely to become trapped in its emotional system and act and react in ways that merely complement others' expectations and demands. My actions are responses to others' needs and activities, and I lose self as I merely react automatically to those about me. In order to be a self I must be able to think as an individual and perceive self and others clearly.

My family relationships are most rigid and binding when I and those emotionally closest to me are anxious. As the level of anxiety in my nuclear family or family of origin is raised, my relationships rigidify, and I become increasingly trapped in my own unproductive, repetitive, and reactive behavior. I am not sufficiently free to be able to think and act for myself in this intense emotional field.

I cannot even become aware of my own beliefs in this anxious climate. I spend most of my time and efforts pleasing others and compromising my own convictions.

In order to strengthen self and function more effectively in my nuclear family and in other social settings, I must try to dilute some of the anxiety I have in self and in my family relationships. One way to do this is to increase the ongoing and meaningful personal contacts I have with members of my family in all possible generations. Additional communications with family members will gradually open up this system and relieve anxiety in the relationships. Although in the long run an increase in the number of relationships I have with family members is itself insufficient to keep the system open, extending my family contacts improves the quality of my relationships and dilutes their intensity.

When I can stay in meaningful contact with large numbers of family members in different generations, the intensity of the anxiety in my nuclear system is diluted. My feelings become more invested outside my nuclear system, and this refocus of emotions creates conditions that lower the level of anxiety in my nuclear family. As I become less involved with members of my nuclear family, this system becomes calmer. This change is particularly apparent where I am able to make a substantial number of contacts with members of older generations in my family.

My engaging in genealogical research of selected life histories of my ancestors can also improve the quality of my relationships in my family and open this system further. In this kind of project I become more emotionally detached and more objective about living generations by gathering data and comparing it to my knowledge of my family. This enlarged perspective on my life situation can assist me to be more objective about myself. Sharing information about deceased relatives with living family members may also increase the flexibility and openness of the overall system. This enables family members to be more objective about living generations and about the complexity of the influences that have affected their lives.

It is through these kinds of interpersonal changes that I can most effectively change self. Political action in an institutional setting, although necessary, is less conducive to more permanent modifications of self at deeper levels than is changing self in the context of my family. I need to deal with my interpersonal emotional bondage before I can be an effective and enlightened political agent in the wider society.

FROM REACTIVITY TO RESPECT

Family members' reactions to the changes I make in my behavior are initially intense and negative. I should expect anger, criticism, and even symptomatic behavior from those who are closest to me when I try to change self. Other family members will pressure me to revert to the behavior of my former self with a variety of reactive responses, even though they may at the same time give me much verbal approval of my efforts to make changes.

When I can look at my family and the part I play in it more objectively, I can tentatively predict who will be most likely to react to changes I may make and how these reactions will be expressed. The more objective I can be about myself and my family, the more accurate my predictions about others' reactions will be. The immediacy and intensity of others' reactions act as strong pressures on me to return to my former behavior. The rapidity and strength of their responses will tend to easily unnerve and undermine my most rigorous endeavors to change self.

At a time of crisis in my family, my efforts to change self may not meet with the more usual immediate negative reactions. My family relationship network may be temporarily loosened by a sudden death or by another kind of traumatic event. In these circumstances, there will generally be sufficient anxiety in the system to make changes in self possible. The family tensions may be diffused throughout the system or focused on critical aspects of relationships like the loss of a key family member. In either pattern of intensity, I can begin to act differently more easily than if all was peaceful and in the usual routine.

When there is no particular crisis in my family, other family members' reactiveness to my continued modifications in behavior will tend to mellow through time. This increased tolerance for my behavior will occur only if I can maintain emotional contact with a sufficiently large number of family members and simultaneously sustain my improved level of functioning. If I am able to make meaningful contacts with members of my family of origin, my changes in self will be considerably more effective than if I restrict contacts to my nuclear family and my in-law relationships.

When I make efforts to change self primarily in relation to my family of origin, others' reactivity to my changed functioning position will surface more in my family of origin than in my nuclear family. The greater the extent to which negative reactions to my changes of self can be confined to my family of origin, the less the likelihood that negative reactions will appear in my nuclear family. If my efforts to modify my functioning are concentrated in my family of origin, divorce and interpersonal behavior symptoms will be less likely to occur than if I focus my adaptations in my nuclear family. If my nuclear family is overloaded with anxiety, and I increase this tension by trying to change self only in relation to my nuclear family, it is quite likely that the intensity in this system could explode and sever some relationships. It is my family of origin that is my most long-standing and permanent group affiliation, not my nuclear family. Compared to my family of origin, my nuclear family may be transient. My need for my family of origin will remain as a basic personal and intimate need whether or not my nuclear family continues to exist.

If my marital relationship becomes overly fused and overly bonded, the only way I can get out of such restrictions may be to break away from my spouse. However, emotional estrangement, distancing, or geographical separation and divorce would not necessarily be a mature separation of me and my spouse. An immediate and predictable consequence of a premature severance of our relationship is that I would have a great propensity to become equally emotionally fused or entangled in another twosome or marriage. In order to avoid this dilemma, I need to move through the phase of reactivity to respect in my relationship with my spouse, with the knowledge that my spouse will continue to be more reactive to my changes of self than will other family members.

CHILD DEVELOPMENT

My children will have a stronger sense of self if I can successfully strengthen my own self. The degree of self of my children is in many respects a product of their parents' levels of self. Child-parent dependency is so great that the intense interrelatedness will prompt children to behave in ways congruent with their parents' development of self.

I select a spouse who is at approximately the same stage of development of self as I am. My overall level of differentiation of self will tend to be so close to that of my spouse that I can say that I select a spouse who has the same functional range of differentiation of self as myself. Although I may make visible functional shifts in my behavior after my marriage, it is difficult to make substantial moves away from my original level of differentiation of self. My children, as a consequence of their dependency on both my spouse and I, will generally be restricted to behavior patterns based on this same relatively narrow range of possibilities for differentiating self.

Even though my children will react negatively when I change my behavior, in the long run they will benefit directly from any moves I can make in the direction of my increased effectiveness in functioning. My children are less capable of finding ways to make me revert to my former functioning position than my spouse or my parents are. My children's limited capacity to pressure me effectively is due to their greater dependence on me to satisfy their basic physical and emotional needs. My children are also generally less able to maintain their negative reactions to any changes in my behavior as they have fewer resources to call upon for this task. My children's greater adaptiveness also indicates more flexible responsiveness and greater dependency on me than the responsiveness and dependency of my spouse or parents.

I am a more effective parent when I act as a self. If I can act decisively in accordance with my own integrated beliefs, my children will be actively encouraged to make life decisions for themselves that are congruent with their own real interest. When I annihilate self by engaging in overly dependent and overly fused exchanges with my spouse and my parents, I will not be able to maintain a clear posture in these intimate relationships. One consequence of my inability to be an effective self is that I will be a weak parent. My children will be more likely to have behavior problems if I am an ambiguous self and an ineffective parent than if I am a more clearly differentiated self.

In contrast to traditional and popular views, my children will be freer to make their own choices and decisions if my spouse and I do not present a united front to them in day-to-day disciplinary matters. Presenting a united front is a no-self posture of fusion and overdependence in my relationship with my spouse. This twosome can be overwhelming to any of my children, so that a child is discouraged from thinking of self in this context. If I can develop meaningful personal relationships with each of my children based on my own genuine concerns and beliefs, my children will be better able to relate to me as a person than if my spouse and I decide to present a contrived and artifical togetherness that suggests we equally share all our beliefs and principles. To the extent that my children become overpowered by the united twosome of my spouse and myself, they will be unable to respond to either one of their parents except by distancing or overreactive behavior. The reality of my marital relationship is that my spouse and I are two distinct and separate individuals, even though we are at the same time very dependent on each other. If I compromise self in relating to my spouse, I lose self in that critically vital relationship and simultaneously negate my effectiveness as a parent.

OVERRESPONSIBILITY AS IRRESPONSIBILITY

Woman is traditionally viewed as a helper in the family. I am expected to be nurturing and emotionally supportive in my relationships with all family members. I am also expected to be responsible for the health and well-being of young and old, especially of my children, parents, and spouse.

These and related expectations generally demand more than a reasonable share of my responsibilities for others. However, if I focus on others' needs too much, I essentially suffocate some of their options and ability to choose for self. When I allow myself to do this, I manipulate the dependent others' behavior and ultimately act irresponsibly in relation to my own priorities. My overresponsibility is irresponsibility.

In making changes for self and strengthening self, I move toward a more reflective and a more responsible functioning position in relation to those who are emotionally closest to me. When I act from my own integrated beliefs, I become more responsible. I increase my control of my own feeling and thinking behavior, and I discard the artificial manipulative controls I have been wielding over others.

Traditional family responsibilities continue to be particularly demanding and onerous for both woman and man. I am viewed as less of a person if I do not help or serve other family members. I am considered to be strong to the extent that I become a focal support person in my family network. Traditional helping and caring-for postures are generally forms of overresponsibility and irresponsibility, however. Although I will precipitate negative reactions from those I have helped in the past if I decide to discontinue my caretaking, they will gradually become more responsible for themselves. Those I assisted to become dependent on me will gain some independence when I cease my habitual assistance. If I refuse to do all that is requested or demanded by other family members, I may gradually increase my own responsibility and theirs.

I can change self by moving toward a more responsible functioning position in my family. My becoming more objective about my responsibility in my family must precede an effective change in self.

Responsibility is a quality of feeling, thinking, and acting. I am responsible for my perception of self and others, and for the quality of my thoughts that precede behavior as well as for my action. I change self when I decide to move in the direction of increased responsibility for self rather than toward increased responsibility for others. I can approach this goal only slowly, however, even when I have strong commitment and motivation. I may partially attain this objective through persisting in my efforts over a lifetime.

Chapter 6

On Selling Self at a Sacrifice Price _____

I can perhaps think more clearly about what it means to be a self and to value self if I use some selling and pricing analogies. I cannot stretch these analogies too far, however, without distorting some essential meanings of self.

In order to know self, I must imagine that "I" and "self" are synonymous. Holding that idea in my mind will involve some effort, as I will not necessarily begin with an automatic realization that I and self are the same. My most advantageous life plan is to know that I and self can be mutually reinforced to the extent that my actions are responsible in relation to self and others. My behavior must be based on my own inner beliefs, rather than on others' beliefs, if it is to be responsible. I cannot do things for others effectively unless I decide to act with integrity at each opportunity for action that presents itself. My automatic responses to the stresses of a particular situation or to emotionally significant others' pressures cannot relieve me of my obligation to consider my own integrity as the ultimate basis of my behavior.

Even though I might imply, by using selling and pricing analogies and metaphors, that self is my most precious possession, I must not objectify self. Self is my vital life stream and essential being, rather than an object or series of roles that are removed and separate from me.

I may choose to respond directly to others'

expectations and demands or to deny the existence of self, but self continues to be a critical reality for me and others. If I habitually choose to sacrifice self or to trade it for others' approval, I will eventually run my life less effectively and lose some degree of control over my affairs. I will lose my autonomy. My most vital concern must be to maintain my awareness of self and at the same time to act in accordance with my own integrated inner beliefs.

COMPROMISE AS SACRIFICE

If I sacrifice self, I give self away to others for a price that is below the value I should accept in such exchanges. Self may be described as my most precious possession, state of being, or activity. I cannot grow and develop either by holding on to self in a closed and restrictive manner or by giving self to others too easily.

If I passively go along with others' demands and expectations, I sacrifice self. Unless I am to suffer the consequences of compromise of self, I can act only with genuine belief-based agreement. In order to function effectively and to lead a purposeful life, I must deliberate about my decisions to act, and consider the detailed implications of my options seriously. I must try to ensure that all my actions are congruent with my strongest inner beliefs and with each other.

A surfeit of compromise with others is characteristic of emotional togetherness or fusion. It is supremely difficult to avoid overcompromising in my relationships with those who are emotionally close to me. However, some degree of compromise of self may be unavoidable and necessary for my day-to-day survival. A posture of not compromising with others at all is generally suspect of immature rigidity and an unproductive lack of shared beliefs with others.

Compromise can be a manifestation of my tolerance and respect. Where compromise is linked directly to my inner integrity, it is not a dissipation of self. If I compromise when I do not know all the facts of a situation, or when I am not fully aware of my own beliefs, I may increase the flexibility of my responses. Such a compromise will not generally be harmful to my overall well-being if it exists only for a temporary period of time, and if my own awareness of self is gradually heightened to eliminate any discrepancy between my beliefs and the conditions of the situation.

I can avoid unnecessary compromise and sacrifice of self by focusing my interest and motivational energies on defining and acting from self. I will be less inclined to compromise and support relationships of togetherness and fusion with those who are emotionally close to me when my efforts are aimed at differentiating self from others. I need a strong focus on self to neutralize my automatic inclination to meet others' demands and expectations directly. Although I must maintain some degree of adaptiveness in order to keep my relationships with intimate others flexible and viable, overadaptiveness is characteristic of a loss of self. An exaggeration of a "we-ness" posture to others occurs only as I become a "no-self," and as fusion or togetherness permeates my intimate relationships.

Excessive emotional involvement in my personal relationships impedes my growth and development. When I am emotionally entangled with others, I lose touch with my own beliefs and sell self at a sacrifice price. This situation occurs most readily in my nuclear family and in my family of origin. If I can work toward defining self effectively in these most intense relationship systems, however, I will be able to avoid sacrificing self in other social settings.

OVERRESPONSIBILITY AS SACRIFICE

Being responsible for self frequently involves my doing considerably less for others. If a great proportion of my energies is absorbed by my meeting what I perceive to be others' needs and demands, my vital resources may be rapidly depleted without my behavior necessarily being responsible. I will be unable to conduct my own life responsibly and effectively if I disguise my personal weaknesses by presenting myself as a helper or a caretaker to others. My supportive posture to those who function less adequately than I will reinforce and perpetuate already existing overly dependent and overly adaptive behavior patterns.

Although in all my helping or caretaking relationships both parties are losers in that each loses self, I must become aware of the extent of my own losses and the extent to which I encourage the other to lose self. If I am overly responsible in a relationship where the other is helped or looked after, I can begin to retrieve self only when I see my overresponsibility toward the other as both an irresponsibility and a sacrifice of self.

When I am able to maintain a focus on self and my own responsibilities, both my exploitation of others through their dependency and my sacrifice of self will decrease. Traditional expectations of my behavior as a woman generally perpetuate my tendency toward this kind of irresponsibility. Social and cultural influences add pressure to my intimate others' expectations that I should nurture and support those who are emotionally closest to me before seeking out or satisfying my own interests.

I may also easily become too responsible for the day-to-day running of my home under the influence of traditional expectations for woman. If I become overly active in filling routine demands in my home, I may lose self and eventually be unable to retrieve self. My sacrifice of self in this context may undermine my effectiveness as a person just as much as the inadequate satisfaction of other of my basic needs.

One positive consequence of being programmed by traditional expectations to be an overresponsible family member is that it is easier to stop overfunctioning than to cease being overly adaptive or overly submissive. I can cut down on my overresponsible overactivity more easily than I can generate energy and motivation to change underfunctioning and passivity. Although I may presently be irresponsibly adaptive in some of my activities, I can capitalize on my overresponsibility in my family relationships and grow toward increased responsibility and decreased sacrifice of self more easily than if I am in an underfunctioning position in my family.

INVESTING IN SELF

Investing in self is frequently criticized by others as narrowly "selfish" and self-centered. I will be a more effective person to the extent that I become focused on self, however. My most rewarding investments in self will result from my becoming increasingly self-centered in responsible ways. I may make investments in self and avoid sacrifice of self when I do less for my children and protect them less, as well as do less caretaking for incapacitated or overly dependent family members. Only when I release superfluous claims of dependency on others can I behave responsibly and allow others to discover self and live from self.

When I invest in self, I simultaneously make myself

vulnerable to criticism and disapproval from others. In order to grow and mature, however, I need to experience these kinds of painful direct consequences of my actions. I must deal responsibly with the predictable and unpredictable impact of my actions. I must also do what I can to allow those who are emotionally close to me to experience the consequences of their own actions directly and to deal with those same consequences responsibly. When I unambiguously invest in self and select my responsibility to self as my highest action priority, I will automatically loosen any overly protective and manipulative grip I have on those close to me. My growth and theirs can occur only when our interdependent relationships are sufficiently flexible to allow for free interaction with a variety of others.

My investment in self must necessarily manifest itself in activity. Even though I may increase my feelings of self-respect, and thereby appear to invest in self, this change in feelings toward self will not necessarily lead to changes in my behavior. The most vital aspects of my existential being are represented by what I do, rather than by what I feel or say. I am ultimately valued considerably more on the basis of my actions than on the basis of my thoughts, sentiments, and intentions, even though changes in my inner self are a necessary component of modifications in my external behavior.

My actions indicate the price at which I knowingly or unknowingly sell self. When my behavior is relatively disintegrated and replete with contradictions, I sacrifice self. When my behavior becomes more integrated and more consistent with my inner beliefs, I have been able to invest in self. My success in investing in self depends on the strength of my motivation and the existence of the emotional courage necessary to consider my personal integrity before the immediacy of pressing demands of others and my needs to meet others' approval.

Investment in self is not an automatic pattern of behavior. I must consciously and consistently direct my actions toward increasing my responsibility for self if I am to be successful in my efforts to invest in self. Although this process is inevitably painful or provokes anxiety, the ultimate rewards and dividends of meeting the difficulties of such a challenge are considerable.

As I continue to invest in self, I become increasingly aware of the distinctions that can be made between my feelings, thoughts, and overt behavior. In selecting my action options, however, I may consciously combine different levels of activity. I may choose to speak a language of togetherness but act from self, for example. I will generally find that I will be accepted more readily by a particular group if I speak togetherness rather than difference, and at the same time act from my inner beliefs. By choosing not to verbalize an "anti" or adversary position when I take an unpopular action stand, I will be more protected by approval based on my past performance than if I constantly voice disagreement. I may speak to others about my beliefs, but if my actions contradict my words, then I will essentially be striving for togetherness in my behavior rather than for the actualization of my own genuine beliefs. Responsibility for self and investment in self do not necessarily include a verbal articulation of my inner beliefs, although my behavior must be integrated with my beliefs if I am to invest in self effectively.

OTHERS' EXPECTATIONS AND SACRIFICE

One way I may be able to discover the extent to which I have sold self for a sacrifice price is to observe the emotional intensity with which others respond to me and how they react to changes I make in my behavior.

Although it will be more difficult for me to observe and be objective about the range of behavior of those who are emotionally closest to me, it is their actions and reactions that will give me my clearest indication of whether or not I sell self at a sacrifice price. The patterns of interaction I engage in with those who are emotionally most significant to me are more repetitive and more clearly visible than patterns of interaction in other behavioral settings. Also, the changes I make in relation to my most intimate relationship system will have more reactive and more visible responses from others than those generated by modifications in my contributions to other groups.

My family of origin is the most significant arena in which I can evaluate the extent to which I act to satisfy others' expectations of me rather than acting according to my own beliefs and convictions. When pleasing others or seeking approval is my primary objective, I sacrifice self. When I react to a crisis situation by meeting others' needs rather than my own, I sacrifice self. I may choose to lead a life of sacrifice for others, but this choice will be responsible only if I base each of my decisions to act on my own integrity, rather than respond automatically to others' demands.

As a child, I unquestioningly sacrificed self to my parents' emotional demands and needs due to my strong developmental dependency on them. I behaved in ways that first and foremost pleased my parents or reinforced their approval of me. I made constant efforts to be obedient and to respect family rules as I was convinced that such behavior was expected of me. I was tremendously fearful of my parents' displeasure, and thought their disapproval would surely follow if I was disobedient or disrespectful to their wishes and expectations. As a child I also easily fell into patterns of behavior based on what others wanted me to do, rather than on what I had decided to do. With these habits and tendencies, I could not sustain the continuous effort necessary to pursue my own goals or objectives.

As an adult, I still find it much easier to perpetuate my established patterns of dependent behavior, rather than to act in thoughtful accordance with my own inner beliefs. The programming I received in my earliest years continues to nurture a strong inclination to meet others' demands, rather than to select my own priorities.

I find it extremely difficult to base my actions on my inner beliefs and convictions in order to avoid my sacrifice of self through responding directly to others' expectations. If I continue to behave primarily in accordance with others' wishes, however, my sacrifice of self will gain momentum and will subsequently become considerably magnified. I may ultimately annihilate my sense of self and my personal integrity unless I refuse to sacrifice self to others' demands.

JUST PRICE

I must express self in personal, individuated action in order to live my life productively. However, on a variety of occasions I must make reasonable and responsible compromises in relation to others' demands at an action level. I must necessarily sell or give self to others to some extent in order to honor self and my integrity.

When I can successfully integrate my personal responsibilities with broader social concerns, perhaps I can be said to have arrived at an awareness of a just price for self. My just price for self is essentially a balancing point between my integrity and what I perceive to be the legitimate or reasonable claims of others for my attention and energy. When I am my most responsible self, I can be thought of as making decisions based on giving or selling self for a just price.

My integrity, inner beliefs, and convictions must optimally include some degree of concern and consideration for others. In fact, unless I orient at least some of my behavior toward broad social goals, I run the risk of being irresponsibly narrow and rigid in my overall individual behavior. A lack of breadth in my personal objectives can be equated with my being unresponsive to vital dimensions of social reality. When I am able to select a few broad-ranging social concerns for personal priorities, I begin to know my just price for self.

I can invest in self more meaningfully and more effectively when I give self in responsible ways. The more engaged I become in activity that manifests my inner beliefs and convictions and responds to some social concerns, the more opportunities I will have to grow and develop as a self.

In order to apply the just price idea of responsibility to self and my intimate others, I must try to reverse or neutralize some of the more entrenched programming and patterns of behavior that have persisted since my earliest interaction with emotionally significant members of my family. If I increase the number of personal contacts I have with members of my family of origin, and improve the quality of these relationships, I may be able to begin to loosen the tenacity of some established expectations for my behavior.

In order to become more objective about my family relationships, I can view my family as a network of triangles. I may try to change my relationships in this system through my awareness of this substructure of triangles, by contacting someone who is close to a person with whom I have an overly intense relationship. I may qualitatively change my relationship with my mother, for example, by modifying my established patterns of behavior with my father. If I relate to my father in a more open and personal way, my relationship with my mother will change and may eventually become more mature. I will sell self for a just price only if I act in relation to those closest to me with belief and conviction rather than with emotional reactivity. I do not act responsibly if I allow tensions in a particular situation to determine my behavior.

My success in exacting a just price for self in the sum total of my relationships with others depends on my capacity to withstand the sale of self at a sacrifice price. I must become aware of my own irresponsibility before I can take steps to successfully eliminate imbalances and inconsistencies in my behavior. Awareness of my inadequacies alone is insufficient for this difficult task. I must be able to see the ways in which I nurture and encourage these contradictions, and then put my responsible self into action.

In order to actualize my choice to express a just price for self in my behavior, I must make difficult decisions. I will have to muster considerable courage in order to modify my behavior. The exacting challenges that come my way must be dealt with consistently and flexibly so that I will be able to survive the variety of pressures and strains that will inevitably follow. My just price for self will become a reality only when I can view self and others objectively and act responsibly.

Chapter 7

Self Is More than a Sum of Roles

I am more than an actor of roles or a combination of roles. I become stronger and more alive when I use initiative and decide on a course of behavior that lies outside my traditionally defined roles and expectations. When I acquiesce to others' demands, I lose self in my emotional reactiveness to the powerful group togetherness.

Role playing consists of behavior that is essentially automatic or conditioned. When I am under pressure from others, role playing is one of my easiest and most practical resorts in the difficult situation. I know that I will not generate resistance or opposition within a particular group if I choose to act in accordance with others' expectations. Although it is possible for me to spend much of my lifetime conforming to others' expectations and making decisions in response to others' demands, I will not be a strong person if I choose merely to follow previously defined roles and to commit myself only to traditional expectations. Behavior that is other-directed to this extent will not be sufficiently consistent for me to be able to be effective as a whole person. However, the contradictions that exist in the action responses I make to different role demands may appear to me to be unimportant. I may continue to imitate preestablished patterns of behavior without an awareness of my own beliefs and convictions. It is difficult to perceive self as more than a sum of roles.

"I" TRANSCENDS AND INTEGRATES ROLES

Self is expressed by "I." My I positions on a variety of issues may be described as a range of different but related manifestations of self. I will be credible to self and others only to the extent that my behavior is integrated and based on my own inner beliefs and convictions. Respect from others follows my clear action communication of where I stand on separate concerns and issues.

In the same way that self is more than the sum of my roles, my I transcends and integrates the roles I play. My wholeness as a person cannot easily be incorporated by the idea that I am an actor of roles. My I has special unique qualities that transcend the sets of expectations related to the roles I perform. The quintessence of self may be said to lie in those activities of my I that go beyond my role playing.

The transcendent and integrative characteristics of my I are to some extent composed of my complementary and automatic behavior in relation to others. Although I may not be aware of the decisions I make in order to play certain roles, some elements of self are latent in the range of roles I select. When I am an effective self, my I personalizes or modifies the roles I play, rather than merely fitting in with or conforming to others' traditional expectations. My individual interpretations of the roles I play have some crucial shared characteristics. The ways in which I respond to others' demands have similar tendencies and patterns in all the roles I play. The common denominators that can be traced in different variations of my role activity are manifestations of my I and self.

Optimally, I will be able to integrate all the roles I choose to play. If I am able to influence and substantially modify the ways in which I respond to others' emotional demands and expectations, I will be more consistent in my behavior than if I conform to these pressures. When I am strong, the roles I choose to play will themselves be more integrated due to my own thoughtful selection. However, I can only express self in the roles I play when I have achieved a certain level of awareness of my own inner beliefs and convictions, as well as of the objectives or long-range goals I want to pursue. If my beliefs and aims are contradictory and inconsistent within themselves and between each other, I will not be able to express self clearly to others in action.

When I am aware of both the necessity for and the potential of my I in all levels of my behavior, my self more obviously becomes more than a sum total of traditional or normative roles. My being and my doing are vital interdependent aspects of self. I can have some degree of control over my behavior only when I am able to reflect on self and those who are emotionally closest to me, and predict fairly accurately the extent of others' influences on me and the nature of their reactions to my behavior. This kind of observation or reflection both transcends my habitual role playing and becomes an integral part of my acting self. My ultimate freedom, although narrowly restricted, is essentially based on my choice of whether to act or not act, and how to act or not act. If I choose to follow the dictates of traditionally or socially prescribed roles, I am usually not as free as if I select or create my own individualized patterns of behavior. When I play established roles, I tend to react to others' pressures and traditional expectations automatically, rather than to act in accordance with my own reflections and deliberations.

If I act in ways that reverse traditional expectations or that are contrary to others' demands, I may be just as emotionally bound to the pressures and influences of a particular situation as if I unquestioningly and automatically conformed to these demands. My strength and course for future development and growth lie more in my individual interpretation of particular situations at a variety of action levels than in either conforming with or rebelling against the more clearly defined role expectations of others. I must maintain a difficult and precarious balance of being simultaneously inside and outside the roles I play. In order to actualize self, both the integrative and the transcendental aspects of my I must be manifested in my behavior. I transcend my roles, and at the same time I integrate them. I must maintain emotional contact with others' role expectations for me, as well as stand outside my roles, in order to observe self and modify the quality of my participation with others.

ACTIVITY OUTSIDE ROLES

When I am able to maintain some of the shared and recognized characteristics of traditional role playing in my behavior, I will not lose meaningful emotional contact with others as quickly as if I act in opposition to conventional expectations. I need to conform with at least some traditional expectations for woman in order to be a viable and credible member of my group. It is useful to be able to maintain sufficient conformity in my behavior and in my perception of others' role expectations in order not to antagonize too many people in the wider society. Although I cannot compromise my integrity through this awareness, it is perhaps accurate to say that I can be an effective agent for change only if I share certain overt aspects of my role behavior with others. Distancing and estranging self from others will put me in a disadvantageous position in relation to the group as a whole.

It is my creative and individualized action responses to the demands of the roles I am expected to perform that indicate the strength of my self. I will generally find it easy to know others' traditional expectations and to imitate others' prescribed role behavior. However, it will be extraordinarily difficult for me to break out of patterns that are very strongly influenced by others' traditional and emotional expectations.

My behavior outside the roles I play is a vital and necessary component of my strengthening self. Activity beyond my roles is difficult to maintain over long periods of time and in stressful situations. I am not able to act "automatically" outside role expectations for me. In contrast, role playing is fairly mechanical and unplanned.

Unpredictable aspects of my behavior may represent vital components of self and my most significant personal beliefs more accurately than predictable aspects do. My unexpected responses to others in unforeseen situations may be clearest evidence of the existence of self for me and for others. I begin to know who I am and what I believe in more decisively when I allow myself to respond to others genuinely, rather than in strict accord with past habits or precedents. I quash self when I restrict my behavior to traditional role expectations and to what others expect of me.

I can initiate and maintain changes in self only through interaction with emotionally significant others. I cannot change self passively in a vacuum or by thought alone. However much I reflect and consider options for self, the only effective means of modifying my beliefs is through my behavior in relation to others.

In order to succeed in changing my behavior, I must first observe the complex interdependencies in my intimate relationship systems. To a certain extent I must plan my changed participation with emotionally significant others before I act. This forethought will facilitate change in self as my consciously modified role playing will contribute directly to my growth and integration of self.

Within a program of action such as this, it is especially my behavior outside my roles that will modify my I position and self. I must be able to delineate specific ways in which I can go beyond my traditional roles and move away from the binding influence of others' expectations in order to individuate and differentiate self from others. My conventional roles are too frequently paths toward entrenched togetherness with others, which reverse the direction of my growth and development as a self.

INTEGRATION OF PERSONALIZED ROLES

When I interpret the demands of others and modify traditional role expectations to be consistent with my inner beliefs, I personalize my roles. I must choose to play those roles most meaningful to me and most congruent with my own convictions if I am to be an effective self. When the roles I choose to play and the ways in which I choose to meet others' demands are consistent with my personal integrity and objectives, I will be a stronger self than when I habitually accommodate the demands of others in a given situation.

Only when I am able to effectively personalize the roles I play can I have some degree of control over my life decisions. If I merely follow behavior patterns preestablished by others, or those that are an extension of my earlier programming and socialization, I cannot actualize my potential. If I behave automatically and mechanically in different situations, I must question the extent to which self is invested in these repeated activities.

As there are many intrinsic inconsistencies and contradictions in the traditional roles of woman, it is inordinately difficult for me to integrate the diverse variety of expectations implied by these roles with my own personal beliefs. In light of this difficulty, only my personal interpretations of traditional roles can be successfully integrated with my inner convictions. The degree to which my personalized roles eventually become integrated with my beliefs also reflects the degree of consistency of my inner beliefs.

The core of the different modes or levels of integration of my behavior is self. I will be stronger and more effective if my deepest layers of self are integrated and relatively free from inconsistency. I cannot be scattered or lack persistence in my attention to my own priorities without suffering some loss of self.

I must reflect seriously on self before I can act as a self. I must believe in self and act as a self before others will recognize and respect any contributions I may make to a particular relationship system. As my self becomes increasingly integrated at all the different levels of action expression, the degree of compartmentalization that necessarily exists between the roles I choose to play decreases. Contradictions between the roles I play will also be minimized. I decrease estrangement and alienation from others when I am able to personalize the roles I play and integrate my roles with my inner beliefs.

LAYERS OF SELF

Self can be conceptualized as having different levels or layers. My most deep-seated beliefs and convictions make up my innermost or "hard-core" self. This is the most solid and most essential part of my being. I cannot compromise my hard-core self without having destructive consequences in my life and relationships with others. I cannot sell hard-core self at a sacrifice price and continue to live my life fully. I must exact a just price for hard-core self, as I cannot exist without honoring my deepest beliefs and convictions. When I give away or sacrifice hard-core self, I annihilate self.

My most responsible behavior is based on and generated by the qualities of my hard-core self. I can commit myself more genuinely to goals and objectives that represent or reflect my basic beliefs and values. My position on concerns related to my personal beliefs will be easier to define clearly than my views on issues peripheral to my central interests. I have a greater awareness of self when I respond to subjects or situations that are emotionally and intellectually meaningful to me than when I am confronted with more distant topics. I act more effectively whenever my behavior is based on my own inner convictions. In spite of this self-knowledge, I will find it difficult not to negotiate hard-core self with others, even if the consequences of such negotiations will ultimately be to annihilate self. I will be strongly tempted to give up my hard-core self to the other in an emotionally close twosome. The resulting togetherness will eventually undermine my integrity and debilitate or annihilate self. The twosome will not be a viable relationship if this happens. I cannot make such a sacrifice of self if I am to survive in relation to others.

Hard-core self represents my innermost and most integrated layers of self. These central beliefs will optimally manifest themselves in behavior that has maintained some degree of flexibility. If I take a rigid posture in my daily transactions with others, this inflexibility will suggest that I do not have many firm convictions of my own. When I know that my beliefs are strong, I can allow myself to be flexible in my behavior without compromising my beliefs.

"Pseudo-self" refers to the outer layers or relatively fluid and vacillating aspects of self. This peripheral or superficial part of self is characterized by my automatic responsiveness to the role-playing demands of others and to traditional or stereotype expectations. Whereas hard-core self is essentially nonnegotiable in my relationship systems, pseudo-self is fairly easy to negotiate with others. As pseudo-self is made up of attitudes and opinions that are not as deep-seated as the convictions of hard-core self, the consequences of compromising pseudo-self are less deleterious than the consequences of compromising hard-core self. In some instances, I can benefit from trading my opinions with others, but relinquishing my most basic beliefs cannot be profitable for me. I will find it extremely difficult not to absorb both the opinions and the beliefs of others, especially the beliefs and opinions of those who are emotionally closest to me.

To be persistently strong in my diverse transactions with others, I must develop a substantial hard-core self. If I sacrifice self to a relationship system or to another person, I dilute or neutralize my hard-core self. The ensuing fused relationships I have with others will leave me with little or no hard-core self and a weak pseudo-self.

In order to grow in the midst of my many dependencies and responsibilities, I must value my hard-core self more than any other part of me and more than a particular relationship or relationships in general. I can thrive and develop self satisfactorily only when I place my highest premium on honoring my innermost convictions through action. By freeing self I allow others to free self. My growth as a woman may be followed by man's growth. Each person's development is characterized by a similar sequence of action and interaction.

FLEXIBILITY AND STRENGTH

I must be resourceful if I am to accomplish what I believe to be my most responsible long-range objectives. In many ways, personal strength depends on the extent of my flexibility. When I am arbitrary, rigid, and dogmatic, I am weak.

Although intellectually I may agree that my self is more complex and more comprehensive than the sum total of the roles I play, I will tend to repeat patterns of behavior that are familiar to me. The tenacity with which I adhere to my established role playing is directly correlated to my weakness of self: The more I mechanically conform with others' expectations and demands in the roles I choose to play, the more ineffective I will be in relation to others. When I can personalize my roles and express hard-core self through my actions, I will be stronger and more flexible in my different relationships. I can most fully honor the other by respecting my own innermost convictions and by perceiving self to be both in and beyond the roles I am expected to play.

Togetherness with others can be viewed as a force or drive that moves in the opposite direction to individuation of self. When I am primarily concerned with seeking others' approval or with maintaining equilibrium in my personal relationships, I cannot simultaneously give adequate attention to honoring hard-core self by differentiating or individuating self from others in my relationship systems.

Conventional role playing is representative of a shared

togetherness orientation in behavior. When I choose to duplicate traditional roles, I sacrifice self for others' approval by conforming to their expectations with prescribed rules of behavior. When I respond so directly and impersonally to others, I conduct myself as a pseudo-self and, at the same time, risk destroying hard-core self. Traditional role playing is generally so ingrained that I cannot strengthen or develop self through these kinds of activities. The transactions of role playing are largely based only on pseudo-self. My personal beliefs may not be called into question by these kinds of automatic habits or established patterns of behavior.

Roles reflect others' norms and, even though they may be inconsistent or contradictory within and between themselves to some extent, they are generally more compatible with conventional or societal goals than with personal goals. Some degree of deviating from role expectations is an essential element in individuating self. If I want to grow as a self, others' expectations must become less influential in my decision making and general behavior. My new strength as a self depends, in large part, on the flexibility of my responses and activities.

Successful individuating is synonymous with strengthening self. Individuating promotes increased flexibility in self and in my position in my most significant relationship system, as well as a heightened awareness of my hard-core self. I must be able to create and re-create flexibility in my behavior at the same time that I maintain firm stands in relation to others, if I am to grow and strengthen self effectively.

When I focus my attention on traditional role playing and attaining others' approval, rather than on self, I will become rigid in my behavior. To the extent that individuation serves to increase my flexibility and strength, role playing weakens self through its implicit denial of hard-core self and its unquestioning and rigid adherence to previously established patterns of behavior.

If I can substitute action generated by self for some of my automatic role playing, my behavior will gradually have a more constructive impact on broad social change processes. When I am able to change self and take more control over some facets of my life, I will be more able to influence far-reaching kinds of social change. When I have strengthened self, I can become more effectively engaged in conventional political action, and more able to inspire others to change self. To a certain extent, my increasingly differentiated self will compel those who are emotionally closest to me to change self through the intensity of their dependency on me. As I become a self, others will have to change their functioning due to their emotional investment in my behavior. Others need my responses as much and sometimes more than I need their responses.

Changes in self are qualitatively different from mechanical or technical exchanges of roles with others. Playing a different role is not the same as self development. I can be flexible and strong only when I am able to release myself from the necessity or obligation of ingrained role playing and act for self. My flexibility and strength lie essentially outside the roles I play, although I need to maintain an awareness of role expectations and some degree of role playing in my overall behavior. My strongest and most flexible I is both the essence of the roles I play and the transcendence of my roles. My versatility in perceiving self is a source of my strength and flexibility. I am part of my roles but I am more than the roles I play.

Chapter 8

Economic Independence and Being a Self

In order to be an effective self, I must have economic independence. The success of my efforts to gain economic independence is largely dependent on the success of my attempts to differentiate self from those who are emotionally close to me. Only when I have economic independence from my parents, spouse, children, and others who are emotionally close to me, can I act decisively for self. If I am economically dependent on family members, I risk having my funds cut off when my behavior does not gain sufficient approval from them.

Conditions of economic independence do not necessarily entail having a substantial income. I can pursue my own goals responsibly with relatively minimal financial means. I do need to be able to provide adequate subsistence for myself, however, so that I can live and die responsibly. I do not need to keep abreast with current fashions and luxuries.

I must become a breadwinner, to some extent, so that I can shoulder my part of the economic burden of family commitments. I can neither shirk financial responsibilities nor assume too much economic responsibility for others without losing self. My financial dependencies are a fairly accurate reflection of the nature of my emotional dependencies. Where economic dependencies are extreme and complex in their relatedness, I will be relatively trapped in the underlying emotional network of the economic dependencies.

Economic independence cannot be confused with having a profession or a career. Although I may get a stronger sense of self and personal fulfillment from being a professional or from having a career, I can easily lose self by overinvesting in a work system. I am able to preserve self in a work setting when I am able to retain a certain degree of autonomy in complex professional obligations and responsibilities. I may be a successful professional when I have been able to differentiate self successfully, but having a successful career is no guarantee that I am a strong self.

Differentiation and individuation of self are not dependent on certain levels of educational attainment or occupational standing. The accoutrements of professional success may lull me into a false sense of self-differentiation, when in reality I continue to be unproductively dependent on those I work with, as well as on those who are intimately close to me. My basic need is for minimum economic independence, rather than for social mobility and high achievement in a career.

ECONOMIC ADAPTIVENESS

Woman is traditionally viewed as both economically and emotionally dependent on man. However, woman is inherently no more economically or emotionally dependent on man than man is inherently economically or emotionally dependent on woman.

To the extent that woman is emotionally adaptive to man, she is also economically adaptive to him. The extent of woman's economic adaptiveness is also a fairly accurate measure of the extent of her emotional adaptiveness.

Historically, woman's economic standing has been determined almost exclusively by her dependency on other family members and on workers in the economy. Woman has tended to be more malleable and more compromising than man in most social and emotional situations. Some consequences of these patterns of adaptation are that I will easily fill a role or position that complements man's activities, or I will find myself strongly inclined to remain visibly dependent on man.

Stereotype views of woman suggest that I cannot be actively assertive and follow my interests without denying my femininity. I am thought of as having my existence in the shadow of man's dominance. I may conclude from these perceptions of woman that my roles as wife and mother, in spite of being socially acceptable, are not directly advantageous to me in market bargaining processes. Although this may be a fairly accurate view of my general economic standing, I need not think that my family experiences have weakened my effectiveness as a person. I can make many gains for self in being wife and mother. The essence of my freedom lies in the choices I have in perceiving self. I need not accept others' perceptions of who I am or what I should do.

In order to change self and maintain those changes, I must move out of my posture of economic adaptiveness. The existence of economic dominance in my intimate relationships is as potentially destructive to my being as the presence of emotional dominance. Although the moves I must make toward becoming a stronger self will predictably precipitate negative responses from my spouse, parents, and children, I must have sufficient economic independence in relation to those who are emotionally closest to me in order to maintain my changed position of self.

When I am a stronger self, I will be better able to make

an accurate estimate of my economic worth on the job market. If I am able to break through my adaptiveness with my most emotionally significant others, I will be able to gain a certain degree of economic independence from them. The kind of work I do or the ways in which I gain my economic independence are not as important in this sequence of events as the fact that I receive sufficient income to claim my own economic independence. Although my selection of a particular occupation is undoubtedly a serious and important concern and a meaningful aspect of my self-fulfillment, my personal freedom is ultimately based on my economic autonomy, rather than on the particular work style or occupation I choose.

ECONOMIC AND EMOTIONAL DEPENDENCE

Woman is characterized primarily by her emotional and economic dependencies. Economic dependence implies excessive emotional dependence. When I can identify the different kinds of economic dependencies and transactions in my family, I will be able to delineate the intensity of the network of emotional dependencies in this system.

I may not necessarily have to hold a job in order to have an income and economic independence, although this is usual. To the extent that I have an income that does not depend on living members of my family, I will be able to be sufficiently independent in my actions and emotional relationships. The source of my economic independence is not as vital a component of my emotional independence as the fact that I have financial resources that are not supplied by a living family member. Although there may be strong emotional continuities in my dependency on living family members when my income is the bequest of a deceased relative, these attachments are not as restrictive as if my financial assets were supplied by a living family member. When I am supported by a bequest, I may be overly concerned about those who were emotionally closest to the person who left me the funds. However, this involvement is less threatening to my freedom than is economic dependence on living relatives. Bequeathed resources cannot be terminated if I do not meet the approval of the living close relatives. However, if I am economically dependent on living family members, I will constantly be vulnerable to the possibility that my funds will be terminated unless I gain sufficient approval. Financial dependence on a living family member is precarious in that resources can be terminated arbitrarily, without any consideration of my responsibilities beyond that person's perception of my part in the emotional fusion of the twosome.

Although other family members may initially object to my seeking economic independence in the same way that they resist any change I make in my behavior, in the long run they will respect my economic independence. My spouse may disapprove of my working out of the home, for example, but eventually he will acknowledge some of the benefits he gains from having less overall financial responsibility for our family, an additional income, and increased emotional independence. Economic changes are an integral part of the more significant modifications of my family emotional system that occur in response to my changes in self. I cannot change self sufficiently by focusing solely on economic aspects of my behavior, however. Above all I must continuously heighten my awareness of my emotional functioning.

TERRITORIALITY

A significant aspect of my necessary economic independence is my ability to maintain some territory of my own. I need a place where I know that my thinking and reflections will be mine, rather than responses or reactions to others' expectations and demands. When I can think clearly for myself, I will be more likely to make decisions and act in accordance with my own beliefs. My expression of self is made more possible and more probable by having my own territory.

Although my territorial needs may be most easily met by my arranging individual living quarters, geographical separation from others to create conditions where I can clear my thinking and make decisions about self is not necessary. I can share a residence and function effectively as a self, if I have access there to quarters that are essentially mine. My needs for privacy and a place of my own are deep-seated. I easily lose self when I use only areas that are already occupied, managed, or owned by others.

As a woman, I am conditioned to think that man provides a house for his family and that woman stays there and maintains it. I will be freer if I contribute directly toward the provision and maintenance of my home, with the knowledge that I have earned my share of the owned or rented property. I have a responsibility to supply my own territory and the resources to maintain it.

My living space may be a corner of a room, or it may be a substantial residence. Whether my living space is large or small, the contribution I make toward its purchase or support will enable me to be freer than if I did not assume a responsibility for its existence. I become stronger as a self through providing my own territory. The personal place I inhabit is also an important means of my becoming more of a self, although merely having territory cannot change self for me. My living space is significant to my differentiating self when I actively select my territory and maintain my awareness that this personal area is conducive to my growth and development.

My needs for privacy and territory are so fundamental

to my being that I can view them as manifestations of my animal origins and continuities in my relatedness with all members of the animal kingdom. I cannot deny basic needs of this kind and at the same time continue to grow and develop as a self. Only when I am aware of some of my limitations of change in self, as well as of my potential for change, can I control my life. When I respect my territorial needs, I increase my awareness of both my limitations and my potential.

LAST WILL AND TESTAMENT

Responsible economic independence includes some long-range planning for a variety of contingencies. I need to provide for my old age, for example, as well as for my more immediate needs. I need to contribute my fair share to the expenses involved in the support of my children or elderly parents. I need some assurance that my assets will be disposed of adequately and responsibly after my own death.

The ways I choose to distribute my possessions at my death represent self in the same way that the patterns of my earning and spending money during my lifetime do. My planned gifts to others at my death reflect many of the emotional dependencies I have in my lifetime. The flow of money and possessions in the direction of either giving or receiving draws into sharp relief the network of feelings and interdependence in my personal relationships. I am emotionally most dependent on those from whom I receive gifts and on those to whom I give gifts.

My will has a characteristic of finality and a special significance for self and others that my routine day-to-day transactions do not have. My will continues to have this personal importance, even though I may choose to deny my death and to deny the advantages of making my own will. I may encourage my spouse to assume the responsibility of making a will for us both, for example, without acknowledging my responsibility to make decisions and plans for the distribution of my own economic assets. One of my first steps in economic independence may be to make my own will.

My will is one of the most personal statements I can make; it may be viewed as an expression of my most vital thoughts, interests, and feelings. If I examine the bequests of significant deceased members of my family, I will be able to delineate the most intense dependencies and feelings in past generations, and repetitions of these entrenched patterns in present generations. Although the wills of deceased members of my family are not sufficiently detailed to give accurate information on the complete range of sources of income and disposition of income in my family, the patterns of distribution of assets at death can suggest the major trends of dominance and adaptiveness over several generations.

If I am to free self, I must become as aware as possible of the network of dependencies that has stretched through many generations of my family. I will be able to take a firm stand in relation to impairing and inhibiting intensities in living generations of my family only when I am able to recognize a variety of patterns of dependence in past generations. When I am sufficiently aware of economic and emotional trends in several generations of my family of origin, I will be able to assume my economic responsibilities for effective long-range planning. Making my last will and testament is one way to free myself from some of the more immediate economic and emotional dependencies in my family, as well as a way to invest in self.

MATERIAL NEEDS

In order to grow and develop as a self, I must have sufficient means of my own so that I can act autonomously. I cannot allow others to impinge on my freedom to be a self without losing self. However, I do not need a great abundance of material goods and conveniences in order to grow and develop. In most circumstances, I will be able to be a stronger self when my access to material goods is limited. My total economic resources should be adequate, rather than overly abundant, in order to facilitate my efforts to differentiate self. If I prolong my efforts to change self throughout my life, my awareness of the advantages of having limited economic resources may have a variety of implications for my daily activity. I need not place a high premium on economic achievement when other activities would be more meaningful to me.

Acquiring or experimenting with different lifestyles may be an integral part of my personal growth, especially if I find it difficult to break away from the emotional tightness of my family. A change in lifestyle does not necessarily signal a change of self, however, and a change in lifestyle could in fact indicate that there has been no change in self. A complete transformation of my lifestyle suggests as much continued emotional dependency on patterns of living in my family of origin as a repetition of parental living patterns does. Also, to the extent that my changed lifestyle is merely an expression of increased opulence, the underlying network of emotional dependencies in my relationship system remains unchanged, in spite of the modifications in surface appearance.

Economic independence and emotional maturation frequently include a move in the direction of subsistence living, rather than toward expensive habits. I can be more aware of my own beliefs and convictions when unrest and discomfort are not lulled out of my awareness by largesse. Relative poverty appears to be more conducive to serious and responsible reflection than are riches and creature comforts. Economic and emotional autonomy are not dependent on the satisfaction of a large variety of material needs.

Social mobility and class-oriented behavior are characteristic of strivings for emotional togetherness rather than individuation. Emotional and economic independence are qualities that are more directly related to who I am and what I stand for than to current customs, fashions, or fads in the wider society. Conforming with others as I satisfy my material wants serve to keep the economic machinery of society moving in the direction of maintaining the status quo. In contrast, economic and emotional independence are integral parts of my own personal change and usually involve limiting my demand for material goods. As I gain increased economic and emotional independence, there will be some corresponding qualitative changes in the broader social system. When economic independence is sufficiently pervasive, there will be an increase in the flexibility of society's complex relationship systems. By striving for economic independence and making efforts to be a self, I can have a part in these broader social change processes.

Chapter 9

Woman in the Home and Out

I am more than a combination or sequence of roles that I play in my family. However, there appears to be a strong relationship between how I interact with members of my family and how I behave in other social settings. Usually my activities in the home influence my activities outside the home, rather than the other way around.

Throughout my efforts to differentiate self, I continuously clarify the boundaries of my relatedness with others. As I am a participant in many relationship systems, I will be able to define self clearly only when I can distinguish my position from others in these different groups. My awareness of my own inner beliefs and convictions is inextricably linked with the degree of my emotional dependence on those who are emotionally closest to me.

The conditions that surround and influence woman in the home and out are not qualitatively different from the conditions that surround and influence man in the home and out. I share many of the same kinds of difficulties and limitations in changing self as man. My time and energy are scarce resources for me in the same way that man's time and energy are scarce resources for him. I share most human characteristics with man. Both woman and man need to work toward individuation or differentiation of self in order to improve their quality of life experiences.

To the extent that I can differentiate self effectively only in relation to my family, the quality of my activity out of my home will depend on the ways in which I behave in my home. However, as my most long-standing significant emotional relationships are with members of my family of origin rather than with members of my nuclear family, a retreat into my nuclear family may not be productive for my growth and development. Although my behavior out of the home is strongly influenced by my behavior in the home, both phases of my activity are ultimately dependent on the quality of my participation in my family of origin. When these complex interdependencies are considered more fully, it appears that a literal interpretation of the traditional view that woman is more appropriately occupied by staying in her nuclear family home can be detrimental to woman's well-being.

FAMILY INFLUENCES

My family emotional system, with its manifold complexities, generally exerts a very powerful influence on my life decisions and day-to-day behavior. The nature of my relationships in my family of origin in large part determines my behavior in my nuclear family and in other social settings. One way to become more objective about self is to observe the extent to which my behavior changes according to whether I am at home with my family or out of my home and with a particular social group. Even though my behavior may appear to be distinctively different in these two settings, my awareness of self and my effectiveness as a self have many common denominators in each situation. The linkages of interdependence in my family are so intense and so potent that my activity in other social settings is more influenced by these programmed patterns than my participation in social systems is able to modify my family behavior.

My behavior at home is a fairly reliable indicator of how I perform out of the home. If I want to predict how effectively I may respond to a set of particular circumstances out of the home, for example, I must first observe and assess the strengths and weaknesses of my participation in relation to my family. If I am able to take a strong stand for self when communicating with my spouse or a parent, I will usually be able to hold a similarly strong stand in relation to my boss, partner, or friend. If I am able to maintain a strong stand with my boss, partner, or friend, however, it does not necessarily follow that I will be able to take a strong position with my spouse or a parent.

The different relationship systems I belong to overlap with each other in many complex ways. I cannot compartmentalize my roles and relationships without losing my sense of self and some personal integrity. In order to strengthen self, I must seek out the interconnectedness between the different facets of my behavior, rather than fragment my activities. Compartmentalization is an unproductive process, which, if it persists, will tend to be interrupted by breakdowns of self in symptomatic behavior. The broad and deep-seated interdependencies between my relationship systems in and out of the home will continue to exist even if I choose to deny their significance. Unless I am able to recognize and exert some control over these different role and relationship influences in my life, they will take more and more control of me.

Using more scientific language, family relatedness may be viewed as an independent variable in complex situations produced by broad ranges of human behavior. This idea expressed artistically includes the portrayal or symbolization of family relatedness in all human interaction. As a woman, I can also view my family relationships and my emotional bondedness with other human beings as parts of my kinship with the animal kingdom. When I rationalize my behavior and articulate what I consider to be logical and credible explanations of why I act in particular ways, I deny the influence of my emotional relatedness with others. Most of the animal qualities of being and behavior are manifested primarily in my family and secondarily in other social settings. Woman in the home may be thought of as being more animal than woman out of the home, but both aspects of my behavior are animal and are closely related to each other.

SHARED RESPONSIBILITIES

Among my unique characteristics as a human being are my reflective awareness and my sense of responsibility. Being responsible for self may include pursuing my thrust for crude animal survival, but ideally my sense of responsibility goes far beyond my having a preoccupation with merely staying alive. My responsibility for self must ultimately be primarily concerned with the fact that my life consists of activity that involves others and extends further than my own bodily survival.

I am unique in that my understanding of my own responsibility is distinct from how others view my responsibility. As a woman, however, I do not have a qualitatively different responsibility from man. I share the same ranges and varieties of responsibilities with man. Both woman and man have the critical responsibility to express their inner beliefs through behavior directed toward long-range goals, rather than through behavior that relieves tension.

My responsibility to self and others is not influenced by my being woman or man. I must necessarily choose how to respond as a woman, even though the pressure of others' expectations and perceptions of how a woman behaves responsibly may be considerable. In many instances, others' views of my responsibility will differ substantially from my own perception of how I can and should behave.

I am ultimately responsible for all my actions. Woman and man share their responsibility, which I express through the effectiveness of my ability to control my decisions on how I feel, think, and act. The integrity of my behavior in the home and out involves many of the same issues as the integrity of man's behavior in the home and out. The challenges I meet as I express my responsibility for self are not qualitatively different from the challenges man meets in expressing his responsibility. I am faced with and must deal with the same complexities and intricacies of interdependencies in my relationship system as man, and I have the same difficulties and limitations in changing self. Although the content of programming influences and traditional cultural expectations for woman and man differ, both woman and man have the same degree of responsibility for their choices of behavior. Woman and man each face the dilemma of deciding whether or not responsibility for self lies in conforming with others' expectations or gaining approval in particular situations.

I cannot assume responsibility for others without losing self and thereby becoming irresponsible. Due to the inextricable relatedness of my behavior in and out of the home, only after I have assumed a responsible posture in the context of my family will I be able to behave responsibly in other social settings. I share these aspects of interrelated influences in my behavior and characteristics of responsibility with man. If I deny the extent to which I manifest a common human condition and share common responsibilities with man, I cannot view self objectively and I cannot behave effectively as a self. I undermine my own interests in setting woman apart from man, especially in relation to an issue such as responsibilities in the home and out of the home.

BOUNDARIES OF SELF

I find it difficult and sometimes impossible to draw boundaries to separate self from those with whom I am most emotionally involved. However, my capacity to delineate meaningful boundaries or definitions for self is a crucial component of my understanding of how I can act most effectively. My activities and my being must aim to extend and capitalize on my corporeal existence, although the physical dimensions of my body are ultimately limiting factors of self. In addition to my more observable animal characteristics, I am an active participant in a number of different relationship systems. Due to the intensity of my family dependencies, I move from particular functioning positions in relation to emotionally significant others to similar positions in different social groups.

When I undertake the task of defining self in the network of my intimate relationships, I find that I am more able to draw consistent and effective boundaries for self in my family of origin than in my nuclear family. It is markedly easier for me to separate self from my parents and my siblings than it is to delineate boundaries between self and my spouse or self and my children. The dependencies inherent in marriage and parenting are too intense and too binding to allow me to have a manageable degree of objectivity about these relationships and my participation in them.

The intensity of my emotional involvement with my spouse may be characterized as positive or negative. It is the factor of depth of involvement with my spouse that creates the relationship conditions that make it overwhelmingly difficult for me to gauge accurately where self ends and my spouse begins. A positive, congenial emotional field between me and my spouse may be more inhibiting and more difficult to manage in my task of defining boundaries for self than a negative, conflictual emotional field. If I have an emotionally fused conflict with my spouse, my repeated "anti" positions may give me a clearer sense of self than my perpetual use of "we" or a "me too" stand, which are characteristics of an intensely shared togetherness. Also, although much of the conflict between me and my spouse may be habitual and nonproductive, serving the general purpose of sporadically exploding or violently diffusing the intensity of the emotional boundedness in our twosome, some of the marital conflict could contribute toward creating boundaries for self.

In an intense togetherness with my spouse, I will tend either to dominate or to become adaptive and submissive. If I become less dominant or less submissive, my spouse will become correspondingly more dominant or more submissive. My spouse's level of adaptation depends on my functioning position. In this complex process of complementary interdependency, the reciprocal "seesaw" moves to high- or low-functioning positions to create temporary or pseudoboundaries of self. Shifts in the boundaries of self in this kind of twosome are precipitated by the level of anxiety in their relationship system and in the families and other significant groups of each spouse. When there is a sufficiently pervasive high level of anxiety, the boundaries will become fixed in artificial positions. Subsequent fluidity and shifts in this intense togetherness will depend on lowering the level of anxiety in the shared and interdependent relationship systems.

The emotional dependency between me and my spouse is so intense that I cannot define boundaries for self in this context. I need to draw closer to emotionally significant others in order to get increased distance and objectivity in my relationship with my spouse. I can only pull away from my spouse sufficiently and begin to consider boundaries of self realistically when I am involved in a different emotional field.

The most effective way I can "triangle" or "detriangle" self in my intimate relationships is to become increasingly involved with members of my family of origin. For example, when I can activate my emotional dependency on my mother, my relationship with my spouse will become less anxious, and I will be able to perceive boundaries of self more realistically in my relationship with my spouse. A diffusion of anxiety will also occur, but to a lesser extent, if I triangle someone who is not a member of my family into the intensity of my twosome with my spouse. Any triangle or three-person relationship will dilute the intensity of the anxiety between my spouse and myself, but having one of my parents as a third person in the triangle will activate more feelings and dilute more anxiety than having a person who is not a member of my family. If the third member of the triangle is not a family member, the newly created three person relationship system is less stable, and this third person may have to be substituted or replaced frequently in order to keep the anxiety in the twosome low enough to make defining the boundaries of self a possibility. My participation in groups out of my home may seem to be emotionally significant, but within a full spectrum of degrees of intensity it is less strong than my family relationships.

It is easy to think that I can effectively define boundaries for self in the work, friendship, or religious groups I belong to, but in several essential respects such an assumption is inaccurate. In order to define self productively, I must have both the challenge of intense emotional involvement in a particular group and the reality and security of continuing group membership. My boundaries of self express my deepest beliefs and convictions. By implication, my boundaries of self must be manifested in my participation in my most intense and most intimate relationships. If I define my boundaries of self effectively, however, I will precipitate resistance from those who are emotionally most involved with me. Consequently, I can only define my boundaries through action when I can be sure that the group I interact with will not exclude me as I try to establish my boundaries.

Work, friendship, and religious systems are relatively temporary groups compared to my family. Social groups of this kind can exclude me fairly easily if I do not conform sufficiently to their expectations. I can be sure that I have activated my own boundaries of self only when I consciously plan my behavior in relation to my primary emotional investment in my family. The definition of effective boundaries of self in relationship systems out of my home automatically follows my successful definition of boundaries of self in my family. When I have surmounted some of the difficulties involved in defining self in my family, I will function differently in other social settings.

TIME AND ENERGY

My decisions to invest time and energy in action in or out of the home are vital aspects of self. The ways I choose to spend my time and energy in large part determine my effectiveness and productivity. My time and energy are my most valuable personal resources. They are scarce commodities of my being and action.

My expenditures of time and energy reflect my innermost beliefs and convictions. When my behavior is productively integrated, my allocation of time and energy will appear to be more balanced than if my beliefs and convictions are contradictory or inconsistent with each other. In order to cope respectfully and efficiently with my most intimate dependencies, I must decide what amount of time and energy I should invest in family interaction and how much time and energy I should invest in other social settings.

I lose my personal effectiveness when I overinvest in relationships with others. In contrast, if I maintain a strong emotional interest in an unattainable goal, I may be able to increase the overall productivity of my other, seemingly unrelated investments of time and energy. If I select objectives I can accomplish easily and adequately, I must constantly replace them with other goals in order to avoid manifesting my automatic tendency to overinvest time and energy in relationships.

The more I am able to gain some degree of objectivity in my life, the more easily I will be able to control my allocation of time and energy. I can make satisfactory decisions about spending my time and energy efficiently only when I can observe and evaluate my behavior fairly objectively. I will be pushed and pulled by the immediacy and exigencies of particular situations unless I can view my life from a broad perspective. My long-range goals are an effective guide for my decision making and investments of time and energy.

My plans must necessarily supersede day-to-day transactions and interactions with my family if they are to be useful. My expression of self relates to my family and at the same time transcends my family. However abstract or remote my long-range goals seem to be, I cannot allow these objectives to justify means that would deny my dependence on others. I need to maintain a high level of awareness and respect both for my own strengths and frailties and for those of others if I am to be responsible in all facets of my behavior.

I can meet my needs for others effectively and responsibly when I ensure that the quality of time and energy spent with them has a higher priority than the amount of time and energy invested. My efforts to strive toward goals that transcend my family generally have the effect of increasing family members' respect for my activities.

My family relationships become more enjoyable and more flexible when I spend some of my time and energy outside my home. The intensity in my nuclear family is diluted by my action decisions to invest time and energy in activities that transcend these relationships. My spouse and my children are freer to be autonomous when my activities allow them to be responsible and to function more or less independently of my needs. My contact with those emotionally closest to me gains in respect and tolerance when I turn away from, rather than persistently toward, members of my nuclear family.

One of the most productive ways to invest my time and energy is to increase the quality of my contacts with my family of origin. If in the past I have not had frequent contact with my parental families, I may increase my contacts as a first step toward enhancing their quality. If I have had very frequent contact with particular members of my extended families in the past, however, I will be well advised to decrease these contacts somewhat, or at least to communicate with family members with whom I have not had a viable relationship. Throughout all exchanges with members of my family of origin, I must remain focused on self and at the same time sufficiently responsive to others in order to be productive and effective as a self.

When I evaluate my options in deciding how and where to invest my precious limited supply of time and energy, I may be able to establish priorities in terms of their usefulness for my development of self. The more time and energy I invest outside my immediate family relationships, the more flexible my nuclear relationships will become. This sequence of events is especially important as the usual tendency in my nuclear family is toward emotional overload. The more time and energy I invest in my family of origin, the more autonomously I will function in my nuclear family and in the other groups I participate in.

LIMITATIONS

It is only after I have identified my personal limitations fairly accurately that I will be able to be effective in my behavior in the home and out. When I know the limitations of my time and energy, for example, I will be able to plan my use of these scarce resources more effectively than if I was not aware of my limitations. I can become stronger through my recognition and acceptance of my limitations. The restrictions inherent in my human condition dictate much of my behavior. When I can assess my shared weaknesses and frailties, I am more likely to respect self and others realistically.

One of my most significant characteristics as a human being is my emotional need for others. This dependency consists of my need for emotional closeness and responses from significant others, rather than for mere crude physical survival. The satisfaction of my need for emotional dependence is perhaps as vital to my survival and general well-being in important respects as the satisfaction of my physical survival needs. When I am aware of my need for interdependence, essentially a significant and forceful limitation on my autonomy and activity, I can at the same time choose to be a little more independent of others.

My recognition and acceptance for my limitations will enable me to be more objective about planning my activity in the home and out. If I cannot strengthen self through total investment in my nuclear family, I can sometimes increase my effectiveness by becoming more involved in groups out of my home, especially if I build relationships in my family of origin. I am usually more responsible if I divide my activities between my nuclear family and other groups.

When I believe that responsibility for self must necessarily include assessing my limitations and respecting my dependencies, I will be more able and more likely to curb my strong inclination to overextend my feelings of being responsible for others. When I value and respect my weaknesses as well as my strengths, I will delegate tasks and responsibilities to others efficiently. When I draw boundaries for self, I can simultaneously recognize and value my limitations. Only when these conditions have been acknowledged can I assume my responsibility for self in the home and out.

I may be a more effective self if I overtly acknowledge that I am not omnipotent, and if I assume that I am more or less powerless to determine my destiny. I must be self-focused before I can contribute to others productively. When I examine my beliefs and convictions closely, I find that I cannot be infinitely flexible in my relationships and transactions with others. However, I must maintain at least a minimum degree of flexibility in order to adapt to others and survive. When I am aware of my hard-core self, I will know that my innermost beliefs and convictions cannot be compromised without a destructive loss of self. It is perhaps in my "weakness" or shortcoming of inflexibility that my strength as a self lies. My behavior in the home and out must be based on uncompromised integrated beliefs if I am to be a responsible self.

In some ways, my vital uniqueness as a self can be perceived as a collection of patterns of behavior that indicate where my limited ability to conform with others is most marked. When I discover and accept the spectrum of the varied dimensions of my uniqueness, I will be better able to decide how to use my time and energy in and out of the home responsibly and effectively. After I have recognized my own limitations and uniqueness, I can appreciate the uniqueness of others and respect their limitations. The personal balance I achieve between activities in my home and in the outside world can be created and maintained only in an atmosphere of tolerance and understanding of human limitations.

Chapter 10

And They All Lived Happily Ever After . . .

Perhaps it is only in fairy stories or in fantasy that everlasting happiness for all is the most appropriate or most usual outcome for disparate sets of circumstances and individuals. Happiness is such an elusive human quality that it is difficult for me to be sure that it actually exists. If happiness can be found or earned, perhaps individuals, rather than a whole group, are more likely to find or earn it. To the extent that happiness has been part of my own experience, I may question whether it is possible for me to share my happiness or experience it with others. Perhaps the exploitation of others rather than the sharing of happiness, is an intrinsic characteristic of human existence and the human condition.

Although issues and questions of this kind are largely unfathomable, I can and inevitably must select some assumptions to use in relation to the multitudinous dimensions of my perception and the myriad ways I interact with others. Furthermore, I must have sufficient confidence in the assumptions I make about self and others so that I am able to depend on at least some of my guesses in order to survive. I have to delineate a few facts in my daily life in order to make a modicum of sense out of the complex whole of my impressions and interactions. However, it may be constitutionally impossible for me to utterly disbelieve in happiness or in its availability to all.

I cannot scientifically prove hypotheses that substantiate the quantity or quality of happiness in human relationships, but I can conceptualize happiness in more scientific terms than are customarily used. Happiness may be viewed as a component of the emotional field of a relationship system, for example, rather than as a moral dimension of utopian vision. My personal happiness may be thought of as resulting more from my responsible realization of self and my mature interaction with others than from a titillation of my sense. If I tentatively accept a definition of happiness that derives from my actualization of self in relationship systems, I will begin to recognize different manifestations of happiness in my daily activities. Although many traditional and conventional meanings have been given to happiness, the essence of the term can perhaps be more satisfactorily captured by pinpointing relationship characteristics of happiness than by emphasizing random transient saccharine qualities of feelings of happiness.

Happiness is a process rather than a final state, a journey rather than a point of departure or a point of arrival. Happiness suggests conditions where an individual's flow of activity is possible along with a mutual give-and-take between self and others. I am happy when I am flexible in my behavior without compromising self. This quality of happiness is perhaps closer to fulfillment than to pleasure.

I must travel with woman and man toward increased mutual respect if I am to be relatively free. My autonomy and security will grow if my efforts extend over sufficiently long periods of time. It is only when I make a conscious and effective effort to define self clearly that I can move from the pain of suffocating togetherness and compromising adaptiveness toward fulfillment of self.

HAPPINESS AS RESPECT

My differentiation of self enriches the quality of my life experience to such an extent that it is easy for me to conclude that the difficulties and tortuous efforts involved in the individuation process have a direct bearing on the personal happiness that results. One of the major salient characteristics of the improvements in my life is my enhanced respect for self and for others. I am better able to feel and show respect for self and others at emotional, thinking, and action levels of my behavior. I give respect to self and others more responsibly; I am more genuinely appreciative of self and others. In return for this posture, I receive more respect from self and others. This ambience or emotional climate of tolerant give-and-take is a vital dimension of happiness that includes but transcends feelings of superficial enjoyment.

In the initial stages of my definition of self, however, and throughout my continued efforts to grow and develop as a self, I will have to deal with negative feelings of self and others. I will probably feel unhappy, for example, when I realize that my personal freedom can be achieved only when I am willing to risk estranging or alienating emotionally significant others. Those closest to me communicate that they are unhappy, that they believe I make them unhappy when I define self, and they reactively try to exert pressure on me to revert to my former behavior. The necessary loneliness or aloneness involved in differentiation of self tends to increase my anxiety and may contribute to my automatically feeling unhappy during my most diligent efforts to differentiate self.

If I can survive the painful initial stages of differentiating self without relinquishing my attempts to grow and develop self, I will gradually experience some fulfillment and increased respect. I will not lose my tendency to feel fearful and unhappy, however successful I may be in strengthening self, or however much emotional courage I may be able to muster. Although my family may be observably calm and congenial during my efforts to differentiate self, a latent but pervasive inclination toward anxiety exists at all times. Unrest, disturbances of the status quo, and crises with shock waves may easily reverberate throughout the whole system. The earlier traumas related to my differentiating self may erupt with seemingly little or no provocation, for example.

Although happiness cannot be thought of as being synonymous with respect, perhaps respect is a necessary condition of my living happily ever after. Unless I have respect for self and others, I will not be able to make productive long-range plans for my life. Unless I continually preserve my awareness of the importance of respect in all my relationships, my happiness will be transient.

To some extent, both happiness and respect are components of the contagion that is endemic to relationship systems. My happiness and respect for self and others are products of the emotional systems I participate in as well as products of my individuating efforts. My dependency on others is painfully exposed by my pronounced physical and emotional inability to become autonomous. There is such a high degree of reciprocity and emotional contagion in my relationship systems that my respect for self and happiness may be shortlived unless those close to me acknowledge these qualities also. In reality, my respect and happiness may not be ultimately recognized and accepted by others, however. My effective differentiation of self will precipitate some change in others' behavior, even though these changes may be largely adaptive, functional changes rather than real modifications of differentiation. If these complex interactive processes include an emulation of my own respect and happiness by others, my decision to live happily ever after may encourage others' abilities and decisions to live happily ever after.

WOMAN AND MAN

Respect and happiness are integral parts of my mature and responsible recognition of the mutual emotional dependence of woman and woman and woman and man. If I can respect woman and man and acknowledge the fact that to some extent my happiness is dependent on both woman and man, I will be more likely to be both respected and happy. This recognition of mutual dependency does not postulate the necessity of either dominance or submission in relationships between woman and woman or woman and man.

Absolute equality between woman and man does not exist and is an impossible goal, as is absolute equality between woman and woman. Human beings are unequal in several respects, and man is as weak in his personal characteristics as woman is in hers. Man is not necessarily dominant and woman submissive, for example, in the same way that woman is not necessarily dominant and man submissive. Although I am culturally conditioned to behave in submissive ways more than man, if I believe that I am as much a self as man, I will be able to act more freely than if I did not have this belief. I cannot consciously strive to be more than man or less than man if I am to be responsible and act responsibly.

I have a variety of contacts with man, even though I might be most aware of my age-peer relationships with him. I participate in woman-man relationships that cross different generations, for example. As my most meaningful and most vital emotional relationships are in my family, the quality of my relationships with my father, my brothers, and my sons will tend to influence my relationships with man. If my closeness to my father or sons is overly intense, I can gain some degree of freedom or flexibility in these relationships by getting closer to my mother or to my daughters. The complex interdependency between woman and man is both potent and pervasive. The degree of dependency I perceive and actualize between woman and man underlies all my most intimate and most significant emotional relationships, including my relationships with woman. If I want to improve the quality of my relationships with woman, I must improve the quality of my relationships with man as well as with woman directly. I cannot sacrifice self to man and gain respect from woman. My respect for woman grows out of and is dependent on my respect for man, as my respect for man is based on my respect for woman. Traditional submissive-dominant patterns of behavior between woman and man are not respectful and are not conducive to my happiness or to others' happiness. I must define self through responsible action and allow man to define self through responsible action if change in traditional roles is to become sufficiently pervasive to bring about broader shifts in behavior.

I will usually be compelled to relate to man through my mother, sisters, and daughters. My daughters may effectively introduce man to my most intimate relationships system with or without my approval, for example. Man is a constant reality I must deal with. I cannot develop maturity in my relationships with woman or man by cutting myself off from man. I may find that I can improve the quality of my relationships with man more effectively by improving the quality of my contacts with woman, but I cannot relate to woman exclusively or acknowledge woman as superior to man without some loss of self. Woman is as superior a human being as man is superior. If I am to be successful in my thrust to live happily ever after, I must allow man to live happily ever after without sacrificing self. In the long run, man is unable to survive woman's sacrifices. If woman sacrifices self to man and man sacrifices self to woman, both woman and man will become extinct due to their irresponsibility to self and life.

CONTINUOUS GROWTH

I perhaps act most responsibly if I am able to make a decision and commitment to differentiate self over a lifetime. This is a weighty decision and a difficult and elusive commitment, however, and I may choose to avoid the burden of such a responsibility. Under most circumstances, my tendency is to avoid the anxieties that accompany differentiation of self.

Although I may eventually receive respect from those emotionally closest to me who initially responded to my individuation by disapproval, criticism, threats and other attempts to preserve togetherness, I cannot relax my efforts to grow and develop self. If I and those emotionally closest to me are to live happily ever after, I must persist in my attempts to differentiate self. As I persevere in my individuation, I should optimally realize that to a considerable extent I will not be able to differentiate self. Such an acknowledgement of my limitations may preserve my most human qualities in my task of differentiating self. The resistance of others may discourage my individuation, but I must continue to act responsibly, with a full awareness of my strengths and weaknesses. I cannot succumb to the automatic behavior patterns and conditioning of my past if I am to develop self.

Both woman and man will continue to differentiate self if they choose to live happily ever after. Continuities in the growth of both woman and man are vital for my well-being, for woman and for man. Selecting my own goals and objectives, as well as making meaningful decisions about my limited resources of time and energy, are characteristic of continuities in my growth toward personal fulfillment. My happiness is a dividend of my increased maturity, rather than an end in itself, however. Continuities in my growth are preconditions of my happiness, although growth alone cannot guarantee my happiness. After I have accomplished other changes in my life, I will be able to choose happiness, although I cannot focus exclusively on happiness and achieve it.

Although the emotional climate of current times suggests that I can find my most satisfying happiness in personal relationships, this kind of enjoyment or pleasure is in fact generally short-lived and narrow in its scope of expression. Due to my strong tendency to move too close to those who are emotionally significant to me, I can easily become either stifled in the fused sharing of my dependency or limited in my objectives and perspectives. I will eventually lose self and assume the other's objectives and beliefs in this process of togetherness, or dominate the other who will then assume my goals and convictions.

These patterns of interaction suggest that my happiness and the happiness of all cannot occur where conditions of acute and chronic fusion exist in personal relationships and other groups. If I orient my behavior exclusively toward maintaining equilibrium in an intimate twosome, for example, I will become less selective in my behavior and less concerned about my responsibility to formulate a life plan. By seeking peace and approval of the other, I essentially lower my chances of being happy and reduce my opportunities to contribute towards others' happiness. By becoming overly adaptive to others, I lose self, together with the personal fulfillment that accompanies my development and expression of self. I lose the dream and reality of living happily ever after at the same time that I lose my ability to choose and control my life. Even though I can have only a relatively miniscule influence over my activities, the improved quality of relationships and accomplishments within this narrow range of influence is very significant. My life will be distinctly enriched if I can maintain my ability to choose my own objectives and control my behavior. My continuing happiness depends on my continuing growth, even though the increments of my development throughout my lifetime are fractional.

AUTONOMY AND SECURITY

My autonomy and my security are important dimensions of my happiness. The quality of my individual being and the nature of my intimate relationships are interdependent. Each aspect of my autonomy and security derives from my most significant emotional systems. My happiness is contingent upon my ability to act with autonomy and to gain increased autonomy. Independence is a dividend of my self-development and growth.

The quality of my relationships in my family of origin is the strongest determining factor in my quest to strengthen self and my decision of whether or not to allow myself to be happy. Similarly, my behavior influences members of my family more than it influences members of other groups. My own happiness has a greater and more contagious impact on my family than on other groups.

Although I can work to increase my autonomy, independence is an impossible goal for me to attain. A vital human characteristic is that I am physically and emotionally unable to be autonomous. As I am the product of many different kinds of internal and external influences, in particular the emotional forces in my relationship systems, my happiness lies in my efforts to become more autonomous and to apply a working knowledge that absolute autonomy is impossible. One of the most ambitious goals I can have is to increase my autonomy. When I recognize my limitations, I am likely to attain growth and meaningful happiness than if I believe that I have no limitations. I can easily deceive and delude myself with an unrealistic view of my potential, and I will be unable to act responsibly as a consequence.

My security, if it is to be as durable as is humanly possible, must be security in self. The expresssion of my inner beliefs and convictions will be my highest priority if my action is responsible. Only when I actively place my security in self can I give of self productively and contribute meaningfully to others. When I value and realize this quality of personal security in my daily transactions, I will act responsibly in relation to others due to the consistency of my focus on self. When I am more responsible, I allow others to be more responsible and more secure.

As a woman, both my autonor iy and my security must be consciously derived from self. My responsible action for self effectively neutralizes some of the deleterious effects of traditional models of woman. I have been conditioned to believe that man is independent and woman is dependent. However, in reality both woman and man have an equal propensity to define self in terms of autonomy. I have been conditioned to believe that a woman can gain security only if she is submissive or adaptive to man and his goals.

Woman's security is thought to be man. These patterns of highly dependent attitudes and behavior are destructive to both woman and man. I cannot be responsible for self without some degree of autonomy and security in self. As man becomes responsible for woman, he becomes irresponsible.

A utopia of equality and freedom for all is not imminent. Woman and man will probably not be able to live happily ever after. The challenge of the possibility of some changes in this direction is omnipresent, however, and perhaps it is my responsibility to invest my efforts in this direction. In order to become more effective in each decision I make, I must have vision of self and others. My vision optimally includes an expressed sense of quality, respect, and appreciation in human relationships. I cannot change the world to ensure that all live happily ever after, but I can modify self a little and thereby make it more likely that I and others will gain personal and social fulfillment through responsible action. I can attain more autonomy and more security, for example, even though I can be neither autonomous nor secure. At each point of individuation or development of self I am dependent on others, however. Woman's happiness depends on man's happiness to the same extent that man's happiness depends on woman's happiness. Human problems cannot be resolved through exploiting others, even though I may be strongly tempted or inclined to do so. If I allow myself to dominate or to be dominated, I lose self together with my autonomy and security.

FROM PAIN TO FULFILLMENT

A continuum that may be perceived as stretching between personal pain and fulfillment is generally not aligned with gradations of individual political involvement or legislative activities. Although transitions between pain and fulfillment may accompany sectarian militant participation in political liberation movements, these feelings are usually superficial and transient. Only rarely does political participation become an integral part of my efforts to modify and integrate my inner beliefs. However, only my deepest and most personal fulfillment can generate my most valuable and vital happiness.

My most painful feelings generally result from my being trapped in my intimate relationship systems and caught in others' stereotype expectations and demands. Personal fulfillment and happiness accompany or follow my successful efforts to move out of these bonds and traditional roles. When I act more freely, I encourage others to become free.

My "I" activity is the most critical dimension of my existence. My increased focus on I and self guide my action, heighten my sense of responsibility, and promote my effectiveness. The happiness I gain through maximizing the responsibility of my action is in large part due to my strengthened ability to remain outside the restrictive togetherness of my most intimate emotional relationships without becoming isolated. Happiness is essentially being able to choose togetherness without being compelled to fuse with others whenever I enter into a relationship with them. I can be happier when my relationships are flexible. As I develop self, I become increasingly capable of choosing whether or not I will be emotionally close to or distant from others.

I can vary the intensity of my togetherness with others to the extent that I can perceive self objectively and act responsibly. The ways in which I perceive self, the social setting I am in, and the quality of my personal fulfillment are largely dependent on my functioning position in my most intimate relationship systems. The level of anxiety in my personal relationships is another determining influence on my capacity to be objective about self and to act responsibly. If I "deserious" the emotional climate of my intimate relationships, for example, I add human and personal dimensions to the tone and impact of exchanges in this context. Levity and lightheartedness ease tension and create conditions where increased respect and happiness can be cultivated.

My happiness and the happiness of those about me is closely related to self-knowledge and a historical awareness of how those closest to me behave and have behaved in past generations. I can be more sure of successful transition from pain to happiness if I can predict fairly accurately some of the feeling responses and patterns of behavior in my intimate relationships. My ability to predict others' reactions to my individuating activity may not necessarily decrease the pain I feel from precipitating their disapproval. However, I am more likely to be secure as a self and to move from experiencing pain to finding fulfillment if I know the basic feeling and behavior characteristics of my family and other emotionally significant groups.

Political liberation implies that at a certain time a sufficient number of laws can be passed so that I will consider myself to be free from the legal and social shackles that have impeded the development of my potential. There is an unrealistic utopian element in the political liberation ideology and model of human nature, which itself can inhibit growth. The concept of differentiation or individuation of self, in contrast, suggests a continuous process that brings with it no guarantee of complete freedom and no assurance that I can make a definitive move from pain to fulfillment. Differentiation of self is extremely difficult to accomplish. There are also definite limits to the possibility of achieving a substantial increase in my personal level of differentiation. I can only become and act as a self through my own continuous efforts to make responsible decisions.

If I decide to place a high value on my efforts to differentiate self, I can be assured that there will be an increase in more deep-seated aspects of what I know to be happiness. Although pain cannot be eliminated from my day-to-day experience, my chances for personal fulfillment will be increased if I at least try to differentiate self. When I can fully respect my personhood, I will be less likely to regress to patterns of dependence and behavior characteristic of my initial programming and conditioning, and less likely to react automatically to the emotional demands of others. I will not choose the more conventional and traditional interpretations of happiness associated with fused togetherness in intimate relationships, as emotional cosiness of this kind annihilates self. I seek durable happiness rather than fleeting pleasure.

I must maintain my capacity to change self if I am to have some degree of control over my decision of whether or not to experience pain or fulfillment in my different activities. My potential for change of self is narrowly restricted, especially when I view self from biological or evolutionary perspectives. I cannot be sure that anyone will live happily ever after. In spite of the difficulties and limitations involved in freeing self, however, the enriching gains from my knowing self through action surpass many of the pseudogains thought to be produced by political and legal liberation.

Appendix

The Bowen Family Theory

Murray Bowen, M.D., is a pioneer in the development of family theory, especially family systems theory, in the United States. Bowen is currently clinical professor of psychiatry and director of the Family Center, Georgetown University Medical Center, Washington, D.C., and clinical professor and chairman, Division of Family and Social Psychiatry, Virginia Commonwealth University, Medical College of Virginia, Richmond. Although the eight basic concepts of the Bowen theory have not been empirically verified, detailed multigenerational case history data from many hundreds of families provide some evidence to substantiate theoretical synthesis. Bowen has directed clinical and formal research projects on family emotional processes for more than two decades, and has worked with several of the same families throughout this period.

At the outset of his work in theory construction, Bowen purposely selected biological models as the basis for his conceptualization of family emotional processes. He consistently formulated hypotheses congruent with the accepted body of scientific knowledge. Bowen's systematic observations, and those of the researchers who work with him, are used to accumulate facts. This information serves to develop and refine the concepts of family process. The formulations that have evolved are essentially tools to facilitate the collection of data that are intrinsically extremely difficult to describe, order, and quantify. The concepts and hypotheses are generated from a new spectrum of facts and a different dimension of reality in human interaction.

One important premise used in science and in the Bowen family theory is that the natural and human universe is orderly and that some degree of regularity exists in those human events and relationships that appear to be most random. Bowen views the family as the most emotionally intense human relationship system, which characteristically has more repeated patterns of behavior and more reactive interaction than other human groups. Although it is very difficult for individuals to observe their own families accurately, it is possible for an entire family system to change its level of functioning if one family member successfuly modifies habitual functioning positions and, at the same time, stays in emotional contact with a sufficient number of other family members. The possibility of this occurrence generates hypotheses about the potential and limitations of change for one person, one family, and society at large.

To the extent that the Bowen family theory can be viewed as an integral part of science, interaction precipitated by emotional dependencies in families and other human groups may be thought of as components of broad evolutionary processes. Bowen's use of biological models and his insistence and emphasis on the relatedness between human behavior and animal behavior further clarify the holistic evolutionary perspective of his theory. Bowen's key concept of differentiation of self represents and abstracts some of the broadest constructively adaptive aspects of evolution, as well as some of the most miniscule constructively adaptive processes. Maladaptive evolutionary processes, in contrast, are conceptualized as transitions or tendencies toward fusion and togetherness in human relationships.

Some concepts of the Bowen family theory, such as emotional process in society, are specific attempts to describe certain aspects of evolutionary processes in families and larger groups. To the extent that a family emotional system can be compared to other groups with respect to the shared characteristics of intensity of relatedness between members, the Bowen theory can be applied to a variety of social settings. At its present stage of development, however, the empirical base of the Bowen theory is primarily composed of family data, rather than of data from other kinds of groups or from broader social processes. Bowen's theoretical propositions about evolution and evolutionary change continue to be impressionistic, tentative, and somewhat speculative.

As Bowen has focused on patterns of family interaction over extended periods of time, including genealogical research across several hundred years where possible, this family systems theory has a multigenerational perspective for the observation and description of different kinds of interaction. In contrast to much contemporary research on families that examines patterns of family behavior in a typical single life cycle, the Bowen theory suggests that there are many complex and vital linkages between succeeding generations in the same family. The Bowen theory attempts to go beyond the cultural descriptions predominant in contemporary sociological and anthropological family research by postulating that some predictions can be made about a family's tendency to repeat particular patterns of behavior, especially in stressful circumstances.

The Bowen family theory suggests a variety of

applications and implications for the wider society and for further research in the behavioral sciences. Just as the systems thinking underlying Bowen's work is distinctive in the explicitness of its statement of the intricate relatedness of phenomena, the overall view of the universe suggested by the Bowen theory is innovative and perhaps startling. After exposure to the Bowen theory, one is encouraged to reexamine one's preconceived assumptions of cause-effect thinking, as well as the position one has in one's family and the influence this location has on one's behavior in other social settings. Bowen views human emotional dependency as a cornerstone in understanding the many varieties of personal and social interaction that can be observed and described.

HISTORICAL DEVELOPMENT

Bowen has used a family perspective for his studies of human behavior since the early 1950s. The data, which clarify and substantiate different family systems hypotheses, have been accumulated from the early 1950s to the present. As the information collected for some of the families covers several past generations, the facts and patterns of behavior documented have a pronounced longitudinal perspective. Bowen's examination of family interaction over long period of time contrasts with the more conventional, relatively short-range experimental or survey family research, which usually focuses on present circumstances and recent behavior.

Bowen developed his family theory from some of the concepts and techniques of psychoanalysis, although Bowen's frame of reference for the description of individual behavior is consistently the family unit and not the individual. In contrast to psychoanalysis, Bowen emphasizes the significance of the emotional field in several generations of family. With respect to clinical practice, Bowen specifies that a therapist will be more effective when able to stay relatively outside the emotional exchanges of family members than when participating in the transference.

Other intellectual and professional disciplines have their own distinctive research traditions in family studies, but their separate and collective influence on Bowen is not as great as the influence of psychoanalysis. Findings from anthropology, sociology, psychology, social work, and, more recently, general systems theory have all had some impact, however, as have recent studies in zoology, natural history, and sociobiology.

Bowen's original family research in the early 1950s explored the reciprocal influences between a mother's behavior and that of her schizophrenic child. Findings derived from this research prompted Bowen to change his conceptualization of family influences in the symptomatic manifestation of schizophrenia. In later phases of the development of his family theory, Bowen examined the behavior of the father and other members of different generations of the same family in order to more fully understand schizophrenia. In Bowen's most recent research, emotional processes in society are postulated to have some influence on family, individual, and social behavior, such as the manifestation of behavior symptoms or social problems.

Bowen's contributions to family theory have several unique characteristics. However, many of Bowen's pioneering studies were completed at a time when, in retrospect, it can be observed that an entire family movement began to burgeon in the United States. A similar awakening of professional interest in family research appeared a little later in Europe. Important speakers and sessions at meetings in medical and social sciences reported on family studies and family therapy, and increased attention was paid to the idea that professional performance is related to individual family history.

The Bowen family theory, like science, is an open thought system. The Bowen system may include additional concepts or exclude concepts from the present eight formulations. Some of these eight basic concepts were defined very recently. Due to the nature of the interdependence between these concepts, several working hypotheses can be proposed. At present, there are insufficient data to verify such hypotheses, however, and much of the data necessary for substantiation will be difficult or impossible to collect for years to come, unless other means of recording and measuring information on family behavior can be devised. Some of the more recently developed objective techniques of recording and measuring family behavior currently used at the Family Center, Georgetown University Medical Center, where Bowen is director, include videotapes of clinical sessions with families over long periods of time and biofeedback laboratory studies of individual levels of anxiety and ranges of control over symptomatic behavior. Clinical and formal research projects at the Family Center also serve to increase and diversify the family data already collected by Bowen and his staff.

CONCEPTS

One of the first and most developmentally significant concepts Bowen formulated is "undifferentiated family ego mass," although Bowen has not used this concept in recent years. Undifferentiated family ego mass describes the emotional unit of a family with its primary characteristic of relentless compulsion toward fusion or togetherness in all its relationships. Bowen's emphasis on the functional significance of a family's strong tendency toward fusion or togetherness, as well as his recognition of the importance of levels of anxiety in individual family members and the family group as a whole, were eventually expressed by his other family concepts. Bowen also suggested working hypotheses to articulate differences between open and closed family emotional systems.

The eight basic concepts that Bowen currently uses in his family theory are differentiation of self, triangles, nuclear family emotional system, family projection process, emotional cutoff, multigenerational transmission process, sibling position, and emotional process in society. Emotional cutoff and emotional process in society are the most recently formulated concepts in this group.

Differentiation of self describes fundamental processes that relate to individuals and their ability to function within a range of levels of expression of emotions, feelings, and thoughts. A more differentiated person, for example, is aware of the distinctions that can be made between emotions, feelings, and thoughts, and controls behavior sufficiently so that self is not lost in the togetherness forces of relationship systems. "Hard-core" or basic self and "pseudo-self" denote innermost beliefs and convictions and more variable attitudes and opinions of self, respectively.

Triangles are three-person relationship systems that overlap and interconnect throughout the broadest emotional network of a family. The tightest and most potent triangle of a family is usually between two parents and a child. A triangle may be activated at any time, this activation being most likely to occur when there is a raised level of anxiety in a two-person relationship. A third person is drawn into the anxious twosome and serves to dilute the stress in the two-person relationship. The most advantageous position in a triangle is to stay in touch with the emotions of the system but at the same time to remain relatively outside the emotional field of the triangle.

Nuclear family emotional system is the two-generational family group composed of parents and children. There are several nuclear families in any family system, and emotional intensity is most concentrated in each of these relationship units. As surplus anxiety in a nuclear family must be absorbed in order for its members to survive without manifesting behavior symptoms, there are three mechanisms that families use variously to reduce the overload of anxiety. These mechanisms are conflict between spouses, dysfunction of a spouse, and projection to a child.

Family projection process is the concept that describes how a child becomes trapped in the emotional fusion between parents. The mechanism of projection of parental undifferentiation to a child is generally used to cope with one of the highest levels of anxiety in a nuclear family. The consequences of family projection are severe, and a child's behavior may be impaired for a lifetime by this complex and intense process. Families that project undifferentiation to a child are generally the most resistant to clinical intervention of any kind.

Emotional cutoff describes extreme distancing or acute estrangement in the systemness of the emotional field of a family. Individuals and segments of a family may be excluded and may exclude themselves from the family "relatedness" in crisis circumstances or for a variety of reasons. Pervasive cutoffs or emotional divorces in a family precipitate much symptomatic behavior and are characteristic of a relatively closed family system.

Multigenerational transmission process describes family projection and related repeated patterns of behavior over several generations. Some of the linkages between daughter, mother, grandmother, great-grandmother, and so forth or son, father, grandfather, great-grandfather, and so forth appear to be salient factors in describing individual behavior objectively in present generations.

Sibling position describes some of the impact of seniority and sex distribution in a family system. Characteristic patterns of behavior can be predicted for particular sibling positions, although actual behavior is usually more influenced by the patterns of emotional intensity in the emotional relationships systems than by a particular chronology or sex distribution. However, the functioning position a person has in a family appears to be more significant than crude sibling position for accurately predicting behavior.

Emotional process in society describes the broadest differentiating and individuating or fusing and togetherness influences in society at large. A high level of anxiety in the emotional process of society precipitates symptomatic or regressive behavior, and a low level of anxiety in the emotional process of society precipitates asymptomatic or progressive behavior. The manifestation of either of these tendencies creates a specific emotional climate conducive to certain patterns of interaction and encourages a particular range of social behavior.

APPLICATIONS

The Bowen family theory has been developed largely from clinical data. Bowen also uses his findings and concepts as a basis for training in family systems psychotherapy. Many of the clinical applications of Bowen's concepts are an extension of his original research with families with a schizophrenic child. Current applications focus largely on families that do not have severe behavior disorders or symptoms, however.

One of the most distinctive characteristics of the variety of different clinical applications of the Bowen family theory is that the family systems therapist usually works with only the two spouses or parents of a family, rather than with the whole family or adult and child family members. Multiple therapy sessions given by a systems family therapist generally include spouses from three or four families, with sequential questions and answers between the therapist and each family group, rather than simultaneous or mixed discussion with all present. Children are purposely excluded from multiple family sessions and also from most therapy with a single family. A child's symptomatic behavior is thought of as being precipitated by the interaction and emotional dependencies of members of the parent and grandparent generations of the same family, rather than as a consequence of the child's individual characteristics.

The Bowen family theory is a general theory of emotional systems and can be applied, to some extent, to many disparate kinds of groups. Friendship systems, work systems, religious systems, and political systems manifest similar kinds of emotional interdependency and patterns of interaction as families, for example, although the interdependencies and patterns of interaction in these groups are less extreme and less impairing in their long-range consequences than those in families. Although it is possible to apply the Bowen family theory to any social group, including transient groups, the specific concepts are more meaningful and more useful when applied to groups that persist through time. Relatively permanent groups exhibit observably marked patterns of behavior among their continuing members.

The Bowen family theory can be applied to problem dimensions of social behavior in addition to clinical symptoms. The theory can provide a useful perspective for the study and description of minority group relations, aging, deviancy, crime, and social change, for example. Family data related to the manifestations of these specific interest areas may be combined and examined as specific independent variables, although the Bowen theory represents an express attempt to move away from traditional and conventional cause-effect analyses of human behavior.

One of the most valuable uses of the Bowen theory is a personal application to one's own life and to one's view of one's family. The theory can provide a blueprint for action to free self from some of the emotional entrapments of day-to-day family living. The Bowen theory is more than a series of formal research statements. The concepts create personal opportunities to see new options for action through perceiving self and others more objectively. The theory is essentially tentative, however, and in no way guarantees that accurate predictions about self or others can be made. The theory suggests various directions and options, with the overall implication that one's life can be enriched by such a personal application. Relating the Bowen theory to one's own life may also contribute toward more effective applications of the theory in a variety of research and clinical settings.

Although each of these specific applications can be described in further detail, perhaps more important is the view that the entire Bowen theory is also a contribution to basic research in general human behavior. The overall potential of the Bowen family theory lies in its individual, social, and medical usefulness, and in its versatility as a frame of reference for the observation and documentation of a new order of phenomena in human interaction, social change, and perhaps evolutionary processes.

SYSTEMS THINKING

Bowen attempts to describe and define some of the complex interdependencies and intense emotional reactivity in human relationships. In order to represent the nature of these manifold intricacies, he formulated interrelated concepts to reflect observed empirical aspects of emotional dependencies in human relationships. Although the general thrust of the Bowen theory suggests a marked predominance of family influences in human behavior, which implies that certain patterns of family relatedness precipitate certain patterns of behavior, the theory also illustrates the degrees of systemic human and animal emotional behavior in different kinds of settings.

Bowen views cause-effect thinking as a product of feelings, rather than as a dividend of individual reflection. He considers a cause as an arbitrarily selected phenomenon or variable, which does not in and of itself create a completely different phenomenon or variable that is generally thought of as an effect. Bowen suggests that a more accurate way to perceive seemingly qualitatively different phenomena is to describe the separate manifestations as a chain of events or reactions, or as sequences and patterns in behavior. Systems thinking, the core of the Bowen family theory, is a direct attempt to conceptualize the relatedness within and between chains of events or sequences and patterns.

Systems thinking in the Bowen theory makes use of biological and natural systems as basic frames of reference. Although a historian could perhaps substantiate the hypothesis that the first effective systems thinking was used to describe the solar system, systems thinking in the study of human behavior is fairly recent. It has proved inordinately difficult for human beings to apply principles of systems thinking to their own interaction. Until the last few decades, human beings have found it too difficult to maintain the degree of objectivity necessary to observe facts of human behavior and thereby change their traditional perceptions of reality. Conventional cause-effect models of explanation try to accomplish an impossibility by specifying the "why" of human behavior, whereas the systems thinking of the Bowen theory attempts to describe and define some of the orderly processes that exist in a wide range of seemingly unrelated and contradictory phenomena.

Bowen's systems thinking is an extension of natural systems models, rather than an application of mechanical systems to the study of human behavior. Although some of the input-output terms of cybernetics may be used to describe particular aspects of family interaction, Bowen makes primary use of biological models to suggest an animal relatedness between all living creatures, rather than a mechanically or artificially engineered interreactiveness between human beings. Within a natural systems perspective, family is viewed as the most basic human group due to its continuous preoccupation with vital life processes and events such as birth, marriage, and death. The most instinctive and most primitive aspects of human behavior are thought of as being manifested in this particular relationship system.

As well as the Bowen system of concepts and the Bowen conceptualization of the systemic nature of the universe, society, and families, the individual can be viewed as a system. A more differentiated person, for example, recognizes a wide range of behavior options and is able to control action at emotional, feeling, and thinking levels. This broad awareness of choices enables the more differentiated individual to become effective, integrated, and responsible as an open system, whereas a less differentiated person will function restrictively as a more closed system.

The Bowen family theory suggests that the human condition can be ameliorated through opening different relationship systems. A relatively open relationship system leads predictably toward conditions of constructive adaptation, but a relatively closed system is characterized by symptomatic behavior and gradual extinction. As all individuals play a part in the degree of openness or closedness of the relationship systems they belong to, each person can be thought of as a participant in broad evolutionary processes.

IMPLICATIONS

The systems thinking core of the Bowen family theory provides a new way of looking at human beings, human nature, and human interaction. The systems focus may be described as a potential, theoretical breakthrough by virtue of its synthesis of seemingly disparate data and its provision of a broad base for the observation of many different kinds of human behavior. Perhaps the greatest contribution of the Bowen systems perspective lies in its deemphasis on thinking in terms of individuals with its explicit refusal to conceptualize individual behavior as a product of self-contained individual characteristics.

The Bowen theory is extremely versatile. The theory has a wide range of diverse applications, and the concepts are useful tools in specifying the nature of the kinship between human beings and animals. The theory suggests order and regularity in a seemingly disordered universe of human emotions and feelings, and points up the influential significance of nonrational components of human behavior. Bowen's concepts describe ways in which patterns of interaction become symptomatic. The destructive consequences of denying the existence of problems or dependencies in human relationships are postulated as outweighing the consequences of overemphasizing the existence of problems or dependencies in human relationships. A congenial family system may be more lethal to individual survival and growth, for example, than a conflictual family system is.

Bowen's focus on an individual's relatedness to the emotional unit of the family and his focus on the limits of change for an individual and a family are presented in a universalistic frame of reference. These interdependencies and limitations are salient points in making the perception of a different order of reality possible. The emphasis placed on one's own position and one's own functioning level in different relationship systems suggests real but limited options of change for oneself. Perhaps the implied "pessimistic" view of human nature and human potential is more humble and more objective than the alternative "optimistic" view that many different kinds of change are possible and probable.

Experience in interpreting family data suggests that conditions of stress in a family may be as conducive to productive change as to impairment. An individual family member will be more likely to change patterns of functioning and make efforts to define self when a crisis is at hand. The individual effort necessary to deal with the emotional intensity generated by a crisis generally brings some important dividends of growth and maturation. In these and other instances, Bowen suggests that relationship crises can become constructive phases of emotional maturation.

One of the most important implications of the Bowen family theory is the meaning each person gives it after being exposed to the substance of the concepts. As the theory describes emotional functioning, it is difficult for anyone to hear its content without becoming somewhat caught up in the feelings the ideas generate.

The innovative approach of the theory has precipitated extremely divergent and contradictory responses. The concepts have been dismissed as sheer nonsense, and at the same time elevated almost to the status of a cult or religion. However, the Bowen theory appears to make a substantial contribution to basic and applied research in human behavior, which would justify responses somewhere between the extremes described.

Individual responses to the Bowen family theory will be varied. Bowen's ideas may be absorbed, stored away for later use, or discarded. Optimally, the theory provides a fuller understanding of human behavior and offers some means of improving the quality of human experience. Although many different applications of the Bowen theory exist, the implications of Bowen's contribution for individuals can be more easily actualized than those for society at large. One can best hear and make use of ideas that make sense in one's own life.

Bibliography

Bowen, M., A family concept of schizophrenia. In D. Jackson (Ed.), *The etiology of schizophrenia.* New York: Basic, 1960.

Bowen, M. Family psychotherapy. *American Journal of Orthopsychiatry*, 1961, *30*, 40-60.

Bowen, M. Family psychotherapy with schizophrenia in the hospital and in private practice. In I. Boszormenyi-Nagy & J. L. Framo (Eds.), *Intensive family therapy.* New York: Harper and Row, 1965.

Bowen, M. Intrafamily dynamics in emotional illness. In A. D'Agostino (Ed.), *Family, church and community.* New York: P. J. Kennedy and Sons, 1965.

Bowen, M. The use of family theory in clinical practice. *Comprehensive Psychiatry*, 1966, *7*, 345-374. Also in J. Haley (Ed.), *Changing families.* New York: Grune and Stratton; and in B. N. Ard and C. C. Ard (Eds.), *The handbook of marriage counseling.* Palo Alto: Science and Behavior Books, 1969.

Bowen, M. Family and family group therapy. In H. I. Kaplan & B. J. Sadock (Eds.), *Comprehensive group psychotherapy.* Baltimore: Williams and Wilkins, 1971.

Bowen, M. Principles and techniques of multiple family therapy. In J. Bradt & C. Moynihan (Eds.), *Systems therapy.* Washington, D.C., 1971; and in P. Guerin (Ed.), *Family therapy.* New York: Gardner Press, 1976.

Bowen, M. The systems viewpoint of human behavior. In J. Gerba (Ed.), *Alternative futures and environmental quality.* Washington, D.C.: Office of Research and Development, U.S. Environmental Protection Agency, 1973.

Bowen, M. Cultural myths and realities of problem solving. *Ekistics,* 1974, *37* (220), 173-180.

Bowen, M. Societal regression viewed through family systems theory. In A. Schmalz (Ed.), *Energy: Today's choices, tomorrow's opportunities.* Washington, D.C.: World Future Society, 1974.

Bowen, M. Toward the differentiation of self in one's family of origin. In F. Andres & P. Lorio (Eds.), *Georgetown family symposia, Volume I 1971-1972.* Washington, D.C.: Georgetown University Medical Center, 1974.

Bowen, M., Dysinger, R. H., & Basamania, B. The role of the father in families with a schizophrenic patient. *American Journal of Psychiatry,* 1959, *115,* 117-120.

On the differentiation of self. In J. Framo (Ed.), *Family interaction.* New York: Springer, 1972.

Index

Autonomy, 76, 111, 112, 132, 134, 139–141

Behavior:
  adaptive, 20, 56–57, 121
  dominant, 20, 56–57, 121
  integrated, 30–33, 39, 75, 89–95, 98–100
  intergenerational influences on, 35–36, 49–50, 52, 154–155
  over-responsible, 70–71, 78–79
  patterns of, 54–55, 61–62, 64–65, 82, 143, 144, 148
  reactive, 64–65, 67–68, 82, 148
  regressive, 54–55
  sibling position influences on, 52, 155
  symptomatic, 40, 60, 151, 154, 166
Boundaries:
  political, 3–7
  of self, 4–5, 115, 120–123

Bowen family systems theory, 147–162
  applications of, 155–157
  concepts of, 147–150, 152–155
  development of, 150–152
  and evolution, 148–149, 157
  implications of, 160–162
  and psychoanalysis, 150, 151
  research on, 147, 152, 155
  and science, 147, 152
  and systems theory, 150, 151, 158–160
  and therapy, 150–152, 156
Bowen, M., 147, 152

Children:
  dependency of, 41, 68–70, 82–83
  and differentiation of self, 41–42, 68–70
  and projection process, 154
  and symptomatic behavior, 154, 156
  in therapy, 156

Compromise, 56, 76–77
Conflict, 121, 154, 161
Conformity, 89–93
Crisis, 36–38, 67, 161

Death, 37, 67, 159
Decision making, 56, 76, 123, 138
Dependency (see Emotional dependency)
Detriangling, 122
Differentiation of self:
   and children, 41–42, 68–70
   and contact with family, 23, 33–36, 47–52. 54–55, 57, 64–68, 84–85, 116–118, 148
   in crisis, 36–38, 67, 161
   definition of, 153
   and economic independence, 103–107, 111–112
   and family of origin, 42, 47–52, 65–68
   and functional behavior, 63, 159–160
   and happiness, 132–135, 137–144
   importance of, 141–144
   levels of, 69, 121
   limitations of, 143–144, 148, 161
   and nuclear family, 47–48, 54, 64–65, 77, 116
   and political action, 8–13, 22–24, 30–31, 66, 100, 141–142

Differentiation of self (*Cont.*):
   reactions to, 38–43, 61–63, 66–70
   and role integration, 29–33, 38–39, 56–57, 89–95, 98–100
   and social change, 8, 14, 63, 100, 112, 141, 142
   and spouse, 40–42, 57, 67–69, 121–122
   and territoriality, 107–109
   and work system, 47–48
Divorce:
   emotional, 34, 51, 68
   marital, 35, 67–68

Economic independence, 103–112
   and differentiation of self, 103–107, 111–112
   and emotional dependency, 103–107, 111–112
   and territoriality, 107–109
   and will, 109–110
Emotional cutoff, 34, 35, 47, 51, 154
Emotional dependency:
   and autonomy, 33–36, 111, 112, 134, 139–141
   and boundaries of self, 4–5, 115, 120–123
   of children, 41, 68–70, 82–83
   and economic independence, 103–107, 111–112

INDEX

Emotional dependency (*Cont.*):
- and emotional distance, 34, 51, 68, 154
- and evolution, 148–149
- and family of origin, 33–36, 47–52, 54–56
- in human behavior, 20, 148, 150, 156–158, 161
- and in-law family system, 52–54
- as need, 33–36, 48, 127
- and nuclear family, 33–36, 47–49, 54–56
- and political action, 10–11, 18, 20–21, 30, 35
- and security, 139–141
- of sexes, 24–25, 135–137
- of spouses, 34–35, 48, 55, 121–122
- in work system, 47–48, 123

Emotional field, 20, 151, 154
Emotional process in society, 5, 19–21, 149, 151, 155
Emotional system, 18, 20, 116–117, 149, 152–154, 156, 160
Evolution, 144, 148–149, 157
Extended family (*see* Family)

Family:
- and legal measures, 19
- nuclear, 33–36, 47–48, 54–56, 64–65, 116, 154
- of origin, 23, 33–36, 42, 47–52, 54–56, 65–68, 116–117

Family (*Cont.*):

Family process (*see* Bowen family systems theory)

Family system:
- anxiety in, 40–43, 48, 64–68, 121–122, 153, 154
- closure of, 51, 153, 154, 160
- conflict in, 121, 154, 161
- as emotional unit, 18, 116–117, 148, 149, 152–154, 161
- and self, 18

Family therapy, 150, 151
- movement, 151–152
- of Murray Bowen, M.D., 156

Father, 36, 136, 151

Functioning:
- in family system, 62–63, 67–70, 120–121, 148, 155, 161
- in society, 19–20, 120
- of women, 19–20, 56, 70

Fusion:
- definition of, 152–153
- in emotional system, 138, 142, 144, 149, 152–153
- in family of origin, 62–63, 152–153
- in human behavior, 76, 77, 112, 138, 142, 144, 149, 155
- in nuclear family, 62–63, 152–153
- with spouse, 68, 70, 121–122

Goals, 49, 56, 103, 118, 124, 138, 140
Geneological research, 65–66, 149

Happiness, 131–144
  and differentiation of self, 132–135, 137–144
  and interdependency of sexes, 135–137, 141
  and respect, 133–135
Hard-core self, 96–100, 128, 153

In-law family system, 52–54
Interdependency of sexes, 9, 24–25, 135–137, 141

Legal measures:
  and family, 19
  and social change, 5, 7, 11, 17, 21–22
  and woman, 13, 21–22

Minority groups, 19–20, 157
  and woman, 19–20
Mother, 35–36, 42, 49–50, 54, 151
Motherhood, 29, 31–33, 43
Mother-in-law, 42, 54
Multigenerational transmission process, 149, 154–155

Nuclear family (*see* Family; Family system)

Parents:
  and dependency of children, 41, 68–70, 82–83
  and projection process, 154,
Personhood, 8, 30, 33, 36, 42, 43, 144
Polarization of sexes, 9, 24, 119–120
Political action, 3–14, 17–25
  and differentiation of self, 8–13, 22–24, 30–31, 66, 100, 141–142
  and emotional dependency, 10–11, 18, 20–21, 30, 35
  and social change, 5–14, 22–23
  and woman, 6–7, 9, 11–12, 14, 17, 18, 21–25
Political boundaries, 3–7
Projection process, 154
Pseudo-self, 97–99, 153

Role:
  integration of, 30–33, 38–39, 56–57, 89–95, 98–100
  personalization of, 94–95
  playing, 89–100
  traditional, 29–33, 38–39, 42, 56–57, 70–71, 78–79, 89–100

INDEX

Schizophrenia, 151, 155
Security, 132, 139–141
Self:
   and autonomy, 76, 111, 132, 139–144
   boundaries of, 4–5, 115, 120–123
   and family system, 18
   hard-core, 96–100, 128, 153
   integration of, 30–33, 38–39, 56–57, 75–85, 86–95, 98–100
   investment in, 79–81
   layers of, 95–98
   losing, 29–33, 56–57, 64, 69–70, 76–85, 89–100, 103–111, 119–120, 137–139
   pseudo, 97–99, 153
Self-awareness (*see* Differentiation of self)
Self-development (*see* Differentiation of self)
Self-growth (*see* Differentiation of self)
Selfhood, 30, 33, 36, 42, 43
Separation:
   geographical, 34, 51, 68
   marital, 35, 55–56
Sexes:
   interdependency of, 9, 24–25, 135–137, 141
   polarization of, 9, 24, 119–120
Sibling position, 52, 155
Sisterhood, 29, 31–33, 43
Social change, 5–14, 23–24, 63, 100, 112, 157

Social problems, 19–21, 151, 156, 157
Spouse:
   and anxiety, 48, 121–122, 154
   and conflict, 121, 154
   and differentiation of self, 40–42, 57, 67–69, 121–122
   and emotional dependency, 34–35, 48, 55, 121–122
   and fusion, 68, 70, 121–122
   and symptomatic behavior, 40, 151
   in therapy, 156
Symptomatic behavior, 40, 151, 160, 166
Systems theory, 150, 151, 158–160

Territoriality, 107–109
Therapy (*see* Family therapy)
Triangles, 84–85, 122, 153–154
Triangling, 122

Underprivileged, 19–20
Undifferentiated family ego mass, 152–153

Will, 109–110
Woman:
   and autonomy, 103–112, 140–141

Woman (*Cont.*):
  and career, 57, 104, 106
  and dependency, 103–112
  and economic independence, 103–112
  and family system, 63
  functioning of, 19–20, 56, 76
  and goals, 103, 118
  and happiness, 135–137, 141
  intergenerational influences on, 35–36, 49–50, 52

Woman (*Cont.*):
  and minority groups, 19–20
  and political action, 6–7, 9, 11–12, 14, 17, 18, 21–25
  and responsibilities, 103–112, 118–120
  and security, 140–141
  and sibling position, 52

Womanhood, 29, 32–33, 43
Women's movement, 12, 30
Work system, 23, 47–48, 123

Separation Without Hope?

Essays on the Relation
between the Church and the Poor
During the Industrial Revolution
and the Western Colonial Expansion

ORBIS BOOKS
Maryknoll, New York 10545

Acknowledgements

— To the authors of the different chapters of this book, who have contributed so well to the achievement of this project.
— To Claudiana Editrice, Torino, Italy, who kindly agreed to translate two chapters of Mario Miegge's book, *Il Protestante nella Storia* (1969), into English.
— To Mr J. Victor Koilpillai and Mr Jan H. Kok for their assistance in giving this book its final form.
— To Miss Erna Haller and Miss Angela Horton, who untiringly attended to production details of this book and cared for it at different stages of its progress.

The Catholic Foreign Mission Society of America (Maryknoll) recruits and trains people for overseas missionary service. Through Orbis Books Maryknoll aims to foster the international dialogue that is essential to mission. The books published, however, reflect the opinions of their authors and are not meant to represent the official position of the society.

Library of Congress Cataloging in Publication Data

Main entry under title:

Separation without hope?

1. Church and the poor—History—Addresses, essays, lectures. 2. Church and social problems—History—Addresses, essays, lectures. I. Santa Ana, Julio de.
BV639.P6S46   1980   261.8   80-12831
ISBN 0-88344-456-9 (pbk.)

© 1978 by World Council of Churches, Geneva

All rights reserved

U.S. edition 1980 by Orbis Books, Maryknoll, NY 10545

Typeset in Switzerland; printed and bound in the United States of America

Contents

Editor's preface, *Julio de Santa Ana* vii

1. Gradual Awareness of Social, Economic Problems (1750-1900), *André Biéler* 3

2. The Church and the Trade Union Movement in Britain in the 19th Century, *John Kent* 30

3. German Protestantism and the Social Question in the 19th Century, *Günter Brakelmann* 38

4. Social Reform and the Social Gospel in America, *Ronald C. White, Jr* 50

5. The Russian Orthodox Church and the Poor in the 19th and 20th Centuries, *Nicolai A. Zabolotsky* 60

6. The Protestant in Bourgeois History, *Mario Miegge* . . 87

7. Social Action and Thought Among Arab Orthodox Christians (1800-1920), *George Khodr* 111

8. Rejection of Christianity by the Indigenous Peoples of Latin America, *Julio Barreiro* 127

9. The Church and the Poor in Asian History, *C. I. Itty* . . 137

10. The Christian Mission and the African Peoples in the 19th Century, *Sam M. Kobia* 155

Conclusion, *Julio de Santa Ana* 171

About the Authors 190

Editor's preface

This is the second volume in the series of studies CCPD is publishing on the Church and its relations with the poor. The first volume [1] examined various situations and the problems in them during the early centuries of church history up to the end of the Middle Ages in the West. It dealt with a number of problems which persist in the life of Christian communities today, despite the historical changes that have taken place, and which underlie their social programmes, the attitudes of church members and their views on political and economic issues.

Before embarking on a discussion of present-day relations between the poor and the Church, we feel it is essential to take time to reflect on what these relations were during the industrial revolution and the period of western colonial expansion (1800-1914), when the attitudes directly affecting the nature of the problem as we face them today first developed. This second volume sets out to analyse the nature of these relationships in a number of situations, placing them against a general view of what was happening at the time, and bearing in mind the ideological background.

The contributors to this second volume [2] are authorities on the subject, people for whom the issues are not purely theoretical and who are actively involved in the life of the churches, helping to develop a relationship of service to and solidarity with the least privileged sectors of society. The concluding chapter presents a synthesis of the major problems arising, preparing the way for the third volume in the series which will reflect on relations between the Church and the poor at the present time.

It is hoped that the material published here will give rise to reflection and discussion in the churches, and prompt them to take steps to show their solidarity with those to whom Christ said: "Blessed are you poor, for yours is the Kingdom of God" (Luke 6 : 20).

JULIO DE SANTA ANA

---

[1] JULIO DE SANTA ANA: *Good News to the Poor*. Geneva: WCC, 1977.

[2] A list of contributors with brief curriculum vitae may be found on p. 190.

Julio de Santa Ana / Separation Without Hope?

1 • Gradual Awareness of Social, Economic Problems (1750-1900)

André Biéler

Can we really speak at the present time of a historical process of growth of understanding on the part of Christian churches and sects in the West of the social and economic problems created by the industrial revolution, when in fact the extent, complexity and speed of the upheavals that mark the spread of technological civilization appear increasingly to escape the notice of our contemporaries?

The tortoise chasing the hare
Would it not be truer to say that far from growth of awareness, what has come about is that as the human sciences, following the pattern of the natural sciences, discover certain aspects of the human phenomena connected with industrialization, new segments of that complex reality come into view like gigantic unknown factors which only deliver up their secret by revealing new and unexplored abysses?

There are, of course, good grounds for some observations on the gradual growth of awareness of these phenomena, yet the first thing that has to be said is an odd paradox. The more scientific knowledge develops and the more numerous its technological applications, the greater our ignorance of their effects on nature and mankind. And man's vanity increases in equal proportion, so that with no idea where he is going, he hurries on faster than ever in blind pursuit of ever more science and technology. These, of course, advance with no other purpose than their own expansion. Once they were thought to be tools at man's service, but they have now become ends in themselves, blind and groping, and are turning against mankind.

Where do the Christian churches and sects stand in this process? Although they were partly responsible for the development in its initial stages, and subsequently became its active accomplices, overt or tacit, it must be recognized that so far, speaking generally, we cannot say that concern about it has been one of their daily preoccupations, with the exception, that is, of some notable minorities. These latter are disturbingly conscious of a widening gap between the purposes of human life which they confess in their creed, and the divergent purposes (or purposelessness)

Translated from the French by the Language Service, WCC.

of the sciences and their technological applications; they are alarmed to see how completely these condition the life of industrial societies, and the extent to which, as powerful and daily conditioning factors, they contradict the Christian motives for human individual and social conduct.

The astonishing fact of runaway development

It must be admitted, then, that viewed in a long-term perspective of human history, the scientific and industrial revolution, as a phenomenon with radically subversive consequences for all societies, has *never* yet been completely analysed and understood. To a great extent it is still mysterious. It is not at all the case that science, of which we are so proud, has succeeded in identifying all its elements, discovering its unknown factors, working out all its mechanisms.

Since the process has only been partially understood, it has only been partially possible to master it. Its future course is therefore completely unknown. No human group at the present time, in east or west, north or south, whatever its ideology, can claim to have succeeded in mastering it. That is why the havoc it caused in the past, and even more the damage which its exponential growth (even if this has slowed down a little since 1974) is actually doing to the human and planetary ecosystem, disconcerts and baffles even those who are contributing to its explosion. The growing complexity of its component elements, at a time when it is assuming worldwide, all-embracing proportions, is so great that the imbroglio of contemporary history is becoming more entangled than ever. Causes of conflicts are multiplying at the same time as techniques of subversion and instruments of repression are being perfected. While more and more arsenals stockpile increasingly monstrous weapons of apocalyptic destruction, countless masses crushed by want and dependence proliferate. There are hordes of people in every continent camped at the very gates of cities radiant with the luxury and wealth of a proportionately smaller and smaller minority.

This explosive phenomenon which astonishes us all today is, however, only one stage in a cultural revolution, with roots reaching back into Greco-Roman antiquity, that only began to produce its innumerable, galloping and all-transforming effects in the 19th century. This, then, is the moment of its history which must be studied if it is to be understood, just as a chemical phenomenon is studied in its initial stage the better to observe its nature and effects.

We must also note two very important facts which have to be borne in mind if the complexity of these phenomena is to be appreciated.

In the first place, the gigantic and unsolved problems which face us today were interconnected from the start, as belonging to a total process which binds together the various phenomena, while they by their mutual interaction constitute it. To study them each in isolation, as is commonly done by the various university departments, just as our churches and their historians are too inclined to isolate spiritual and church life from other aspects of existence, is an arbitrary method which is scientifically justified only at the provisional stage of small-scale analysis.

It is also necessary to take into account the fact that certain features of industrialization, such as the impoverishment of some and the enrichment of others, place observers (Christians included, despite their assertions of spiritual emancipation) in a position that debars them from any pretension to objective, morally and ideologically neutral observation. The place they occupy in the conflicting social process makes them liable to experience the individual and social effects of feelings of guilt and self-justification, resulting in the adoption of aggressive and defence mechanisms. These affect their analyses and reflections with patches of obscurity or ignorance that completely conceal certain aspects of reality, while excessive importance is attributed to others. We shall see that the churches and sects, far from being immune to distortions of that kind, are in fact prone to reinforce them precisely on account of their faith, which inclines them to give a sacred colouring to the decisions at which they arrive.

If we provisionally distinguish, for the better understanding of certain particular aspects, the main interdependent features of the worldwide process of industrialization as it developed and continues to develop in the various zones of industrial capitalism (liberal capitalism with originally decentralized decision making, and state capitalism with centralized decision making), we may note the following characteristics:

a) industrialization itself, that is, the creation of methods of production and distribution, closely linked (by action and reaction) with the development of science and technology;

b) urbanization and movements of population; in particular their concentration in centres of production and exchange, with consequent crowding into inadequately equipped urban areas;

c) colonial expansion, that is to say, colonization of other continents by the continent first in possession of the new industrial power;

d) the simultaneous impoverishment of the industrial urban masses and of colonized societies as compared with the relatively small proportion of the remaining population which is enriched;

e) the proliferation of these impoverished masses, sometimes amounting to a population explosion, as the combined effect of migrations towards the centres of industrial concentration, a rising birth rate, lengthened life-expectation and a drop in mortality rates;

f) the formation of conflicting ideologies parallel to the directly opposed interests of various groups of the population. The Christian churches and sects, whose message is not tied to these ideologies, are nevertheless, as we shall see, their unwitting and often fanatical instruments, for they have a very great capacity for unconsciously attributing a sacred character to the ideologies and existing structures of their social or national environment.

All these interlocking phenomena, among which it is difficult to decide which are primary to such an extent do they react dialectically on one another, first appeared in the West, then gradually spread to the whole world in step with the colonial, technological and cultural expansion of the western countries and then, more recently, of the industrial society of Eastern Europe.

The Christian churches and sects as source and victim of events

If it is true that industrial societies sprang up and carried all over the world the uncontrolled effects of their mode of development without ever succeeding in fully understanding or above all in mastering that mode of development, the Christian churches and sects, and their theologians shared in promoting it for good and ill by not understanding and therefore not controlling, except in a very limited way, the forms it took. Today, most of them are as disconcerted as everyone else at the extent and complexity of events, and few are equipped with the institutions and personnel necessary to cope with them as the nature of their own mission requires.

It is noticeable, however, that a small minority of believers, forming what the majority has called the Christian social movement, and often regarded with contempt, did initiate a close investigation into the human sufferings caused by the subversive process of industrialization. Endeavouring more and more to understand the source of such sufferings, this minority was and remains actively engaged in alleviating them and in eradicating their causes.

Furthermore, it is noteworthy, too, that apart from that minority, the majority of Christians and their theologians were and are passive in regard to the development of technological society without overmuch concern about the human dramas to which it gives rise. These Christians and these theologians were unaware, and sometimes still pretend to be unaware that they have actively contributed, both by their own individual daily political, economic and commercial activities and by their ignorance of the collective effects of these activities, in promoting more and more intensely an ill-considered and irresponsible development under cover of the alleged neutrality of their spiritual and church life. Even today, growth of awareness of the ethical and therefore theological importance of all these phenomena is taking place only in some restricted circles of Christian churches and sects and in marginal sectors of the faculties of theology which train the theologians of the future.

Why is it that this growth of awareness, which we are going to study in its various stages, was, and still is achieved only by minorities in the churches?

1. Account must be taken of the fact that the mental and cultural structure of the Christian churches and sects and their theologians is still to a large extent pre-industrial. This is due to the power of tradition in theological and religious matters and to the force of inertia affecting the storage of information in the collective unconscious.

2. The phenomenon is further complicated by the additional difficulty arising from the fact that the cultural framework of the Bible, that irreplaceable authority to which the Christian religion appeals, is itself rural and artisanal, pre-industrial. Its consequent unfamiliarity demands, if the Christian message is to be faithfully reinterpreted in a technological world, a considerable effort of intellectual imagination and spiritual creativity to translate into new terms the concrete ethical implications of the gospel teaching. Now systematic efforts to do this are very rarely undertaken in the churches and theological faculties, for they lack knowledge of political, economic and social mechanisms. It follows that preaching and catechetics, for example, seldom go beyond the framework of private life and personal relationships. Consequently, it needs to be stated emphatically how great is the merit of those few people who, following in the footsteps of the pioneers of the minority social Christian movements, originated the ecumenical movement of the last few decades; they have alerted the churches, their authorities and theologians, and have courageously brought them face to face with the complex realities of the contemporary world. They have only partly succeeded, for that matter, and not without difficulty, not without meeting with fierce resistance, and often with caustic and unjust criticism.

3. Another important historical fact explains the time-lag between theological and ethical teaching and the lightning-swift development of industrial societies. Topographically, the new industries and the new working-class quarters mostly developed outside the traditional geographical bounds of old-established parishes. The new textile and metallurgical industries which were the basis of the "take-off" of technological development, sought the energy they required outside the ancient mediaeval cities, by the water courses, or near coal supplies needed for the steam engines. In England, for example, in the mid-18th century, there was an average of 15,000 people per parish in Sheffield. A century later there were 100,000, but no particular change had taken place in the territorial distribution of the churches.[1] It is often said that the Church lost the working classes. To some extent this is true, but it must also be said that to a large extent the working class was never "lost"; it came into existence and pursued its painful growth quite simply outside the range of action of the traditional churches. This is, for that matter, still in fact more or less the case for the greater part of the proletarian masses, despite the laudable and persevering efforts of some dynamic evangelical movements. Precisely because

those movements came in from outside, and were very often culturally alien and ideologically hostile to the milieu in which they were conducting their mission, they only made very superficial contact with the proletarian masses in comparison with their influence on the middle classes, for example, whose ideology was in the end adopted by western Christianity and tacitly incorporated into Christian teaching, generally without this being realized and even when pains were taken to avoid it happening.

4. This clandestine identification of the Christian message with the ethics of the western middle classes, has been so considerable that it has to a large extent distorted Christians' own awareness of the part they have played in the ambiguous development of society. The way in which ecclesiastical history has generally been written is very revealing in this respect, and has certainly contributed to reinforcing the distortion. Most histories of the Church, in fact, make a very revealing assumption. They deal with that history as if the daily life of the great majority of Christians and their ideology were neutral in economic, social and political matters, and as if only the so-called Christian social movements had or have any influence on the course of the history of industrial societies. Apart from the general relations of faith with secular philosophical and literary culture and from questions concerning the property of the churches in relation to the state, the history of the Church is written as if that history has taken place in a sphere of its own, without reciprocal relations with socio-economic life. Such relations, which are of course very considerable, are passed over for the simple reason that Christians are not clearly conscious of them. As a result, only the Christian social movements, usually representing minorities, are taken into consideration as in any way relevant.

Now in the light of present-day social sciences, it appears increasingly evident that this unawareness by Christians of their real participation in the process of development is a defence mechanism designed to hide the important action they exert on society by reason of their faith and of the ideology which they often combine with it. It is not true that, apart from the so-called Christian social circles, the Christian churches and sects are economically, socially and politically neutral, and do not take an active part in economic expansion, in the choice of its structures with their multiple good and bad effects. It is therefore important to demonstrate the fact of this participation and the forms it takes by displaying its more or less visible links with the various forms of ethical and consequent theological expression of the Christian faith. It is important to escape from the oversimplified schematic presentation given in ecclesiastical history books by bringing out of isolation the sector termed "social Christianity" and setting it in due relation with the whole body of Christians and their action in society. It is important to render explicit the theological and ethical assumptions which condition the tacit socio-political conformity of the great majority of Christians and to make clear the active character of their implicit involvement, which they look upon as neutrality. The weight of that conformity must be taken into account as one of the factors contributing to determine the course taken by industrial societies and the balance sheet of their fortunes and misfortunes.

Industrial capitalism, dynamic factor of progress and subversive force

No revolution has so radically and permanently transformed the social order, habits, morals, mentalities and economic and political structures of all human societies as the industrial and technological revolution.[2] For two centuries, that revolution has been inspired by the two types of subversive capitalism operative in the world, private capitalism and state capitalism.[3] People have been and still are slow to realize just what these profound changes mean, because the revolutionary process is a continuous one and modifies human consciousness at the same time as it transforms the structures of society.

The balance sheet of industrialization includes both credit and debit entries. It would be particularly unjust to deny the good it has done, since many enterprising Christians were responsible for it. However, as disciples of Christ we must direct our attention primarily to human sufferings, their causes and remedies. We shall therefore consider only the growth of awareness of this aspect of the balance sheet.

The most destructive feature of the industrial revolution was and is the proletarianization of ever-increasing masses of human beings, caused by the migration of immense human groups crowding in search of work into zones of industrial concentration ill-prepared to receive them, and of their impoverishment consequent on the rapid drop in wages and working conditions produced simultaneously by competition from machines and the growth of population. Everyone knows what dreadful extremes of human exploitation were and still are produced by this unfortunate conjunction of circumstances, despite a perceptible improvement in the living conditions of the working classes in the industrial countries of West and East, which, however, are only a minority on the worldwide scale.

Industrial serfdom in the new urban centres, spreading like tentacles on the European continent, went side by side with the exploitation of natives in the colonies. The capital yield in continental industry was based on the same extreme conditions as in the colonial plantations or mines; while accumulation of profits prompted the rapid expansion of new industries as well as the conquest of new colonies. The pressure of capital led to this all the more surely, because the financial costs of the infrastructure needed for industrial expansion at home and the military forces needed for colonial expansion abroad were both borne by the state, which in most industrial countries had just been taken over by the commercial middle classes.

Now proletarianization should have alerted Christians, because it is something that radically destroys man's nature as a creature of God. "The phenomenon of proletarianization", writes Max Pietsch,[4] "is characterized by a dangerous sociological and anthropological situation in which man is stripped of property, deprived in every respect of resources to fall back on, detached from family and neighbourhood ties. He falls into a state of economic dependence, is torn from his roots, militarized in his work, estranged from nature and mechanized in his daily activities. In short, the characteristic feature of proletarianization is human devitalization and depersonalization." Furthermore, it includes a powerful factor of demoralization. "The means of living the interior life", Max Pietsch continues,[5] "work, becomes nothing more than a servile means to an end, and the hours employed in work are written off on the debit of the balance sheet of existence whereas in normal conditions they should represent a positive gain. The more conscious the workers become of the inner emptiness of their work, the more they seek compensation by squandering their wages, only too often in amusements and pleasures that are no less mechanical and empty than their work. It is not surprising that these drifting human beings, modern nomads, long with particular intensity for precisely what is most lacking in their lives, security and stability."

What understanding have Christians shown for these new things, unprecedented in their history? How did they react and deal with them?

In the growth of awareness by the West and the churches, several levels can be distinguished, often corresponding to successive stages. But from the chronological point of view, these levels are superimposed rather than successive, and there are no strict divisions between them. We shall give a few examples, but it should be noted from the start that these examples are simply intended as illustrations and are not exhaustive on any of the levels in any country. In any case, they are chosen from three countries only, England, France and Germany which, though the three main industrial powers of the 19th century, were not the only ones.

First stage in growth of awareness: charitable work

In face of suffering, the first impulse of Christian charity is to give direct and immediate aid. Works of charity are traditional fruits of faith, multiplying as faith awakens; they are so sure a barometer of faith that from the historical point of view they can serve as a sort of external index of the vitality of authentic Christianity in a society.

From the very dawn of the industrial revolution, Christian charity actively responded to the growing sufferings of the people.

In England, the ground had been prepared by the religious revival promoted by the work of John Wesley and the rapid spread of Methodism. Once more, a minority of Christians had rediscovered the predilection of the Christ of the gospels for the material, moral and spiritual salvation of the most destitute of his people. Penetrating even the most abandoned strata of the proletariat, even the notorious slums which were increasing with dizzy speed in the mining and industrial regions, and then in the colonies, Methodist evangelization promoted training for adults, schooling for the children, prison reform, and the anti-slave movement. (The Sunday School Society was founded in 1785; Hannah More's schools were started at Cheddar in 1789, giving religious education and training in spinning.) This exceptional religious movement succeeded in awakening a minority of the industrial working class to its own lot, and encouraged it to take over responsibility for its own fate. As a result, when the trade unions were founded later on, they bore the stamp of Christian ethics and their development took quite a different course from that in other industrial countries. Attentive to the new social ills born of proletarian despair and destitution, the Methodists were among the first, from 1830 onwards, to give systematic aid to alcoholics, in collaboration with other Christian minorities, Baptists, Quakers and Plymouth Brethren.[6]

John Wesley's influence affected even the most torpid traditional churches. The evangelicals represented a spiritual dynamism which stirred the Anglican Church and helped the court, the upper and middle classes to discover to some extent at least the sufferings and needs of the people. This was at the root of William Wilberforce's anti-slavery movement and of Lord Shaftesbury's philanthropic activities, which inspired many religious and social societies.

The evangelical revival in Scotland was similarly marked by sensitivity to social problems. At the beginning of the 19th century, Thomas Chalmers tried to interest the established Church in the condition of the proletarians. Especially among the poor of Glasgow he promoted education and works of Christian solidarity, notably by the reestablishment of diaconal ministries.

The same concern for the total salvation of the human person and of the lot of the most deprived inspired the minority of Christians preoccupied with the gospel mission among the distant peoples who had been subjected to the double domination of conquering capitalism and imperialist nationalism. Thanks to the tireless work of William Wilberforce, public opinion was gradually won over to the new idea of the liberation of the blacks. Wilberforce had founded in 1784 the Society for the Reformation of Manners, and in a work published in 1797 he presented *A Practical View of the Prevailing System of Professed Christians in the Higher and Middle Classes in the Country Contrasted with Real Christianity.*[7] For, in fact, missionaries were coming into conflict with the interests of the East India Company; the refusal of the latter to allow schoolmasters to be sent to India was only ended in 1813, when the Company's charter was renewed, by the insertion of an appropriate clause.[8] Nevertheless, the missions were organized. A humble cobbler, William Carey, who became a Baptist minister and who was called a lunatic because he was concerned about the fate of distant peoples, had founded in 1792 the Baptist Missionary Society. Then in succession came the London Missionary Society (1795), the Church Missionary Society (1799), the Religious Tract Society (1799) and the British and Foreign Bible Society (1804).

By a strange historical convergence, religious revival movements inspired by social concern developed all over the European continent at the same time as the proletarianization and pauperization of the industrial masses. It was a sort of compensation for the increasingly harmful effects of the capitalist and colonialist expansion of Europe. In Switzerland, the Basle Society for the Diffusion of Christian Truth was founded in 1780 and gave rise to a Bible society (1804) and to the famous missionary society (1815) known as the Basle Mission.[9] In France, Baron de Staël, son of the famous writer, campaigned for the abolition of the slave trade,[10] while in Paris in 1822 the Society of Evangelical Missions among the non-Christian Peoples was founded.[11] In Germany, charitable organizations were established to help the unemployed (Baron E. von Kottwitz, 1807), prisoners and the sick (Theodor Fliedner, 1826; Amelie Sieveking, 1830). The German pastor Johann H. Wichern began his work of religious and social revival in 1833 (foundation of the Rauhes Haus institute), and simultaneously in France, the Catholic St Vincent de Paul Society was founded by Frédéric Ozanam, while Victor de Pressensé and Agénor de Gasparin inaugurated the work of the French Evangelical Society.

The period preceding the great spring-time of the European peoples, 1848, was one of the most fertile in religious and social creations, both Catholic and Protestant. In 1825, Clémentine Cuvier, daughter of the great naturalist, brought many prominent persons with her into the Protestant Benevolent Association of Paris, which organized help for the very poorest, and owed its existence to her initiative. The Lutheran pastor Louis Meyer established in 1833 the Society of Friends of the Poor, then the Home Mission in France (1840), the year in which Armand de Melun with some Catholic friends established the St Francis Xavier Society to provide hospitality for working men as the earlier Society of St Joseph had done, but had not survived the 1830 revolution.

The first savings banks date from the end of the 18th century, when they were established in Germany and in England. In the '40s, Benjamin Delessert encouraged their creation in Paris to help working men to save, while the Alsatian industrialist Jean Dollfus, one of the famous Protestant "social employers" of the time, had houses built for his workers at the same period. This was also when the houses of deaconesses were established in France.

In England, William and Catherine Booth were beginning their well-known work of evangelization and assistance to the poorest of the poor. Born of the Christian Revival Association, it was to be known after 1865

Gradual Awareness of Social, Economic Problems (1750-1900)

as the Salvation Army, and was to work effectively in all parts of the world in spite of often stupidly fierce opposition.

Like the Salvation Army, the Young Men's Christian Association, founded by George Williams in 1844, and the Young Women's Christian Association in 1855, spread to innumerable countries at the same time as houses of deaconesses and Protestant reception centres for every kind of moral, physical or mental distress: Asiles de la Force (John Bost) in France, in 1848; hospital centres in Germany at Bad Boll (J. C. Blumhardt) and Bielefeld (Fred. Bodelschwingh); the charitable foundations of Charles Spurgeon in England, etc. With the years, the charitable institutions intended to alleviate the new evils created by the social upheaval consequent on industrial and capitalist subversion grew in number and variety. For most Christians sensitive to the sufferings of their time, these charitable activities continued to be the principle remedy for the pauperization and proletarianization of the industrial centres. This active minority of Christendom was animated by a sentiment of authentic charity which often inspired the unselfish dedication of lives completely devoted to others. However, this minority, being entirely absorbed in its immediate and legitimate concern, hardly attempted at all to seek out either the origins of the social evil whose ravages they perceived, or the means of correcting it. This was the period of so-called paternalist charitable institutions, which for their time were in fact great enterprises; they only became open to criticism when they came to serve as an excuse for refusing other ways of seeking authentic love of the neighbour. A minority of Christians had already entered on those ways.

Second stage of awareness: recognition of the need for state legislative intervention

In face of the social evils arising from industrialization, many Christians were thus content with directly charitable work which, when undertaken seriously with faith, mobilized a great deal of effort, energy, time and money of an active minority, but there were nevertheless those who realized that action of this kind has its limitations. Its main defect is that it does not touch many of the causes of human need. Yet the more active these causes, the greater and more numerous are human sufferings.

An Alsatian industrialist, Daniel Legrand, influenced by the evangelical revival of the early 19th century, and aware of the unfortunate lot of his workmen whom he was trying to help, realized that his efforts encountered limits imposed on his generosity by the action of other industrialists' competition. Far from using this to justify any inertia on his part, or like most of his colleagues contaminated by the ideology of liberal capitalism, to invoke the alleged iron law of socio-economic mechanisms precluding any state intervention, he was convinced on the contrary that the law could modify the industrial system if it imposed simultaneously on all employers at least some of the measures which charity had suggested to the best of them. Otherwise the generosity of the latter would penalize them in competition and would also bring disadvantages with unfortunate repercussions on their workers. Consequently, Legrand began with what he regarded as most urgent and became the convincing promoter of a law designed to improve the tragic working conditions of children in industry and the mines. Masses of children were so employed, of course, sometimes from the age of five, twelve to fifteen hours a day, in conditions almost inconceivable today, and many died.

In 1841, the first French social law was passed, forbidding the employment of children below the age of eight in the mines and factories, and limiting their work to eight hours under the age of twelve.

Legrand was conscious of the fact that competition also operated on the international plane to the disadvantage of the most generous employers. Using his friendship with the statesman Guizot, he therefore endeavoured to get the industrialized nations to adopt an international labour code, but without success. Like the philanthropic English industrialist Robert Owen, who from 1818 on had made similar efforts, Daniel Legrand was a forerunner of the considerable international social legislation which was to be achieved later.[12]

Other Christians were at work from the very dawn of the industrial era, trying to go beyond individual action and to act on society as a whole by giving Christian love a political dimension. We have already referred to William Wilberforce's anti-slavery movement. He was not content merely to influence public opinion, but acted on Parliament which, in 1807, finally passed the law abolishing the slave trade, and then the Abolition of Slavery Act in 1833. (We must not forget that on the continent, serfdom continued to exist in many places. It was only abolished on French royal estates in 1779, in Prussia in 1812, and was actually reinforced by Catherine II of Russia, where it was only abolished in 1861. That was two years before the abolition of slavery in the United States. The age of serfdom or of slavery in what are now two world superpowers is only four or five generations removed from our own.)

We also referred above to the noble work of Lord Shaftesbury. One of his creations was the "ragged schools". He, too, was not satisfied with acts of charity. He campaigned vigorously on working conditions, and in 1847 an Act was passed limiting the length of the working day in textile factories to 10 hours. This law was not, however, fully applied until the Factory Act of 1874. Before that first law regulating adult hours of work, Parliament had already in 1802, under pressure from philanthropic industrialists, regulated the work of parish apprentices in textile mills by limiting their hours of work to not more than twelve hours a day and laying down minimum conditions of hygiene, such as, the provision of dormitories. But no provision was made for enforcement.

In this way, little by little, through the initiative of a minority of Christian or philanthropic industrialists with a sincere desire to improve the condition of the workers, then — because of the inertia and resistance of other employers — under pressure from the workers themselves, strikes and revolutionary threats, labour legislation progressively improved the living conditions of the proletariat. Nevertheless, although legislation contributed to some extent to modify the social position of the workers, this brought no progress in knowledge of the socio-economic mechanisms of industrial society or in the understanding necessary for its transformation.

Third stage of awareness: studies, publications, inquiries and associations for social progress

The dominant circles of the industrial middle classes were guided in their decisions by the socio-economic doctrine of liberalism. This enjoyed special favour because political liberalism, springing from a combination of the Protestant puritan ethic and the philosophy of the Enlightenment, had been the revolutionary doctrine which had enabled the middle classes to overcome the theological, ideological and military resistance of the Ancien Régime. It therefore appeared that the liberty gained in the political field (purely relative as it was in the course of the various revolutionary and counter-revolutionary changes of the 19th century) must likewise, if it were to triumph on the economic and social plane, lead the nations to harmonious development.

However, though optimistic in its early days, with Adam Smith in England and J.-B. Say, Ch. Dunoyer and F. Bastiat in France, it rapidly became pessimistic when brought into contact with reality, for it led to results contrary to those which in theory were to be expected. Anyone who did not possess any economic power apart from his capacity to work, in other words the great majority, the mass of the people, rapidly fell victim to a freedom which gave the rich full liberty to ruin the poorest. The truth of Lacordaire's remark was evident: "Between rich and poor, strong and weak, it is freedom that oppresses and the law that frees." Provided, of course, the law is not made by the powerful alone; in other words, provided the poor succeed in winning their share in government, which the limited franchise of bourgeois democracy refused them.

The new liberals, the Rev. Thomas Malthus and the economist David Ricardo, agreed in observing that the poor man, because he was poor, had no right to more at the banquet of life than a bare subsistence (the iron law of wages). The myth of liberalism continued, nevertheless, to retain its hold on many secularized minds, just as the old theological notion of Providence still dominated conservative Christian consciences. Both led them to believe that invisible powers harmoniously regulated economic life as they did nature, and that it was not man's place to intervene deliberately and responsibly to change their course. (Cf. for example, F. Bastiat, *Les harmonies économiques*, 1838.) This myth of providential harmony was to continue to form the basis of the thought of liberal capitalism right down to the present day, just as the myth of inevitable conflict is at the basis of the thought of socialist state capitalism. The two myths, both western in origin, would be set up against one another as irreconcilable truths, whereas they each account for part of reality, and they would eventually be transplanted into every contemporary culture as a result of the worldwide expansion of industrial civilization in the colonies which we now call the Third World.

Although considered an eminent representative of the liberal school, John Stuart Mill revised his ideas in the light of the crying injustices which liberal capitalism was producing under his very eyes. In 1848, in his *Principles of Political Economy*, he advocated state intervention to set up productive cooperatives and to correct inequalities of wealth by taxation.

One of the first to call in question the actual principle of economic liberalism, the alleged providential balance of socio-economic life, was the Genevan Protestant C. L. S. de Sismondi. He, too, was a liberal at first, but as an attentive witness of the economic crises which England was going through, and of the resulting distress, he advocated state intervention to compensate the inevitable disharmonies created by the accumulation of wealth in a capitalist regime (*Nouveaux principes d'économie politique*, 1819). For this Christian, Providence is not the blind, cold force, insensitive to human sufferings and sanctioning the egotistical mechanisms of accumulation for some and of frustration for others in which the liberal doctrinaires believe. The divinity, whose purpose must also be that of a political economy conscious of its responsibilities, calls for "the spread of happiness on earth" by work and not simply for the production and accumulation of wealth.

The reformers of this period who sought to oppose the liberal *laissez-faire* doctrine formed a very mixed minority. Yet they did have one thing in common. Owing nothing to the influence of Marxist atheism, which would only make itself felt much later, each in his own way believed that, provided it seriously reforms itself, Christianity is the spiritual force capable of transforming society so as to undo the ravages of liberal capitalism. The social reformers, even the agnostics, nearly all assimilate their doctrinal teaching to a sort of renewed Christian catechetics. The pacific revolutionary E. Cabet published in 1825 *Le vrai christianisme* (True Christianity). The posthumous work of Count Saint-Simon, the spiritual father of the small group of French Christian socialists before 1848, is a veritable short treatise of social theology to which its author attached the greatest importance; it is entitled *Le nouveau christianisme* (The New Christianity) (1832). Conservative social Catholicism found expression in the work of A. de Villeneuve-Bargemont, *Economie chrétienne* (Christian

Economy) (1834); revolutionary social Catholicism in that of C.-F. Chevé, *Catholicisme et démocratie ou le règne du Christ* (Catholicism and Democracy or the Reign of Christ) (1842); and reformist social Catholicism in that of the Christian socialist A. Boulland, *Doctrine politique du christianisme* (Political Doctrine of Christianity) (1844). Even the anticlerical A. Comte would later entitle his reforming pamphlet *Catéchisme positiviste* (Positivist Catechism).

In Germany, the Christian revolutionary W. Weitling published in 1843 *Das Evangelium eines armen Sünders* (The Gospel of a Poor Sinner), founding his vision of a new society on the teaching of Christ; it was a sequel to his work *Die Menschheit wie sie ist und wie sie sein soll* (Humanity As It Is and As It Should Be) (1838). He drew inspiration from the theses of Lamennais expressed in *Paroles d'un croyant* (Words of a Believer), in Paris 1834, which summoned the peoples to revolution; this is what immediately brought down papal censure on Lamennais.

In the middle of the century, at the moment of the European revolutionary crisis, two German Christians sounded the alarm for Christendom so that it might change its way of life and renounce the injustices of the new industrial society. On the one hand, there was the Catholic bishop W. von Ketteler, whose *Social Sermons* (1848) roused people's consciences, and on the other, Pastor J.-H. Wichern, who addressed a *Manifesto to the German Nation* (1849). Numerous German social conservatives such as R. Todt, A. Stöcker, then F. Naumann, the two Blumhardts, father and son, and later the Swiss social-Christian pastors L. Ragaz and H. Kutter, developed a reformist Christian doctrine which guided their action and that of a few interested circles, governmental or private.

In the same spirit, and during this same historical period marked by industrialization and the impoverishment of the working masses, some publications attracted attention and gave a section of public opinion food for thought. John Harris, winner out of 145 of a competition organized in 1835, produced a great sensation with a work entitled *Mammon or the Love of Money Considered as the Prevailing Sin in the Christian Church*.

For the Scottish clergyman Thomas Chalmers, whose charitable works we have already referred to, the Bible constitutes the charter of any society that wishes to take its inspiration from Christ and which therefore must make the lot of the poorest its primary concern. He denounced as a great national disaster the condition of the English working class, and proclaimed that it is useless to help the poor without attacking pauperism as a whole. His three volumes (1821-1826) on *Christian and Civic Economy of Large Towns* have been described as "the most eloquent plea for the poor classes ever written".[13] He published numerous writings on aspects of social economy, including in 1844 *The Political Economy of the Bible*, and then a general work on the Christian and economic policy of a nation, a serious attack on the classical political economy which takes into account only the creation of wealth and capital and not men's creative activity. He also deplored the fact that the most pious theologians are not only completely ignorant of political economy, but also think themselves entitled to despise it, while presenting the practice of religion as a solution to the problem of the destitution of the poor. This makes many people think Christianity is synonymous with ignorance. After him, Thomas Arnold of Rugby in his *Christian Politics*, an unfinished work begun in 1827, emphasizes that it is the opposition between rich and poor and class hatred which is at the root of every social crisis.

In the minority of Christians who influenced public opinion to transform capitalist society from the very start, a special place must be made for two very active small groups of "Christian socialists". The English Protestant group, with the clergymen F. D. Maurice and Charles Kingsley and the lawyer J. M. Ludlow, had as great an influence as the French Catholic group. We shall return to these two groups later. For the moment, let us simply note the decisive effect of their writings. The pamphlets of the three Englishmen, signed "a clergyman worker", published during the events of 1848, their weekly paper *Politics for the People*, their *Tracts on Christian Socialism*, and the stories of Charles Kingsley, an eminent representative of the English social novel, had considerable influence in the social education of the English people and authorities. On more conservative lines, mention must also be made of the publications of the Oxford Tractarians, of John Henry Newman and of Cardinal Manning who protested against the harshness of the capitalist system and in particular against the exploitation of women and children in industry.

Even more, perhaps, than this abundant literature, it was the inquiries into the condition of the workers which contributed to open the eyes of the European middle classes and of Christians to the lot of the workers.

Even at the beginning of the 19th century, numerous investigations had been undertaken in various countries and had revealed the extent of working-class distress.

In France, the inquiries of Doctor Villermé [14] and of E. Buret [15] had aroused stupefaction in their readers, as did the work of Frégier on *The Dangerous Classes of the Population in Big Towns*. The Academy of Moral Sciences, which had commissioned Dr Villermé to carry out his researches, concluded that legislative intervention on behalf of the poor was imperative, whereas Villermé himself only considered the value of charitable relief as a remedy for the distress he had uncovered. E. Buret, on the other hand, vehemently attacked the capitalist system, denounced the bankruptcy of the Christian Church and agreed in part with the conclusions of another investigation, that of Friedrich Engels on *The Situation of the Working Class in England in 1844*, published in 1845.

All these publications prompted some of the clearest-minded Christians to deepen their knowledge of the mechanisms of society and to attack those of the multiple causes of pauperization which they were beginning to identify. For this purpose, the Society of Christian Morality was founded in Paris; Alexandre Vinet was a member and so were some of his Protestant friends such as H. Hollard, who with him founded the newspaper *Le Semeur* (The Sower) (1831). Philippe Buchez, though a Catholic, attended the Society for some time. Then he himself brought together some former Saint-Simonians to form the group of Christian socialists. Armand de Melun with some Catholic colleagues founded the Society of Christian Economy (1846), then E. de Pressensé and Pastor H. Lutteroth the Society for the Application of Christianity to Social Questions (1848), while a few years later Fred Le Play took the lead in the Society for Practical Studies in National Economy (1856), which was to give rise to what has been called the Catholic "charitable economy", as opposed to socialism.

On similar lines but with a certain time gap, a group of Germans with F. Hitze founded in 1870 a Catholic Centre of Social Policy, while Protestants such as Todt, Meyer, Stöcker and Wagner formed the Central Association for Social Reform.

The characteristic feature of these associations and publications was that, with a few rare exceptions, they concerned only a limited number of representatives of the two ruling classes, the old aristocracy and the new middle class. For this reason, the reforms which they proposed were hardly sufficient to bring about the transformation of the structures of capitalist industrial society which they suggested.

Thus a certain growth of awareness of the evils produced by the industrial revolution did take place in a minority of Christians, and inspired works of charity. Then progressively, and thanks to the pressure of the working-class world, some legislative reforms were made, and finally some actual inquiry into the causes of pauperization and into the action needed to eradicate it, but little really decisive action was taken to achieve this. For, in fact, the consciously-concerned minority was opposed by a conservative majority that had little wish for real changes in society. This opposition is the root of the dramatic clashes of the age of industrialization.

Fourth stage of awareness: the emancipation of the working classes and the class war

It is evident even from these examples, though additional ones would be needed to give a more exact picture, that throughout the course of development of industrial capitalism in the West, many Christians were actively mitigating its harmful effects and attempting to alter its course. Numerous as they were, however, most of them did not actually belong to the constantly-increasing proletarian masses; furthermore, they were only a minority in the Christian churches and sects. Very often they found themselves flanked by a faithful and clergy who, in face of the tragic events that marked European industrial and colonial expansion, simply gave way to the pull of irresponsible inertia, collaborated in conservative measures designed to strengthen their privileges, or even vented reactionary aggression against the very poorest and added to their sufferings.

In England, the conquest of democratic power by the middle classes began before the emergence of the actual industrial proletariat; the time-lag was less apparent in France and Germany where the triumph of the bourgeoisie coincided more closely with the beginnings of proletarianization. As a consequence, the middle-class revolution had the help of the proletariat in overthrowing the old regime. But the victorious middle classes very soon realized that their interests were not those of the industrial workers, and once their triumph was won, they opposed the liberation of the working class.

This is why from the beginning of the French Revolution, the proletariat which had taken the Bastille was allowed no part in the electoral assemblies of 1789; to demonstrate its discontent with the crisis and the rise in prices due to the drought, it had to take to the streets. The Constituent Assembly, by maintaining the ban on workmen's associations of trade guilds and strikes imposed by Colbert, and by proclaiming the principle that property was inviolable and sacred, directly impaired the rights of the workers and of small peasants accustomed to pasturing their cattle on seigneurial lands. The introduction of a property qualification for electors restricted the vote to people of property, thus excluding the proletariat from the new democracy.

By limiting the franchise in this way, the middle classes in France as in England and the United States created a political regime devoted to their interests. And even before they had ended their class struggle against the nobility, they opened another on a different front — against the proletariat. The first of these, however, though the cause of innumerable conflicts and much bloodshed during a large part of the 19th century, gradually decreased with the growth and consolidation of the bourgeoisie, while the second, extending from the working classes to the lower middle class rapidly proletarianized by industrialization, was to spread to the whole world as industrial capitalism developed in the five continents and as the proletarian masses multiplied there. And it has continued to worsen down to our own day.

In this struggle the working classes had to wage an unequal fight to obtain successively:

a) an improvement in working conditions.

The first half of the 19th century saw a general drop in wages and their collapse in times of food crisis. The constant increase in the supply of labour accentuated this tendency and also favoured a longer working day, already encouraged by the development of machines and the demands of competition, which again forced down wages. Vast numbers of women and children entering the mines and factories to supplement family earnings that had fallen below subsistence level drove down men's wages even further by their competition. In the English textile industry, women represented 50 to 70 percent of the work force, and children were employed from the age of six or seven.

It was only in 1833 that a Factory Act regulated child labour generally in the textile industry; the Mines Act of 1842 prohibited the employment of women and children underground, while in 1847 their working day was limited to ten hours. Prussia in 1839 forbade the employment of children under the age of eight in factories, while in 1841 France limited their work to ten hours in Paris and to eleven hours in the provinces. In fact, this legislation was not applied anywhere, and it was only later, when working men were strong enough to get it respected, that legislation made any progress.

b) liberty of association, the right to combination and the right to strike.

Though prohibited in the chief industrial countries, clandestine working men's associations were formed for the purpose of mutual assistance similar to that of the old guilds.

The endeavour to achieve joint advantages in wages or conditions of work by workmen's combination and sometimes by strikes was just as pitilessly repressed as their attempts to form associations. Large gatherings of working men were dispersed by violence, without regard for the risk of horrible massacres when troops were employed against demonstrators (Peterloo Massacre in England in 1819, so called by analogy with Waterloo; in France, the Lyons shootings in 1831, when 20,000 soldiers were sent to crush the workers' rising).

England repealed the anti-combination laws in 1824 and recognized the legality of the first trade unions, but it was not until 1864 that liberty of association was legally recognized in France, and only in 1884 that trade unions were authorized by law (1881 in Germany). It was in 1864 that the first international workers' association was formed in London (the First International).

c) the right to vote and to be eligible for election.

Observing that neither the philanthropy of humanists, nor the charity of Christians, nor the intervention of a state whose organs were in the hands of the middle class was capable of putting an end to their distress, the workers learnt the lesson of their strikes and trade-union activities and decided it was imperative to gain political power.

In 1796 in Paris, Gracchus Babeuf had organized a conspiracy on the basis that only the expropriation of the rich could lead the proletariat to liberation. He was arrested and executed, but his idea was taken up again a little later by Buonarotti and Blanqui, who were convinced that such expropriation would be impossible without a workers' dictatorship. The League of the Outlaws (1834), then the League of the Just (1836) to which the German Christian revolutionary, W. Weitling, belonged during a stay in Paris, pursued the same line of thought. Members of the League of the Just scattered in London and Brussels met in London in 1847 and made it the Communist League, which was joined by workers' groups in various countries. Two Germans, Karl Marx and Friedrich Engels, were given the task of writing a Manifesto to publicize its doctrines; this was the celebrated *Communist Manifesto* of 1848.

The more moderate English workers, who in 1830 had formed the National Association for the Protection of Labour, demanded universal suffrage in order, they hoped, to establish economic democracy by political action. After a sometimes violent agitation, the working men in conjunction with the middle classes obtained the 1832 Electoral Reform Act which, by widening the electorate, began the end of the supremacy of the landed gentry, but merely in favour of the middle classes. This working-class effort, a failure on the political plane, was followed by a setback on that of trade-union aspirations. The Grand National Consolidated Trades Union, a federation of all the workers' groups, founded on the initiative of the philanthropic industrialist Robert Owen in 1834, unleashed a vast strike movement to obtain the eight-hour day. The employers replied by a lock-out, refusing to employ members of the trade unions, and the movement collapsed.

Working-class revolt then tried to follow a political course of its own. In 1836, the London Working Men's Association proposed to fight for the exclusive rights of the workers to the product of their labour. In 1837, it drew up a political programme, the People's Charter, which demanded annual parliaments, universal male suffrage, secret ballot, the removal of the property qualification for membership of parliament, and payment of members. Under the influence of the aristocrat Feargus O'Connor, this movement, Chartism, became a revolutionary one, advocating insurrection and the general strike, since all other ways were blocked by the two classes in power. A Chartist Convention met in London in 1839, presented a petition to Parliament and decided to reply by a general strike if Parliament rejected the petition and charter. It was a failure, because the workers, threatened with destitution, went back to work. Chartism then split into two tendencies, the "moral force" wing, consisting of the partisans of legality and political alliance with the Radicals, and the advocates of "physical force", under O'Connor, who led the revolutionaries into fresh disturbances followed by more failures. The first joined the free-trade Anti-Corn Law Movement which, under the leadership of the Quaker John Bright and Richard Cobden, brought about the repeal of the protectionist Corn Law in 1846. The latter lost their impetus in a revolutionary

Gradual Awareness of Social, Economic Problems (1750-1900)

attempt at a new petition in April 1848, inspired by the events in Paris in February 1848; this was prevented by the police. Not until 1867 did an electoral reform act make working-class representation in Parliament possible and enable England to become a more complete democracy.

In France, the July revolution of 1830, achieved with the help of the workers, aroused great hopes in them. They expected the political reform to bring about social reforms. But once the liberal bourgeoisie came to power, it immediately set about counter-revolution to put an end to the manœuvres of the workers who, unable to meet except clandestinely, sought to transform the political into a social revolution. As for the February revolution of 1848, which finally established universal suffrage, the great mass of *députés* from the country, whose counter-revolutionary outlook matched that of the bourgeoisie, made it impossible for the representatives of the working class to achieve their demands. The class war was to continue and, after the foundation of the First International in 1864, led to the explosion of the Paris Commune in 1871, the establishment of the Second International in Paris in 1889 and of the Third International in Moscow in 1919.

d) a new status in industrial society.

Neither social legislation, nor the formation of trade unions, nor participation in democratic political power could fundamentally transform the status of the working man in the firm which employed him and in society. Numerous attempts, by philanthropic employers in the first place, by enterprising workers later, endeavoured to change the structure of relationships between the various partners in a business firm. Some examples may serve to indicate the line these took.

The French revolution of 1830 had profoundly impressed a young doctor, Philippe Buchez. A Catholic influenced by Saint-Simon, he founded with some working men the group of French Christian socialists which we mentioned above, and to which we shall return. Their numerous attempts at giving business enterprise a democratic constitution in the form of productive cooperatives were among the first of their kind in 1834, two years after some Alsatian bakers had set up the first consumers' cooperative. It was at this period that the Scottish industrialist Robert Owen himself organized his own industry as a cooperative association. (He was the first in 1819 to call himself a "socialist", and the term was taken up by the Saint-Simonians.) Seven weavers, disciples of his, founded in 1844 the Rochdale Pioneers society which was the origin of the English cooperative movement which eventually spread all over the world. Other attempts by employers can be cited, such as that of the French painter Leclaire, who in 1842 established a profit-sharing scheme for his employees. Schemes for working communities were suggested by Saint-Simon and Fourier, but had little influence on working men. Louis Blanc had more success with his proposal for establishing national workshops. But the way they were established by a commission of the Second Republic was a caricature which only served to discredit them. The Second Empire was at pains to ruin the last attempts at such associations, so that the capitalist pattern prevailed and became the type of industrial enterprise increasingly characteristic of industrialization in the West and then throughout the world.

What was the attitude of Christians at this stage? Only a minority took part in the search for genuine improvement of working men's status, while the vast majority joined with the middle classes and the old society in resisting the emancipation of the proletariat.

A Christian minority fights side by side with the workers

We have passed in review some of the initiatives of Christians in the fields of charity, social legislation, investigation, inquiries and associations for social action. These activities originated either with generous middle-class people, usually from bourgeois circles affected by a religious revival, or with philanthropic conservatives. Many of the latter were all the more attentive to the poverty and distress of the working classes because by birth and tradition they were adversaries of the middle classes and regarded them as responsible for the cruelties of the new industry. They had also preserved a certain tradition of solidarity linking the former privileged class with the small artisans and peasants. Generally speaking, no such tradition had been revived by the individualistic bourgeoisie. In fact, however, neither of the groups, however well-intentioned, made common cause with the working classes in their struggle to improve their status and general position in society. Only a few very small Christian minority groups were the exception.

One of the most typical of these was the Catholic group of French Christian socialists in the first half of the 19th century. The great mass of Catholics still linked Christian theology with the ideology of the old regime, and took an active part in the reactionary and counter-revolutionary enterprises of the period, both against democracy and against the betterment of the working class. As a logical consequence, the movements of middle-class and then of working-class emancipation based their struggle for liberation on anticlerical or even anti-Christian ideologies. It was, however, in a renewed interpretation of the gospel tradition that the small group inspired by Dr Philippe Buchez sought bases of social thought and political action favourable both to working-class emancipation and to the establishment of democracy. In a relatively short space of time, it accomplished an exceptionally fruitful theoretical and practical work. At the head of the first working-class newspaper, *L'Atelier*, composed and distributed by a workers' cooperative, this small group, very adaptable and without formal bonds, produced a considerable number of valuable publications. (The main authors were P. Buchez, P.-C. Roux, A. Ott, D. Laverdant, A. Boulland, C.-F. Chevé, A. Corbon, etc.). It was active on both the economic and social planes by creating business enterprises in the form of cooperative self-managing associations, and by defending working-class political interests. Philippe Buchez was the first president of the French Constituent Assembly in 1848, and A. Corbon its first secretary. They tried without success to put forward a scheme for worker-controlled business in place of the abortive national workshops of the Second Republic, meeting with opposition both from conservative employers and from the utopian socialists. Unfortunately, the events of June 1848 and the reaction which followed and its triumph in the Second Empire scattered the group and put an end to its experiments.

The second group of Christians who can be cited as having fought on the side of the workers is that of the Protestant Christian socialists in England.

The lawyer J. M. Ludlow knew Buchez and his friends in France and studied their workers' cooperatives. Shortly after the February revolution of 1848, he returned to London and witnessed in April the harsh repression of workers' demonstrations. Deeply affected by this, he joined his friends the Rev. F. D. Maurice and the Rev. Charles Kingsley to form the nucleus of the new social action group which was to bear the name of "Christian Socialists". The series of social writings, inaugurated by the puritan Thomas Carlyle, who had broken with the Church (*Chartism*, 1839; *Past and Present*, 1843), and the novels of the social conservative, Benjamin Disraeli (*Coningsby*, 1844; *Sybil*, 1845), included the stories of Charles Kingsley (*Alton Locke*, 1850) and had considerable influence on public opinion. In addition to their intense literary activity, the Christian socialists, like the corresponding French movement, created small groups of working men for education and social action, productive and consumer cooperatives as well as a working men's college in London (1854). They reacted against the all too frequent use of religion by Christians to subdue and dissuade the workers. We have used the Bible, Maurice wrote, as if it were a mere supplementary police manual, "an opium-dose for keeping beasts of burden patient while they were being overloaded". [16] Long before Karl Marx, Christian voices were thus denouncing the misuse of Christianity as opium of the people. The Christian socialists greatly influenced the trade unions, prolonging the influence of the Christian Chartists.

Outside England, the trade unions in the industrial countries met with hostility from most Christian milieux, as we shall see, and this hardened the anti-Christian and anticlerical position of the workers' leaders. There was nothing left for Christians who wanted to act in solidarity with the proletariat except to create denominational trade unions. These had the widest development in Germany under the influence of the Catholic Church, with first of all the "Kolping Families" for journeymen, then actual trade unions, thanks to the efforts of Bishop von Ketteler; corresponding Protestant trade unions came later.

These efforts of a continually active wing of Christianity in solidarity with the workers were due to a minority that was often criticized and sometimes even despised by most Christians.

The majority of Christians indifferent, conservative and often reactionary

We have already noted the parallelism, though with some time-lags, of the inderdependent phenomena common to the European nations: growth of political democracy, industrial development, colonial domination, proletarianization of the working classes (despite a slight general rise in their living standards). The progressive detachment of the proletariat from the traditional sources of recruitment of members of the Christian churches and sects (nobility and peasantry in the old society, middle classes in the new), is explained by a growing ideological opposition bound up with divergent material interests. On the one hand, theological conservatism largely contributed to confer a sacred character on the old social and political structures and to reinforce in Christians a defence mechanism against the advance of political democracy and working-class betterment. On the other hand, that rigidity strongly encouraged in the middle classes first, and then in the working class, a spiritual quest outside the framework of traditional Christianity, since the latter was serving as an ideology of reaction. As a consequence, that quest was inevitably heretical judged by received ideas, since it sought to sap the foundations of a spirituality which was justifying opposition to democratic and social progress. It therefore became increasingly anticlerical and anti-Christian as antagonisms worsened.

Now this heretical character of their adversaries provided the Christians with a supplementary (though not an evangelical) justification for their fanaticism in a combat which gave them the double satisfaction of safeguarding their material interests while fighting in defence of the Christian faith. This religious fanaticism, however, contributed to strengthen the anticlerical ardour of the democratic bourgeois and then the militant atheism of the proletariat. All were convinced they were fighting for the spiritual liberation of the human race still crushed (as was indeed the case, as we shall see) by an authoritarian, hierarchical, elitist and domineering interpretation of Christianity.

There were four historical earthquake shocks in Europe in the course of the 19th century, and each time the epicentre was in Paris. And at each shock, the majority of terrified Christians sought in a reactionary interpretation of Christianity grounds for rejecting the legitimate demands of the peoples.

The reaction against the fall of the Ancien Régime at the beginning of the century was typical. The theology of the period taught that temporal power had of necessity to be exercised by the existing theocratic monarchies. It encouraged the crusade of the Holy Alliance which united Orthodox Russia, Protestant Prussia and Catholic Austria with the involuntary ecumenical blessing of their respective clergy for the purpose of nipping democracy in the bud, having declared it satanic. As always, the sensational excesses of revolutionaries contributed largely to arouse the fear which engendered the defence mechanisms. But the Christian thinkers of the period, Chateaubriand, J. de Maistre, de Bonald, Haller, agreed with the hierarchy and the clergy of the various denominations in recommending a return to the past in which throne and altar were associated. The teaching of the apostle Paul was used to justify the divine right of kings, and the dogma that Providence governed the nations through them was the theological weapon of counter-revolution employed both against liberal democrats accused of naively aiding the revolutionaries, and against republicans.

The English Protestant democratic monarchy, however, remained calm and offered generous hospitality to refugees from the French Revolution, who soon helped to strengthen the conservative tendency of the churches in Great Britain. The Anglican Church opposed, but in vain, the campaigns for electoral reform which resulted in the Reform Act of 1832.

The 1830 July revolution in Paris had a markedly anticlerical character as a result of the preponderant part played by official Christianity in the counter-revolutionary current which had ensured the success of the Restoration in Europe. With the final triumph in 1830 of its adversary, the anticlerical bourgeoisie, the clergy dissociated itself to some extent from this new business and commerical class, and encouraged the charitable tendencies of social conservatism within the churches. At the same time, another current emerged with the gradual conversion to Christianity of a section of the new bourgeoisie, which previously had been philosophically hostile — especially on the Catholic side — for reasons already indicated. This probably goes to explain both a certain tacit agreement between Christians and proletarians in association with the revolutionary lower middle class, against the upper middle class in the events of 1848 (death of Mgr Affre on the barricades), and the immense disappointment of the workers when they found themselves definitively abandoned by the Christian churches and sects after the revolution and the period of harsh reaction that followed. The churches, in fact, increasingly made common cause with the ruling bourgeoisie in proportion as its representatives abandoned the philosophy of the Enlightenment. They developed a new interpretation of Christianity emphasizing middle-class values, which became for the bourgeoisie what Christianity had been for the Ancien Régime: a spiritual weapon of reaction and counter-revolution, directed this time against the working class.

It was only at the end of the century that a new interpretation of the Christian faith by the Christian social movement developed in the various denominations. Leo XIII authorized acceptance of democracy and showed a certain openness to the problems of the working classes in the Encyclical *Rerum Novarum* (1891). A new interest in social problems was now developing among a minority of Protestants. For the working class, however, it was already too late. During this half-century of reaction, the working-class world had found in the atheistic ideology and in the hope given it by the revolutionary doctrine of Karl Marx a substitute for the indifferent and sometimes hostile views held by the majority of Christians and their theologians. The churches and sects had, tacitly or expressly, or at all events uncritically, espoused the interests of capitalism and of the various nationalisms which produced class antagonisms and military clashes between nations. It was not until the ecumenical renewal of the first half of the following century that a different aspect of Christianity would reappear, more faithful to its original tradition and capable of responding anew to the divine inspiration of nations seeking social solidarity and supranational fraternity.

Conclusion

Even a rapid survey of the events which marked the gradual growth of awareness in the West and in the churches of the socio-economic problems created by the industrial revolution permits a few brief conclusions to be drawn.

1. It is obvious that most Christians and their theologians were tempted to confuse the ideologies and interest of the ruling class with the social implications of the Christian faith. The churches' defence of the Ancien Régime was a case in point.

2. A similar temptation recurs after important political and social changes. Christians are inclined once more to identify themselves with the ideologies and interests of the new ruling class. This is shown, for instance, in the rapid and uncritical assimilation of the new bourgeois values by the Christian churches and sects after the rise to power of this new class in the second half of the 19th century. The opposite temptation is also perceptible. In reaction against this kind of infidelity, some Christians cling nostalgically to the previous identification of Christianity with the old ideologies, as in the touching but tragic loyalty of the inconsolable adherents of the Ancien Régime to the old ideology after the triumph of bourgeois democracy.

3. We note the constant presence of a minority within the Christian churches and sects which strives to be faithful to the Gospel by reinterpreting it afresh to meet the new needs of the new poor in society, following Christ's example.

4. We also observe that this minority, seeking the true interests of the poorest, is, like Christ, painfully thrust aside by the majority of conven-

tional Christians attached to the ideologies and interests of the ruling classes. The tension which ensues continually stirs up conflicts inside the churches and sects.

5. It is therefore important for the spiritual health of Christians as a whole that these conflicts should be clearly faced and that, instead of anathemas or pretended neutrality, they should produce continual confrontation within the communities, with the aim of achieving greater common fidelity to the Gospel.

NOTES

[1] Cf. E. R. WICKHAM: *Church and People in an Industrial City*, 1957.

[2] Cf. MAX PIETSCH: *Die Industrielle Revolution*. Freiburg: 1941; French transl.: Paris, 1963.

[3] *The Shorter Oxford English Dictionary:* "Subversion: 1. Overthrow, demolition (of a city, stronghold, etc.); 2. The turning (of a thing) upside down or uprooting it from its position (of an object); 3. In immaterial senses: overthrow, ruin."

[4] MAX PIETSCH: *op. cit.*, French translation, p. 36.

[5] *Ibid.*

[6] ANDRÉ D. TOLÉDANO: *Histoire de l'Angleterre chrétienne*, p. 210 f. Paris: 1955.

[7] *Ibid.*, p. 211.

[8] PAUL FARGUES: *Histoire du Christianisme*, Vol. VI, p. 359. Paris: 1939.

[9] *Ibid.*, p. 352.

[10] *Ibid.*, p. 235.

[11] *Ibid.*, p. 245.

[12] Cf. E. LÉONARD: *Histoire du Protestantisme*, Vol. III, p. 254. Paris: 1964.

[13] L. EPSTEIN: *L'économie et la morale aux débuts du capitalisme industriel en France et en Grande-Bretagne*, p. 254. Paris: 1966.

[14] L. R. VILLERMÉ: *Tableau de l'état physique et moral des ouvriers employés dans les manufactures de coton, de laine et de soie*, 2 vols. Paris: 1840.

[15] E. BURET: *De la misère des classes laborieuses en Angleterre et en France*, 2 vols. Paris: 1840.

[16] In: "Politics for the People" (1848); quoted in A. TOLÉDANO, *op. cit.*, p. 279.

2 · The Church and the Trade Union Movement in Britain in the 19th Century

John Kent

The 19th century in England saw the expansion of both the middle class, among whose institutions was the political party, the urban university, and the "modernized" religious denominations, and of the working class, which set up trade unions as a means of self-defence and self-improvement. The basic theoretical justification of unionism was not an appeal to a Christian concept of love, but the assertion that the relations of employers and employed were governed by natural law.

In the first half of the 19th century, most churchmen were socially conservative. They believed that social harmony had existed in the Ancien Régime and had been fostered by the close links between Church and state. They forgot the steady dehumanization of the poor in the 18th-century parish, and although they deplored the conditions of the new 19th-century industrial towns, they also felt intellectually obliged to accept the intellectual conclusions of the classical economists. As late as the 1840s, the Anglican episcopate doubted the right of the working classes to form independent institutions of power: agitators, socialists (most of whom were atheists) and Chartists led the worker astray from the Church, which only sought to guide them into the proper form of social integration. In this, one sees an episcopal version of what Karl Marx criticized in Hegel, the making of political issues into theological problems, and so taking them out of the realm of the practical: it was this tendency which led F. D. Maurice, for example, to obscure rather than clarify the nature of trade unionism in the mid-century.

Recognition of workers' humanness

On the positive side, however, one must not fall into the error of defining the churches simply in terms of the ordained ministry. Between 1830 and 1850, for example, strenuous efforts were made to increase the amount of elementary popular education on a religious basis. In the same years, Lord Shaftesbury helped to direct a powerful middle-class pressure group in support of working-class aims like the Ten Hours agitation, and made people more aware of the horrors of child labour in a variety of industries. In doing this, Shaftesbury believed himself to be a Tory, a supporter of a traditional, paternalist and Christian society. At this very time, however,

Sir Robert Peel was reorganizing "Toryism" on the basis of the classical economics plus a police force: both Peel, and his famous Home Secretary, Sir James Graham, refused to accept the degree of state interference in industry which Shaftesbury tolerated in his social policies. In social terms, Shaftesbury did much more for the working class than did a theologian like Maurice, and this was partly because he did not convert his reforming programmes into elaborate theologies, but used simpler religious ideas, as for example, that working-class men and children were as human as middle-class men and children. It did not occur to him, however, that this idea could just as easily be developed from the French revolutionary tradition as from Christian principles.

Maurice's "Christian socialism", on the other hand, was a theological rationalization of the view that the business of religious institutions was to reconcile capital and labour, because social conflict was a breach of the Christian concept of love. Maurice did not invent cooperation: the working class had begun to experiment with cooperative societies some years before 1848. His hostile reaction to the strikes of the 1850s, and the consequence that he drew from these theories, that the engineering workers should shame their employers by returning to work and accepting a reduction in wages, was characteristic. His close associates, Hughes and Ludlow, both drew back in later life from working-class unionism as a struggle for economic betterment. Hughes was a romantic utopian, not an hours-and-wages man; Ludlow was much less interested in trade unionism than in cooperative ownership; he wanted to change the existing economic system, and his failure in this direction soured him. Christian socialism, in fact, was always a middle-class affair, an attitude recommended *to* the working class, but never very popular *in* the working class. It is significant that George Howell, one of the ablest early working-class writers on unionism, in *The Conflicts of Capital and Labour* (1878), contrasted political economy (love thyself) with Christianity (love thy neighbour), but he did not quote Maurice nor any other of the familiar theological sources.

The politician and the theologian

The real change of mood took place in the 1870s, as the unions consolidated what power they had. The Gladstone government (which was "liberal") received the report of the Royal Commission on Trades Unionism in 1869 and passed a Criminal Law Amendment Act in 1871 which reflected political liberalism's *laissez-faire* tradition, linked unionism with conspiracy, and maintained the status of the Act of 1825 on the relations between master and servant which had been interpreted so as to put a worker in danger of criminal prosecution for breach of contract if he went on strike. Yet Gladstone, it should be remembered, was quite as much a pillar of the Church of England as any of the episcopate. When Disraeli's (Conservative) administration took over in 1874, it repealed the Liberal Act through the *Conspiracy and Protection of Property Act* and the *Employers and Workmen Act* in 1875: these legalized collective bargaining and removed the concept of a strike as a breach of contract from the criminal code, thus giving strikes a legal basis. Much middle-class and business opinion has never quite accepted the implications of these steps, but they have never been really reversed. On the whole, *clerical* opinion in the 1870s avoided these topics, and this explains why E. R. Norman, for example, can say that: "the Church had no clear opinion".[1] This is a superb instance of a wrong definition of "the Church": he meant the bishops and clergy, of course, but most of the Conservatives concerned in these political changes were far from being *outside* the Church, and they seem to have seen the issues clearly enough. In the past, *laissez-faire* ecclesiastics had opposed unions on the ground that they interfered with economic law. A mid-century generation had argued that the Church should somehow intervene between the conflicting classes; intervention depended either on the theory of arbitration, that there was always a difference which could be split, or on the belief that conflict was inherently and theologically wrong. The new Tory position implied that parties whose interests were not the same would come into conflict, and that such conflicts were not in themselves immoral, nor was the legislature bound to support only one side, a conclusion probably aided in the 1870s by aristocratic Tory dislike of the new industrialism. Disraeli certainly thought that the aristocracy could afford to protect the working classes from the untrammelled power of the industrial middle class.

In this sense, therefore, the politician was a more important representative of the Christian tradition than was the theologian, and this situation was not much affected by the formation in 1889 of the largely clerical Christian Social Union (CSU), whose first president was Bishop Westcott.[2] Membership of the CSU meant little more than an opaque, sentimental adhesion to the ideal of social harmony; in practice, the CSU's attitude to trade unionism was more grudging than that to be found in *Rerum Novarum*, the first important modern Roman Catholic social encyclical, issued in 1891. Part of the trouble was that "progressive" clerics had status in the Liberal Party as a political subculture, within which they had connections with government, channels of communication, and so forth; trade unionism, on the other hand, lay outside their normal field of influence, and they disliked the prospect of independent working-class political organization as a threat to the Liberal Party itself. In a deeply divided city like Bristol, for example, the centre of unionism in the 1890s lay in the old town along the river, far from the great middle-class Victorian churches up on the hill in suburban Clifton and Redland, whence they dominated the institutions of local religious opinion and ecclesiastical politics.[3]

Redistribution of power — a crucial issue

What kind of reaction was trade unionism entitled to expect from religious institutions and opinion? The sympathy was there in the early 19th century from a small but influential group of men like Shaftesbury, who found it possible to stir public emotion, especially about the labour of women and children; this was a public whose sensibility was already exercised over slavery. Even in the 1890s, this method still brought results, as when religious and secular journalists exposed the apalling housing of the urban and rural poor, or when, briefly, the London sweated trades were attacked by Fabians and others. This kind of emotion, which involved pity, guilt and a sense of a common humanity, did little for unionism as such, because the essence of unionism lay in abstract questions of natural justice and political power. The present-day parallel would be that journalists can always hope to arouse sympathy about the sufferings of black groups, but find it much harder to pacify suspicions about black possession of political power.

Here it is necessary to bring in the idea of class. Class was (and is) to be established in differences of experience, especially working experience, not in differences or similarities of income or of cultural aspiration — as though the working class arrived at middle-class status as soon it started to read Henry James in paperback and was able to obtain cheap divorce. Working experiences differed greatly in the 19th century, and industrial experience, that of the shop floor worker, the miner, the bricklayer and so forth, has to be distinguished from the professional experience of the lawyer, doctor, teacher, priest, etc. Factory workers, shop and office workers, domestic workers and so on formed working-class groups because they were perpetually directed, limited, frequently admonished and fired by others. Unionism was concerned with, and rose out of, the directed classes. And what was always implicit, and finally explicit, in both the revolutionary tradition (from 1776) and the distinct socialist tradition (from a slightly later period), was the proposal that some power, even great power, would have to be given (not *ought* to be, but would *have* to be given) to large numbers of people who in the traditional western society had been the directed, the subjects of the power of others. Because unionism always meant some degree of redistribution of economic power, it inevitably threatened the redistribution of all power.

One finds this very clearly stated by George Howell in *The Conflicts of Capital and Labour*. "In the earlier history of industry", he wrote in 1878, "there was political serfdom and social servitude combined; in later times we have political freedom, but there coexists with it a kind of social servitude almost equally to be dreaded with that of the past; it is this fierce struggle for social life and industrial freedom that we now witness; political economy does not tell us how to achieve this, hence it has failed in its assumed mission; the aspiration of the masses, and their efforts to carve out a path for themselves, are stigmatized as rank socialism; even Christianity is declared to be rank sentimentality when applied to social questions. If we cannot destroy servitude, we may at least regulate it." Howell vigorously defended the right of workmen to combine, to form their own centre of power, and although he mentioned Christianity for the sake of its emotional value to the worker when he criticized the classical economy, it is obvious that Howell prefers organization to sentiment. In this connection, it is also interesting to note that when Edward Beesley, the Comtist from University College, addressed a great rally of working men in Hyde Park in 1868, he attacked Shaftesbury as an enemy of trade unions, and as one who praised the kind of working man who rose from the ranks and made himself affluent; Beesley praised trade unionism on the precisely opposite ground that it enabled the ordinary man, who only wanted a fair day's wage for a fair day's work, to look after himself: this was praising the non-Christian aspect of the tradition. (For this speech, see M. Katanka (ed.): *A Year of the Unions*, 1968.)

When one turns from Howell and Beesley to the moulders of religious opinion on the subject, one finds them chary of tackling the question of the redistribution of power in society; there seemed to them to be no theological ground for this, but only for schemes of reconciliation which would bind more tightly together the holders and subjects of social authority. The unions should abandon any aggressive role and abjure the concept of the strike, which was never to their advantage. (See, for example, B. F. Westcott: *Lessons from Work*, 1901, especially pp. 305-326, 418-419.) Westcott wrote as though this reconciliation of employers and employed must be brought about in the ecclesia; the factory did not need to be changed structurally itself, but fellowship in Christ must be made the foundation of closer social intercourse. *Rerum Novarum* (1891) proposed a cultural third element as well, more often seen in practice in France than in England.

Chapel communities and trade unions

In fact, however, if reconciliation was to be possible without any palpable transfer of social power, it had to carried out *within* the factory as well, and this was never done. Part of the trouble was that even at the end of the 19th century middle-class Protestants still had a low expectation for the working classes, whose minimum wage could be fixed at a very low figure, and whose education could still be limited to an appropriate level. The varieties of Christian and guild socialism, which had a vigorous private as much as public life between the 1880s and 1939, were the typical products of a middle-class religious subculture which was always too sure that it knew what kind of society working-class people ought to want; Westcott and his successors were insufficiently interested in what working-class people actually did want. This is why one finds Stewart Headlam's *Church*

Reformer, the organ of his "Christian-socialist" *Guild of St Matthew*, saying in 1893 about the recently-formed Independent Labour Party that "to advocate the introduction of working men as such into Parliament, as the Fabians now seem to be doing, is utterly absurd". In the same style, the Church Socialist League, founded as late as 1906, with its roots in the Community of the Resurrection at Mirfield in Yorkshire, refused as early as 1909 to join broadly with the Labour Party, and retreated into P. E. T. Widdrington's obscurantist "Christian sociology". These middle-class religious groups had no deep interest in the politics of wages and working conditions which was the normal sphere of trade unionism. A book like *The Return of Christendom* (1922), which contained essays by M. B. Reckitt, L. E. Thornton and A. J. Penty, for example, was the ultimate in withdrawal from any such reality.

A further explanation of the slightness of contact between religious institutions and trade unions in the 19th century was to be found in the way in which local congregations of whatever denomination, and even when they were largely working-class, came to live in a common life somewhat withdrawn from the rest of society. It became difficult for full-time, deeply-committed members of local chapel communities to become significantly related to working-class culture. Whatever their class, the chapel members were normally committed to a cult of respectability, which often included teetotalism, the desire to rise socially, and conscious moralism; working-class culture on the other hand, when sophisticated, drew more directly on natural law than on revealed theology, and therefore on natural justice rather than on given moral judgments. Working-class culture had a weakness for entertainment as much as for respectability: entertainment has to be understood as an end in itself, deriving from an aristocratic not a bourgeois model, quite different from the satisfactions which the chapel pursued — and it is significant that in the 20th century the chapels closest to the working class, and by that time in serious decline, themselves tried a modified style of entertainment, the Lancashire pantomime, for example.

Chapel-centred Protestantism, therefore, could make little common concern with trade unionism. Their programmes differed radically, not because of politics, but because of the forms of the underlying subcultures. Chapel and trade union could only blend, and then not for long, in unusual areas like the Durham mining valley examined by Robert Moore,[4] in which for a brief period at the end of the 19th century the Lodge leaders were also chapel-goers. This did not mean a genuine fusion of cultures — in fact, as Moore showed, it meant that between about 1880 and 1910 the mining leadership of the local Wesleyan and Primitive Methodist chapels had more in common with the pit owners in terms of the respectability cult than they had with the other miners as a larger group in terms of life-style.

Obviously, the small, inward-turned chapel community had its own strengths for which it might be valued at certain times. The withdrawal of Christianity from a dominant culture may happen at any time. But a religious group which wanted to affect the trade unions could not simultaneously choose to build a community oriented in another direction. There is little evidence that in the later 19th century religious groups as a whole *did* want a close relationship with trade unions; they were more likely to identify with the Liberal than the Labour Party, and therefore with the employers rather than with the employed at the political level. Exhortations that Christians should attend Lodge meetings and vote down the communists, who have meanwhile been exhorting *their* members to attend and vote down the bosses's men, are still offered as both a social policy and a social possibility. But such actions are not possible if the Christians concerned are already organized in groups which have become a kind of local community-in-itself. Groups which set out not to be working-class could not also lead or influence the working class inside the institutions which formed the core of the working-class culture, the unions and the clubs. The late 19th-century religious groups set themselves a task of double conversion: they sought to convert the workers to Anglo-Catholic or evangelical dogma; they also tried to convert "socialism" into a Christian system. The proletariat usually rejected both approaches. They did not, in any case, owe their conversion to trade unionism to the religious groups: other workers proselytized for unionism in terms of natural justice, solidarity, self-defence and so forth. The case made for the unions was a case neither for a religious nor socialist position, but was a case for the organization of the working classes wherever they worked. Religious groups which aspired both to remain working-class and to play a role in trade unionism would have needed a flexible structure which stopped short of becoming a local centre for a non-working-class subculture in the traditional sense.

Conclusions

a) In 19th-century socio-economic terms, trade unionism was a highly probable growth; it would have developed, and largely did, without assistance from religious institutions, and it drew its morality as much from the Enlightenment as from the gospels.

b) As to the question of a "separation" between the churches and the industrial workers, one might argue that this never took place. There was more of a failure to come together as the new working classes grew in numbers and urban concentration between 1820 and the 1880s. This new subculture never came very close to Christianity (which is not the same thing as saying that it was not in other senses religious, and to some extent para-Christian), because the economic basis of working-class life — its poverty, its working conditions, its lack for decades of real domestic privacy — made the cult of respectability which went with Victorian Christianity neither possible nor very attractive to the vast majority.[5] As a result, when working-class congregations formed, as they sometimes did, they always tended to develop away from, not into, the working-class subculture. (The Roman Catholic working class in England might seem to be an exception, but one has to remember the perpetual importance of Irish nationalism in this instance.) A handful of politically-sympathetic middle-class organizations and of locally brilliant parish priests and ministers had no permanent effect on this fundamental distinction between two worlds, and it is hard to see how it could have done.

c) There was little in Christian theology (of which "respectability" was not an essential part) which was inimical to trade unionism, except for the view that the Christian idea of "love" necessarily entailed reconciliation, so that the acceptance of the idea of "class-war" was "un-Christian". The theological point which was debatable was compounded by the social fact that "reconciliation" often seemed to the trade union world as a device to remove from the hands of the working class its means of self-defence, and as evidence of a kind of ecclesiastical naiveté about the nature of industry. In any case, "reconciliation" undercut most programmes for the reconstruction of society. It was hardly surprising that at this point the churches and the unions were not easily reconciled.

NOTES

[1] E. R. NORMAN: *Church and Society in England 1770-1970*, p. 155. Oxford University Press, 1976.

[2] For Christian-socialist bodies after 1870, see P. D'A. JONES: *The Christian Socialist Revival 1877-1914*. Princeton: 1968.

[3] See J. KENT: "The Role of Religion in the Cultural Structure of the later Victorian City", in *Transactions of the Royal Historical Society*, Series 5, Vol. 23, 1973, pp. 153-175.

[4] R. MOORE: *Pitmen, Preachers and Politics*. Cambridge University Press, 1974.

[5] H. J. DYOS AND M. WOLFF (eds): "Feelings and Festivals" in *Victorian City*, Vol. 2, pp. 855-872. Routledge, Kegan Paul, 1973.

3 · German Protestantism and the Social Question in the 19th Century

Günter Brakelmann

Even the small town of Wittenberg — Martin Luther's town — had its own great moment in the year 1848, quite apart from the revolutionary happenings at that time. Five hundred ministers and laymen from the provincial churches of Germany met there to discuss church matters and political questions. The idea was to redefine the Church's attitude to political developments and to consider ways and means of organizing a united evangelical Church of Germany more in keeping with contemporary needs.

One of those who took part in this conference was Pastor Johann Hinrich Wichern (1808-1881) who pleaded that the conference should also consider social problems. In an impassioned extempore address lasting an hour and a quarter, he tried to show his mainly conservative audience the need for the Church to undertake organized social work. It was the Church's duty to serve and not simply to preach. Faith and love were inseparable. Wichern accused the official Church of having neglected social questions in the past. He urged that the Church should commit itself to Christian social service in a big way and proposed that the conference should form a "Committee for Home Missions".

Wichern's charitable services

Wichern's judgment on the Church's failure was severe, prophetically so. Obviously, he knew that there were exceptions. He knew, for example, of the work of Johann Falk (1768-1826) in his Luther Chapel in Weimar, who had tried to educate orphans to become useful members of Church and society by "prayer and work".

Wichern also knew at first hand of the charitable efforts of Baron von Kottwitz (1757-1843) in Berlin, who had already created a "Voluntary Employment Centre" for the unemployed and made strenuous efforts for the education of poor children.

Last but not least, he was aware of the work of Theodor Fliedner (1800-1864) in Kaiserswerth on the Rhine. Fliedner had been responsible for

---

Translated from the German by the Language Service, WCC.

the revival of women's diaconal work. The service of deaconesses soon became one of the most familiar features of German Protestantism. Altogether it must be said that diaconal work by both men and women in the 19th and 20th centuries constituted a major material and human achievement. In countless hospitals, orphanages and special schools, practical help was provided for people in danger of going to the wall in a bourgeois capitalist society which put a premium on performance.

Wichern himself had for fifteen years been associated with a distinctive pattern of loving service by individual Christians who owed to the revival movement their concern for such work, which was directed to the unfortunate at the margins of society.

Wichern had begun in 1833 in the so-called Rauhes Haus ("ragged school") in the Horn district of Hamburg, where he cared for and educated neglected youngsters. A sizeable "institute" soon developed from these modest beginnings. Wichern worked out and put into practice a type of remedial social work which still retains its interest even today. The aim of this "residential education" was to turn out young people equipped and trained as mature Christians to face the adult world. Wichern's assistants were male deacons who had received special training for their ministry among young people.

For this ministry to the sick and the neglected, Wichern coined the term "home mission". He campaigned for the spread of this social service work throughout Germany by his own travels and by means of his published journal *Die Fliegenden Blätter* (The Winged Pages).

But Wichern realized that the distress of the masses in early capitalistic society was not going to be cured simply by the action of individual Christians. He tried, therefore, to make the institutional Church in Wittenberg realize that the cause of "home mission" was its own deepest concern and draw the necessary organizational conclusions. The organized Church itself should sponsor a wide-ranging social service through which it would influence government and society by the spirit of its teaching and the example of practical Christianity. Wichern's conception of the Church's task and of its "home mission" is best seen in the published programme he issued in 1849, entitled: *The Home Mission of the German Evangelical Church — A Plea to the German People*. This document could be described as a counterpiece to the *Communist Manifesto* of Karl Marx and Friedrich Engels published in 1848.

In his memorandum, Wichern unfolded a huge practical programme for church home service which was to a large extent to be put into practice in the course of the coming decades.

Opposed to structural change

It is an entirely different story when we turn to Wichern's comments on activities which went further than aid for unfortunate individuals. Even before the revolution happened, Wichern had recognized the fact that as well as a "natural" poverty there was also an "artificial" poverty with its roots in the role allotted to the proletariat. He realized clearly that it was impossible to deal effectively with this distress solely by individual help and self-help, and that only by the systematic application of assistance to the masses could their poverty, their pauperization, be eliminated. He therefore called for social reform through government agencies. He evidently knew that the principle of "rescuing love" needed to be complemented by the principle of "organizing justice", in other words, by government-directed social policies. He was also one of the first to grasp the idea that those in need of help should form associations to help themselves, that is, the idea of workers' helping themselves by forming trade unions.

But these two fundamental insights — government social policy and trade union representation of the workers' interests — were not to result in any practical political governments so far as Wichern himself was concerned. After the revolution, the Church's social welfare work increasingly became the essence of home mission, which thus stopped half-way. How did this happen?

Under the impact of the revolution, Wichern tended increasingly to see the work of home mission as part of the struggle against the disintegrating forces in government and society. For him, the struggle against the revolution and its ethos became a battle of faith against unbelief; socialism, communism, atheism, and democracy were all of them simply rebellion against the existing government and the existing social order, against the sanctity of law, against the divine order of things. As a result of this struggle against contemporary developments in the interests of the Christian position, Wichern and the home mission became more and more strongly attached to the restoration society with its marriage of throne and altar. The home mission allied itself with the authoritarian state and society of order in its struggle against liberalism, socialism and democracy. A solution of the social question was unimaginable except within the established framework of government and society. Any tendency in the direction of development or even revolution was labelled anti-Christian, which was the severest theological condemnation in the book.

It was this radically hostile attitude of mind which prevented any critical but constructive dialogue between Wichern and most of his contemporary churchmen, on the one hand, and the other political and social movements of the other. So it was that Wichern, while promoting an undoubtedly magnificient welfare work within the existing structures, was never moved to work for new structures in government and society. He never really moved into the field of social policy in the strict sense. It was also a theological assumption which played a major role in preventing him from taking this further step. Only through evangelization could he imagine any social rebirth of the nation or any renewal of society. The individual had first to be "converted" and then a "Christian society" would follow as a "natural" consequence. For Wichern, a "Christian change of mind" was the prerequisite of any "change in social conditions".

The last point can be put another way. Wichern was unable to understand the modern process of "secularization", the secularizing of social life. For him, secularization meant apostasy from God, the victory of the opponents of Christianity. In opposition to this, he placed his thesis of the evangelization of the whole nation. Wichern's answer to the modern ethos was the Christianization of the individual and the institution, of government and society. But even at that time, this was no longer possible. His conception of Christian society and a Christian state with an active Christian Church at the heart of it inevitably became the political expression of a late-bourgeois Christian ideology. History inevitably rolled on over it. But in spite of fatal errors, Wichern was the first German evangelical theologian to sharpen the social conscience of Protestantism. For this we are still his debtors today.

First evangelical social politician

Yet it was a contemporary of Wichern's who already went a great deal further than this appeal to the individual conscience: Viktor Aimé Huber (1800-1869). He is really the first German evangelical social politician. Huber had spent some time in England in the 1840s studying social questions there. The analysis he gives bears a striking resemblance to that of Friedrich Engels at about the same time in his *The Condition of the Working Class in England* (1845). But their conclusions differ. As Engels sees it, the class struggle and revolution are the only way to the future. Huber, on the contrary, chooses the evolutionary way, the way of reform. He stands, therefore, between a socialist future utopia and a conservative ideology of the past. His own description of his position is "creative conservatism". By this, he means a position which, while preserving the tried and tested elements of the past, at the same time does not shrink from the inescapable claims of the future. For him, the major future task is the incorporation of the "fourth estate", the proletariat, into existing society. But, of course, this development of the position of the proletariat can only be achieved by deliberate efforts towards reform. For Huber, social policy is the answer to the social question.

Huber still hoped initially that the responsible people and groups in society would realize the need to help the proletariat to improve its individual and social position, but he was forced reluctantly to admit later that the ruling propertied classes were not in a position to do what was needed on their own. If there was to be any social policy at all, it would have to be government social policy. But Huber set the principle of self-help alongside this as equally important. Above all, the workers should form associations which would provide them with a means of self-protection against capitalist domination and exploitation. The workers' associations should at the same time help to educate the workers for independence. They should be established as a self-conscious group within existing society. Huber did not regard capital and labour as inevitable opposites. What he was after was an equilibrium between the two elements. He rejected liberalism with its claim that capital should rule, as well as socialism with its claim that labour should rule. He was committed to the discovery of a realistic mediation between the two. He realized that at that time it would be impossible to plead for cooperation between them, and, in order to achieve some sort of balanced relationship, he produced concrete proposals. He advocated that the workers should have a share in industrial profits. He developed the principle of turning "propertyless workers into working proprietors". He claimed for the workers themselves the freedom to form associations, to establish trade unions. So far as relations within industry are concerned, he grasped the basic principle of codetermination.

To have put forward such ideas as this in the '50s and '60s of the last century betokens great independence of mind. But while his contemporaries understood what Huber was saying, they did not follow his advice. He was rejected both by the majority of churchmen and by the ruling classes. He deserves to be remembered for having developed social political ideas based on Christian responsibility. He had deliberately gone a step further than Wichern, that is, had taken the step into social reformism. Unlike Wichern, he realized that it was no longer possible to Christianize society, and that what the condition of the proletarian working class urgently called for were concrete social policies based on Christian responsibility.

Huber was no more successful in persuading German Protestantism as a whole of its social responsibilities than Wichern had been. Most church people continued for a long time to reject social reformist ideas and activities.

Attempt at constructive dialogue with socialism

This was still the position in 1877 when a book appeared which had a sensational impact at the time. It was called *Radical German Socialism and the Christian Society* and was written by a country pastor named Rudolf Todt (1839-1887). Here was the first attempt to enter into a critical, but constructive, dialogue with the socialism of that time. Todt had a detailed knowledge of socialist writings. His analysis of bourgeois capitalist society largely tallies with that of the German socialists. The class struggle, exploitation, alienation and mass poverty are for him facts which can neither be gainsaid nor glossed over. He regards the revolt of the proletariat against an inhuman and unjust society as something legitimate. He can therefore understand socialism only as a moral quantity, a justified movement of emancipation from economic and political tutelage.

Todt inevitably shocked his contemporaries by making such statements. Bismarck even considered whether the book ought not to be banned under the laws dealing with socialists.

On the basis of his analysis, Todt concludes that the choice confronting government and society is either reform or revolution. His own option is for reform and a concrete reformist programme.

The method adopted by Todt in his book is, first of all, to present the socialist proposal and to ask how far it can be reconciled with the spirit of the New Testament, a Christian concept of man and a Christian view of society. In this argument — presented in great detail — the only elements in the socialist stock of ideas he regularly excludes are certain forms of radicalism and utopianism, though without rejecting the basic ideas. In his second section, Todt incorporates the justified concerns of radical socialism in a personal version of Christian socialism. By a critical dialogue with the socialist partner, he thus achieves a distinctive approach to social policy which he is able to develop into a Christian socialist programme.

Central to this programme is the idea of government intervention. The government must intervene in the body politic to regulate and control. Otherwise there will be a general revolution. The government must produce social legislation to protect the workers from exploitation and enslavement. Justice demands that the workers should be safeguarded against the domination of capital by means of written laws and guaranteed rights.

With these ideas, Rudolf Todt became, on the evangelical church side, the man who, theoretically and practically, helped to prepare the way for the later social legislation introduced by Bismark. Already in 1877, a National Association for Social Reform was founded under his leadership, with the *State Socialist* as its weekly paper. Here, for the first time on the evangelical side, we find an association and a newspaper devoted in a systematic and scholarly way to the social problems of the day. The association's statutes included the statement: "The association's aim is to prepare for social reforms in accordance with religious and constitutional monarchical principles."

At the request of the association, Todt himself carried out an energetic practical and literary programme. His special concern was to persuade pastors to take an active part in solving the social question.

First Christian Social Party programme

When we ask with what success, the answer is that on the whole Todt was no more successful in persuading his church to become "involved in the secular" than were the other evangelical social reformers in that century. Most people in the Church were opposed to the objectives of Todt and his few friends. But Todt did not even succeed in winning over the workers themselves to his ideas. For the most part, they continued to be more at home in social democracy. The deeper reason for this was that

Todt, while able to accept even the specific social political demands of the Gotha Programme of 1875 was still unable, because of his monarchical views, to accept political demands for democracy and popular government. But the workers at that time wanted both social *and* political emancipation.

Todt had frequently urged the creation of an independent Christian social labour party in order to have an organized counterpart to oppose the social democrats. In the year 1878, this desideratum was supplied by the next major representative of the evangelical social movement, Adolf Stoecker (1835-1909), who was court and cathedral preacher in Berlin. By his whole bent, he was a political activist. He even entered the party political life of his time. The founding of the Christian Social Labour Party was his achievement. In association with the Protestant political economist Adolf Wagner (1835-1917), he drafted the first Christian Social Party programme, the "general principles" of which were:

1. The Christian Social Labour Party stands on the platform of Christian faith, and love of king and country.

2. It rejects contemporary social democracy as impracticable, un-Christian and unpatriotic.

3. It seeks the peaceful organization of the workers in order to cooperate with the other elements in public life in preparing the necessary practical reforms.

4. Its goal is to reduce the gulf between rich and poor and to achieve a greater economic security.

One of the major practical demands is the protection of the workers by state legislation.

For Stoecker, however — and this was the decisive point — social policy was simply a means of incorporating the workers into the Prussian German state. What he wanted was to reintegrate them into the authoritarian society of the second German Reich, and, in addition to that, to win back the workers for the Church. Neither of these goals was achieved. Stoecker failed both as a tribune of the people and as an evangelist of the people.

Shortly after the creation of the Christian Social Party, in which the proletarian element was still strongly represented, a transformation already took place in the party. Gradually, the petty bourgeois middle-class element made up of artisans, traders, and petty officials began to predominate.

Stoecker's entry into political anti-semitism was connected with this change. He soon became one of the leading exponents of anti-semitism in the imperial era. But his party never became a people's party. Later, it became an appendix of the Conservative Party. Stoecker was a member of the German legislature except for brief intervals. Down to his death he never achieved any political influence worth speaking of. He certainly had more influence in certain church social groups which largely lived by his stock of ideas. Nor did he even achieve his real goal, namely, the reconciliation of the workers with the Kaiser's society, of the proletariat with the imperial regime. Stoecker wanted at one and the same time to be both a tribune of the people *and* a pillar of the established system, both politician *and* missionary, both the Kaiser's paladin *and* spokesman for the working classes. Wanting everything at one and the same time, he lost everything. The marriage of throne and altar, of catechism and bayonet, had long ago ceased to be a historical possibility. Stoecker was the last major representative of this Protestant synthesis, the brittleness of which would be finally demonstrated at the end of the first world war.

Between conservatism and revolution

But a young contemporary of Stocker's in the evangelical social movement experienced, and suffered as a result of, the whole dilemma which the idea of an alliance between Christian state and Christian Church, between politics and faith, between world and the Kingdom of God represented. Friedrich Naumann (1860-1919) was a young minister in an industrial congregation in Saxony and an industrial chaplain with the Home Mission in Frankfurt-on-the-Main. He took an active part in the evangelical social movement. From the beginning, he publicized his ideas with great pedagogical skill. At first, they were still strongly influenced by Wichern, Todt and Stoecker. His views about social politics were summed up in the statement: "There is no such thing as a biblical programme, but there are biblical motives for handling problems of social policy."

Naumann wanted to steer a course between conservatism and revolution. He called this way "Christian socialism", and by this he meant an active pursuit of social reform in a spirit of love and justice. From the outset, he represented an emphatically proletarian branch of Christian social work. This brought him very soon into collision with the "old men" around Stoecker, almost all of whom were members of the Conservative Party. The controversy between the "young men" around Naumann and the "old men" around Stoecker intensified from year to year. The "young men" regarded Stoecker's attempt to win the conservative world over to active social policies as a failure. Soon their slogan was that "Christian social" and "conservative" are incompatible terms. Naumann and his group always thought in proletarian terms. They rejected any form of Christian paternalism in politics and in the organization of the workers. What they were after was an independent worker politics and an independent organization of the workers free from any taint of paternalism, however well intentioned. Even in the appraisal of social democracy, the ways divided. For Stoecker, social democracy was *the* political enemy; Naumann's thought was much more subtle. Although he, too, recognized that the social democrats were hostile to religion and materialist in outlook, the most important thing in his view was to help them to change from a revolutionary party into a party of radical reform. What Naumann wanted was the inner transformation of the main workers' party, not its political and moral destruction. He wanted to work "from below" to renew "the age old alliance between Christianity and the weary and heavy laden". In opposition to Stoecker, he often said: "A friendly relation between the high and the low is just what we don't want!"

Naumann departs from the social movement

The bitterness of these controversies over the position of the evangelical social movement increased when the young Kaiser Wilhelm II, after a brief flirtation with a policy favourable to the workers, came increasingly under the influence of the great industrialist Baron von Stumm (1836-1901) in the middle of the 1890s and joined with him in denouncing the Christian socialists of the Naumann school as more dangerous than the social democrats. Even the Evangelical Supreme Church Council — the highest authority of the Prussian Provincial Church — took a hand in the controversy with "a decree concerning the participation of pastors in the socialist political movement". This decree directed pastors to pay more attention to preaching and pastoral care than to social and political problems. The controversy reached its climax when the Kaiser cabled his old teacher in February 1896: "Christian socialism is nonsense — the reverend gentlemen should concentrate on the souls of their parishioners and leave politics alone as being none of their business."

The church authorities were instructed to stop encouraging Christian social work. Dutifully, they obeyed the Kaiser. But the part played by the Church authorities in the dissolution of the old evangelical social movement was a relatively small one. The main responsibility for this was Naumann's, for in the years 1895-1896 Naumann was one of those who experienced a redirection of intellectual (theological) and political (social) thinking. Influenced by the thought of Rudolf Sohm (1841-1917), the expert in constitutional law, and Max Weber (1864-1920), the sociologist, Naumann swung away from the Christian social position to the national social position. On the basis of a strict view of the so-called Lutheran "two kingdoms doctrine", which made a sharp distinction between the Kingdom of God on the right hand and the kingdom of this world on the left, Sohm concluded that neither a Christian state nor any alliance between the Christian and the social was possible. Weber had pointed out that the necessary presupposition of a far-reaching social policy was a strong overall national policy. "Surely he is right", said Naumann. "What good is the best social policy to me, if the Cossacks come? If we want to pursue good domestic policies, we must first make the people, the fatherland, our boundaries secure. We must see to our national power." Naumann made an increasingly sharp distinction between religion and world, faith and politics, Church and society. The private world of individuals is now all that is left for religion and faith. Naumann also drew conclusions concerning organization from his personal reorientation. In 1897, he founded the National Social Union. He resigned from the ministry and became a professional politician. When the party he himself had created failed, he became a member of the Progressive Union, a party of left-wing liberalism. In 1919, he was a member of the National Assembly in Weimar which drafted the constitution, and president of the German Democratic Party. With his death, German "culture Protestantism" lost its greatest exponent.

Naumann's departure from the evangelical social movement in 1896 meant in practice the end of the movement. After this, all that remained were isolated individuals and groups with an active concern for social policy.

But these groups and individuals had already created a new organization for their work, the Evangelical Social Congress. This had been founded in 1890 with the aid of Stoecker, Naumann and Ludwig Weber, the chairman of the Evangelical Workers' Association. It was designed as a fellowship of study and action for all Christians concerned with social policy. Each year, it organized a great study conference on problems of social policy and social ethics. In the preamble to the statutes, it was stated: "The Congress has set itself the task of studying objectively the social conditions of our people, testing them in the light of the ethical and religious demands of the Gospel, and making the Gospel more fruitful and effective than before in contemporary economic life."

It can fairly be claimed that these congresses provided a meeting place for the theological and intellectual representatives of German Protestantism at that period. All the vital questions of the day and all questions of principle were discussed. There was unanimity about the goal: the establishment of a modern welfare state. But the details gave rise to serious tensions. In the critical year, 1896, the conservatives who supported Stoecker finally walked out of the Congress and founded their own Church Social Conference. Here the orthodox conservative forces found their spiritual home, while the liberal Protestant elements dominated the Evangelical Social Congress. The latter undoubtedly had the edge in intellectual power and political acumen. Adolf von Harnack (1851-1930), the best known theologian of that time, was for many years its president.

The evangelical workers' associations

Our picture of socially-committed Protestantism prior to the first world war would not be complete without a mention of the evangelical workers' associations. These date back to an association founded in the year 1882 by Ludwig Fischer (1851-1930), a miner, in Gelsenkirchen. The essential structure of this union can easily be gathered from its first statute:

"The Evangelical Workers' Association stands on the platform of the Evangelical Confession and its purpose is:

1) to awaken and encourage evangelical awareness among fellow Christians;

2) to work to improve the morality and general education of its members;

3) to maintain and cultivate harmonious relations between employers and employees;

4) to support its members in cases of sickness and death;

5) to be loyal to Kaiser and Reich."

The evangelical workers' associations were gathering points for workers with a strong national outlook, patriotic Christians, most of them conservatively minded in church matters.

In most cases, they generated a vigorous union life and did a great deal for the religious and moral education of their members and families. But they seldom represented the interests of the workers over against the industrialists. The National Union of Evangelical Workers' Associations, founded in 1890, failed at any rate to avoid the same kind of tensions which the Evangelical Social Congress had experienced. Naumann wanted the workers' association movement to be mainly proletarian, organized for economic struggle, and primarily a movement with a social and political commitment. But the socially-conservative group had always been in the majority. Large sections of the movement were attached to Catholic-led Christian trade unions, whereas Naumann's supporters had opted for non-denominational trade unions.

Two men who must certainly be ranked among the committed evangelical social reformers were Theodor Lohmann (1831-1905) and Hans Baron von Berlepsch (1843-1926), both of whom were in government service and accomplished valuable practical work in the legal field. Lohmann worked for many years developing social legislation in Germany. He was at the same time Bismarck's closest collaborator. The sickness insurance laws of 1883 were largely his work. He had a hand in almost all the social legislation in the succeeding years down to his death in 1905. He is coming to be recognized more and more by modern historians as an outstanding social engineer. Wichern and especially Huber were his spiritual fathers.

From 1880 onwards, he was on the central committee of the home mission and tried hard to reawaken its concern for practical social policies over and above its purely charitable duties. He succeeded in doing this to a large extent. In 1884, Lohmann published a memorandum on behalf of the central committee, entitled: *The Task of the Church and Home Mission in Face of Contemporary Economic and Social Conflicts*. This memorandum indicates a renewed concern, even of the home mission, with current social issues. In his book on Friedrich Naumann, Theodor Heuss ventures the judgment that this memorandum "appeared seven years before *Rerum Novarum* and deserves no less praise for its contents than Leo XIII's great encyclical on social questions".

Baron von Berlepsch was appointed by the young and still reformist Kaiser Wilhelm II in 1890 to the staff of a Prussian minister of state. His special responsibility was in the field of social policy. Already in 1890, he presided over the International Conference on Safety at Work held in Berlin in that year. During his tenure of office from 1890 to 1896, a series of important laws were passed, among them the supplementary industrial code. He worked tirelessly to improve the lot of the wage earners by means of government organizational policy. He saw social policy as a concrete expression of love for one's neighbour.

In the critical year 1896, he also quit government service. He found it impossible to reconcile the new reactionary line followed by the Kaiser in what was known as the "silent era" with his social conscience as a Christian. He continued to strive for a consistent continuation of his social policy in a different form. On his initiative, the Society for Social Reform was founded in 1901, and this soon gained the active support and participation of politicians and scientists of widely different persuasions.

A survey of evangelical social reformers and social reform movements down to the first world war forces us to be more than a little suspicious of the usual blanket verdict which concludes that Protestantism made no contribution whatever to the solution of the social question. A more discriminating picture is overdue here. The official institutionalized Church with its organs or government provided hardly any encouragement to the effort to solve social problems. If it spoke at all, it was simply as an extended mouthpiece of government views and policies. What the "king by divine grace" had already indicated as his wish, the official Church usually did no more than interpret and explain. We scarcely find any independence of judgment or individual initiative on the Church's part but — thank God! — the Church is more than just its official organs. Individual Christians and groups of Christians played an enthusiastic part in the struggle for the emancipation of the workers. As a rule they were not revolutionaries but committed pragmatists with an eye for what was possible. They were not ideologies, hawking their utopias, but realists with a sense of Christian responsibility. It is hardly possible to deny today that they were among those who laid the foundations of our present constitutional state and society.

4 · Social Reform and the Social Gospel in America

Ronald C. White, Jr

The study of the American churches' encounter with the challenge of the poor is the story of the changing conceptions of social reform. The impact of the industrial revolution came later to the new world than the old, but most of the results were the same. While much attention has been focused on the political birth pangs of the new United States of America, pangs of another order were evident in the new nation. With the growth of American industrialism, especially after the war of 1812, the increase of the urban poor accompanied the spectacular rise of American cities. Consigned to struggle for survival working twelve to fourteen hours a day, crowded in tenement housing in neighbourhoods victimized by disease and crime, the poor were an anomaly in a nation viewing itself as "a city set upon a hill". If the poor were everywhere present by 1820, it is worth observing that they were still somewhat "hidden" from the American churches at the beginning of the industrial revolution. It is the discovery, first of the poor, and then of the structures of poverty in the remaining years of the 19th century that will culminate in a new emphasis on social justice and poverty evident in the first two decades of the 20th century.

Strategies for reform: voluntaryism

The first responses to the poor were part of a larger reform movement growing up in the years immediately after the war of 1812. Patterned after older British societies, there developed in America hundreds of voluntary societies dedicated to evangelism, education, mission, and moral reform. The manner in which these societies fanned out across the country has prompted a recent historian to speak of them as an "evangelical united front" bent on transforming America.[1] They lay claim to both the burgeoning cities and the expanding West for a Protestant ideal of a Christian America. The principle of organization — voluntaryism — was particularly suited for a new nation where the separation of Church and state helped ensure that no one church would have the kind of dominance often found in the old world. The societies were in fact voluntary associations of individuals, not associations of churches. They were led by lay persons. They were organized around a task, rather than subscription to a creed. Voluntaryism is important for our study because these societies became primary vehicles by which the problem of the poor was encountered. Within the "front", and alongside such reform organizations as the American Anti-Slavery Society (1833) and the American Peace Society (1830), there were societies such as the Association for the Improvement of the Condition of the Poor (New York, 1844), the Female Missionary Society for the Poor of the City of New York (1816), and the Society for Employing the Poor (Boston, 1820). In addition, there were related societies dealing with orphans, widows, immigrants, prisons, and other persons or issues connected with the overarching challenge of the poor.

Revivalism and reform

In seeking to understand the theological content and reform strategy of these societies, one encounters at every turn the nurturing presence of American revivalism. Revivals, or "awakenings", had long been an important part of the American heritage, finding their norm in the Great Awakening associated with Jonathan Edwards in the 1730s and 1740s. In the early years of the 19th century, religious leaders such as Lyman Beecher, Peter Cartwright, Francis Wayland, and Albert Barnes heralded a new awakening that produced not only converts, but workers for the voluntary societies. The best known of these leaders was Charles Grandison Finney, a former lawyer now "on a retainer from the Lord". Beginning in 1826, Finney's revivals spread across New York state, consuming a region that had become known as "the burned over district".[2] But however much revivalism has been associated in the popular mind with rural or frontier camp meetings, Finney's revival measures became focused on the growing urban centres of the East: New York, Philadelphia, and Boston.

There is considerable debate over the relationship between revivalism and social reform. It is important not to see early 19th-century revivalism simply through the lens of 20th-century revivalism. The revivalist preached for conversion and the new birth, but there was considerable emphasis upon the subsequent life of piety and holiness. Piety did mean personal religion in the first instance, but holiness often precipitated an interest in social reform.[3]

As the revivalists encountered the urban poor the question that arose was one of strategy. The compassion that was evoked by coming face to face with squalor and degradation was sometimes muted by older ideologies. Francis Wayland was representative of many who persisted in the notion he believed inherent in Calvinism that accepted economic inequality as a result of divine ordination. The corollary of this belief was that the poor continued to exist in their condition because of sin or sloth. Belief in a divine ordering was accompanied by an implicit faith in a free market system. Lyman Beecher spoke for many when he commended the new societies working with the poor, but objected to public poor relief as a strategy that was both contrary to our economic system and ultimately degrading to the poor themselves. When the hidden and isolated poor began to be organized by an incipient labour movement, nearly all evangelical leaders were arrayed against the new unions. Likewise there were few who raised their voices to complain about the evils of child labour.[4]

A major strategy for working with the poor was the recruitment and instruction of the rich. In dealing with the wealthy, the revivalists were often caught in the midst of conflicting concerns. Their message was consistently against the perils of worldliness, but they were dependent upon the wealthy to support both the revivals and the variegated activities of the Evangelical United Front. The legacy of a Calvinism which believed that poverty was foreordained persisted in affirming that wealth was a sign of the elect. This view-point was not held by the revivalists alone. No less a theological pioneer than Horace Bushnell, known both for his departures from the older Calvinism and as a source for what would become known as "the new theology", spoke for this point of view. In a well known sermon, "Prosperity our Duty", Bushnell asserted that "a state of prosperity is itself one of the truest evidences of character and public virtue, a reward of honour which God delights to bestow upon an upright people".[5]

All of this is not to say that the pursuit of wealth was not questioned during this period. Albert Barnes remarked that "the love of gain ... is still our besetting sin. This passion goads our countrymen, and they forget all other things." Finney went even further in his indictment that "the whole course of business in the world is governed and regulated by the maxims of supreme and unmixed selfishness". Wayland, a Baptist minister whose *Elements of Political Economy* became a textbook in the field, readily followed Adam Smith and David Ricardo and their economic teachings, but did attempt to Christianize these theories by a constant reference to our accountability to God for the stewardship of our possessions.[6]

Stewardship became a vehicle for a strategy of compassion for the poor. Specific measures were developed to deal with both the question of the accumulation of wealth and the issue of dispersal to the poor and other persons. For example, Justin Edwards suggested that merchants devote from ten to twenty-five percent of their income to charitable concerns. His brother-in-law, Nathaniel R. Cobb, had drawn up a resolution stating:

> By the grace of God, I will never be worth more than $50,000.
> By the grace of God, I will give one fourth of the net profits of my business to charitable and religious uses.

Edwards even perfected a sliding scale culminating in the person making $50,000 giving the whole profit for charitable use.[7] Lewis Tappan, leader in the evangelical campaign against slavery, struggled with his own wealth and stewardship. Under the influence of Finney, and after two decades of leadership in social reform, he wrote to his brother telling him that "I have enough property to support my family and I am tired of labouring at the oar to acquire money, when so much can be done in moral enterprise." [8] The question seldom asked in all of the conversations about stewardship was the relationship between the accumulation of wealth and the spreading blight of the urban poor.

Changing understandings of poverty

It may be worthwhile at this point to pause in the historical narrative and ask some questions about the changing American perceptions of the poor (and the rich). As Robert H. Bremner has reminded us, for the first two hundred years of the country's existence, the American people took it for granted that most persons would always be poor. In a country undergirded by an evangelical ethos, the words of Jesus: "The poor always ye have with you", were used to buttress this attitude. It is only in the middle decades of the 19th century that America begins to discover not just the poor but the condition of poverty. The financial panics of 1819 and 1837 relegated many persons to economic dependence and degradation. Although private charity organizations were formed to cope with the problems of the poor, they were quite often dealing with symptoms. A cup of hot soup and a temporary place to stay were needed forms of charity, but these efforts did not come to grips with root causes. Even in the midst of acts of compassion, in which the churches often took the lead, Bremner says it well in observing that still at mid-century "Americans found admiration of wealth a more profitable occupation than contemplation of misery".[9]

After the civil war (1861-1865), the process of urbanization and industrialization accelerated, accompanied now by the flood-tide of immigrants from Europe and Great Britain. It was in these years that a significant shift occurred in the understanding of the cause and cure of poverty. Most importantly, the discussion shifted ground from the poor to poverty. Earlier discussions perceived the problem of the poor as a moral dilemma, focusing on their attitudes and shortcomings, whereas the apprehension of poverty focused on economic causation and social environment. Now the problem began to be seen in all of its interrelatedness: the accumulation of wealth and the spread of poverty, the increase of factories and the reality of slums. The growth of the social sciences, especially sociology, provided the means of more sophisticated assessments of the dimensions of poverty in American cities. The beginnings of a stronger labour movement turned attention back again on the conditions of the labour members. As labour and management met in sometimes bloody confrontations towards the end of the century, the rich and their obligations to labour in particular and society in general came under public scrutiny.

In sum, the discovery of poverty helped to reframe questions about American life. The promise and the problems of life were now set irrevocably in the context of social causation and environment. If the problems of poverty were social, the most powerful religious response that it evoked would also be social in nature.

The social gospel

The most concerted attack upon poverty before our own day was carried out under the banner of the social gospel. The story of the social gospel is one of the most distinctive chapters in the American experience. Historian Carl Degler has observed: "The acceptance of the social gospel spelled the transformation of American Protestantism." [10] The social gospel was born in post civil war America, and grew to maturity in the first two decades of the 20th century.[11] Towards the end of what was known as the progressive era in American history, the social gospel was defined by one of its adherents as "the application of the teachings of Jesus and the total message of the Christian salvation to society, the economic life, and social institutions ... as well as to individuals".[12] Interacting with the changing realities and problems of an increasingly industrialized and urbanized nation, the social gospel viewed itself as a crusade for justice and righteousness in all areas of the common life.

As with any movement it is not possible to pinpoint a date of origin. It is instructive, however, that a beginning date often associated with the social gospel is linked to poverty, unemployment, and the needs of labour. Washington Gladden,[13] later to be called "the father of the social gospel", came to Springfield, Massachusetts, in 1875 to accept a call from the North Congregational Church. Springfield had been hard hit by the industrial depression that followed the panic of 1873. Not long after his arrival, Gladden was invited to speak to a meeting of the unemployed at the City Hall. At the close of his talk, he invited the men to come to his church the following Sunday evening to hear what he would say to their employers, the class of people who attended the North church. Practical results in terms of new sources of employment emerged from what became a series of addresses. In 1876, these talks were printed as *Working People and Their Employers*, the first of a cascade of Gladden books about a social gospel.

The experience of Washington Gladden was repeated again and again in other settings; ministers and laypersons, nurtured in an evangelical religion that emphasized individual salvation, confronted with a new world born of the industrial revolution being forced to rethink their whole understanding of Christian faith and life. It happened to Walter Rauschenbusch when he came to live on the edge of the Hell's Kitchen neighbourhood of New York City. The man who was destined to become the foremost theologian of the social gospel had come to be the pastor of the Second

German Baptist Church. Descended from six generations of Lutheran ministers, following now in the footsteps of his Baptist father, Rauschenbusch was beginning his career with quite traditional understandings of Christian ministry. Soon after arriving, he wrote a piece for a local newspaper entitled "Beneath the Glitter". He described a walk through a neighbourhood in America's leading city. He pictures a woman dying of disease while her husband was unable to be home, away working fourteen hours a day just to preserve their deplorable lodgings. He described children and old people, all in need, but "hidden", according to Rauschenbusch, "beneath the glitter". Rauschenbusch had come to New York, true to his evangelical heritage, to save souls, but in his own words he soon discovered that Hell's Kitchen "was not a safe place for saved souls".[14]

If the social gospel arose as a response to the external events of urbanization and industrialization, it is also true to say that it was part of the continuing dynamic of an internal theological heritage. The experiences of Gladden, Rauschenbusch, and others sent them back to their Bibles and to theological and historical studies to rediscover aspects of their Christian heritage often obscured in the recent past. A perusal of their sermons and books reveals a new consciousness of the Old Testament prophets with their message of good news to the poor. The central teaching that emerged from their study was the Kingdom of God. Rauschenbusch often said, "this doctrine is itself the social gospel". Rauschenbusch, who later became Professor of Church History at Rochester Theological Seminary, liked to assert that the social gospel was nothing alien or new. He recounts what for him is the strange story of how the doctrine of the Kingdom of God, so central in biblical teaching, "was left undeveloped by individualistic theology and finally mislaid by it almost completely ... What a spectacle, that the original teaching of our Lord has become an incongruous element in so-called evangelical theology." Hailing a new day, Rauschenbusch proclaims: "Now, as soon as the social gospel began once more to be preached in our time, the doctrine of the Kingdom was immediately loved and proclaimed afresh, and the ethical principles of Jesus are once more taught without reservation as the only alternative for the greedy ethics of capitalism and militarism." [15] It was the corporate nature of the Kingdom, both in terms of social sin and social salvation, that formed a theological basis upon which to attack poverty and every other social, economic, and political issue. It was confidence in a living Christ now at work in the world, bringing in the Kingdom, that was the basis of the social enthusiasm of the leaders of the social gospel.

If the Kingdom of God was the theological foundation, the watchwords of the social gospel became "the fatherhood of God and the brotherhood of man". These words were a way of depicting what they understood to be the solidarity of men and women in both the Christian community and the world. If all men and women are brothers and sisters, then this can be the basis of a social concern that overcomes barriers of class, sex, and race. A striking example of this theology occurred in a pastoral epistle issued by Henry Cadmon Potter, Episcopal Bishop of New York, shortly after the Haymarket Riot in 1886. Potter challenged the assumption "that labour and the labourer are alike a commodity, to be bought and sold, employed or dismissed, paid or underpaid as the market shall decree". He went on to espouse an alternative environment where "the wellbeing of our fellow men, their homes and food, their pleasures and their higher spiritual necessities, shall be seen to be matters concerning which we may not dare to say, 'Am I my brother's keeper?'" [16]

Growing out of a social gospel theology, the strategies employed for an attack upon poverty were quite diverse. The utilization of the social sciences brought a new sophistication to the attempt for understanding. This was the era of the appropriation of the technique of the social survey, most notably in Hartford, Connecticut, in 1889, and in New York City in 1895. The inclusion of sociology in the curriculum of Protestant seminaries was highlighted by the inauguration of Graham Taylor in the first chair of "Christian Sociology" at Chicago Theological Seminary in 1894. It is to be remembered that these pioneers in sociology approached their task from a strongly ethical point of view. Information was but a platform for action and two years later Taylor established "Chicago Commons", a settlement house in a working-class district of German, Scandinavian, and Irish immigrants.[17]

The social gospel leaders lived in an uneasy coexistence with the concept of wealth and the captains of industry. They preached a strenuous message of stewardship to the wealthy, many of whom were the backbone of city congregations. They were much more willing than their forebearers to confront what Washington Gladden called the forces of "predatory wealth". In 1905, Gladden touched off a national furor by protesting against the acceptance by the Congregational Board of Foreign Missions of a gift of $100,000 from John D. Rockefeller. In Gladden's autobiography, published several years later, he observed:

> It is impossible to deny the existence of a considerable class of persons who have obtained great wealth by predatory methods, by evasion and defiance of the law, by the practice of vast extortions, by getting unfair and generally unlawful advantages over their neighbours, by secret agreements, and the manipulations of railway and government officials ...

The question that emerged for Gladden was whether the Church "ought to go into partnership with them in the business of religion?" Gladden rallied many Congregationalists to his cause, but was ultimately unsuccessful in blocking the gift.[18]

Many different movements within the larger social gospel movement focused their energies on working men and women. Many of these people laboured long hours in miserable conditions and would best be described by the modern term, "the working poor". A most remarkable organization was the Church Association for the Advancement of the Interests of Labour. This Episcopal society, founded in New York in 1887, reversed the aversion of earlier church leaders to labour organizations and boldly asserted a genuine concern for those involved in industry. Imbued with the same kind of vision was Charles Stelzle, founder of Labour Temple in New York. Stelzle, Presbyterian minister and member of the International Association of Machinists, was a frequent delegate and speaker at national labour conventions. In 1901, he became the first secretary of the Department of Church and Labour of the Presbyterian Church. In the six years that followed, the Episcopal, Congregational, Methodist and Northern (now American) Baptist churches each established church agencies for social action. What had begun as voluntary societies now became institutionalized as agencies attempting to bring the corporate muscle of the major denominations to bear on a diversity of economic and social issues. Poverty was never the central focus of these agencies, but it was very much a part of the whole cluster of issues growing out of the central concern for modern industry in the nation's cities.

Official recognition of the social gospel within the churches was solidified in the formation of the Federal Council of Churches in 1908. At the heart of the Federal Council was an ethical thrust that received final formulation in 1912 as "The Social Creed of the Churches". Dealing primarily with issues of modern industrial life, this social creed was both a challenge and a programme to guide the life of the churches.

Lessons to be learned

This period from 1800 to 1914 witnesses the transformation of the United States from a new nation to a world power. Responding to the challenges of the industrial revolution, the American nation amasses great wealth only to slowly discover poverty in its midst. To chronicle the response to that poverty is to chart the changing conceptions of social concern. In the story of this concern, a number of lessons are to be learned.

1. The voluntary societies were the vehicles of reform by which poverty was encountered in the early years of this period. Organized as an association of individuals, nourished by revivalism, these societies emphasized action against specific social problems. A number of societies acted with great compassion to bring help to the growing numbers of urban poor.

2. The discovery of poverty in the middle years of the 19th century was a catalyst evoking changes in strategies of social reform. The whole issue is framed in a new way when discussion shifts from the poor

to the condition of poverty. This shift from individuals to systems (today we might speak of the culture of poverty) calls into question some of the presuppositions and strategies of the voluntary societies.

3. The social gospel, rooted both in a theology of the Kingdom of God, and in a sociology of the solidarity of humankind, brings a new understanding of social reform. The emphasis now shifts from social service to social action. Social service, rooted in charity, works with the poor after the fact — when they are already out of work and out of hope. Social action attempts to deal with problems before the fact; it is concerned to change social structures and systems which encourage unemployment and poverty. Both social service and social action are needed as a fully Christian response to human need. Both were operative within the social gospel movement. But it was the prophetic stance of the social gospel which saw clearly that social action was the best response to the crisis of a changing America.

4. The social gospel was the bridge to a modern understanding of social justice. The leaders of the movement perceived that the real issues involved in the problem of poverty were justice and power. The social gospel has been criticized for its undue optimism about social transformation, and this charge can be levelled about their plans for the abolition of poverty. The leaders of the social gospel can also be faulted in that, although they were courageous advocates for the poor, they failed to see the power of the poor becoming advocates for themselves. Nevertheless, the social gospel's steadfast commitment to social justice is a vital heritage and link undergirding the renewed commitment to the oppressed and the poor in our own day.

NOTES

[1] CHARLES I. FOSTER: *An Errand of Mercy, The Evangelical United Front, 1790-1837*, p. viii. Chapel Hill, North Carolina: University of North Carolina Press, 1960.

[2] See WHITNEY R. CROSS: *The Burned-Over District*. Ithaca, New York: Cornell University Press, 1950.

[3] Two contrasting viewpoints in this debate can be found in CHARLES C. COLE, JR.: *The Social Ideas of the Northern Evangelists, 1826-1860*. New York: Columbia University Press, 1954; and, TIMOTHY L. SMITH: *Revivalism and Social Reform*. Nashville, Tenn.: Abingdon Press, 1957. Smith argues that the reform impulse growing out of the revivals in the twenty-five years before the civil war is a major root of the later social gospel. He also argues that the revivalism from Dwight L. Moody through Billy Graham "reverses" this strong impetus towards social reform.

[4] JOHN R. BODO: *The Protestant Clergy and Public Issues, 1812-1848*, p. 177. Princeton, New Jersey: Princeton University Press, 1954; CHARLES C. COLE, JR., *op. cit.*, pp. 186-187.

[5] HORACE BUSHNELL: *Prosperity Our Duty*, p. 4. Hartford, Conn.: 1847.

[6] ALBERT BARNES: "Revivals of Religion in Cities and Large Towns", *American National Preacher*, XV, No. 1 (1841), 23; and, CHARLES G. FINNEY: *Lectures to Professing Christians*, 95. New York: 1837, cited in CHARLES C. COLE, JR., *op. cit.*, pp. 167, 178.

[7] CHARLES C. COLE, JR., *op. cit.*, p. 168.

[8] LEWIS TAPPAN to Benjamin Tappan, 6 August, 1849, *Benjamin Tappan Papers*, Library of Congress, Washington, D.C. Cited in CHARLES C. COLE, JR., *op. cit.*, p. 169.

[9] ROBERT H. BREMNER: *From the Depths, The Discovery of Poverty in the United States*, p. 4. New York: New York University Press, 1956.

[10] CARL DEGLER: *Out of Our Past, The Forces That Shaped Modern America*, p. 347. New York: Harper & Row, 1950.

[11] The standard account of the social gospel is C. HOWARD HOPKINS: *The Rise of the Social Gospel in American Protestantism 1865-1915*. New Haven, Conn.: Yale University Press, 1940. For a new restatement and revisioning, see RONALD C. WHITE, JR. and C. HOWARD HOPKINS: *The Social Gospel, Religion and Reform in Changing America*. Philadelphia: Temple University Press, 1976.

[12] SHAILER MATHEWS: "Social Gospel", *A Dictionary of Religion and Ethics*, ed. Shailer Mathews and Gerald Birney Smith, 416. New York: 1921.

[13] An excellent biographical study of Gladden is JACOB HENRY DORN: *Washington Gladden*. Columbus, Ohio: Ohio State University Press, 1967.

[14] See DORES R. SHARPE: *Walter Rauschenbusch*. New York: Macmillan, 1942.

[15] WALTER RAUSCHENBUSCH: *A Theology for the Social Gospel*, pp. 25-26. New York: Macmillan, 1917.

[16] HENRY CODMAN POTTER: *Christian Thought*, 4th ser., pp. 289-291. New York: 1886.

[17] RONALD C. WHITE, JR. and C. HOWARD HOPKINS, *op. cit.*, pp. 132-142.

[18] WASHINGTON GLADDEN: *Recollections*, pp. 404-405. New York: Houghton Mifflin, 1909.

5 · The Russian Orthodox Church and the Poor in the 19th and 20th Centuries

Nicolai A. Zabolotsky

The attitude of the Church to those in need (the poor) is determined by the gospel precept expressed in the words of the Sermon on the Mount: "Blessed are the merciful, for they shall obtain mercy" (Matt. 5 : 7). The parable of the good Samaritan (Luke 10 : 25-37), and the words of our Saviour in a number of passages of Scripture (Matt. 5 : 42; 6 : 3-4; 10 : 42; 25 : 34-40; Luke 6 : 30, etc.) explain the meaning and character of this kind of service to one's neighbour. It is imperative to give to everyone who asks, without expecting anything in return or setting any conditions burdening the conscience either of recipient or giver. Alms are to be given in secret, thus giving no occasion for vainglory, or humiliation of the dignity of the petitioner. The Christian is called upon to respond to any necessity; hunger, thirst, nakedness, a stranger's lack of shelter, imprisonment — such are the evangelical examples of works of mercy. Those in need (the poor) are the "least brethren" who are to be served lovingly, without pharisaical vainglory (cf. Luke 18 : 11-12), and with no trace of any paternalism to embarrass them. Pharisaic self-satisfaction at paying the tithe is unfounded, not only because it is opposed to the spirit of evangelical charity, but also because at any moment or even there and then the giver may in fact find himself in a state of need, that is, in some sense one of the "least brethren", appealing for help. This creates the Christian attitude of humility, equally essential for giver and recipient. Should we not then interpret the Lord's words reported by the apostle Paul: "It is more blessed to give than to receive" (Acts 20 : 35), as applying to both parties in an act of charity?

The Russian Orthodox Church, like other churches, was guided by these evangelical principles in admonishing its members to serve their neighbour lovingly with alms giving. As a rule it did not set up special institutions for the service of those in need, but inspired and supported private and communal, parochial, monastic and secular state initiatives in aid of the "least brethren". In old Russia, sermons for the benefit of the poor rang out from the ambos on the lips of Archbishop Luke Zhidiata,

---

Translated from the Russian by the Language Service, WCC.

appointed Novgorodian guardian of the poor of Archbishop Euphymius. In the period after Peter the Great, St Tikhon of Zadonsk was renowned as a preacher of charity to the poor, especially the peasant serfs. In old Russia, there was a saying that "The holy man goes to heaven by alms: the beggar is fed by the rich, but the rich man is saved by the beggar's prayer." The Russian historian V. O. Kliuchevsky, interpreting this popular wisdom, wrote: "When two old-Russian hands met, one with a request for Christ's sake and the other with alms in the name of Christ, it was difficult to say which of them bestowed greater alms on the other. The need of the one and the help of the other flowed together in the reciprocal brotherly love of both." [1] Of course, the ideal of service of the "least brethren" was not always fulfilled in all its perfection, but even in the forms that were employed it resulted in the warmth of a fraternal mutual bond; it helped the formation of a psychology and spirit of communal life, of personal encounter; it called for a change of attitude between people in society and, ultimately, for the rebuilding of the structures of social and state organization.

Unfortunately, Russian historical literature does not deal to any great extent with the service of the poor on the general church level. Traditionally, the Russian Orthodox Church did not have social charitable institutions similar to those that flourished in the West in the Roman Catholic and Protestant churches. Only at a later date was something of that kind created, chiefly under the influence of western experience, but it did not develop sufficiently. It was traditional for charitable service to be private, though from time to time monasteries and associations connected with local churches were drawn in. This is how one work on Christian service to the world describes Russian Orthodox aid to the needy: "Russian ascetics (Observe the personal aspect. — Author's note.) all undertook service to the world, as each was able; one by teaching the ignorant people, another by public denunciation of the Moscovite autocracy, another by giving a piece of bread to a dying child abandoned under the monastery wall by his starving parents, another by feeding thousands of starving people, another by caring for sick and crippled peasant women and by establishing almshouses for them under the auspices of the monasteries." [2] These inadequate words hide the appalling calamity of innumerable unfortunates, an abyss difficult to fill, a wound impossible to heal, at least by church ministry alone. The Church assisted the hungry, gave shelter within monastery walls to the sick, it established monastery almshouses (the Pereyaslavl-Danilov monastery among others); it supported by charity abandoned children, gave aid to the people in times of epidemics, founded schools in the vicinity of the monasteries and in the parishes (church parish schools), promoted the activities of brotherhoods, especially in southwest Russia, encouraged private and communal philanthropy, etc., but for various reasons it was not in a position to change the state of affairs so that

Russia would no longer have any hungry, destitute, sick, forsaken people. The Church was not in a position to solve the problem of the poor, and this constituted the tragedy of its encounter with the world of those in need. This is probably why the literature on the problem is so scanty. There is only a rather short list of articles and a few books written before the revolution, which attempt not so much to draw a picture of church participation in aid to the poor as to compel public opinion in the Church to reflect on the theme of responsibility for the poor and to extend charitable work. That was a feeble answer to the threatening challenge which had arisen. It was an attempt to revive ancient forms of Christian charitable work, while adding to them elements derived from the experience of western churches, a palliative measure, incapable of calming the troubled sea of universal poverty.

Obviously, the problem of the poor could not be solved by philanthropy alone. Nor was the philanthropic activity of clergy in the Russian Orthodox Church or associated with it, in fact, confined solely to charitable work on behalf of the poor. To understand this, a new inquiry is necessary, making use of the literature of sermons and *belles-lettres* and enlisting the services of unpublished materials in archives. In this connection, contemporary Russian church historians are able to do useful work; in particular a scholar as serious and reliable as Archpriest Ioann Belevtsev, a professor in the Leningrad Theological Academy, whose advice and help in the selection of material for what is presented here were extremely important.

I. THE WEALTH AND POVERTY OF RUSSIA AND ITS CHURCH

In one of his poems, the Russian poet N. A. Nekrasov accurately described the condition of Russia in this period as highly contradictory:

You are both poverty-stricken and rich,
You are both mighty and weak, Mother Russia.

In fact, for Russia, the 19th and early 20th centuries were a time of growth of contradiction in all spheres of life; this was the time of the radical reassessment of values and of far-reaching changes leading ultimately to the 1917 socialist revolution. The reassessment of values also concerned the concepts of wealth and poverty, which are relative categories and only take on definite meaning in a concrete situation, in comparison and in application to this or that sphere of human existence.

Let us consider the policy of the Russian empire of the pre-revolutionary period.

Emperor Alexander I (1801-1825), though wanting to preserve peace and neutrality in foreign policy, was obliged to wage war with Sweden and

Turkey and finally with Napoleon I. The patriotic war of 1812 ravaged Russia; Moscow was burnt, but circumstances changed dramatically, and Russian troops marched triumphantly through Europe. In the reign of Nicholas I (1825-1855), Russia waged great wars in the East with Persia and Turkey, and also in Poland, in an effort to influence the Balkan peninsula and Europe as a whole. The success was meagre. The subsequent Crimean campaign with the defence of Sevastopol brought unforgettable glory to its heroes and prompted an upsurge of patriotism in Russia, but contributed nothing to strengthening the country politically. Emperor Alexander II (1855-1881), having concluded the eastern war on harsh terms for Russia, consolidated the power of the empire in the Far East, in Central Asia and the Caucasus, and then waged war on Turkey for the liberation of the Balkan countries, Bulgaria, Serbia and Romania. Although this latter war was successful, its consequences were not entirely satisfactory for the Balkan Slavs, while in Russia as a result of the upsurge of Slavophil and nationalist sentiments created by the war a feeling of disappointment arose because the political aims of the empire were not achieved, and it appeared isolated without allies and friends. Alexander III (1881-1894) had to stabilize the conditions of the state, weakened by the wars of the preceding reigns. A defensive alliance was concluded with France, by which the emperor restored the balance of power in Europe. His reign was marked by peace after a short clash with the Afghans, which resulted in some small territorial gains for Russia. The next emperor, Nicholas II (1894-1917) would have liked to follow his father's pacification policy, and he even inspired the Hague peace conferences (1899 and 1907), with the important aim of seeking means to find a peaceful settlement of international conflicts ("to put an end to the incessant increase in armaments and to seek means of preventing the calamities threatening the whole world"). However, the Boxer Rising in China, the seizure of Manchuria and the subsequent war with Japan, disastrous for Russia, and also the first world war, not only did not confirm the peace-loving intentions of the Tsar but brought the Russian empire to a final crisis." [3]

Fourteen wars waged by Russia in the period under review meant hard times for the nation and intensified its poverty. Particular moments of patriotic enthusiasm, examples of heroism by soldiers and of unselfish labour by civilians, could not counterbalance the impoverishment and weakening of the state. A wealth of political activity turned into poverty for the state structure and for human existence. This was even more clearly the case in internal policy.

Reforms not appropriate

The reign of Alexander I opened with liberal principles, which the son of a village priest, a pupil of the main Petersburg seminary (the Theological Academy), M. M. Speransky, tried to carry into effect. But these principles were implemented solely in the sense of centralization of government control, and contributed to consolidate the bureaucratic system. At the end of the reign, the appearance on the stage of Arakcheev showed that Alexander had lost the ideals of his youth and had given way to open reaction against all the reforms which he had been determined to carry out. With Nicholas I the bureaucratic apparatus of the state was strengthened even more to counterbalance the nobility, suspected of sympathies for the revolutionary movement. The development of His Imperial Majesty's Own Chancery, the promulgation of the Complete Code of Laws, and other legislative enactments of a similar kind, demonstrate the bureaucratization of power. Something was done in this reign to improve the lot of the serfs, but the government continued to be afraid of the liberation of millions of serfs, all the more because there was unrest among the peasants in a number of places. Nicholas I deserves credit for improving the country's education system, yet at the same time enlightenment was feared, and endeavours were apparent to prevent enlightenment leading to any revolutionary ideas in society. Emperor Alexander II, realizing the inevitability of radical reorganization in the state, especially in view of the fact that obsolete forms of economy based on serfdom were hindering the further growth and perfecting of the powers of the state, launched a series of internal reforms. In 1861 serfdom was abolished; in 1864 there followed the *zemstvo* (local administration) and judicial reforms, and in 1870 a new system of municipal administration; in 1874 universal military service was introduced, and a number of measures taken in regard to national education, the censorship and the finances.

The purpose behind all this was the desire for internal renewal in the state, as the imperial manifesto noted: "Let the internal organization of public services and amenities in Russia be strengthened and achieved; may justice and mercy prevail in the courts; let the aspiration towards enlightenment and every useful activity develop everywhere and with new force." However, neither the radical reorganization on the political and social planes, nor the internal renewal which was called for by the times and the conditions of life in the country came about. As a result, the revolutionary movement was strengthened, and so were corresponding acts of repression by the state. Alexander II, a victim of these unresolved conflicts, died by a bomb thrown by the revolutionary organization, People's Will. Alexander III took as the main purpose of his activity the establishment of autocratic power and of the tottering order of the state. This inevitably had to be achieved mainly by firm suppression of all "sedition" (revolutionary movement) and then by the revision and consolidation of the laws and institutions created in the period of reforms under Alexander II. The reign of Alexander III was reactionary in character. Yet despite the secret police measures, the revolutionary movement grew and increasingly assumed the definite direction of a fight against autocracy. The government tried to enhance the importance of the nobility, but history brought out the new social power of the working classes recruited from the proletarianized peasantry estranged from the land. Attempts at better organization of the peasants by measures of migration to unoccupied land in Siberia and Central Asia, and the establishment of a Peasants' Land Bank (1883) proved insufficient. The village proletariat in the country and the town proletariat in the industrial centres were increasingly alienated from the state system. The impoverishment of wide masses of the people and the simultaneous growth of popular consciousness established the material and psychological bases for the break-up of the state political and social structures from within.

An impoverished empire

In the reign of Nicholas II, the external political and internal instabilities of foreign and domestic policy were complicated by natural calamities, such as the failure of crops in 1891-1892, which led to famine in the chiefly grain-producing regions. The sufferings of the people from destitution, famine and exploitation were scandalous. In some circles (the intelligentsia), urgent demands were voiced for some partial political changes, and the government was obliged to introduce these after the revolutionary events of 1905. Russia was reorganized as a constitutional state with national representation in the State Duma. But this did not save the situation, for the influential nobility insisted on their strictly class privileges, while the government now as before pursued a policy based on the police, with recourse to repression and sanguinary measures (the shooting down of the demonstration before the Winter Palace, the Lena shooting, etc.). The first two State Dumas were undisciplined, and the next ones turned into a mere stage-set as a cover for the reactionary reality of the autocracy. In conditions of extreme impoverishment of the people, of military failures, of the obvious real weakness of the state structure, of moral degradation in the upper classes (Rasputin), of corruption from top to bottom of the government apparatus, under the pressure of the popular masses, who in February 1917 started to demonstrate in the streets, shouting for "bread", and were joined by the soldiers who had been brought out against the popular movement, the February Revolution occurred, followed in March by the abdication of Nicholas II, and in October 1917 by the Socialist Revolution, which established in principle a new social, economic and political order in the country, in a new state, the Union of Soviet Socialist Republics.[4]

It is thus evident that the Russian empire, so rich in resources, of such a vast extent, so abounding in human talents, so rich in good wishes and intentions, so mighty in inherent strength, in actual fact was destitute, wretched, disorganized. It is also possible to recognize that the poverty and disorder of human life in Russia nevertheless indicate the wealth of inner national forces, which were able ultimately to break the vicious circle of poverty and to ascend to a new horizon of human existence, to a higher stage of creation and perfection.

We must now, however, turn our attention to the Church.

The Church — rich and poor at the same time

From the time of Peter the Great, the Russian Orthodox Church was subordinated to the state. In 1764, the empire secularized church and monastic lands, thus bringing ecclesiastical institutions even more under state control by gradually giving them official status. Alexander I established the Ministry of Spiritual Affairs and Public Education and entrusted church affairs and education to his favourite, Prince A. N. Golitsyn, on the pretext that "Christian piety was always the basis of true enlightenment". Subsequently, the procurators of the Holy Synod, laymen appointed by the state, were actually in charge of church affairs, deciding the destinies of church dignitaries, and constantly promoting state ideologies and state interests within the Church. In these conditions, the Russian Orthodox Church during the period under consideration was directly involved in state politics both at home and abroad. Inevitably, the Church itself experienced the contradictions of the period and to some extent shared the fate of the Russian empire and its ruling circles.

In speaking of the Church, one must always bear in mind its ecclesiological essence. Organs of church government, hierarchical administrators, monasteries, places of worship, schools, charitable establishments and so on, are not themselves the Church; they are church institutions easily combined with state institutions, and this was the case in the Russian Orthodox Church in the 19th and early 20th centuries. The Church, of course, is composed of believers performing their religious services according to their calling — people living in the world and those living a monastic life, men, women and children, deacons and priests, under the general pastoral supervision of the bishops. In this conception, the Church, though in the state because it is composed of people belonging to the state, nevertheless in its life, services and aims does not necessarily coincide or have to be combined with the order, tasks and aims of the state. In its most important capacity and content, relating to the sphere of salvation, spiritual life and liturgical experience, the Church is not involved in the framework of state order and administration. What was imposed on the Russian Orthodox Church in the Russian empire proved to be a "Procrustean bed", but it was not to be the state that cut the bonds of this non-interfering element, which in the end, after passing through the trials of the pre-revolutionary period and after the fires of the revolution, proved to be living and free for further growth and fruitfulness.

From this, we can form some opinion of the wealth and poverty of the Russian Orthodox Church in the period under consideration. The Church appeared to be rich because it had many splendid churches and monasteries, magnificient divine services, material incomes, competent and well-provided-for hierarchs, and so on. It looked rich because the state power made use of its authority and influence. Nevertheless, it was poor, because all it owned was combined with the possessions of the state, because the will of the state weighed on it, because its incomes were devoured by the state and were allotted under state control, because the lower clergy were poor and unsettled, because the majority of its members were poor folk. It was also poor because it was not in a position to fight the poverty around it properly, and sometimes in fact, in the person of some hierarchs and other influential clerics, it came out against measures capable of relieving the sufferings of the unfortunate.[5]

Poverty of the clergy

Speaking of the actual poverty of the Orthodox lower clergy, Professor N. N. Glubokovsky wrote: "The material provision for the clergy was always casual and beggarly." [6] Another scholar dealing with this question, P. V. Znamensky, notes: "It (the clergy) was far from being spoilt with benefactions and solicitude about its fate." [7] N. Glubokovsky noted the grievous condition of the town clergy and the bleak, dreary existence of the clergy in the down-graded provincial towns, where they were almost completely devoid of material support. Extremely harsh, too, was the lot of the widows and orphans of priests, deacons and other clerics. Aleksei Tolstoy in his *Peter the Great* painted a depressing picture of the mode of life of the supernumerary priests at the street corners in Moscow pestering passers-by for the celebration of liturgies and religious rites. In the works of N. S. Leskov (*Soboryane* — Cathedral Folk, etc.) sadness for their misfortune is affectionately veiled by warm sympathy for the clerical characters. The conditions of the country clergy was humiliating. Before the abolition of serfdom, there were cases of clerics who were serfs. But even when not actually serfs, they were despised and oppressed by the landed gentry, were slavishly dependent on the higher ecclesiastical authorities, and bore the burdens of country labour side by side with their parishioners. Usually what was most derogatory to human dignity was to have to go the rounds of the parish, collecting produce for the upkeep of the clergy. In this connection, it is possible to refer to data from private archives which indicate the straitened circumstances of the priest, in charge successively of the churches of the villages of Gribna and Ploskoe in Tver province, George Smerdynsky (the author's great-grandfather); the annual income of the clergy of a parish (priest, deacon and reader) scarcely amounted to 500 roubles; consequently, it was necessary to raise funds for the building of the church in Ploskoe village, and this occupied Fr George very nearly all his life. The poverty of the lower clergy is easily explained; their income was drawn solely from the voluntary sacrifices of parishioners, the majority of whom were even poorer themselves. However, it was not only the lower clergy who lived in indigence and want; very often venerable hierarchs, although personally sufficiently provided for from the exchequer, were obliged to turn to noblemen, merchants and other monied people with humble requests for donations for the needs of charity, education and even of the mission.

Moral and spiritual poverty

The material indigence of the clergy, however, to some extent justified by gospel proclamation, was not as terrible as the grievous moral and spiritual poverty described by authors of that period, which had the negative result of impoverishing faith among the people.

When, under Alexander I, Prince A. N. Golitsyn, a humane and gentle person, distinguished by mystical sentiment, was appointed head of the Ministry for Spiritual Affairs and Public Education, an appeal was made to correct the deficiencies of secular and clerical schools and to eradicate "pseudo-philosophizing". The practical application of this idea to people's lives was not notable for real insight, and attention was directed to the latter part of the assignment. Some leading officials in the ministry, especially Magnitsky, were intolerant of anything that seemed to them "atheistic" and "free-thinking". Faith and morals among students and white-collar workers were usually promoted in their directives by fear and violence, threats and punishment. As a result, hypocrisy and bigotry developed, and not sentiments of genuine piety; petty surveillance of behaviour and ways of thinking led to delation and victimization.[8]

The writer N. G. Pomialovsky in his *Seminary Studies* [9] speaks of the upbringing and training of the future pastors of the Church. The grotesque characters and system they describe is horrifying. The conclusions which he draws testify to the extreme spiritual and moral poverty of teachers and taught. The description of the final year seminary students is interesting. Most of them seem to have been little versed in matters of faith and piety, and displayed "a blend of wild fanaticism with complete personal apathy in the matter of faith", without the slightest suggestion of "a feeling of all-forgiving, all-reconciling, all-equalizing Christian love". Their religiosity, in the opinion of N. Pomialovsky, was analogous to "complete, absolute atheism — not to conscious atheism, but to the organic atheism of the uneducated person". Such people could at best become conscientious masters of ceremonies — "a pipe, through which the voice of God passes, but ... does not touch". Were such pastors capable of educating, spiritually and morally, a nation crushed by oppression and poverty? N. Pomialovsky divides the minority of more intelligent graduates into three groups.

The first of these were the "idealists, spirituals, mystics", and at the same time were by nature "honest and nice, good people". Sincerely believing graduates of this kind, having managed to transform the crumbs of seminary information into solid theological knowledge, or having created by independent reflection "a new faith of their own, a human one", then preach it under the name of the Orthodox faith when later on in their parishes they have put on cassocks and become priests. In fact, these made good pastors, whom "the people love and the so-called nihilists respect, because these priests are good people".

Another type of seminarist was materialistic by nature, people who had broken with their beliefs and become deliberate, honest atheists, adhering to strict rules of non-interference in matters of conscience, refusing to preach terror of atheism on the one hand, and on the other considering it dishonourable "to preach what they themselves do not understand and live at the parishioners' expense for doing so". These graduates did not enter the ranks of the clergy, finding employment for their powers elsewhere. These two groups — honest believers and honest atheists — could not feel mutual estrangement. "The honest priest", N. Pomialovsky writes, "meeting with an atheist, a comrade, gladly shakes his hand, provided he is essentially a decent man", because the "honest theist and the honest atheist always seek for points on which they can agree". It is important here to emphasize the historical context of the times under consideration, for one of the points on which atheists and theists were both able to find common ground was that of meeting the need of their time — the service of the poor.

Finally, the third type of seminarist, whom N. Pomialovsky does not find agreeable, consisted of the kind of people who "having become atheists, cover their unbelief with the priest's cassock". "These cassock-clad atheists", the author writes, "develop egotism in themselves, the source from which every atheist acts ... they preach with fervour, not because they fear for the eternal damnation of their parish, but because they are afraid of losing their income once and for all ... having capacious pockets holding the money of believers and zealous parishioners, they are often unwilling to lift a finger to help some starving widow or other of their department". They talk louder than anyone about morality and religion, and "generally preach the most extreme, stupid intolerance", in order to hide their own unbelief. Profoundly imbued with the "stinking lie" which "kills in them all shame and honour", "servants of the altar" of that kind deserve the contempt of honest seminarians, who consider themselves not entitled "to wear the cassock" and of forming part of the faithful clergy. Precisely such people cast a shadow on the Russian Orthodox Church in the pre-revolutionary period, and produced the estrangement from it of many, many of the "least brethren".[10]

That is the kind of picture spiritual impoverishment in the 19th century presents. At the end of the century and the beginning of the 20th century, it changed to some extent, thanks to improved education and training in the ecclesiastical seminaries and academies, and to the abolition of the censorship, which opened out opportunity for the circulation of theological works, articles on religious and moral themes and so on to the general advantage of the parochial work of the clergy.

The wealth of the Church, of course, consisted of convinced, believing pastors, capable intelligently and sincerely of educating the Russian people in faith and piety. Such were the Moscow Metropolitan Philaret Drozdov, and also the Moscow Metropolitan, now a canonized saint, Innocent Veniaminov, Nicolai Kasatkin, the apostle of Japan, the Petersburg Metropolitan Antonii Vadkovsky, the Kronstadt pastor, Fr John Sergiev, and many others of less prominent position whose names are unknown but whose deeds bore good fruit in the believing Russian people and sowed the seeds of faith in the new field of the age that followed. The wealth of the Church consisted of the known and unknown ascetics of the Optino hermitage and other monasteries, but also of simple Russian people patiently bearing their heavy cross of poverty and trouble. The Church's wealth also consisted of those of its members who interpreted the course of events properly, actively responding to the sorrow and needs of their time, concerned for the poor, the humble, the unfortunate, the exploited, and who on this account suffered the displeasure and condemnation of the powers-that-be; history to this day is silent about them, but their story will perhaps be told when some solicitous hand opens the available archives.

As we see, the life of the state was full of contradictions, and so was the life of the Church. Wealth was dialectically coupled with poverty and poverty with wealth in the same place. Aleksei, Ivan and Dimitri Karamazov lived side by side, diverse in nature and spiritual substance; at the same time their father Fyodor Karamazov and his murderer Smerdiakov and starets Zosima influenced their world; one and the same cloister harboured the sagacity, lucid simplicity and the wisdom of age, and the obscurantist, ignorant bigotry of those attracted by the death of Zosima. Here indeed the shadow of the "Great Inquisitor" loomed dark, and dim was the light of him who for the second time appeared in court for Christianity after the trial concluded under Pontius Pilate.[11]

II. PRACTICAL STEPS IN AID OF THE POOR

Aid to the poor on the part of the Russian Orthodox Church could take two directions, that of welfare work and that of support for social, economic and political reforms.

Welfare work in the period under consideration was the responsibility of the Ministry of the Interior, the Department of Orthodox Faith, the Department of Empress Maria Feodorovna, district councils and municipal authorities. The Church on the communal, parish level was involved in the welfare activities of all these bodies, but the initiative to a large extent came from state organizations and private individuals.

One scholar who has investigated church charitable work, V. M. Benzin, does not rank it very high. He notes that "the real tasks of welfare work were not yet fully clear to the general mind of the Church" in the 19th century, and considers that "public and church initiative" in regard to welfare work "was little developed".[12] The government had taken welfare work into its own hands; in the words of the same historian, it "was in advance of the society of the time, and determined the real tasks of welfare work ... Only instead of promoting in every way the development of public initiative by means of grants for the organization of public welfare associations, the government undertook to achieve its aims independently by establishing government institutions, maintained by church and monastic as well as by government funds."[13]

A. Vertelovsky in his *Studies in the History of Charitable Work in the Russian Church* lists a series of governmental measures in this connection.

Charitable institutions

Government initiative in philanthropy was due to the Empress Maria Feodorovna, who established a system of charitable institutions. Then, in 1816, Emperor Alexander I founded the Imperial Philanthropic Society with branches in Petersburg, Kazan, Kharkov, Voronezh, 27 establishments in all in various towns in Russia. In the next period to the middle of the 19th century, institutions were established for blind boys and girls, the Nurdzinsky almshouse in Odessa and various societies for distributing bread, fuel, etc., to the needy. In the '60s, the clergy joined in the government initiative for the purpose of religious instruction, mission and charity. It is possible to point to the following societies in which clerics played a direct part: Moscow (St Peter), Vladimir (St Alexander Nevsky), Kazan (St Gurii), Kiev (St Vladimir), that of St Euphrosinia in Polotsk, Holy Cross in Saratov, the St Andrew parish Board of Guardians in Kronstadt, the Ropshinsky Board of Guardians for the poor peasants near Petersburg, the Board of Guardians at the St Sergius monastic church in the Bezhetsk district of Tver province, etc.[14]

Some examples of work done for the poor may be cited. Charitable associations usually organized free canteens, workhouses, hospitals, asylums, distributed grants in money, in foodstuffs and in goods, provided cheap housing, etc. In the years 1878-1879, for example, 55,917 persons received free meals. In Saratov every week, the free canteen fed 100-120 unskilled workers. In Kronstadt, the St Andrew parish Board of Guardians established a workhouse with 300 places, a handicraft school for children with 150 places, a kindergarten for 75, a home for 15 orphans, a clinic for parishioners. A society for poor assistance at the Znamensky Church in Petersburg had an old women's home, a day nursery; here once-only grants were made to people in need, a free medical service was provided, and there was a Sunday school. In Moscow, the Novo-Pimenov Board of Guardians helped those in poor circumstances. In Tver, the guardians at the Skorbiashchenskaia Church let out flats and made grants to young people setting up house. In 1900 in Petersburg, 29 parish charitable associations and 4 fraternities were at work. According to the statistics for that year, the almshouses of the capital housed 1,000 old women, there were 800 children in the orphanages, 200 flats were rented to poor women and 250 flats at reduced rents had been taken for the families of the poor, 200,000 meals were distributed, and 40,000 monthly and weekly grants paid out. The funds for all this were raised from donations. Thus, as a result of 40 years activity down to 1900, the Petersburg charitable associations had 2 million roubles of basic capital with a yearly increase of funds of half a million, reckoned as follows: members' payments — 40,000 roubles; collection in places of worship — 55,000 roubles; collection by subscription list — 20,000 roubles; income from real estate — 80,000 roubles; interest from capital — 90,000 roubles.[15] Provincial church periodicals, such as diocesan gazettes, regularly published details of fund raising for charitable purposes, with lists of the donors. Collections of this kind were particularly intensive in war time in aid of the wounded and for grants to families who had lost their breadwinner on the battlefield. A characteristic feature of war years was the private initiative shown in caring for the wounded (voluntary nursing brothers and sisters), and in the preparation and dispatch to hospitals of bandages and dressings (in many families women and children prepared lint).

Hospitality to strangers has always been cultivated in Russia. It was practised in monasteries, for example, where pilgrims, mostly poor people, found food and shelter. Innumerable wanderers from one end of the country to the other, especially pilgrims heading for the holy places in Palestine or on their way back, met with hospitality from Russian readiness to share even a poor crust of bread.

Hundreds of thousands of destitute people, begging their way home or congregating by church porches, were fed by means of voluntary contributions. The Russian expression "to live by begging" (literally " to walk through the world") applied to the destitute, signified that "the world", that is, society, had in principle the duty to take responsibility for those in need, but further expressed an unwritten right to ask the "world" for help. Although mendicancy sometimes turned into a profession and "those living by begging" occasionally amassed sizeable funds, Russian people left this out of account and gave charitably for Christ's sake, without respect of persons. Various parishes helped to organize assistance for beggars in hospices and doss houses. However, there was no real fight against mendicancy, which throve, and though in fact a social evil, was mostly regarded as something to be taken for granted.

Society was induced by the clergy to be concerned about orphans and abandoned children; many families in Russia adopted boys and girls left without parents or deserted by them.

One of the forms of assistance to the poor was the organization of church parish schools, and in particular of schools for the village population. However poor these schools, they played an important part in the education of the Russian people in the 19th and early 20th centuries. The clergy was directly involved in the business of national education.

We thus observe various forms of welfare work accomplished by the government, by the Church in conjunction with civic institutions, by the Church directly on the monastic and parish level, by society with the help of the clergy, by private individuals. Those of the clergy who responsibly performed their pastoral ministry encouraged philanthropy by word and personal example. An excellent instance of this is John of Kronstadt's personal, self-sacrificing ministry to the poor.

Serious deficiencies

Unfortunately, like the whole life of Russian society of that time, welfare work was not without its deficiencies and contradictions. Charitable institutions were sometimes bad ones, and if a "government inspector" as in Gogol's immortal comedy had turned up, they would have come in for severe criticism. There were patently not enough charitable institutions, and their contribution to helping the immense number of poor was paltry. In society, side by side with charitable people, there were enormous numbers who were indifferent. The customary Russian sympathy was often turned aside by the consciousness of personal poverty, and a request for alms be answered: "But, look here, we haven't anything ourselves." Destitution led to widespread bitterness and callousness in many hearts, and produced the tragic cases we read about in Chekhov, Maxim Gorky and other Russian writers. The migration of former serfs to the towns in search of a living estranged them from society, and exploitation contributed to coarsen their habits and to vices of which drunkenness was the most malignant and led to even greater impoverishment, bitterness and violence. In short, there were plenty of factors bringing to nothing all endeavours to oppose poverty whether by traditional or by newly-devised measures.

The deficiencies in the domain of welfare work in Russia have led those who have investigated this problem to the conclusion that its best form was not governmental, by district or municipal authorities, but the social, church parish form. A. Vertelovsky concludes his essay on the history of charitable work in the Russian Church with the words: "The most important condition of fruitful charitable welfare work, it must be recognized, is its voluntary performance for religious moral motives out of true Christian love of the neighbour, assisted by consciousness of their substantial material and spiritual needs." The author emphasizes the central significance of the place of worship as a starting point for the service of the poor, the role of the clergy as guiding and directing the efforts, and the importance of society as the medium and fundamental instrument for the treatment and cure of poverty. "Only if welfare work springs from the place of worship and is guided towards its aims by the church hierarchy can it be stable, free from the influence of the pride of the do-gooder ... But if it issues from the Church as a central point, and is directed to a definite goal by members of the hierarchy, charitable work can be successfully carried out with the greatest possible active participation of society itself." [16] These statements are, unfortunately, to a large extent merely a pious wish.

The second direction taken by aid to the poor, that of promoting social, economic and political reforms, although it had some place in the Russian Church was not felt to be a priority task. This is perhaps explained by the traditional fidelity of ecclesiastics to well-tried forms, uncritical submissiveness to the autocrats as the "Lord's anointed" and also by the fact that in Russian church society there was no agreement about how the historical processes that were taking place were to be understood. The Church called upon its members to be obedient to the Tsar, to respect the existing institutions of government, to beware of free-thinking and of anything that in one way or another might disturb the established order. Among the clergy, especially in its higher ranks, there were quite a lot of conservatives, although there were also persons of wide progressive views.

A constant problem for the Church was its own disorder as a class. In the first half of the 19th century, the state firmly adhered to the principle that the clergy, as an estate of the realm, formed an exclusive caste, so that there was no other career for clergymen's sons than to follow their father's profession. This created psychological and moral difficulties and filled the parish clergy with men discontented with their position. By the end of the century, this problem of estrangement had been solved to some extent. The existing sharp division between the regular and secular clergy also added to professional difficulties. A striking instance was the disparity between the higher and lower clergy. As has already been noted, the latter were humiliated and badly provided for. There was constantly a question of the widows and orphans of clerical families, who had the first claim to assistance. All this disturbed the Church and distracted it from raising and solving the wider problems of service to society. Clerical harmony was not established until the very end of the period. Metropolitan Antony Vadkovsky, for example, like other hierarchs, could do nothing for poor people from clerical resources, but only help them from personal funds (scholarships for poor students to children of the clergy).

Emancipation attempted from above

A most important matter from the religious and moral point of view for the Church was the emancipation of the peasants. But what did the Church actually do for this? Were the appeals for humanity in the treatment of the serfs on the part of individual figures in the Church effective? How are we to understand metropolitan Philaret Drozdov, who was opposed to the emancipation of the peasants and became the author of the 1861 manifesto? It is quite evident, however, that a large majority of the hierarchy agreed with what Alexander II had to say in discussion with noblemen deputies in Moscow: "It is better to abolish serfdom from above, rather than wait for the time when they will start to abolish it for themselves from below." [17] It is also evident that a substantial proportion of the Church — the laity and the lower clergy — were expecting the reform and welcomed it.

It is well known that the accomplishment of the emancipation of the serfs was attended by difficulties and did not satisfy the new free citizens of the Russian empire because they were set free without land. The clergy were called upon to play the part of peacemakers. Prof. N. N. Glubokovsky rated this role very highly: "In the emancipation of the serfs, attended by not inconsiderable complications, the clergy was a real peacemaker, successfully defending the conception and propagation of the Russian people's freedom." [18]

After the 1861 reform, capitalist attitudes began to take shape in the countryside; a stratum of village rich men emerged (kulaks, landlords of public houses, shopkeepers), oppressing the poor peasants. The local priests and the appointed Guardians of the Poor had to come forward in defence of the weak, to protect the poor peasants from the oppression and extortions of the new exploiters. This brought the clergy into conflict with the rich, who were starting to obstruct pastoral work and care for the poor.[19]

The clergy encountered serious difficulty in the struggle against drunkenness. Temperance societies were organized everywhere in Russia with the participation and on the initiative of the clergy, and were successfully beginning their work with good results. But persons interested in the sale of alcoholic liquors and then the government itself started to obstruct their work by sending secret instructions to parish priests and leaders of the temperance societies to curb their activities. However, the temperance societies continued their work, although it was very difficult.[20]

Before the revolution, there was intense activity by societies for religious and moral education; people's reading rooms were established, discussions were held, and the question was raised about the most appropriate communal life and activity in the parishes of the Russian Orthodox Church.[21]

The Church was thus gradually involved in the socio-political and to some extent economic changes, considering them from a religious and moral standpoint and bringing its own conceptions into them. Members of the Church were directly concerned in such changes, especially lay people, who not only encouraged the changes but were active participants in bringing them about. There were believers among those who supported the revolutionary process. The peaceful demonstration, for example, gunned down outside the Winter Palace, marched under church banners with a priest at its head. In the revolutionary circles, there were seminarists and students from theological academies. It is not out of place to recall here a professor of the Leningrad theological academy, the late A. I. Makarovsky, who bore on his head the scar of a sabre-cut inflicted on him by a Cossack during the dispersal of the demonstration. After 1905, the students of ecclesiastical schools and their professors vigorously opposed the tsarist regime. Revolts took place in clerical educational institutions. Certain pupils of church schools later became leading revolutionary figures (I. V. Stalin, for example). All this shows that the Russian Orthodox Church was not inert in regard to the political and socio-economic changes that were taking place. It is true that, in most cases, it interpreted them in its own way, but there was always a response in the Church to any kind of good work that was not limited to palliative measures but was concerned with radical reorganization to overcome the difficult problems that were emerging, in this case, poverty in both the literal and figurative sense.

In order to form some impression of the direction and effectiveness of the practical steps taken by the Russian Orthodox Church in aid of the poor, it is useful to read N. S. Leskov's book *Soboryane* (1872; English translation, *Cathedral Folk*, 1924). The main character is Archpriest Savely Tuberozov, a truth seeker and truth lover, firm in defence of religious convictions and at the same time full of humane tolerance for those who believe and think differently, an exposer of falsehood, a fighter against injustice. But he is surrounded by a secular and ecclesiastical order with which it is difficult to struggle, and Tuberozov outwardly submits while inwardly remaining "a rebel in a cassock". The book presents examples of simplicity of heart in Fr Savely's comrade-in-arms, deacon Akhilla; it tells of the love and tenderness which links the heoes of the book in bonds of indissoluble friendship, and relates the difficult existence of the priest with a large family, Zachary Benefaktov. It is full of sympathy for the clerics who stood on the lowest rung of the church hierarchy and whose life appeared to the author little different from the calamitous condition of the "simple" people. On the occasion of the publication of the book in 1872, the author wrote, "... from childhood I have not shared the contemptuous opinions and attitudes of the 'cultured' people of my country in regard to the poor country clergy. Thanks to the Orlovsky monastic settlement, I know that among the suffering and belittled clergy of the Russian Church not all are merely the small-minded skinflints and whippersnappers that many storytellers have presented, and I dared to write *Soboryane*".[22]

Both things, then, the direction and the effectiveness, are rather different in character from what is thought in the present-day theology of liberation or on which questions are raised in the ecumenical movement when WCC programmes are being worked out. But we shall return to this later.

III. AID TO THE POOR BESIDE THE CHURCH WALLS

Social movements seeking changes in the internal order of the Russian empire were connected to a certain extent with the religious outlook of some circles of believers, but their driving force came from the ideas of the French Revolution and of later German philosophy; consequently they were not the direct affair of the Church (of the hierarchy); they took place, to use the expression of the contemporary German theologian R. Slesky, "by the church walls" or "at the church doors", forming part of what is now known in the ecumenical movement as "post-liturgical liturgy" (service after the service).[23]

After the European military campaigns that followed the 1812 war with Napoleon, political societies were formed among the educated army officers, and civilians also joined with the aim of preparing liberal governmental and social reforms in Russia. Appealing to religious morality, these circles cultivated a humane attitude to the common people and to soldiers, promoted the teaching of reading and writing, encouraged thought about reforms in the Russian mode of life, which were essential if political reaction and general national poverty were to be overcome. Under Alexander I the most important of these societies was the Union of Salvation, which was later reorganized into the revolutionary "northern" and "southern" groups. At the head of the Northern Union were the Muravev brothers, Prince Trubetskoy, the poet Ryleev; it was active in Petersburg. At the head of the Southern Union, active in the Kiev and Podolsky provinces, was Colonel Pestel. The political programme of both unions was the overthrow of the autocracy. The result was the rebellion in Petersburg on 14 December 1825, and the subsequent repressive measures against the "Decembrists" in the reign of Nicholas I. The political reaction of the empire affected not only those directly involved in the Decembrist rising, but also many other people, in particular the great Russian poets A. S. Pushkin and M. Y. Lermontov. The grievous fate of the Decembrists and their sympathizers covered them with glory as heroes and martyrs of the righteous cause, and this was of great importance in strengthening Russian national consciousness.

An important role in the formation of national sentiment was played by the philosophical societies which assumed two forms: the Slavophils and the westernizers. The Slavophils — A. S. Khomiakov, the Kireevsky brothers, Y. Ph. Samarin, the brothers Aksakov, etc., — called for the strengthening of the national soul, for the establishment of a communal "village commune" organization of life in Russia, for renewed warmth of the "inner truth of genuine Christianity". The westernizers — V. G. Belinsky, T. N. Granovsky, A. I. Herzen, etc., — considered that the task of Russian society of their time was to form closer links with the European West, in assimilating the achievements of European science, in embodying in social and political life the models of the most advanced European countries. Movements of this kind captivated the intelligentsia of Nicholas's time and the ensuing period. On the one hand, they influenced the internal theological, liturgical and communal-synodal renewal in the Russian Church; on the other, they set themselves in opposition both to existing administrative forms in the Church, and to the political order of the empire.

Two movements: one revolutionary

The controversy between these tendencies in philosophical outlook had practical consequences, on the one hand in the populist movement, devoted to the schooling and education of the Russian people in its poorest, especially peasant strata, and on the other in the formation of extreme revolutionary groups, in particular the *Narodnaia volia* (People's Will) party, which endeavoured by means of terrorism and political assassinations to bring about social and political changes. Both of these had in view the problem of poverty and the poor. At the same time arose the Nihilist movement, demanding absolute individual freedom and rejecting as a consequence any obligations whatsoever in regard to the contemporary social, ecclesiastical, family and political order.[24] The ferment in public opinion became more intense after the reforms of Alexander II, increased even more in the time of the repression of the 1863 Polish rising, and was met by government measures for a "war against sedition", which exacerbated Russian society even more and culminated in the assassination of the "Tsar of emancipation".

In the reign of Alexander III, the revolutionary movement was driven underground. The government slogan "Orthodoxy, autocracy, nationality", supported by the official Church chiefly in regard to its first two items, lent itself to public criticism and split Russian society even more, while on the other hand it gave rise to the estrangement from the Church of a considerable part of the intelligentsia and that section of the ordinary people influenced by revolutionary Marxist ideas.

Under the next regime, the social movement on the revolutionary side moved further and further away from the church walls and became secularized in forms of party conflict, not only anti-government but also anti-clerical, emphatically atheistic, opposed not so much to the essence of religion as to those educated in the Church in submission to "the Lord's anointed", in patience and non-resistance, self-restraint, etc.[25]

Aid to the poor, however, did not leave the church porches, so to speak, even if it was at a distance, and even in the case of complete secularization; it continued its course "beside the church walls". For, in the first place, the poor formed an integral part of the Church, and care for those in need — whether it arose from within or from without, whether it took the form of philosophical currents or of the revolutionary movement — was care for those who were embraced by the Church. And in the second place, religious ideas, even when called in question by the revolutionary process, constituted and continue to constitute the abiding essence of the Church's reality — the essence of authentic liturgy — service; they might be manifested to a greater or less extent, or be understood in this or that way, but it is precisely those ideas which constituted and continue to constitute the force of what is done in aid of the poor — it is they that ensured and continue to ensure the "liturgy after the liturgy", even though it were done in contradiction to and alienation from the Church. In this sense, the union of Church and state in welfare work and the support given by the Church to governmental reforms in the 19th century, as well as public protest against the imperfection and inadequacy of both, when in the end the revolution had taken place, mirrored exactly the dialectical process of "liturgy after the liturgy". The very fact of the defection of believers from the Church in the pre-revolutionary period, the formation of Protestant groups, for example of Baptists, the bitterness of the anti-religious struggle in the first decades after the revolution, all show that the movement in aid of the poor went on precisely at the very doors of the Church. The reconciliatory position of the Church in the mitigation of dialectical tension, whether understood or not, the actions of the Church in aid of the poor, whether approved or criticized, the Church itself whether supported or rejected, the Church with all its contradictions, all its own wealth and its own poverty, was the point around which one way or another the question of Russian poverty turned and was decided.

Outburst of literary work

Service of the people by the Church or in connection with the Church in the 19th and early 20th centuries flowed into various forms of theological, literary and journalistic work. It was a period of blossoming talents and emerging reputations that left an indelible trace. In the domain of learned theology, the following were of that kind: Filaret Drozdov (1782-1867), Metropolitan of Moscow; Grigorii Postnikov (1784-1860), Metropolitan of Novgorod; Filaret Amfiteatrov (1789-1857), Metropolitan of Kiev; Makarii Bulgakov (1816-1882), Metropolitan of Moscow; Filaret Gumilevsky (1805-1866), Archbishop of Chernigov; Professor A. V. Gorsky (1812-1875); Professor Ioann Sokolov (1818-1869); Professor Y. K. Amfiteatrov (1802-1848); Archpriest I. L. Yanyshev (1826-1910); the church historian E. E. Golubinsky (1834-1912); Professor N. F. Kapterev (1847-

1917); Bishop Porfirii Uspensky (1804-1855); Professor P. V. Znamensky (1836-1910); Professor I. E. Troitsky (1832-1902); Professor V. V. Bolotov (1853-1900); Professor A. L. Katansky (1836-1919); Silivestr Malevansky (1828-1908); and finally Archbishop Sergei Starogorodsky (subsequently Patriarch of Moscow and of all Russia), and many others. In the domain of religious thought, the following may be mentioned: Petr Chaadaev (1794-1856); Nicolai Gogol (1809-1852), who at the same time was a great literary artist; Ivan Kireevsky (1806-1856); Aleksei Khomiakov (1804-1860); Aleksandr Bukharev (1822-1871); Vladimir Soloviev (1853-1900), among others. The thought and activities of the Russian Orthodox Church of that age were mirrored in periodicals: *Khristianskoe Chtenie* (Christian Reading), Petersburg; *Pravoslavnii Sobesednik* (Orthodox Companion), Kazan; *Pravoslavnoe Obozrenie* (Orthodox Review) and *Dushepoleznoe Chtenie* (Edifying Reading), Moscow; *Strannik* (The Pilgrim), Petersburg; *Rukovodstvo dlia pastyrei* (Guide for Pastors), Kiev; *Trudy Kievskoi dukhovnoi akademii* (Transactions of the Kiev Theological Academy), Kiev; *Chteniia obshchestva liubitelei religioznogo prosveshcheniia* (Readings of the Society of Friends of Religious Education), Moscow.[26] In the literary field, everyone knows the names of Pushkin, Lermontov, Gogol, Belinsky Nekrasov, Saltykov-Shchedrin, Ostrovsky, Dostoyevsky, Aleksei Tolstoy, Leo Tolstoy and many others. It would be possible to list numerous famous names of scientists, doctors, artists, architects, who marked that period with the deathless works of their minds and hands. It is important to stress that a humane spirit, care for the "humiliated and insulted", love for the "least brethren", permeated the majority of the greatest creations of the pre-revolutionary period. They contain the answer of the human heart to the cry of poverty and distress that rises around it. In the works of genius of that age a religious and moral context is very frequently apparent; it is a reflection of an authentic liturgy — creation and activity alongside the church walls. Possibly better than anywhere a reflection of that kind is perceptible in the creations of the Russian composers of that age: Glinka, Tchaikovsky, Rimsky-Korsakov, Kastalsky, etc. The musicians frequently based themselves directly on religious themes; at all events they raised the soul to something purer, more elevated and humane, mirroring at once the grief of the Russian people, the depth of its soul and its hope for a better future.

Thus in every aspect of Russian life of that time the movement alongside the church walls was not uniform, but multiple and contradictory, revealing an upsurge in a situation of crisis, and a crisis in the upsurge itself.

The academic theology, for example, was not always consonant with what religious thinkers put forward in their theologico-philosophical constructions. Philosophical views were divergent, as was plain from the mutual opposition between Slavophils and westernizers. Protestant tendencies differed from traditional Orthodoxy, and this led to the withdrawal of believers into sects of a mystical and rationalist character. Individual opinions came into conflict with the mind of the Church, as happened with Leo Tolstoy. To some extent, differences of views sprang from an analytical form of thought which ruled out the possibility of a creative synthesis.

In this critical conjuncture the tragedy of the great Russian writer Leo Tolstoy is full of significance. It was a tragedy of family life, for Tolstoy's simplified way of life, his increasing closeness to the common people, the poor, provoked a conflict in his family, aggravated by a social conflict. It was a religious tragedy, for Tolstoy's religio-philosophical views were condemned by the Church. It was a moral tragedy, because Tolstoy's teaching about non-resistance to evil was not consonant with the inescapable urgency in every existing society of combating political and social evil. Tolstoy wanted to help the poor by renouncing wealth, by simplifying his life to the level of the simple peasant; although simplicity was praiseworthy from the ascetic point of view, it was no solution to the problem of poverty. The life of one of the greatest men of the age ended up in a knot of contradictions.

Be that as it may, the movement alongside the walls of the Church played a significant role in the approach to a solution of the problem of poverty. It accompanied the revolutionary process, helping it with the contribution of the best of humane ideals founded on religious consciousness.

IV. THE SPECIFIC ROLE OF THE RUSSIAN ORTHODOX CHURCH

It can be said with certainty that, although the Russian Orthodox Church in the 19th century did not attempt directly and specifically to solve the problem of national poverty, it was involved in a kind of dialogue which is set in motion by life itself and which of necessity leads to constructive decisions.[27] Welfare work and support of government measures aimed at achieving reforms in poor relief, participation in popular education, the campaign against vice, educational work in the pre-revolutionary period, etc., — all this argues very definite involvement. But the Church, let us repeat, did not possess its own explicitly formulated programme of political and socio-economic reconstruction of life in Russia; above all, it refrained from that kind of activity, not without reason, believing that precisely as Church it has a much more important field of responsibility.

First and foremost, the Church's responsibility consisted (in the actually existing conditions of relations with the state) of maintaining its own proper identity as an institute of salvation in the proclamation of the Gospel, that is, in its internal and external mission, in the moral education of the faithful, in the celebration of the liturgy, the sacraments and rites of the Church, in pastoral care of souls. Concern for the purity of Orthodox faith and for virtuous life is what characterizes most of the writings of church authors, including the sermon literature of that age. In this connection, it is useful to refer to the spiritual experience and practical work of St Seraphim of Sarov (1759-1833), of the elders of the Optino hermitage, Leonid, Macarius, Ambrose, Anatole and others, toiling in central Russia down into the early 20th century, of Ignatius Brianchaninov (1807-1867), Bishop of Stavropol, Feofan Zatvornik (1815-1894), Bishop of Tambov, etc. Their example of virtuous life and their writings exercised a profound influence on the Russian people, inwardly strengthened the Church and promoted the growth of piety. It was also promoted by the theological works of authors such as professor Sergius Zarin, who wrote a fundamental inquiry into the nature and function in practical life of Orthodox asceticism, or Archbishop Sergii Starogorodsky, already referred to above, whose book *The Orthodox Doctrine of Salvation* to this day serves as a handbook in the theology of the Russian Orthodox Church.

As always, the focus of spiritual life was the liturgy and liturgical functions celebrated in church, in the homes of the faithful, in hospitals, welfare institutions, in army and navy. At divine service, the liturgical activities and sermon created that special spiritual condition in which the faithful whoever they might be found spiritual peace and calm, received moral support for overcoming everyday difficulties, and derived inspiration for the practice of good works. It is important to note that the liturgy was open to all without exception, poor and rich, just and sinners, young and old. Liturgical life accompanied the whole life of the faithful from earliest childhood, when they entered the Church by baptism, "chrismation" (confirmation) and first holy communion, until death, when kinsfolk brought the deceased to the church to pay their last respects, and even after death, because prayers for the dead formed and continue to form an obligatory part of Orthodox worship. The liturgy formed that interior bond between the members of the Church which makes them the organic unity of the Body of Christ, and which is indispensable for the enduring sense of spiritual plenitude and for the realization of the indissolubility of heavenly and earthly, where the heavenly is the sole firm and unshakeable foundation of faith, love and hope in the incessant struggle for holiness of the earthly Church and each of its members.

In the course of liturgical practices, patriotism was fostered in the faithful — an active love for their mother country, selflessness in the service of their neighbour, particularly in the ordeals of the war years, as well as the patience and restraint in meeting difficulties which is essential for self-discipline and that constancy and energy of spirit that is capable of flowing into active forms of service.

Friend of the poor at all times

Whatever his ecclesiastical status, the servant of the altar shared in the common function of the Church, that of the spiritual education of the people, precisely through the liturgy and liturgical practices. However poor or weighed down by his daily affairs the priest might be, he was bound at any hour of the day or night, in any weather, whatever the circumstances, to hasten with spiritual consolation to anyone who stood in need thereof. In churches, in private homes, in the field, on ships, in army camps, in prisons, hospitals, etc., the clergy were ready to serve anyone in spiritual need. They were spiritual physicians; by their example they set a standard of genuine personal relations in the Church; through sacraments and prayers they united the members of the Church on earth with the Church triumphant in heaven.

The special mission of the Russian Church consisted precisely in constantly testifying to the intercommunication of earthly and heavenly Church, in furthering the coming of the Kingdom of God in the hearts of men. It was guided in this by the teaching of the ancient church fathers, and in the first place by the words of St Athanasius of Alexandria who said that God, the Word, became man in Christ in order that, through Christ, believers in him should become capable of deification, attaining holiness by cultivating in themselves the virtues.

The fundamental concern of the Church consequently led to men's acquiring spiritual wealth. It is scarcely possible, therefore, to measure the importance of the pastoral care of those who were most in need of consolation, care of the sick and weak, of abandoned relatives, of those in material need and in misfortunes of every kind. Does not a loving word sometimes play a greater part than a piece of bread? Not for nothing is it written in Scripture: "Man shall not live by bread alone, but by every word that proceeds from the mouth of God" (Matt. 4:4).

The Church appealed to the Christian fidelity of each, to his calling, to his duty, to his responsibility before God, his country, his neighbours, before his own self. This undoubtedly had far-reaching social, economic and political consequences, for fidelity, conscientiousness, responsibility are absolutely necessary for every human organization — even if later a collision of various kinds of fidelity occurred. The principles inculcated by the Church did not lose their significance on that account.

The Church in the 19th and early 20th centuries was concerned that the liturgical rubrics should be understood by the faithful. Translations of sacred Scripture into the various languages of the peoples of Russia, new editions of the church-Slavonic texts of the liturgical books, wide liturgical use of mixed and people's choirs, as well as the introduction into divine worship of the works of church composers who combined in their works the ancient canons of Russian singing with a harmonious contemporary style, the introduction of new features popular with the people, for example, acathistus (series of doxological prayers) — all this served the one purpose of educating the people thoroughly in Orthodox spirituality so as to bring it home to the heart and mind of each member of the Church.

In the later years of the period under consideration in the Russian Orthodox Church, there was a strong inclination both for a renewal of life and for the restoration of ancient forms of Christian community, and to the kind of regulation of relations between Church and state which would not prevent freedom of conscience and the establishment of an order of church government on independent, canonical principles. Abundant materials concerning this are contained in the documents prepared for the synod of 1917-1918.

The end of the 19th century was remarkable for the ecumenical enterprises of the Russian Orthodox Church. Bishop Porfiry Uspensky, Professor V. V. Bolotov of the St Petersburg Academy, Metropolitan Antony Vadkovsky of St Petersburg and others, promoted "rapprochement" between the Russian Church and the ancient Eastern Churches: Coptic, Ethiopian, Armenian, Chaldean. In 1885 an important ecumenical event took place — the reunion with the Russian Orthodox Church of a part of the Persian Nestorians. Contacts on the question of union with the Anglican and Old Catholic Churches date back to that time. Thus, the Church did not shrink into itself in defence of its own Orthodox identity, but opened up the way for understanding and mutual assistance to other Christian communities, both within the frontiers of the Russian empire and beyond its limits.

It must not be overlooked on that account that the Russian Orthodox Church gave spiritual and material assistance to fellow-Orthodox churches in the Balkans and Near East; nor must it be forgotten that the foreign mission of the Church in Siberia, in the Far East, in Alaska and in other parts of the world was accompanied by direct help to poor people, that it was concerned with education, with a better quality of life.

It can thus be seen that in the dialectical tension of the pre-revolutionary period, the Russian Orthodox Church found the right way of creating interior wealth in the hearts of those who in reality and not merely in name were "the people of God". The people of God, nurtured and educated by the Church in the 19th and early 20th centuries, was not shaken in its faith, love and hope in the storms of the ensuing revolution. It showed itself capable of grasping the new age conscientiously and responsibly. Supported by the people of God, the Russian Orthodox Church integrated itself into the new epoch, bowing before the all-powerful sign of the cross and remembering the general resurrection.

NOTES

[1] V. M. BENZIN: *Tserkovno-prikhodskaia blagotvoritel'nost' na Rusi* (Church Parish Charity in Russia). St Petersburg: 1903.

² S. SMIRNOV: "Kak sluzhili miru podvizhniki Drevnei Rusi" (How the Hermits of Old Russia Served the World), in *Bogoslovskii Vestnik* (Theological Herald). Sviato-Troitskaia Lavra: 1903.

³ PROF. S. F. PLATONOV: *Sokrashchennyi kurs Russkoi istorii* (Abridged Manual of Russian History). Petrograd: 1917.

⁴ *Ibid.*

⁵ See, for example, the polemic with Archimandrite Nikon in the article by S. SMIRNOV quoted above, No. 2; cf. also E. F. GERKULOV: *Russkaia Tserkov' v roli pomeshchika i kapitalista* (The Russian Church in the Role of Landowner and Capitalist). Soviet publication.

⁶ *Pravoslavnoe beloe dukhovenstvo po ego polozheniiu i znacheniiu v istorii* (The Orthodox Secular Clergy: Its Historical Status and Significance). Petrograd: 1917.

⁷ *Ibid.*

⁸ PROF. S. F. PLATONOV: *op. cit.*, pp. 352-353.

⁹ *Ocherku bursy*. Chita: 1954. First published under the title *Fiziologicheskii ocherk* (Physiological Study) in the periodical *Vremia* (Time), 1862, No. 5. Cf. similar reminiscences of contemporaries: A. V. GUMILEVSKY: *Prikhodskii sviashchennik* (Parish Priest). St Petersburg: 1971; D. N. ROSTISLAVOV: "S-Peterburgskaia dukhovnaia akademiia" (The St Petersburg Theological Academy), in *Vestnik Evropy* (European Herald), 1883, No. 7-9; A. N. NADEZHDIN: *Istoriia S-Peterburgskoi dukhovnoi seminarii* (History of the St Petersburg Church Seminary), 1885.

¹⁰ See N. POMIALOVSKY: *op. cit.*, pp. 148-153.

¹¹ Cf. F. M. DOSTOIEVSKY: *The Brothers Karamazov*, and also M. BULGAKOV: *Master i Margerita* (Engl. Transl. *Master and Margarita*), 1967.

¹² V. M. BENZIN: *op. cit.*, No. 1 above.

¹³ *Ibid.*

¹⁴ A. VERTELOVSKY: The studies referred to appeared in the periodical *Vera i razum* (Faith and Reason), pp. 676-775. Kharkov: 1884.

¹⁵ Cf. A. VERTELOVSKY: *op. cit.*, and also S. RUNKEVICH: *Prikhodskaia blagotvoritel'nost' v Peterburge* (Parish Charity in Petersburg). St Petersburg: 1900.

¹⁶ A. VERTELOVSKY: *op. cit.*

¹⁷ PROF. S. F. PLATONOV: *op. cit.*, pp. 387-388.

¹⁸ *Op. cit.*, No. 6 above.

¹⁹ A. VERTELOVSKY: *op. cit.*

²⁰ P. I. POLIAKOV: *Pravoslavnoe dukhovenstvo v bor'be s narodnym p'ianstvom* (The Orthodox Clergy in the Fight Against National Drunkenness). St Petersburg: 1900.

²¹ ARCHPRIEST NICOLAI BLAGORAZUMOV: *K voprosu o vozrozhdenii pravoslavnogo russkogo prikhoda i obnovlenii tserkovno-obshchestvennoi zhizni v nem* (On the Question of the Revival of the Russian Orthodox Parish and the Renewal of Church Social Life in It). Moscow: 1904.

²² A. LESKOV: *Zhizn' Nicolaia Leskova* (Life of Nicolai Leskov), p. 274. Moscow: 1954. Quoted from the postscript by A. BATIUTO in the 1960 Leningrad edition of *Soboryane*.

[23] Cf. the materials of the Orthodox symposium in New Balaam Monastery, Finland, in September 1977.

[24] Cf. TURGENEV's novel, *Fathers and Children*.

[25] Cf. PROF. S. F. PLATONOV: *op. cit*.

[26] See on this in more detail: HANS-DIETER DÖPMANN: *Die Russische Orthodoxe Kirche in Geschichte und Gegenwart*. Berlin: VOB, 1977.

[27] See the author's essay, "Dialog v obshchestve" (Dialogue in Society), in: *ZhMP* (Journal of the Moscow Patriarchate), 10, 1977, and also *Faith in the Midst of Faiths: Reflections on Dialogue in Community*, Geneva: WCC, 1977.

6 • The Protestant in Bourgeois History

Mario Miegge

I. PROTESTANT ETHIC AND CAPITALIST RATIONALITY

The fundamental interest of the researches of Max Weber (1864-1920) lies in determining what constitutes modern capitalism in its historical individuality. This cannot be done on the economic plane alone; according to Weber, capitalism is a "sociological type" and a form of culture. This is the field of inquiry to which Weber's famous essay on *The Protestant Ethic and the Spirit of Capitalism* belongs (published 1904-1905, translated into English by Talcott Parsons, 1930).

Capitalist rationality and the struggle against tradition
1. According to Weber, capitalism takes shape as a "formally rational" economic activity, that is, a systematic activity, based on calculation, and carried out within the continuity of a business enterprise. The capitalist enterprise (and above all the industrial enterprise) is not concerned simply with meeting needs ("domestic" economy) and is not limited to the production-consumption cycle, but is aimed at profit. The capitalist economy is one of accumulation. This does not mean hoarding (putting earnings aside); it means economic development. Profits are reinvested and the enterprise grows of itself. Enterprises which do not develop, drop out of the competition. Development itself takes place through exchanges in a market economy. But precisely because the capitalist enterprise develops in time through operations which are not exclusively tied to the cycle of nature (as in traditional agricultural enterprises), it involves systematic forecasting on the basis of strict calculation of all the present and future "utilities".[1] This means, therefore, that all the "utilities" are reduced to measurable homogeneity, that is to say, subjected to monetary calculation; this applies equally whether the utilities are things (resources and available plant) or human beings. Labour in particular has to be reduced to a commodity (wage labour).

2. The capitalist enterprise therefore reduces the economy to a measurable order. According to Weber, this involves the establishment of a "formally rational" (technically efficient) order on all levels: the entrepreneur's mode

---

Translated from the Italian by the Language Service, WCC.

of life (self-control and methodical habits), use of goods (frugality and investment), behaviour of the labour force (rational division of labour and factory discipline), and ultimately the actual organization of power and legal system which have to correspond to the demands of production and exchange. It is therefore obvious that the development of the capitalist economy calls for the formation of a particular *ethos*, a set of models of conduct, typical values.

3. Modern capitalism, however, emerged and developed through a long and hard conflict (from the 16th to the 19th century) against the forces, forms of organization and values of mediaeval society.

In fact, feudal society stands in antithesis to the world of calculable homogeneity where everything is reduced to a commodity, the world of the capitalist economy. Mediaeval society is hierarchical, and the differences of rank are seen as qualitative; social performances and roles are heterogeneous. From the economic point of view the ruling class (the feudal nobility) is a parasitic class (living on income), its parasitic character being masked by caste privilege. As a warrior, the nobleman claims to be different from commoners, the serfs and labouring masses. He appears as the man who risks his life in battle. His performance therefore cannot be measured in economic terms; it is heroism or brigandage and violence (according to different points of view).

As a consequence, the feudal economy does not aim at profit and accumulation, but only at meeting domestic needs, and these will be qualitatively different for nobleman and commoner. By the brilliance of court life, again, the nobleman is distinguished from the serfs tied to the soil and from the middle classes of the towns: by squandering his revenues on festivities, tournaments, religious ceremonies, he shows his contempt for economic matters and the productive classes.

In conclusion, from every point of view the nobleman's mode of life is non-systematic; if it has rules, they are rituals (such as those of chivalry), not rational patterns of behaviour. To the nascent middle class, therefore, the nobleman's performances appear negative (feudal wars are brigandage), his social role parasitic, his ostentation mere waste, his religious life and his rites irrational and superstitious. It is easy to see why mortal conflict broke out between bourgeoisie and nobility.

4. The establishment of capitalist rationality, however, involved not only the destruction of the whole economic and cultural world of the feudal nobility, but also a struggle against the traditional attitude of the working classes who had to become available (as a wage-earning labour force) for the process of industrial production. The parasitic nobility had to be destroyed, but capitalism also had to create the proletariat, by transforming the serfs and mediaeval artisans into industrial workers capable of continuous methodical performance under conditions of factory discipline.

This formation of the industrial proletariat was not achieved by economic coercion alone or, on occasion, by class violence, but by a gradual transformation of the mentality and patterns of conduct of the past.

It is against the background of this struggle on two fronts against traditional attitudes that the contribution of the Protestant ethic to the development of capitalism is gradually defined.

Protestant ethic and "spirit of capitalism": "inner-worldly asceticism"

The systematic regulation of conduct which constitutes a fundamental element in what Weber calls the "spirit of capitalism" at first operates to a large extent in the forms of Protestant "inner-worldly asceticism". According to Weber, the great ethical innovation of the Reformation consisted in transferring the Christian asceticism of the Middle Ages to the secular domain. Whereas the monks sought the perfection of Christian life outside the "world" (in monasteries), Calvinism and the Protestant sects (up to the Quakers) imposed a strict religious discipline on worldly activities and, in particular, on the domain of economic action (work, use of possessions and money, relations of production and exchange). What has to be determined is, firstly, what religious attitude gave rise to the "inner-worldly asceticism" and, secondly, what ethical elements were relevant to the development of capitalism.

1. At first sight, it might seem paradoxical that Protestantism, which arose as a reaffirmation of salvation by grace and opposed "faith alone" to the "religious works" (penitential and ascetical practices) typical of mediaeval Christianity, should become an "asceticism in the world". The connection between theology and Protestant ethic is, in Weber's opinion, to be found in the actual doctrine of gratuitous election by God and in the increasing failure of institutional guarantees (which were still quite strong in the Lutheran churches and in Calvin's Geneva). Calvinism insists on the absolute sovereignty of God *(Soli Deo gloria)* and hence on the inscrutability of the divine decree of election of the "saints". Now, the more the relation between man and God is withdrawn from human mediations (priests and sacraments), the more dramatic becomes the question of the individual believer: Am I numbered among the elect? So, when the reformed are a scattered minority under attack from the official churches, and when within the very ambit of Protestantism the cry for independence is raised, together with the affirmation that the true Church is constituted solely by those professing faith, the question of knowing one's state of grace tends to be transferred to the ethical plane: Is it possible to distinguish the elect from the reprobate on the basis of conduct? Undoubtedly, as Luther had already observed in his *Freedom of the Christian Man* (1520): "Good and devout works never make a man good and devout, but a good and devout man does good and devout works ... As Christ says, a bad tree does not bear good fruit, a good tree does not bear bad fruit ..." (XXIII).

But while salvation does not depend on the works of man but on grace alone and divine election, the fruits of grace and election must be visible. And for the Calvinists and sectarians of the later 16th and early 17th centuries, the fruits of sin and of divine reprobation were easily identifiable. Disorder, idleness, waste of time and property, arbitrary violence, were amply represented by the daily behaviour of the feudal nobility, but they were also found in the lower ranks of society, in the country people driven out of decaying feudal estates and reduced to vagrancy. When contrasted with this historically-perceptible reality, the regular and sober life of the Calvinists, of those who in England would be called "Puritans", appeared as a sign of divine election. And in this setting, the world of economics (despised by the nobles and the hermits of the Middle Ages) and even the very banality of the daily discipline of work, assumed religious significance and value. "... Only in the Protestant ethic of vocation", says Weber, "does the world, despite all its creaturely imperfections, possess unique and religious significance as the object through which one fulfills his duties by rational behaviour according to the will of an absolutely transcendent God. When success crowns (...) purposive behaviour, such success is constructed as a sign that God's blessing rests upon such behaviour." [2]

2. Some typical elements of the ethics of "ascetic Protestantism" [3] must now be noted:

a) *Self-control and disciplined use of time*
Time is a gift of God, and life is short but infinitely precious because in it the vocation of the elect is accomplished. The Puritan of the 17th century did not yet say, as a century later the secularized Protestant, Benjamin Franklin, would, that "time is money", but by means of rational self-control and daily examination of conscience (How have I employed my day? Have I used every moment of my time to the glory of God?), he transformed the cyclical time of mediaeval life determined by nature and custom into a methodical construction, a regulated and calculated time. The management of Christian life on the path of sanctification, Weber observes, is organized like the book-keeping of a commercial enterprise.

b) *Labour as vocation and professional ethic*
Following in this respect the tradition of western monasticism *(Ora et labora)*, Luther regarded labour first and foremost as a harsh discipline imposed on the body (man's animal nature), a means of representing the passions. But to this ascetic significance (which persists throughout Protestant ethics), Luther added a decidedly vocational meaning. In fact, the actual word which in German means "vocation" or "calling" *(Beruf)* was coined by Luther. In the Middle Ages, "vocation" was predominantly understood in the clerical or monastic sense. The Reformation affirmed

that vocation is something addressed to every Christian, and is therefore accomplished in the state of life of each, by steady and continuous work devoted to the service of the neighbour in the midst of secular society. Luther, however, held a traditional and very conservative view of secular society. Consequently, he affirms that to accomplish his own vocation one must remain in his "status", respecting the rigid order of the mediaeval classes (serfs remain serfs, etc.). Calvin, on the other hand, who consciously accepted the new development of the market economy, already admits that fulfilment of one's vocation need not be incompatible with change of status. And a century later, the Puritan Baxter praises what nowadays is called "social mobility" within the framework of an economy based on exchange and on the division of labour. In this way, the accomplishment of one's vocation was translated into professional diligence and spirit of initiative; and social advancement (measured no longer by the mediaeval hierarchy of classes, but by increase of property and development of economic enterprises) was now regarded as a divine blessing and sign of election.

c) *The regulation of sexual relations*

To the chastity and sexual repression of the monks, ascetic Protestantism opposed the discipline of monogamous marriage. Just as rigid a discipline is involved, though fundamentally different because established in the bilateral relationship of the couple. Marriage and family thus become a place for the fulfilment of the Christian vocation (and extra-marital relations were considered in Reformed communities to be one of the gravest sins).

d) *The management of possessions: austerity, thrift, standardization of consumption*

Calvinism (and "ascetic Protestantism" in general) affirms that we are only administrators of the riches that God places at our disposal. Wealth is not condemned in itself (as in monasticism and in the poverty movements of the Middle Ages), but the unregulated use of possessions is. The worldly ostentation, pomp and waste, characteristic of the nobility, was contrasted with the thrift and frugality of the Puritan bourgeois. But, as John Wesley was acutely to remark towards the middle of the 18th century, the industry and frugality of the pious Protestant necessarily produce new wealth. And because this wealth cannot either be squandered in irrational consumption or stored up and left unused (for this would be a bad administration of God's gifts), the cycle of capitalist accumulation now opens out: thrift becomes investment. The well-to-do Puritan will use his money to "redeem" the vagrants by subjecting them to the discipline of wage labour in his own firm. And in the meagreness of the wages, Puritan austerity is linked with the "rational exploitation" of the labour force! The growth of a business enterprise thus appears to correspond to its social utility.

Finally, Puritan austerity encourages standardized consumption. For what causes diversification of consumption (the luxury of the ruling aristocracies) is the will for distinction and prestige. This stands in contrast to the norm of *Soli Deo gloria*. But the requirement of uniform and impersonal consumption (that all should dress soberly and more or less in the same fashion) falls into line very well with the new forms of production just when the industrial enterprise organized on the basis of division of labour is beginning to supplant the artisan's workshop, and mass production is replacing the mediaeval master-craftsman.

e) *The new concept of charity and the impersonal regulation of social relations*

Weber notes that Calvinism and Puritanism profoundly transformed the concept of charity. In the Catholic Middle Ages, charity tended to be identified with a particular sector of religious good works, those done for the needy or suffering neighbour. By insisting on acts of charity, Catholicism brings out the personal and emotional aspect of this relation with one's neighbour (alms and the kiss to the leper are regarded as meritorious, provided there is an intention of sympathy and benevolence towards the poor). On the other hand, this tends to perpetuate the presence of the poor, as an opportunity for the exercise of charity by the devout.

The Calvinist regards this attitude as impiety pure and simple — You think to save yourself by your works of charity and your good sentiments, but you are simply giving man the glory which belongs to God alone. You are divinizing the creature! The Puritan especially distrusts the "heart", because he knows that sin is a spiritual fact and that the inner man is corrupt. Furthermore, the very presence of those who are the objects of Catholic charity (beggars, etc.) is regarded as a sign of that human disorder which is an outrage to the glory of God. Mendicity, like vagrancy, must be got rid of. But at this point, Weber observes, charity comes to take the form of impersonal action directed towards the common good; by giving my offering to public welfare institutions, I will avoid exalting the creature (in me and other people) and at the same time contribute in some measure to limit and correct the disorder of the world. And this will also be a sign of election.

The main features of the "Puritan order" of the life of society thus emerge. Without deluding himself that he is building the heavenly Jerusalem on this earth, the Puritan tends to promote a provisional order which will be to the glory of God, not of man. You must neither indulge in looking on man defaced by sin, nor even claim to see clearly the face of the new man, but by hard labour you must establish and regulate social life so that the outcome of human action be at the same time visible and anonymous as a balance of profit.

In a similar way, the rationalist philosophy of the 17th century (which is not a typically Protestant phenomenon, seeing that Galilei, Descartes and Father Malebranche were Catholics and Spinoza a Jew), in its polemic with scholasticism, affirmed that the glory of God is manifested in the simplicity and impersonal mathematical rigour of the laws of the universe which the new physics was working out.

The Puritan ethic and the rationalist philosophy form part of the same historical conjuncture in which modern capitalism arose and developed.

II. THE LIMITS OF MAX WEBER'S INTERPRETATION
1. Max Weber's study and historical materialism

In the central essay of *History and Class Consciousness* (1923), entitled "Reification and Proletarian Consciousness", George Lukács notes at one point that "... the Calvinist linking of an ethic of putting to the proof (inner-worldly asceticism) and the complete transcendence of the objective powers which move the world and determine the content of human destiny (*Deus absconditus* and predestination) represent in mythological form, but in their pure state, the bourgeois structure of the reified consciousness *(das Ding an sich)*". [4] He refers in a footnote to the essays of Max Weber, and adds: "It is quite immaterial, for an appreciation of the facts, whether one approves or not of his causal interpretation."

The importance of Weber's study of the Protestant ethic and the spirit of capitalism,[5] the central elements of which were to be presented again in the systematic framework of *Wirtschaft und Gesellschaft*,[6] appears, therefore, to be confirmed by the fact that his findings seem significant even when viewed in the quite different perspective of Lukács in *History and Class Consciousness*.

Now Lukács regards Weber's findings as significant because "the fundamental problem which had emerged" in Weber's researches, particularly in the sociology of religion, and which "forms the background of *Wirtschaft und Gesellschaft*", is that of the "individuality of modern capitalism".[7]

The difference obviously consists in the fact that for Lukács (in the years 1919-1923) the fundamental question was not to define the "historical individuality" of modern capitalism, but to determine the historical conditions of its overthrow. But precisely in the context of a revolutionary strategy, the questions of class-consciousness crop up again with extreme urgency and in quite different terms from those that had prevailed in the last years of the 19th century and the beginning of the 20th century from the point of view of reformism and the Second International. In *Geschichte und Klassenbewusstsein*, the class-consciousness of the proletariat (as the consciousness of an antagonistic relation in society) is not assumed as a "natural" factual datum reducible to the psychological mechanism of the "reflex". Undoubtedly, the proletariat's class-consciousness expresses its position within the capitalist system. But it represents for the proletariat the alternative to a "reified consciousness". For reified consciousness, as a "fundamental ideological structure of capitalism", is not found only in the bourgeois but also establishes itself in the proletarian, obliterating class relations and conditioning the actual conduct of the workers' movement (reformism). Class-consciousness therefore represents for the proletariat a qualitative transition, and its actual formation is a revolutionary task.

When historical materialism was thus reinserted in the dynamism of the revolution and rid of positivist deformations, the connections between the plane of economic and social structures and that of consciousness had to be replaced in a dialectical perspective. And from this point of view, certain elements of Max Weber's study could be used to define the "historical individuality" of the "fundamental ideological structure of capitalism" (the reified consciousness), without accepting the type of causal connection suggested by Weber.

Besides, Weber's aim was not to "substitute for a one-sided materialistic an equally one-sided spiritualistic causal interpretation of culture and of history".[8] In the essay on the Protestant ethic, he opposes an "abstract", one-sided materialism ("... we must free ourselves from the idea that it is possible to deduce the Reformation as a historically necessary result from certain economic changes") and continues: "On the other hand, however, we have no intention whatever of maintaining such a foolish and doctrinaire thesis as that the spirit of capitalism ... could only have arisen as the result of certain effects of the Reformation, or even that capitalism as an economic system is a creation of the Reformation." The aim of the inquiry is therefore presented as follows: "We only wish to ascertain whether and to what extent religious forces have taken part in the qualitative formation and the quantitative expansion of that spirit over the world. Furthermore, what concrete aspects of our capitalistic culture can be traced to them?" [9]

The delimitation of the field of inquiry does not concern only the type of connections that are to be laid bare, however; it also concerns the extension of the terms "Protestant ethic" on the one hand, and "spirit of capitalism" on the other. Although Weber does not present strict definitions at the beginning of the essay, he nevertheless establishes quite a precise frame of historical reference. On the one hand, he explains that the Protestantism which he has in mind applies to the phase of Dutch and English Calvinism of the 17th century, and of the dissenting sects of the 17th and 18th centuries more than to the initial phases of the Reformation (including Genevan Calvinism).[10] On the other hand, he distinguishes between the various phases in the development of modern capitalism and the position of the various strata of the bourgeoisie in this process of development, observing that "... at the beginning of modern times, it was by no means the capitalistic entrepreneurs of the commercial aristocracy who were either the sole or the predominant bearers of the attitude we are here calling the spirit of capitalism. It was much more the rising strata of the lower industrial middle classes." [11] The formation of this new entrepreneurial bourgeoisie, the protagonist of the industrial revolution of the 17th and 18th centuries,[12] is therefore in the centre of Weber's inquiry. "The rising middle and small bourgeoisie, from which entrepreneurs were principally recruited, were for the most part here (in Holland) and elsewhere typical representatives of capitalistic ethics and of Calvinistic religion." [13]

The way in which Weber, within this frame of reference, brings out the interconnections between religious attitudes and the conduct of secular life, and describes the passage from the "inner-worldly asceticism" of Calvinism and the sects to the forms of rational action "orientated to a system of discrete individual ends" *(zweckrational)*, typical of capitalist enterprise, is well known and we shall not repeat it. In a page of *Wirtschaft und Gesellschaft*, Weber presented afresh the basic features of that ethico-religious historical phenomenon. "But an unbroken unity, integrating in systematic fashion an ethic of vocation in the world with assurance of religious salvation, was the unique creation of ascetic Protestantism alone. Furthermore, only in the Protestant ethic of vocation does the world, despite all its creaturely imperfections, possess unique and religious significance as the object through which one fulfills his duties by rational behaviour according to the will of an absolutely transcendent God. When success crowns rational, sober, purposive behaviour of the sort not oriented exclusively to worldly acquisition, such success is construed as a sign that God's blessing rests upon such behaviour. This inner-worldly asceticism had a number of distinctive consequences not found in any other religion. This religion demanded of the believer, not celibacy, as in the case of the monk, but the avoidance of all erotic pleasure; not poverty, but the elimination of all idle and exploitative enjoyment of unearned wealth and income, and the avoidance of all feudalistic, sensuous ostentation of wealth; not the ascetic death-life of the cloister, but an alert, rationally-controlled patterning of life, and the avoidance of all surrender to the beauty of the world, to art, or to one's own moods and emotions. The clear and uniform goal of this asceticism was the disciplining and methodical organization of the whole pattern of life. Its typical representative was the 'man of a vocation' and its unique result was the rational organization and institutionalization of social relationships." [14]

We should only like to note that in the essay on the Protestant ethic and the spirit of capitalism the analysis of the progressive emancipation of a "formally rational" economic action from the fetters of tradition, an emancipation which in the first place came about in the religious context of Calvinism and the sects,[15] is carried out by Weber in connection with the two classes composing the capitalist industrial structure. On the one hand (by far the most important part of Weber's essay), in regard to the formation of the spirit of capitalism in the entrepreneurial bourgeoisie;[16] on the other, in regard to the formation of the labour forces available for the capitalist enterprise.[17]

Weber's observations on the availability of labour, gathered on the subjective level by means of patterns of professional ethics in "ascetic Protestantism", are among the most interesting items in his study, and they can be utilized even in a heuristic selection different from Weber's. Undoubtedly, Weber's analysis leaves in the background the objective components of the availability of labour within the framework of the market economy and the capitalist enterprise. It leaves in the shade the process described by Marx in the fourth section of *Capital* (Book I), by which labour reduced to a commodity is progressively socialized and incorporated into capital, in the various stages of development of modern industry: "simple cooperation", "division of labour in manufacture", "mechanized large-scale industry".

It might be said that the subjective elements were of greater importance precisely in the initial stages of industrial capitalism, while the economic mechanism was still in formation. And this could be the case both on the plane of the competition between entrepreneurs and on that of the availability of labour.

"But victorious capitalism, since it rests on mechanical foundations",[18] "has become emancipated from its old supports. But as it could at one time destroy the old forms of mediaeval regulation of economic life only in alliance with the growing power of the modern state, the same, we may say provisionally, may have been the case in its relations with religious forces." [19]

2. The limits of Weber's inquiry: some general questions

The scope of Weber's study of the Protestant ethic and the spirit of capitalism therefore determines to a large extent the results that can be expected from it.

But it still has to be asked whether its deliberately restricted scope accounts entirely for the limits of the inquiry itself. Weber's heuristic choice implies a selection and arrangement of the data according to a typical pattern. But reexamination of certain elements that have been excluded, or at least obliterated by the choice made, might bring to light a somewhat different and perhaps even more problematic pattern of connections between the ethico-religious attitudes of Calvinist or sectarian Protestantism and the structures of nascent bourgeois society.

Is a reexamination of this kind possible within the framework of Weber's thesis? Or would it involve a different heuristic choice? And would such a new choice not itself depend on a different evaluation? This reopens the disputed question of the relations between heuristic choices and value judgments.

In fact, the use of a selective and ordering "type" in view of identifying the historical individuality of a phenomenon implies that certain "value relations" are being taken to be significant while others are being excluded as not significant within the proposed framework. Weber, however, also insisted on the non-evaluative character of this choice in the sense that it does not imply approval or disapproval of the value relations identified and described.

"The fact that one investigates the influence of certain ethical or religious convictions on economic life and estimates it to be large under certain circumstances does not, for instance, imply the necessity of sharing or even esteeming those causally very significant convictions (...) The empirical-psychological and historical analysis of certain evaluations with respect to the individual social conditions of their emergence and continued existence can never, under any circumstances, lead to anything other than an 'understanding' explanation. This is by no means negligible." [20]

But now, if "understanding" depends on the elaboration of a type pattern, does this elaboration itself even allow other heuristic choices and a wider "understanding"?

Since the ethico-religious attitudes of Protestantism of the 16th and 17th centuries are identified and selected in relation to the emerging "type" of capitalist rationality, could the elements which are excluded as not significant not in fact become significant within a different type pattern? And if this were possible, how could a unitary view of the historical process be reestablished? Would not the relations revealed on the basis of the various different heuristic choices turn out in the end to be insignificant when set side by side?

Undoubtedly, Weber affirms more than once the relative and "partial" character of the "formal" economic rationality realized by modern capitalism.[21] But does this very affirmation not itself imply in some way a value judgment? And has the value judgment a rational or irrational basis? In fact, according to Weber: "It is really a question not only of alternatives between values, but of an irreconcilable death struggle, like that between 'God' and the 'Devil'." [22]

But in face of the elaborated "type" of a capitalist rationality, will not any suggestion of a different rationality, whether emerging in the past historical process or posited in the present by political action, appear purely irrational?

These questions, of course, need above all to be given formulation in the domain of historical research by a brief reexamination of some elements which are taken into consideration or excluded from Weber's inquiry. At the end of this reexamination, it will be possible to raise the problem again on a better basis.

3. The doctrine of election, and Calvin's position

Seeking to determine in the context of "ascetic Protestantism" the links between the religious attitude and the general pattern of life, in particular on the plane of professional ethics, Weber gave prominence to the subjective and individual element. He left in the background, on one side, certain doctrinal features (for instance, the theological structure of Calvinism) and, on the other side, the attitudes and views toward community, whether on the strictly ecclesiastical plane (concept of the Church and actual historical forms of organization) or on that of social projects, more or less utopian schemes of reform, and actual experiments made to found "republics of the saints" within the ambit of ascetic Protestantism.

It is then obvious that the doctrine of gratuitous election inevitably appeared as the most characteristic doctrine of Calvinism.[23]

Moreover, Weber examines the doctrine of predestination in its most rigorous formulations in the 17th century (such as the Westminster Confession of 1647)[24] and at a stage in the history of Protestantism in which the subjective and individual problem of the *certitudo salutis* (the confirmation of election) had become of great importance in consequence of the vanishing of any sacramental intermediaries[25] in the process of transition from the original Calvinist ecclesiastical model to the communities of the "Confessions" (Independents and Calvinist Baptists).[26] This was at a time, therefore, when the connection between the discipline of the secular life of the "saints" and the assurance of the state of grace had become rather closer than in the early days of Calvinism.

In this perspective, Weber could insist on the "inner loneliness" of the elect in relation to the *Deus absconditus*[27] and on the repercussions of such an attitude on the conduct of life: in the field of professional activity ("... in order to attain that self-confidence, intense worldly activity is recommended as the most suitable means"),[28] in the control of time and management of worldly possessions, and also in the field of social relations where the conception of love of the neighbour, subordinated to the imperative *Soli Deo gloria*, tended to promote an impersonal regulation which anticipates the terminology of utilitarian liberalism.[29] Hence it is no accident that inner-worldly asceticism reached its most consistent development on the foundation of the Calvinist God's absolute inexplicability, utter remoteness from every human criterion, and unsearchableness as to his motives. Thus, the inner-worldly ascetic is the recognized "man of vocation", who neither inquires about nor finds it necessary to inquire about the meaning of his actual practice of a vocation within the world, the total framework of which is not his responsibility but his God's. For him, it suffices that, through his rational actions in this world, he is personally executing the will of God which is unsearchable in its ultimate significance.[30]

The doctrine of election, therefore, acted in the "saints" as a sort of power of determination promoting a new self-awareness and coherence in the conduct of life, while stimulating impersonal activism in the direction of the nascent capitalist rationality.

Weber more than once stressed that this development was nevertheless already far from Calvinism in its origins.[31] The difference between Calvin's doctrine and the position of his Puritan successors is concretely shown in the question of the *certitudo salutis*, the assurance of election: "For Calvin himself", Weber observes, "this was not a problem. He felt himself to be a chosen agent of the Lord, and was certain of his own salvation. Accordingly, to the question of how the individual can be certain of his own election, he has at bottom only the answer that we should be content with the knowledge that God has chosen, and depend further on that implicit trust in Christ which is the result of true faith." [32]

And yet the doctrine of election as relationship to the *Deus absconditus* is taken by Weber to be the central element of Calvinist religious sentiment (and this theme is once again taken up, as we have seen, by Lukács also). In fact, the reexamination of Calvin's work which has been carried out in recent years (to a large extent in the context of Barthian neo-Calvinism) has considerably modified this so-to-speak traditional view.

So, it is to be borne in mind that the most complete formulation of the Calvinist doctrine of election is late [33] and, furthermore, is undoubtedly conditioned by the polemics of the years of the Council of Trent. But above all, the doctrine in Calvin is invariably characterized by two elements: the transcendent sovereignty and the revealed action of God, an action which unfolds according to a precise design in the alliance and promises of the Old Testament, and in the Incarnation and the Gospel. If, therefore, according to Calvin (as Weber himself acknowledges), the certainty of election is attained solely in faith, faith itself is not a relation to the *Deus absconditus*, but to the God who acts and is manifested in Jesus Christ.[34] And hence, in Chapter 24 of Book III of the *Institutes* (1560 edition), which deals precisely with the theme, that "election is confirmed by God's call", Calvin declares: "But if we have been chosen in Christ, we shall not find assurance of our election in ourselves; and not even in God the Father, if we conceive him as severed from his Son. Christ, then, is the mirror wherein we must, and without self-deception may, contemplate our own election." And he adds: "If this is our ultimate goal, how insane are we to seek outside him what we have already obtained in him, and can find in him alone?"

These specific features of Calvin's doctrine have been pointed out once again in the invaluable study of Calvin's economic and social doctrine by André Biéler.[35] As this work shows, Calvinist dynamism, extending and applying its theological principles to the understanding of economic and social life, finds its driving force not in the doctrine of election, but in the whole conception of God's design and redemptive action, manifested in the Word, the Gospel of Christ. And consequently, the vocation, the "call" addressed to the elect, is not the simple summons to submit to the "hidden decree", but rather the imperative of the "new creation": the promise and divine command to *"instaurare omnia in Christo"*, and this in the life of the redeemed will take shape as the path of "sanctification".[36]

If, then, election and vocation have their foundation in the Gospel of Jesus Christ, their practical consequences likewise have always and solely to be judged by reference thereto.

The secular accomplishment of a vocation which can no longer be fulfilled in the cloister and in "ecclesiastical works", is therefore verified in the context of human relationships based on the evangelical norm of love of the neighbour. Consequently, professional vocation is measured by social utility. "And so, just as we must always bear in mind that, whatever our station in life, God must go before as if He were calling us to himself and we must follow the path he shows us by his word, it is certain that no trade or occupation will ever be approved by him unless it is useful and of general service, and redounds to the advantage of all." [37]

Here, however, the new feature of Calvin's attitude in relation to bourgeois society emerges, for the evaluation of the social utility of professional vocation is expressed quite directly in market economy terms: "The life of the faithful is aptly compared to dealing in merchandise, because they must exchange and barter with one another for the upkeep of the company. Furthermore, the diligence with which each fulfils his charge, and the vocation itself, the skill of good management and other graces, are like commodities, because the purpose and use of them is to be mutual communication among men." [38]

Moreover, the vocation to service of one's neighbour is not linked with the traditional order of "status",[39] but is compatible with a certain amount of social mobility.[40] In contrast to Luther, the profession of merchant [41] is regarded as having positive value in the perspective of that circulation of services and goods which is recognized as corresponding to the divine plan of creation.[42] Material goods and even their unequal distribution (wealth and poverty) are no longer regarded as a natural datum, a matter of indifference in the last resort in regard to salvation, but take on a certain significance in the dynamism of the relations between God and man: [43] both wealth and poverty are a test to which the faith of the individual is subjected in the context of the community.[44]

Finally, in contrast to the rigidity of the "political" order (which is reaffirmed as corresponding to the demands of a provisional order in a world disordered by sin and in a perverted society),[45] the Church is called upon to achieve within itself a different communication between its members, beyond all distinction of nationality, class and economic circumstances. This communication foreshadows the restoration of the order of creation which will come about in the Kingdom of God,[46] and it also applies to worldly goods.[47] The reorganization of the Church and its ministries through the demolition of the hierarchical structures of Catholicism [48] implies the active participation of the laity in the government of the congregation (which constitutes perhaps the most revolutionary aspect of Calvin's work). The "elders" are placed in charge of the discipline of its members and the "deacons" are placed in charge of a service of redistribution of possessions, which is no longer simply a work of beneficence (for the very idea of meritorious works has been eliminated), but opens out the prospect of a different kind of relations among men in the light of the Gospel.

If, then, these are some of the new things introduced by Calvinism, their connections with the nascent bourgeois world are not difficult to discern.

On the one hand, these links appear to be even more direct than Weber himself supposed. But they also indicate that Calvin was consciously adapting to the economic and social changes which were already perceptible in the first half of the 16th century. This was so, of course, in the question of loans at interest which Weber deals with. Here, Calvin first draws a distinction between a loan for consumption, which gives rise to usury, and a loan for investment, which he recognizes as licit. And, in working out this distinction, the Genevan reformer does not scruple to call in question (despite the most venerable authorities) the classical Aristotelian theory adopted by Patristic and scholastic tradition, that "money does not breed money".

On the other hand, this account of Calvin's views and their sociological links gives a quite different and less relevant dimension to the themes of *Deus absconditus* and the "inner loneliness of the elect" which, after all, is one of the hinges on which Weber's thesis turns (and of course of Lukács contentions mentioned above).

4. The vanguards and the crisis of Puritanism

Nevertheless, these remarks on Calvinism may appear non-conclusive for the purpose of a critical revision of Weber's theses in view of the fact that he deliberately centred his study on the period between the emergence of Puritan dissent in England in the first decades of the 17th century and the Methodist revival of the 18th.

Moreover, while Weber takes his chief terms of reference from the works of the English preachers of the 17th century (in particular, Richard Baxter), the paradigm illustrations of the fundamental theme consist of two texts from the 18th century presented one towards the beginning and the other at the end of the study: the utilitarian admonition of Benjamin Franklin ("Remember that time is money", etc.),[49] and the reflections of John Wesley on the relation between religious piety and wealth: "I fear, wherever riches have increased, the essence of religion has decreased in the same proportion. Therefore, I do not see how it is possible, in the nature of things, for any revival of true religion to continue long. For religion must necessarily produce both industry and frugality, and these cannot but produce riches. But as riches increase, so will pride, anger and love of the world in all its branches. How then is it possible that Methodism, that is, a religion of the heart, though it flourishes now as a green bay tree, should continue in this state? For the Methodists in every place grow diligent and frugal; consequently they increase in goods. Hence they proportionately increase in pride, in anger, in the desire of the flesh, the desire of the eyes, and the pride of life. So, although the form of religion remains, the spirit is swiftly vanishing away." [50]

Ultimately, therefore, it was on this last Puritan generation (Franklin and Wesley, contemporaries and both long-lived, died in 1790 and 1791 respectively) that Weber's attention concentrated; for it was in this generation that the crisis of Puritanism was unmistakably manifest, whether in a completely secularized professional ethics, such as Franklin's, or in Wesley's express misgivings.

But once the paradox that Puritan asceticism produces riches is acknowledged,[51] it still has to be determined whether the crisis of Puritanism sprang from that paradox or whether the very paradox itself did not depend to some degree on a crisis which has to be sought further back: namely, in the failure of the Puritan project to establish an order in harmony with the glory of God, not only in the conduct of the individual, but also in civil society (Commonwealth).

If this were the case, the markedly individualistic pattern of the Protestant ethos ("inner loneliness of the elect") would then appear, at least in part, to be the consequence of a defeat suffered in the political domain.

Even leaving out of account events in Geneva (and the conflicts that occurred there in the time of Calvin and Theodore Beza between the preachers and the civil authorities), some mention would have to be made at this point of the English Puritan revolution and its radical and egalitarian vanguards. Weber did not deal with this in *The Protestant Ethic and the Spirit of Capitalism*, though interesting hints may be found elsewhere.[52]

It was, in fact, in these circles of Puritan radicals and revolutionary Baptists that demands for a reordering of society on an egalitarian basis were associated with the "concern" for election.

Now, in this respect, it does not seem sufficient merely to restate the thesis of the "mysticism remote from the world" of the sects and of its "aristocratic" outcome,[53] a thesis which reappears in the Lukács' essay already quoted: "... It is not by chance that the revolutionary religious sentiment of the sects provided the purest forms of capitalism (England, America), with their ideology. For this connection between an interiority purified to the highest pitch of abstraction and freed from the weight of the 'creature', and a transcendent philosophy of history, matches the fundamental ideological structure of capitalism." [54] In fact, what this thesis lacks is precise reference to actual historical process, to its real conflicts and dramatic events, which, if taken into consideration, obscure somewhat the track of the dialectic.

It will only be possible to establish that the nexus between sectarian utopianism and the "spirit" or, if it be preferred, the "fundamental ideological structure" of Anglo-Saxon capitalism was not merely accidental if account is taken above all of the links between the Puritan and sectarian vanguards who were defeated in the English revolution (1640-1660), and the later regroupings and attitudes of the dissenter "saints".

For, in fact, it is not entirely by chance that John Lilburne, leader of the Levellers, "ultimately found a refuge in the quiet haven of Quakerism" [55] and that Gerard Winstanley, the communist Digger, "disillusioned in the same way as Lilburne, finally found a home among the Quakers, together with many of his followers".[56]

And yet Weber states that "programmes of ethical reform never were at the centre of interest for any of the religious reformers (among whom, for our purposes, we must include men like Menno, George Fox, and Wesley [...] The salvation of the soul and that alone was the centre of their life and work".[57]

But precisely in regard to the founder of the Society of Friends, Christopher Hill writes: "A man like George Fox, the Quaker, later an apostle of non-violence, felt that the revolution had been betrayed." [58]

The origins of the most representative Protestant sect of the second half of the 17th century (the Quakers, who were to promote the "sacred experiment" of Pennsylvania in the final liquidation of which about the year 1756 Benjamin Franklin took an outstanding part — can this too be pure chance?) [59] must therefore, it would seem, be related to the ebb of the revolutionary tide in the years of the English civil war.

In those crucial years, the radical agitators of the new model army, the visionaries of the fifth monarchy, the regicide "saints" (among whom it is sufficient to mention the Anabaptist, Colonel Harrison, later executed under Charles II) [60] before acquiescing in the sectarian-bourgeois combination of "purified interiority" and "transcendent philosophy of history", were capable of translating the egalitarian demands of radical Puritanism into political proposals and, for the first time in modern history, into an internationalist programme,[61] and to adopt subversive political options. They were defeated and repressed. The outlook of the revolutionary Baptists was exposed for the last time in the left wing of the "Parliament of the Saints" [62] summoned (1653) and hastily purged and then dissolved by Oliver Cromwell.

It would appear probable, and in fact reasonably well established, that *after this* the Puritan vanguards defeated in the course of the revolution and the protectorate and then — more generally — the dissenters excluded from political life after the restoration (1660) did withdraw into an individual, productive "inner-wordly asceticism" such as had already been successfully tried out by some *possidentes*, supporters of the civil war, like Cromwell himself; [63] that, ultimately speaking, dissent did constitute a milieu extremely favourable to initiative and to the management of private business (a "spirit of shopkeepers" [64]).[65]

It is no accident, either, that in the end the Methodist Revival in the 18th century, aimed at the conversion of individuals,[66] bearer of a completely non-political message, found itself faced with the dilemma of "religion which produces riches" (and also produces the availability of the labour force in the context of the industrial revolution, as Weber notes.[67] But Wesley does not seem to have realized that).

This process, however, did not take place without hindrances and contradictions. If this is so, Weber's thesis must be modified. If, in fact, the rationality of the capitalist enterprise developed to some extent in symbiosis with the Protestant ethic, the actual picture of the Protestant ethic drawn by Weber itself bears signs of *mutilation*. And in a sense, Weber cannot be blamed for such a mutilation, because it is a product of history. But he must be blamed for not having recognized it as such. The *ideological* character of bourgeois learning is ultimately shown by its stating only a part of the truth and leaving out the rest, even when its researches are pursued in a serious scientific spirit.

5. Conclusions

It therefore seems that the structures of nascent bourgeois society carried out a sort of sifting process in the richly complex phenomenon of Calvinism and the sects, in the course of which inappropriate attitudes and values (and in particular, the egalitarian proposals of the Puritan vanguards and the utopian subversive demands of the sects) were pushed out of the way and dismissed as irrational.

Since this was not a matter of natural selection, that sifting took place either through class violence (as in England in the years of the protectorate and the restoration) or through integration into that economico-social mechanism which Weber certainly recognized in the result,[68] but underestimated in the process of formation of the capitalist structures.

In fact, even at the start of his study, Weber had to deal with the subject of selection: "Thus, the capitalism of today, which has come to dominate economic life, educates and selects the economic subjects which it needs through a process of economic survival of the fittest. But here one can easily see the limits of the concept of selection as a means of historical explanation. In order that a manner of life so well adapted to the peculiarities of capitalism could be selected at all, i.e. should come to dominate others, it had to originate somewhere, and not in isolated individuals alone, but as a way of life common to whole groups of men. This origin is what really needs explanation." [69]

Here, however, we can also perceive the limits of Weber's thesis. He assumes that the "way of life and work" sprang up almost as a complete whole, and then flowed into the complex of conditions that constitute modern capitalism and "our capitalistic culture",[70] rather than being itself to some extent the product of a history in which economico-social forces were already active.

On the basis of what has been said about Calvin and about the crisis of Puritanism, the following hypotheses might be suggested:

a) that the riches of the religious phenomena of Calvinist Protestantism and of the sects is far greater than would appear from Weber's essay;

b) that these phenomena from the beginning and throughout the course of their development stand in quite precise relations with the already forming structures of the capitalist economy and of bourgeois society;

c) that these relations are not, however, all of the same kind. If, ultimately, the Protestant ethic took the form of the "bourgeois ethic",[71] and the religious attitude of later Calvinism and of the sects anticipated in some ways the "fundamental ideological structure of capitalism" (Lukács), this happened in a historical process which was not without conflicts. Those who were defeated, and all the elements marginalized by capitalist rationality, are not without significance.

It must be said in this connection that more justice has been done to the Puritan vanguard by an English Marxist historian, Christopher Hill. At the end of his essay on *The English Revolution and the Brotherhood of Man*, he observes, "... during those two decades, words had been spoken and principles proclaimed which were never to be forgotten. Despite all the hypocrisy which sullied the principles of internationalism and human equality, it is worth recalling when and by whom they were first enunciated as a programme possible of attainment on earth. 'I believe', wrote a New England Puritan in 1647, 'that the light which is now discovered in England ... will never be wholly put out, though I suspect that contrary principles will prevail for a time.' He [John Davenport] proved right on both points." [72]

It will be retorted that this different reading of the phenomenon of Puritanism corresponds to a very definite value judgment. That is so. But does it mean that we fall back into the "endless multiplicity of possible evaluations which can be reduced to manageability only by reducing them to their ultimate axioms'? [73] Even without any wish to put forward once more a view of history in which "reason will prevail in the end", we have to get out of Weber's blind alley.

In fact, at the end of the essay on *The Protestant Ethic and the Spirit of Capitalism*, the plane of value judgments emerges in a doubt he expresses about the full rationality of the capitalist system: "No one knows who will live in this cage in the future, or whether at the end of this tremendous development entirely new prophets will arise, or there will be a great rebirth of old ideas and ideals, or, if neither, mechanized petrification, embellished with a sort of convulsive self-importance (...) But this brings us to the world of judgments of value and of faith, with which this purely historical discussion need not be burdened." [74]

But, in Max Weber's sociology, "the value judgment" displays scant rational consistency. It is true, of course, that in *Wirtschaft und Gesellschaft* Weber distinguishes rationality "in terms of rational orientation to an absolute value" *(Wertrationalität)* from rationality "in terms of rational orientation to a system of discrete individual ends" *(Zweckrationalität)*.[75] But Weber adds immediately that, from the point of view of *Zweckrationalitat*, *Wertrationalität* appears always irrational! [76] Now, it is clear that "the attitude of rationality in regard to ends forms the basis of understanding of the other forms of social action; it is an ideal type in relation to which the others constitute derivative ideal types ..." [77]

If, then, in economic activity and the ways power is organized, the "rationality in regard to ends" coincides with capitalist rationality, how will it be possible to determine (rationally!) the internal contradictions of the latter and to form the project of a *different* kind of social rationality?

It is symptomatic that, in Weber's text quoted above, the transition to the "value judgments" ends in a call for "new prophets" or a "rebirth of old ideas and ideals".[78] But this nostalgia and helplessness in face of the future are quite different from the commitment and sober lack of illusions about man which characterized the Puritan believers.

NOTES

[1] By "utilities" *(Nutzleistungen)*, Weber means everything that can give rise to economic action: the land at one's disposal, raw materials, plant and machinery, labour (one's own or that of others), possibilities of exchange, etc. Cf. MAX WEBER: *The Theory of Social and Economic Organization*, p. 164. (A. M. Henderson and T. Parsons, trans; edited with an introduction by Talcott Parsons.) Glencoe, Illinois: 1947.

[2] MAX WEBER: *The Sociology of Religion*, p. 182. (Ephraim Fischoff, trans.; introduction by Talcott Parsons) London: 1965.

[3] In his essay on the Protestant ethic, Weber mainly refers to English Puritanism of the 17th century and draws his illustrations in particular from the works of Richard Baxter, a famous preacher and contemporary of Cromwell.

[4] G. LUKÁCS: *Geschichte und Klassenbewusstsein*, III, 5 ; (French translation by Kostas Axelos and Jacqueline Bois: *Histoire et Conscience de Classe*, p. 237.) Paris: 1960.

[5] MAX WEBER: *Die protestantische Ethik und der Geist des Kapitalismus* in *Archiv für Sozialwissenschaft und Sozialpolitik*, 1904-1905; republished *Gesammelte Aufsätze zur Religionssoziologie, I*. Tübingen: 1920. (English translation by Talcott Parsons: *The Protestant Ethic and the Spirit of Capitalism*.) London: 1930.

[6] MAX WEBER: *Wirtschaft und Gesellschaft, Vol. I, Religionssoziologie*, 1922. (English translation by Ephraim Fischoff; introduction by Talcott Parsons: *The Sociology of Religion*.) London: 1965. Cf. pp. 166-168; 173, 182, 203-206; 220-221; 227; 257; 269.

[7] P. ROSSI: Introduction to Italian translation of *Wirtschaft und Gesellschaft: Economia e Società*, p. xxxviii. Milan: 1961.

[8] *Die protestantische Ethik und der Geist des Kapitalismus, op. cit.*, p. 183.

[9] *Ibid.*, pp. 90-91.

[10] *Ibid.*, p. 99, No. 7 (p. 220), p. 110, p. 129, No. 110 (p. 242).

[11] *Ibid.*, p. 65. Cf. p. 179, p. 200, No. 23.

[12] If the industrial revolution was not a solely technological but, above all, a structural fact, the term can undoubtedly be applied in the 17th century, even though it usually refers to the stage when industrial enterprises were mechanized.

[13] *Die protestantische Ethik und der Geist des Kapitalismus, op. cit.*, p. 65, No. 23 (p. 200).

[14] *The Sociology of Religion, op. cit.*, pp. 182-183.

[15] *Die protestantische Ethik und der Geist des Kapitalismus, op. cit.*, pp. 54 ff. On the "great historical process in the development of religions, the elimination of magic from the world": see p. 105 (Puritanism), and p. 149 (Baptists and Quakers). Cf. *The Sociology of Religion, op. cit.*, p. 269: "Only ascetic Protestantism completely eliminated magic, etc."

[16] In this connection, see in particular on the new valuation of labour and on professional ethics: *Die protestantische Ethik und der Geist des Kapitalismus, op. cit.*, pp. 79-81, pp. 84-86, pp. 204-211 (Lutheran concept of *Beruf*); p. 158, p. 161 (the conception of work in Baxter); on systematic organization and control of behaviour: p. 124 ("The process of sanctifying life could thus almost take on the character of a business enterprise."); pp. 157-158 (disciplined use of time); p. 163, p. 169, p. 171, p. 172 (management of property, disciplined consumption, standardization of production, thrift); on the division of labour and social mobility: pp. 160-163.

[17] *Ibid.*, pp. 62-63 and pp. 177-179.

[18] *Ibid.*, p. 181.

[19] *Ibid.*, p. 72.

[20] MAX WEBER: *The Methodology of the Social Sciences*, pp. 13-14. (Translated and edited by E. A. Shils and H. A. Finch.) Glencoe, Illinois: 1949. The quotation comes from the essay on "The Meaning of 'Ethical Neutrality' in Sociology and Economics".

[21] Cf. among others in the essay just quoted the discussion of "the concept of 'rational' progress", pp. 34-39.

[22] *Ibid.*, p. 17.

[23] *Die protestantische Ethik und der Geist des Kapitalismus, op. cit.*, p. 98.

[24] *Ibid.*, pp. 99-101.

[25] *Ibid.*, pp. 104-105, p. 106.

[26] *Ibid.*, p. 122.

[27] *Ibid.*, p. 104: "In its extreme inhumanity, this doctrine must, above all, have had one consequence for the life of a generation which surrendered to its magnificent consistency. That was a feeling of unprecedented inner loneliness of the single individual. In what was for the man of the Reformation the most important thing in life, his eternal salvation, he was forced to follow his path alone to meet a destiny which had been decreed for him from eternity. No one could help him."

[28] *Ibid.*, p. 112.

[29] *Ibid.*, pp. 108-109.

[30] *The Sociology of Religion, op. cit.*, p. 173.

[31] *Die protestantische Ethik und der Geist des Kapitalismus, op. cit.*, pp. 102-103, p. 110, p. 111, No. 41 (p. 228).

[32] *Ibid.*, p. 110.

[33] Only in the 1560 edition of the *Institutio Christianae Religionis* does the doctrine of election receive separate treatment, and in the actual plan of the work it is not prominent, for it only appears in the final chapters of Book III.

[34] Cf. *Institutes of the Christian Religion*, Book III, c. II, 7. *Library of Christian Classics*, Vols. XX and XXI. (Translated by F. L. Battles; edited by J. T. McNeill.) London: 1961. Vol. XX, p. 551: "Now we shall possess a right definition of faith if we call it a firm and certain knowledge of God's benevolence towards us, founded upon the truth of the freely-given promise in Christ, both revealed to our minds and sealed upon our hearts through the Holy Spirit." The quotations that follow (Book III, c. 24) are in Vol. XXI, pp. 970-971.

[35] A. Biéler: *La Pensée Economique et Sociale de Calvin.* Geneva: 1959.

[36] Cf. *Ibid.*, pp. 355-356, p. 408.

[37] "Sermon XXI on the Epistle to the Ephesians 24 : 26-28" quoted in *ibid.*, p. 405.

[38] J. Calvin: *Commentaires sur le Nouveau Testament*, 1561: Mathew 25 : 20. Cf. *La Pensée Economique et Sociale de Calvin, op. cit.*, p. 411.

[39] *La Pensée Economique et Sociale de Calvin, op. cit.*, pp. 413-414.

[40] *Ibid.*, p. 264.

[41] *Ibid.*, p. 448 ff.

[42] *Ibid.*, pp. 235-236, pp. 335-338.

[43] *Ibid.*, p. 306 ff.

[44] *Ibid.*, p. 314 ff.

[45] *Ibid.*, p. 256 ff.

[46] *Ibid.*, pp. 253-256, pp. 273-274.

[47] *Ibid.*, p. 345 ff.

[48] *Ibid.*, p. 279.

⁴⁹ *Die protestantische Ethik und der Geist des Kapitalismus, op. cit.*, pp. 48-50.
⁵⁰ *Ibid.*, p. 175.
⁵¹ "By a unique paradox, asceticism actually resulted in the contradictory situation ... that its rationally ascetic character ... led to the accumulation of wealth." — *The Sociology of Religion, op. cit.* Cf. *Die protestantische Ethik und der Geist des Kapitalismus, op. cit.*, p. 172.
⁵² Cf. *The Sociology of Religion, op. cit.*, p. 166: In the description of "innerworldly asceticism", "the world is presented to the religious virtuoso as his responsibility. He may have the obligation to transform the world in accordance with his ascetic ideals, in which case the ascetic will become a rational reformer or revolutionary on the basis of a theory of natural rights. Examples of this were seen in the 'Parliament of the Saints' under Cromwell, in the Quaker state of Pennsylvania, and in other types of radically pietistic conventicle communism." See also p. 175, pp. 227-228.
⁵³ Cf. *Ibid.*, p. 166, p. 175.
⁵⁴ *Geschichte und Klassenbewusstsein, III, 5, op. cit.* French translation, p. 237.
⁵⁵ ERNST TROELTSCH: *Die Soziallehren der christlichen Kirchen und Gruppen* (1912), p. 821. Munich: 1922. English translation by Olive Wyon: *The Social Teachings of the Christian Churches*, Vol. 2, pp. 710-711. London: 1931. Cf. *The Sociology of Religion, op. cit.*, p. 175.
⁵⁶ *The Social Teachings of the Christian Churches, op. cit.*, Vol. 2, p. 712.
⁵⁷ *Die protestantische Ethik und der Geist des Kapitalismus, op. cit.*, pp. 89-90.
⁵⁸ CHRISTOPHER HILL: *Puritanism and Revolution*, p. 145. London: 1958.
⁵⁹ Cf. ROLAND H. BAINTON: *Christian Attitudes Toward War and Peace*, pp. 171-172. London: 1961.
⁶⁰ *Puritanism and Revolution, op. cit.*, p. vii, p. 327.
⁶¹ *Ibid.*, pp. 123-152.
⁶² Cf. *The Social Teachings of the Christian Churches, op. cit.*, pp. 708-710, pp. 712-713; Cf. also *The Sociology of Religion, op. cit.*, p. 166.
⁶³ Cf. BRUNO REVEL: *Storia di Cromwell*, pp. 24-52. Rome: 1930. See also *Die protestantische Ethik und der Geist des Kapitalismus, op. cit.*, p. 82, No. 13 (p. 213 ff.) and p. 174.
⁶⁴ *Ibid.*, p. 180.
⁶⁵ In the close discussion which is pursued in the course of the footnotes of *The Social Teachings of the Christian Churches (op. cit.)*, Ernst Troeltsch insists even more than Weber does on the connection between the political exclusion of the Calvinist and sectarian minorities and the development of "inner-worldly asceticism" in private economic activity. See, in particular, note 344 (Vol. 2, p. 894): "I would like to emphasize as an explanation of the 'bourgeois' spirit in this later Calvinism still more than Weber does the setting, the exclusion from the official world, from feudalism and from the right to hold large estates." And also note 392 (Vol. 2, p. 918): "It is also clear ... that the experience of religious oppression and exclusion favours the growth of those business qualities and, finally, that those qualities are connected with moral and religious principles. We might produce similar arguments in favour of the Baptist and Pietist sects (...)

It is not Calvinism itself which is here being considered, but Calvinism as it has developed in the school of oppression and as a minority."

But it must be remarked that Troeltsch was referring to exclusions in the context of social and political structures that were still partly traditional and feudal, or in the context of absolute monarchy. What we have said above, however, refers to an exclusion that had taken place in the framework of the bourgeois revolution of 1640-1660, and, subsequently, in that of the compromise of the restoration and of the second English revolution.

[66] As far as Wesley is concerned, Weber's remark (*Die protestantische Ethik und der Geist des Kapitalismus, op. cit.*, pp. 89-90), quoted earlier (see No. 57 above), is certainly justified.

[67] *Ibid.*, pp. 61-63, p. 177.

[68] *Ibid.*, p. 72, p. 181.

[69] *Ibid.*, p. 55.

[70] *Ibid.*, p. 91.

[71] *Ibid.*, pp. 176-177.

[72] *Puritanism and Revolution, op. cit.*, p. 152.

[73] *The Methodology of the Social Sciences, op. cit.*, p. 38.

[74] *Die protestantische Ethik und der Geist des Kapitalismus, op. cit.*, p. 182.

[75] *The Theory of Social and Economic Organization, op. cit.*, pp. 115-118.

[76] *Ibid.*, p. 117.

[77] *Economia e Società, op. cit.*, p. xxxv.

[78] *Die protestantische Ethik und der Geist des Kapitalismus, op. cit.*, p. 182.

7 • Social Action and Thought Among Arab Orthodox Christians (1800-1920)

George Khodr

The Arab Orthodox have always constituted a distinct socio-cultural entity which earns them separate treatment in any study of the social history of the Church. Those Orthodox living in the areas of Alexandria and Jerusalem come under the jurisdiction of two Greek hierarchies. In the first hundred years of the period under review here, Christians belonging to the Church of Antioch were also under a Greek patriarch. But all Orthodox living in the apostolic territories of Antioch and Jerusalem are members of the Arab-speaking Syrian people, while a majority of the Chalcedonian Christians in Egypt in this period was of Syrian extraction. In social matters the whole of Arab Orthodoxy in the Middle East followed the Antiochene pattern, not only because the Orthodox Syro-Lebanese Christians pioneered the ecclesial revival in the region but also because, awakening to their historical and cultural identity in face of the West, they created charitable organizations which from the '60s onwards grew to considerable proportions.

All these countries were dominated by the same religious outlook. Their historical unity was, moreover, guaranteed by the Ottoman Empire. Even the freedom of thought practised by Christian intellectuals in Egypt under the British occupation derived its inspiration from anti-Turkish sentiments. The same longing for liberation in the Church gave birth to institutions which, though perpetuating the Byzantine tradition of *philanthropia*, tried to model themselves on the same lines as the socio-cultural developments in the Syrian East. While the pattern was western and Russian, the heart and soul of these charitable organizations retained this Arab character, still romantic but at that time experiencing a powerful literary and political renewal. In these countries, therefore, social concern was intimately related to both education and national awakening. It had still to find its own distinctive style. This explains why the following account inevitably suffers from a certain heterogeneity.

I have explained the limits of this study by appealing to the religious and cultural unity of the Orthodox nation in the history of Syria and its

---

Translated from the French by the Language Service, WCC.

extension to Egyptian territory. Despite this common background, however, the different contexts of these three eastern patriarchates cannot be ignored. The inventory of the charitable institutions will necessarily differ in each of the three autocephalous churches. In addition to charitable and educational work, however, we must also consider the development of ideas in these three countries, which was stimulated by Arab Christian intellectuals, some of them nurtured in Orthodoxy. Some, of course, sat loose to doctrine and even adopted a scientific approach bordering on agnosticism. They themselves had firsthand experience of the poverty of the ecclesial conscience and were themselves products of this crisis, particularly in the territory which in 1920 was proclaimed the Great Lebanon. But the confessional identity of the individual in this pluralist religious civilization went so deep that it is impossible to leave out of account writers who remained on the margin of Christian life.[1]

Where the Church was awakened to social issues in countries in which the industrial revolution originated, the problems arising concerned labour conditions, relations between employer and workers, in the sense of the economic factor in daily life. The social and the humane factors were inseparably mingled and these in turn, therefore, with the spiritual life of the whole nation. But the East was still unfamiliar with the " nation " in the modern sense of the term. There a human being belonged exclusively to just one collective, namely, that of his religion. A person's identity was determined by his confessional group, his *millet*, a Koranic term meaning both a religious faith and the community professing this faith. The current term for " nation " is *Umma*, which has always referred to the Islamic community, and the term "Maronite nation", used in consular documents and in some Lebanese history books and in many pamphlets, still refers to this global identity, which is both spiritual and temporal and contemplated in its distinctive destiny.

From this standpoint, Christians, like the Jews, are *dhimmis*, that is, *protégés* of the Islamic community, who in virtue of this status, enjoy considerable internal autonomy. Because of the theocratic character of the Islamic community, they are not liable to military service and have no social service to perform for the Islamic community. Of course, charity was practised in both directions and the Arab poets praise monastic hospitality. Except in periods of crisis or oppression, relations between the different religious groups were marked by an often very gentle human conviviality. This does not alter the fact that the social has always been an integral aspect of the religious confession.

This was accentuated when the Ottomans occupied Syria in 1516. The Orthodox, or *Rum millet*, were at once placed under the protection and responsibility of the Ecumenical Patriarch, who in this way acquired *de facto* control over Christians who canonically were ecclesiastically independent of him.[2] Once again the Orthodox found their destiny bound up with that of the Empire. Empires rise and fall, but imperials remain. Recognition of their patriarchs by the *Sublime Porte* was a token that they had a large measure of autonomy in the management not only of their strictly religious affairs but even in administrative and legal matters. As civil law developed in the Empire the Ottomans reduced the legal competences of bishops from the middle of the 19th century onwards. But the Church still kept its tribunals for dealing with personal affairs, since in the absence of any concept of secularity civil marriage was quite inconceivable, as well as retaining control of the Church's inalienable property for the maintenance of places of worship and for any charitable organization which might be created.

While this system does not explain the survival of the Orthodox Church in the Fertile Crescent, as a contemporary author claims,[3] it obviously provided a factor making continuity, especially in face of Uniatism, and stimulated among the Syrian Orthodox a rich development of various charitable organizations which have strengthened their unity and encouraged them to remain outward-looking.

While it is fairly easy to explain the growth of churches in communion with Rome by pointing to their westernization, that is, their political promotion, it is not so easy to establish the ideological explanation of Orthodox growth. It was Maronite and Druse Lebanon [4] which constituted the sickness of the Eastern Mediterranean. The Maronites were the pillars of French influence in the East. Their agricultural skill, their determination to remain in power (they became the masters of the country with the conversion of the Chebab Emirs to Maronite Christianity) and to liberate themselves with the assistance of their Patriarchate and the great feudal Maronite and Druse families, placed them very much at the centre of social developments in the Lebanon.

Constituting a minority in this mountainous region of Lebanon which was then making Syrian history, the Orthodox were at the mercy of other historical factors, those connected more with the Russo-Ottoman alliance and with the Greek-Arab tension within the Eastern Church. True, the period of Mahomet Ali (1831-1840) was a favourable one so far as the freedom of the Christians was concerned. But it was chiefly the Maronites and the Greek Melchites who benefited from his occupation of Syria. In the long run, their alliance with the Egyptian was disastrous for them and for all the countries, for it was partly in reaction against it that the various confessional massacres took place in Lebanon between 1841 and 1860. The Orthodox in Beirut and Shwaifat refused to take up arms with the Maronites.[5] In the whole of the region [6] they stayed neutral in 1860, but this neutrality was unrecognized and they lost several thousands of victims in Rashayya, Hasbayya, and in the region of Damascus. Yet in 1845, during the partition of Lebanon into two provinces, one Druse and one Christian, they rejected the "Christian" government.[7] The events of 1860 sealed the confessional division of the country. An administrative Council constitutes the government of autonomous Little Lebanon. The Orthodox are represented at the various administrative levels in proportion to their numerical strength. This structure strengthens the monolithic character of the Orthodox of Mount Lebanon and paves the way for a fuller expression of their liberties. But a liberal law for non-Muslims, the famous *Hat Hamayun* of 1856, stimulated in all the provinces of the Empire the internal organization of each Christian community and led to the creation of lay councils with access to the patriarch and the bishops. Being representative of the various professions, these councils had the feeling of being in charge of the affairs of their communities. The laity, who have never been a negligible quantity among the Orthodox, were recognized by the Sultan and the ecclesiastical hierarchy as responsible for all the Church's institutions and schools. Only doctrine and the administration of the sacraments were reserved to the clergy.

Moreover, the protection of Lebanon by the Powers and the intervention of the latter in the whole life of the Empire, together with the presence of both Catholic and Protestant missionaries and their establishment of a large number of educational institutions stimulated the Orthodox to seek their own identity. This identity was conceivable only as they imitated the West, creating their own charitable organizations.

But the main strength of the Orthodox derived from Russia. Article 7 of the Treaty of 1774 which Russia imposed on the Turks stipulated: "The *Sublime Porte* (that is, the Ottoman government) promises a constant protection of the Christian religion and the churches of this religion. It permits the Minister of the Russian Imperial Court at all times to make representations to the *Porte* on behalf of the Church established in Constantinople as well as of all those who serve that Church..." The Slavophile dream of Holy Russia was to save the Slav brothers and to create a "great Graeco-Russian Orthodox Empire". In similar messianic vein, the great Russian missionary Porfiri Uspenski, distinguished for his great piety, zeal and learning, wrote: "Russia has been ordained from all eternity to illumine all Asia and to unite all Slavs. There will be a union of all Slav races with Armenia, Syria, Arabia and Ethiopia, and they will all praise God for this in Saint Sophia."[8] That was never the ambition of the Syrian Orthodox. They had the feeling that in order to survive in what was "no continuing city", Russian protection represented the catholicity and solidarity of all Christian peoples. In 1841, the Russian mission was established in Jerusalem. It was headed by Uspenski. The Orthodox of Syria and Palestine gave him their support. In many villages he struggled against proselytism, distributed his own money, encouraged Patriarch Cyril of Jerusalem to found schools. At the monastery of the Cross in Jerusalem, he established a seminary intended first for young Arabs and then for Greeks. But very few Arabs studied there and in any case they were excluded from the ranks of the entirely Greek hierarchy. He encouraged the Patriarch to establish an Arab printing house in Jerusalem. It was this printing house which furnished liturgical books to all the Orthodox Churches of the Arab world.

Defeated by the Turks, Russia signed the Treaty of Paris in 1856 and had to give up the protection of the Ottoman Orthodox. It nevertheless decided to continue its mission in Jerusalem. "Now that our influence in the East has weakened, we must on the contrary try to behave in such a way that we shall not sink in the esteem of the Orthodox population who still believe in us as of old... The Ministry finds it necessary to place a bishop at the head of the Jerusalem mission instead of an archimandrite... A service taken by a bishop together with Slavs and Arabs would be most impressive for Greeks and Arabs. Jerusalem is the centre of the world and our mission must be there."[9]

The mission was continued until 1917, and since then down to the present time it has persevered with its monastic life, a testimony to an unfulfilled dream, namely, the liberation of Orthodox Christianity.

For the Syrian Orthodox the foundation of the Imperial Orthodox Palestine Society was even more important than the Jerusalem mission. After the Russo-Turkish War of 1877-78, the time came for the Russian presence to make itself felt in the East. In 1840, the Orthodox population of Palestine represented 90% of the Christians there. In 1880, it was considerably less. The Russians blamed the Greek Patriarch for this decline. "There is not one school and the less said about the churches the better. The only concern (of every Greek) is to obtain more money to be able to intrigue, and the purpose of the intrigue is to become patriarch."[10] This increased concern for Arab Orthodoxy led to the foundation of the Imperial Orthodox Palestine Society, a private society in receipt of no government subsidy. The inaugural meeting was held in St Petersburg in May 1882. The object of the society was to keep Russia informed about the holy places in the East, to assist Orthodox pilgrims, to found schools, hospitals and hostels, and to furnish material aid to churches, monasteries, clergy and faithful.

But the fierce opposition of the Jerusalem hierarchy to the society made it turn towards the Church of Antioch. It was in Syria that it began to flourish from 1896 onwards. It was here, too, that it cooperated closely with the Arabs down to 1914. In 1913, after a quarter of a century's work, the society had eight hostels for 10,000 pilgrims, a hospital and six clinics, and 101 schools in the Levant.

These schools made an important contribution because they taught Arabic at a higher level than did other foreign schools. Their former pupils (and the author of these lines has received the personal testimony of a number of them) had no sense of political alienation. Moreover, it was the poor who went to these schools, which a Protestant pastor dismissed in scornful terms when he said of them: "Pupils in Russian schools learned some love poems by Umar Ibn al Farid and recited some of them on their way from school to church."[11] The teachers, Arabs who had never been outside their own country, used to read Turgenev or Chekov, "even the recently appearing green fascicles of Znaniya, and sometimes literature that was banned in Russia itself".[12]

It is of interest to note that the Imperial Orthodox Palestine Society deliberately made primary education its main task, apart from two secondary schools at Nazareth and Beit Zala. "Higher courses would cause a split among local people. The only results would be higher expenditure for the Society and the satisfaction of a few rich citizens, which would gain us nothing."[13]

Obviously, bourgeois society as a whole was not affected by this immense effort of the Russians, and it was thus abandoned to western Christian influence. But the love of the ordinary people for Russia was to provide the emotional force which led so many poor Orthodox to join the Communist Party founded by the Maronites of Lebanon in 1920.

The Russian presence in the East was closely connected with the Greek-Arab conflict within Syrian Orthodoxy. It was the independence of Greece which created a gulf between the Greek Patriarch of Antioch and his Arab flock. What once had been the cultural universalism of Hellenism soon turned into a western-style nationalism. But the Arabs were still Ottomans. The Russians spoke of being shocked by the want of experience of this or that Greek Patriarch, his neglect of pastoral responsibilities, his simony. They backed the demands of the Arabs for an Arab Patriarch in Antioch. One party of Arab Orthodox were opposed to this. "Composed largely of the Orthodox notables of Damascus, it feared that an Arab Patriarch would no longer need to seek their support to retain office."[14]

In 1899, reinforced by the backing of the Sultan, the bishops and the laity "nominated" three bishops, including one—Meletios—who was elected by the Holy Synod. At a moment of vacillation the bourgeoisie regained its influence and remained all powerful in the Church right down to the end of the period under review. As a rule, the poor had no say in the election of the Patriarch or his bishops. But despite the fact that notable laity took over the administration of the Church, Negib Azoury, the great nationalist, after his visit to Damascus, the patriarchal seat in 1904, could still speak of "the penury of the diocesan treasury."[15]

The election of an Arab Patriarch of Antioch was undoubtedly "the first real victory for Arab nationalism."[16] Immediately following his election, he founded a theological college in which the first generation of bishops consecrated by his two successors Gregory and Alexander were trained. Most of these ecclesiastics came from among the ordinary people. Among the Arabs who were consecrated under the Greek Patriarchate of Antioch there were admittedly bishops who were outstanding for their learning, their pastoral gifts and their sanctity of life. They were all animated by a great compassion for the poor. For example, Metropolitan Gabriel (Shatila) founded the St George hospital for the poor in Beirut. Patriarch Gregory (Haddad) distributed more than 20,000 Ottoman sovereigns to feed the starving during the First World War, irrespective of their religious affiliation.[17]

The situation in Jerusalem was much worse. Arabs were kept from membership of the Holy Sepulchre Fraternity and thus had no access to the episcopate to which only monks were called. Clergy of Palestinian origin were obliged to marry and thus disqualified from seeking an episcopal charge. In 1909, the guardians of the Holy Sepulchre were about 400 monks scattered over all Palestine. All the Arab priests were poor. Wealth was in the hands of the top clerics and a very small section of the population. Villages were often divided into *hamoules*, small tribes coming from the same extended family and subject to the authority of the oldest among them. Dissensions often arose if the priest was chosen from a clan considered to be an enemy. It is the same in all the villages of the East, since the priest acquires a certain social status. In some regions of the Levant, he enjoys certain privileges, such as the right to the income from his agricultural lands. In some places they continue to cultivate the land. At Shuyair, in Lebanon, master masons continue to build houses even after their ordination to the priesthood.

Conflict was over the administration of property, apparently. A foreign review estimated the income of the Patriarchate at the time to be in the region of Fr. 1,800,000.[18] The Greek religious press pointed out that there were moneylending monks in Jerusalem who had amassed considerable wealth. "But all these riches amassed so greedily by the hagiotaphic congregation represent an enormous temptation to the Arabs who can only gather the crumbs that fall from so richly furnished a table. This is why the Arab-speaking people demand a part in the administration. If this demand were met, it would gradually give them control of the Patriarchate as has already happened in the case of Antioch."[19]

One reason for the desire for joint administration of church property was that certain families were housed at the expense of the Patriarchate and the latter wished to evict them. The Patriarchate decided that as leases ran out it would only continue to provide accommodation for the necessitous. After the expiry of leases on 24 January, the rest were to be evicted forcibly. The leaders of the people requested the Russian ambassador to suspend its payments to the Patriarchate, arguing that this money belonged to the Orthodox community as a whole.

On 5 December 1908, therefore, the *Palestinios Kyrix* (Palestine Herald) wrote of the need:

1) to maintain the *status quo* so far as the sanctuaries and their clergy personnel were concerned. The traditional rights of the Greek nation

over the Holy Places must be defended. To defend this *status quo* was to defend the peace, tranquillity and integrity of the Ottoman Empire.

2) to oppose all propagandist acts and efforts and, above all, to defend Orthodox against proselytism.

3) to inform the Orthodox of Palestine of their origins and to reestablish forgotten national traditions.

The editor added the comment: "From a political and religious standpoint, the Arabic-speaking Orthodox of Palestine and all Syria form part of the Hellenic nation. But political vicissitudes in the countries where they live have made them forget the national language and, along with this ancestral speech, some of their ancient customs. To teach them this language and to reestablish these customs will therefore be to render service both to the Arabs and to the whole Greek nation."[20]

The Holy Sepulchre Fraternity was defending the notion of the Hellenic character of the Syrian Orthodox people, though every student of history knows it to be pure fantasy. Yet it was not, in fact, this which annoyed the Arabs. It is clear from their struggle, which was renewed again and again within the Arabized Patriarchate of Antioch, that what they wanted was joint reflection within the Church in the form of a council composed of both laity and clergy (the latter of course were Greeks). The real point of these demands was that the Church of Palestine was in fact the whole Orthodox community composed of both clergy and people, and not just one of the custodians of the Holy Places nor merely a church of monks. It was this Church of Jerusalem, capable of protecting the Holy Places certainly, but also capable of devoting itself to the service of the poor. In fact, the struggle for the poor was the expression of an ecclesiological conflict. It was an affirmation that the Church should no longer be a church of monks, even of monks defending the Holy Sepulchre, but really and truly a church of pastors and flock, a flock each member of which is called by name by the pastor, and therefore in the mother tongue in which its members have been brought up, the language of its heart and of its prayers.

There was a similar Arabizing movement in Egypt. The Syrians who had migrated to Egypt had taken with them their Arab awareness, but what chiefly provoked their hostility to Hellenism was the negative attitude which the Greeks finally adopted in the matter of union with the Copts. Their Patriarch Macarius, who had contacts with Uspenski, was ready for union. But when he died, Patriarch Callinicos left the patriarchal seat, and the Syrians of Egypt from 1860 to 1870 demanded a share in administering the affairs of the Church.

In 1899, the Hellenes still refused to accept Patriarch Cyril of the Catholic Copts into the Orthodox family. In any union with the Orthodox or Catholic Copts they believed they would lose the Patriarchate, which would fall to the indigenous Orthodox. The Syrians of the Patriarchate of Alexandria then demanded a part in the patriarchal election, in the administration of the property of the Greek Patriarchate, the training of priests, the use of Arabic as well as Greek in the ecclesiastical tribunals, and the consecration of Arab bishops. They were at last granted a bishop who was assigned residence in Ethiopia.

In this social historical context I have just outlined, how was the concern for the poor expressed in concrete terms?

The Patriarchate of Alexandria

Between 1766 and the beginning of the 19th century, a sort of Basiliad was at work in old Cairo, consisting of a hospital, an old people's home, and a restaurant for the poor. In the Greek quarter, there was still a school, established in 1775, which was in part supported by the mainly Arab parish of Damietta. There was also another school in Cairo where in 1812 there were Arab and Greek teachers teaching literature in both languages.

Over long stretches this was a period of persecution. The historian, Al Jabarti,[21] gives an account of these harassments and discriminatory measures. Heavy taxes were imposed. Napoleon levied a tax of Fr. 100,000 on the Syrians, who were mostly Orthodox. Nor did Bonaparte repair the damages inflicted on the Christians by the Muslim mob when the latter rebelled against the French occupation.

At the beginning of the 19th century, there was an Orthodox school in Damietta with courses in Arabic, French, Greek and modern sciences. Pupils from this school entered the civil service, the consular service, or went into commerce. The school was still functioning at the end of the century.[22]

After their sufferings at the start of Mahomet Ali's reign (discriminatory measures concerning dress, equipment, etc.), from 1855 onwards Christians no longer paid the poll tax which had been imposed on them as *dhimmis*. Orthodox Christians began to enter the administration, but most of them chose independent occupations.

In 1856, Hierotheos II founded the Greek Orthodox Society of Cairo, whose membership included both Hellenes and Arabs. Its objects were to maintain the schools, to give medical treatment to indigent sick people, and to assist the needy. This society was responsible for starting new schools in Alexandria and Cairo.

More specifically, the Arabic-speaking community in Alexandria had two associations connected with the Church. In Cairo at this time there were two large charitable societies with workshop, free school and a dispensary.

Tanta had three benevolent associations. Each of the towns of Mansoura, Port Said and Suez had its benevolent association. The Syrian Orthodox, especially those of Alexandria, generally belonged to this fairly prosperous cosmopolitan society.

The Patriarchate of Antioch

Statistics exist for the benevolent societies in the two republics of Syria and Lebanon. These statistics cover only the names of associations known officially to the government, however. In fact, since the work was non-governmental, religious statistics would have been unavailable. From 1856 onwards, there was not a single parish which did not have its organized voluntary social work by means of religious charitable associations. The work was concerned with a variety of needs, in particular, regular direct aid to the needy. Orphanages, old people's homes, medical care, scholarships, religious circles, anti-illiteracy campaigns—these were the main objects of these associations, always under the leadership of the laity, both men and women. More than one of these societies had rules stipulating that aid should be given to people of all confessions, which was remarkable for that period.

In an anonymous Russian report drawn up in 1850 and published in an appendix to J. M. Neale's book on the Church of Antioch, we read the following: "The churches in the Syrian towns are decent; in the villages they are poor enough. The number of extremely poor churches, or of churches which have been plundered by the Albanians and the Druses during the last troubles in the Lebanon, or have been ruined by earthquakes, or which have fallen in from time and want of repair, or which have never been completed or properly furnished, owing to the poverty of the parishioners, are as many as seventy in all the dioceses of the See of Antioch. There is need to restore and furnish all of these churches."[23]

In this period, when organized aid was still in the future, possibly because of the lack of liberties, J. M. Neale also reports: "In the Syrian churches on Sundays and festivals, they make a collection of money on three plates; and this collection goes to the sick and the poor, for the purchase of oil and candles, and for the support of the clergy and teachers; according to the disposition made of it by the churchwardens, who are elected annually by the people and confirmed by the bishop."[24]

But even before the charitable work, social service began with the parish and monastic schools.

In 1833, the Archimandrite Athanasius founded at the abbey of Belmont the first ecclesiastical school, which lasted only a short time. In 1836, the priest Youssef M. al Haddad founded in Damascus a school in which Greek, Turkish, and Italian were taught along with Arabic and which was profoundly religious in orientation. "In the 50s of the last century in Tripoli, part of the church land revenue was devoted by the Greek Orthodox to expand educational facilities and the opening of schools for both boys and girls."[25]

Under the Egyptian occupation the Orthodox established three schools, in Jerusalem, Damascus and Beirut. But the Levantine educational system had long been tied to the parish or the mosque. "The priest passed on what he knew: some elements of arithmetic and readings in the psalms, gospel and a liturgical book. The poor of the Lebanon learned in order to serve the feudals who needed learn nothing except war and hunting."[26] The Orthodox, however, never having known the feudal system, were in this period equals in this elementary institution. "A poor economy, a conservative society and an oral tradition" tended to preserve this system until the day when the blessing of education was extended to large sectors of society as a result of the awakening provoked by the Egyptian occupation, the Russian presence, and the rediscovery of national identity.

At the Zahrat il-Ihssan Girls' College, the Three Doctors' College, both in Beirut, and at the secondary school of Homs and that of Bkeftine in the Tripoli region, to mention only the most important, the level achieved was such as to open great prospects of social emancipation to a large number of pupils.

In small villages, such as Shwayr, Enfeh, Amiun, Souk and Gharb etc., in Little Lebanon, schools were established which made illiteracy almost non-existent among the Orthodox on the eve of the First World War, except in a few isolated places. In Beirut in 1899, there were nine Orthodox schools with 1210 pupils, a third of them girls. Most of the pupils belonged to the middle and poorer classes.

In 1925, there were 16 schools in the Patriarchate of Jerusalem, the two largest being at Jerusalem and Jaffa, the total school population being 800 pupils.[27]

Outside the educational work and charitable services, the Church's social work was shouldered by the convents.

The convent's land ownership

Convents and monasteries of the Greek Orthodox Church of Antioch in Syria and Lebanon own tremendous areas of land belonging to different land-fertility classes. But the convent building and other fertility buildings were always built on fertile, often irrigated land.

The monks were hard field workers and they produced agricultural commodities of high market value. Their life was very simple and thus they saved money and bought more land around their convents.

Today, we have evidence to believe that the monks were innovators in the field of agricultural development. In the area of Koura, North Lebanon, the first banana seedling and the first cypress tree in the whole district were introduced by the Convent of Kaftoun which also had an elementary school.

Similarly, the Convent of Balamand had special permission from Sultan Abdul Hameed to produce first quality tobacco in the area. No other person or institution at the time had a similar privilege.

When during the 19th century the whole of North Lebanon, and to a lesser extent the whole country, relied exclusively on the production of mulberry trees for the support of the natural silkworm, the convents had diversified cropping systems. The convents and monasteries produced, besides mulberry trees, olive trees, grape vine, almond and fig trees, to mention only a few.

When the natural silk industry in Lebanon went broke and the producers were all bankrupt, the people had no longer any need for the mulberry trees. The population, however, did not know what to do or what to produce in order to make a living. The convents and monasteries who already had a diversified cropping system and had mastered the now-called land management science, rushed to the aid of the people, to solve the problem at a national level. Shifting from one crop to the other is not only a technical problem, but a socio-economic and political problem. It is true, because agriculture is a way of life and livelihood for these people. The same problem recently faced the Algerian Government when there was a shift from growing grape vines for wine-making not consumed by the nationals to durum wheat, very much needed in the country and imported in large quantities.

The monks in their convents and monasteries, therefore, were attending to more than the spiritual needs of the people living in their areas. The whole Koura area is noted for its olive crop since the early '20s, and thanks to the role of the monks in this conversion of agricultural production from natural silk-fibre to the olive-oil crop. Their know-how, training, fellowship and financial help were unhesitatingly given to the suffering population around the convents.[28]

Another aspect of the social and economic development undertaken by the convents and monasteries is the important question of share-cropping as a form of land tenure in this country. Although there are many kinds of share-cropping and share-croppers, the system devised by the church is of special importance.

When the monks acquired more land as property of the convents and monasteries, they shared it with the people, who became share-croppers.[29] The people were not workers in the full sense of the word; they were trained to grow something on the land, normally horticultural crops and trees. Since the people were not workers, they had no fixed wages; although the records show clearly that workers were employed by the monks and that wages were paid in cash. The people were to acquire one fourth of the land and the crop trees on it as their share of the agricultural enterprise or undertaking and, as the unwritten law has it, "the share-croppers own one fourth of the roots of the trees". The word "roots" was put there on purpose to emphasize the ownership, not only of the land, but also of whatever grows on it in the proportions of one fourth for the tenant and three fourths for the convent.

Today, this system may seem very bad or at best judged as unjust to the tenant. This may be true, but in the early 19th century it provided many facilities for the people.

First, in order to become a share-cropper, one must be trained to become a better farmer and not a worker or subsistence farmer.

Second, the share-cropper benefited from all the innovations and technical know-how of the convent and monasteries and consequently increase of yield was achieved at the expense of the convent property. If any new variety was to be tested it was always done on the convent's land first. If, on the other hand, it was a failure, only the convent's land would suffer. In this respect, the convent was the "ministry of agriculture" of the people and, at the same time, the "agricultural extension service".

Third, the convent and monastery was exempted from taxes levied at will by the corrupt empire on land and water resources. The convents and monasteries paid only token amounts of money as taxes. The sharecroppers were also exempted from paying any tax because, according to the law, the land was not their property.

Before leaving this section on the human economy, it is of interest to note that prior to the First World War, one bishop (Athanasius of Homs) created a limited company, with himself as chairman, for the development of technology and the training of workers; this was named "Economic Society for the Development of Homs".

The pattern of charitable associations was adopted in the whole of the Arab Orthodox East. It is unnecessary for us to provide a catalogue for the whole of Palestine. The main thing is to grasp the purpose of this religious programme.

In fact, human development was the achievement of these societies and schools. This is why I felt it important to dwell on this. As a religious association, the school was the expression of a milieu. The school was directed by a local council, often the same as that of the benevolent society. The school was the centre for festivals, for artistic competitions. The theatre was more often than not that of the school. The service of the handicapped, the promotion of crafts (needlework, embroidery, etc.) were linked with the school. The teaching of accountancy, elements of commercial arithmetic and the teaching of law at the Bkeftine all helped to make the Orthodox institutions practically attractive.

The main tragedy of this epoch was that social thinking was conducted outside the Church. Before the end of the last century, thinking had already become secularized. Girgi Zaydan (14 December 1861 to 21 August 1914), one of the greatest of modern Arab thinkers, was born into a poor Orthodox family in Beirut. He learned to read from the psalter, though his mother rarely attended church. Trained at the American University, he belonged to that tragic group of those who see religion as an existential concern, as a social solidarity. He asked himself whether religion was not a means for securing political leadership, but he recognized that the greatest good in the world is so in the name of religion.[30] But it was as an Islamic specialist that he was outstanding. He was the only one produced by Arab Christianity in that period. He contributed enormously to the understanding of and love for the Arab heritage. But he suffered because of his "Christian allegiance". Commissioned by the Egyptian University to give a course on Muslim history, he found himself refused entry to the University on the grounds that he was a Christian.

This hospitality towards Islam was evoked by Patriarch Gregory of Antioch in a speech at Zahle on 22 November 1911: "I love all my compatriots of all religions equally.... Are we not all the work of one and the same creator? Do we not all inhabit the same earth? Are not we and the Muslims bound together as belonging to one territory...?"[31]

More important than Zaydan on the social level was Farah Antun (1874-1922), an Orthodox Christian from Tripoli. He, too, was born into a poor family, but remained deeply impressed by the fact that the Bkeftine College, founded by a bishop in a monastery, had a Protestant headmaster, and an *Ulema* as professor of Arabic.

Two quotations will suffice to illustrate his thinking: "You see two classes of people", he wrote in his *New Jerusalem*, "one happy and the other unhappy. One class is clothed in silks, adorned with jewels, lives in vast palaces, drinks wine of all sorts and feeds itself and its domestic animals on all that is sweetest and pleasantest in the earth; the other class, neglected and poor, begs a little bread to appease its hunger and sinks down exhausted on the ground. Seeking shelter but finding none, it stretches out under the open vault of heaven, on the pavements and amid the dust of the great highways. It lives like the wild beasts exposed to the cold of the night and the heat of the day... I have fears for you, not because of the injustice of the mighty, but I fear God's curse on you if you ever raise your hands in blessing on happy humanity and, by doing so, bless the social injustices which are the cause of our miseries."

In another passage in the same work, he writes: "I see the people improving itself by the machine which it directs and becoming the associate of its boss, lifting itself to the same social level and in this way bridging the huge gap which separates them. I see the labouring poor becoming the masters of empires by universal suffrage. I see the coming of the kingdom of true equality..."[32]

Like Zaydan, Farah Antun was also interested in Islamic thought. Moreover, he rejected the Christianity of the Crusaders and called himself a Christian of the East. What a strange sentiment it is to have an Orthodox identity which one is unwilling to reject even though subjectively its dogmatic content is very thin.

Even at the very heart of the Church, we live rather than reflect theologically on the situation of the poor. On being elected as Patriarch in 1899, Meletios wrote a pastoral letter showing that the Christian community is a global reality, both spiritual and social. He struggled against every kind of excess and preached sobriety in festivities, seeking to diminish worldliness and to introduce an almost ascetic style of life.

Christians may have believed that works of charity were sufficient to solve the social problem in a closed society. In a lecture given by a young woman of Homs in 1902, we find a theoretical basis for this vast enterprise of charity. It may be summarized as follows. The fall of man created situations of inequality between human beings, both at the moral level and at the level of fortune. This inequality engenders disorder in the cosmos. But disorder is contrary to the divine justice. Yet God has implanted in us tenderness and compassion for our brothers, so that we may identify ourselves with them in solidarity. The concerted efforts of many are required if solidarity is to become possible. It demands the cooperation of intelligence and noble feeling so that the human community may progress, may establish and maintain the laws of fraternity and non-destruction.[33]

Salwa Salameh had certainly never read St Maximus the Confessor. The restoration of "the order of the cosmos" by educational and charitable enterprises—that was the utopia of the century to which she belonged. But in the abandoned and humbled condition in which Eastern Christianity found itself between 1800 and the end of the First World War, compassion was the great mystery of life. Faith and tenderness remained the special characteristics of the Church of the poor.

NOTES

[1] JEAN FONTAINE: *Le désaveu chez les écrivains libanais chrétiens de 1825 à 1940* ("The Disavowal among Lebanese Christian Writers Between 1825 and 1940") Doctoral thesis presented to the Faculty of Arts, Paris. (Roneoed text.)

[2] ALBERT HURANI: *Arabic Thought in the Liberal Age: 1798-1939*, p. 273. Oxford: 1970.

[3] DEREK HOPWOOD: *The Russian Presence in Syria and Palestine: 1843-1914*, pp. 19 and 21. Oxford: 1969.

[4] On the social study of the Lebanese society of the 19th century, see DOMINIQUE CHEVALLIER: *La société du Mont Liban à l'époque de la révolution industrielle en Europe*. Paris: 1971; TOUFIC TOUMA: *Paysans et institutions chez les Druzes et les Maronites du Liban du 17e siècle à 1914*. Beirut: 1971-1972; WAGIH KAOUTHARANY: *Les tendances socio-politiques au Liban et dans l'Orient arabe: 1860-1920*, second edition. Beirut: 1978. (In Arabic).

[5] YOUSSEF MUZHER: *Histoire générale du Liban*, Vol. I, p. 676 (in Arabic). Beirut.

[6] SOPHRONIUS, the Metropolitan of Tyre and Sidon, launched an appeal to arms in his diocese. His pastoral letter is reproduced *in extenso* in *Histoire générale du Liban*, *op. cit.*, pp. 676 ff.

[7] KAMAL SALIBY: *Histoire du Liban nouveau*, second edition (in Arabic), p. 103. Beirut: 1969.

[8] Cited by DEREK HOPWOOD: *op. cit.*, p. 7.

[9] From the archives of the Russian Synod 1857, cited by DEREK HOPWOOD: *op. cit.*, p. 51.

[10] Dmitrievski, cited by DEREK HOPWOOD: *op. cit.*, p. 101.

[11] See A. L. TIBAWI: *American Interests in Syria: 1800-1901*, p. 226. Oxford: 1966.

[12] This was reported by the orientalist KRACHKOVSKI, speaking about Russian schools in Lebanon which he visited during his stay there from 1908-1910. Cited by DEREK HOPWOOD: *op. cit.*, pp. 152-153.

[13] DEREK HOPWOOD: *op. cit.*, p. 153.

[14] DEREK HOPWOOD: *op. cit.*, p. 163.

[15] See his book, *Le réveil de la nation arabe* (Awakening of the Arab Nation), p. 73. Paris: 1905.

[16] SATI'AL-HUSRI: *Addresses on the Birth of the Nationalist Idea*, first edition, (in Arabic), p. 171. Cairo: 1951.

[17] Cf. ASSAD RUSTOM: *The Church of Antioch the Great City of God*, Vol. 3, (in Arabic). p. 371.

[18] *Jerusalem Review*, sixth year, No. 55, 24 January, 1909, p. 296.

[19] *Ibid.*, p. 296.

[20] *Jerusalem Review*, *op. cit.*, p. 298.

[21] Also JACQUES TAQUER: *Muslims and Copts in Cairo*, (in Arabic), pp. 200 ff. 1951.

[22] Cf. CH. PAPADOPOULOS: *History of the See of Alexandria* (in Greek), p. 782.

[23] J. M. NEALE: *The Patriarchate of Antioch*, p. 227. London: 1873.

[24] *Ibid.*

[25] A. L. TIBAWI: op. cit., p. 158.

[26] LAHD KHATER: *Lebanese Customs and Traditions*, Vol. I (in Arabic), pp. 371 ff. Beirut: 1974.

[27] SHEHADE AND NICOLAS KHOURY: *Khulasat Tarikh Kanisat Orashalim al Orthodoxiyya*, p. 350. Jerusalem: 1925.

[28] G. H. GEHA: *Memorandum about Land and Water Resources of the Diocese of Mount Lebanon*. Greek Orthodox Church of Antioch: 1974.

[29] *Ibid.*

[30] JEAN FONTAINE: *op. cit.*, p. 108.

[31] Cf. ASSAD RUSTOM: *op. cit.*, p. 351.

[32] These two passages are cited by K. I. KHAIRALLAH: *La Syrie*, pp. 107 and 109. Paris: 1912.

[33] See the review, *Al Mahabba*, 1902, No. 152, pp. 45 ff.

8 . Rejection of Christianity by the Indigenous Peoples of Latin America

Julio Barreiro

Of all the countries which make up the vast continent of Latin America, only two, Uruguay and Costa Rica, are now untroubled by what has been called the "Indian problem". The indigenous peoples who lived in these areas have disappeared or have been absorbed by primitive groups in the regions which border on what are today Uruguay and Costa Rica.

One of the most remarkable cases in the history of the ancient American indigenous groups is the *Charrúas*, whose "territory" covered more than half of what is now known as Uruguay, spreading into areas which today belong to Paraguay, Argentina and some southern parts of Brazil. The Charrúas tribes, whose civilization never advanced beyond the late Neolithic stage, were never conquered by white men — either Spanish or Portuguese. Those who survived the battles with the *conquistadores* disappeared into the woods and mountains of Paraguay, Uruguay and the Chaco, or mingled with neighbouring tribes until their own characteristics were no longer distinguishable. The few groups who stayed on in the land they had occupied between the courses of the rivers Negro, Uruguay and Plate of their own accord joined the first bands of gauchos in their struggle against the Spaniards. Later, they too vanished. We know practically nothing of their gods, their worship and religious habits. They never knew the Gospel.

I mention the Charrúas in particular because this is one of the few cases we know of in the history of the conquest of America of an indigenous group which escaped having the Gospel forced upon it.

In other words, I use this particular case in American history to support my claim *a contrario sensu* that Christianity has never been voluntarily accepted by the indigenous people of Latin America.

Apart from the exceptions which prove every rule, the indigenous people of Latin America saw Christianity as one more weapon in the conquistador's plan to impose slavery and exploitation. To the Indian, the religion of the conquistadores throughout the continent was equivalent to the use of the horse, the first fire arms, iron armour and later the humili-

---

Translated from the Spanish by the Language Service, WCC.

ating use of forced service and tithing. For the Indians, there was never much difference between the cross and the sword, not only because the conquistadores' swords were shaped like crosses, but also because the practices and customs which went with the preaching of the cross bore a closer resemblance to the use of the sword than to the proclaimed gentleness of a Gospel which they never really knew.

In the light of modern history and scientific knowledge of how the conquest and colonization of America was carried out by the Spanish and Portuguese, it is not difficult to understand *why* the Indians rejected Christianity. But the question of *how* this rejection took place — in other words, the many ways in which the Indian, though vanquished and subdued, persisted and still persists in forms of resistance to the religion and ideology of the white man — calls for closer analysis.

Their ways of cultivating a religiosity which we call "popular" is perhaps one of the most pronounced features of this resistance and one of the most authentic traits of their ethnic personality.

Unfortunately, for reasons of space, I cannot deal here with both aspects, and I must concentrate on the more homogeneous elements in the rich and complex history of the various indigenous cultures which developed in Latin America before the arrival of the conquistadores from Europe. I cannot, therefore, refer to particular cases among the indigenous races which people our vast continent.

I must also leave aside, after this explicit mention, historical situations which were later created by other forms of religious penetration among the indigenous people; although, in more recent years, missionary practice has been modernized to a certain extent, it has often suffered from old faults due to the piety of men and women whose vocation has been nurtured by a mistaken reading of Latin American history or simply by the absence of such basic knowledge. I am referring, of course, to the practices of the Protestant missions and missionaries. But, for the reasons mentioned above, I cannot deal with this subject here.

The work of the first Catholic conquistadores had such dire effects that, four hundred years later, Protestant missionaries have inevitably experienced the same forms of rejection that the Catholics experienced and still experience at the hands of the Indians.

With a few honourable exceptions — individuals rather than religious groups — modern Protestant and Catholic missions go about their task with little reference to historical factors which would make their efforts worthwhile. They continue to work as they have always done on the basis of abstractions which serve to justify their purely ideological reasoning: they use formulas, evangelical principles, theological assessments, and so on, which mean that sooner or later their labour will prove as fruitless as that of their predecessors in earlier years. This situation becomes much more serious when that abstract reasoning is manipulated by powerful economic interests which use "mission" as a means of invading areas still occupied by indigenous groups whose vast natural resources are coveted by the great centres of international capital.

Historical reasoning, on the other hand, is narrative reasoning — it is the kind of human reasoning which allows us to understand others through their history. It is the understanding which comes from bearing in mind particular stories and facts about the real sufferings of a community or people.

Christian evangelization cannot be authentic if its exponents know nothing of the events which constitute the history of the Incas, the Aztecs or the Mayas, to mention only three of the greatest indigenous cultures which forged the ancient history of vast regions of Latin America. Their history, though scorned by classical historians, is no less real for being less well known or publicized.

We cannot proclaim the Gospel to the families — men and women, young people and adults — who make up the indigenous nations of the Quechuas, Guaranís, Mapuches, Quichuas, Secoyas, Guajiros, Guanás, Tobas, and so on (to name but a few among thousands),[1] unless we are familiar with their history, customs, habits, deities, systems of production, laws, values, traditions, etc.

We must remember that, before the Spanish and Portuguese arrived, Latin America was inhabited and *cultivated* — in the Latin sense of the word — by a rich indigenous stock who had more right than the conquistador to the fruits of the earth and the goods of a civilization which, though it did not call itself Christian, was in no way inferior to those which claimed this title for themselves.

Historical reasoning is left aside when it is a case of trying to explain why the indigenous peoples of Latin America rejected *that* type of Christianity. We turn, then, to abstract reasoning, which easily leads us to think in terms of *infidels*, *pagans* or *barbarians* in our efforts to explain why the preaching of the Gospel to these people failed. The close link shown by historical reasoning between *conquest-colonization-mission-Christianity* is so strong that modern missionaries cannot evade its conclusions. Having made these necessary clarifications, I will continue with my analysis.

Colonial's attitude towards Indian

If we are to discover the real reasons why the American Indians rejected Christianity, we must first define certain categories of thought. Thus, for example, the term "Indian" always seemed to the colonial (and even neo-colonial) mentality to be synonymous with "pagan" and "infidel" — in other words, to refer to an inferior, barbarous creature, marked out for domination. In a way, to adapt a phrase, the Indian would become for the European conquistador "Hegel's slave". "The indigenist policy", says Guillermo Bonfil Batalla, "is simply one particular form of the relationships established by the dominant society with the dominated peoples within a colonial situation." And he adds: "The end of the Indian as a colonial category leads to the vigorous appearance of the many ethnic groups which represent one of America's most precious potential riches." [2]

If we consider the relationship between the Christian conquistador or the missionary Christian and the uncivilized and pagan Indian as if it were the fulfilment of the religious call to "go and preach the Gospel to every creature", forgetting the social, cultural and especially the economic aspects of that relationship, we distort history, forgetting the terrible injustices and cruelties perpetrated by the white man in the conquest of America, and we are guilty of the greatest disservice to the true Gospel of our Lord Jesus Christ.

From the beginning of the Spanish conquest, there were a few men like Fray Bartolomé de Las Casas, a Dominican monk, whose Christian conscience led him to defend the Indians against the abuse of the white man. For the conquistadores, the conquest and colonization of America were conceived as a missionary undertaking rather than an endless campaign of atrocities. The Indians were "infidels" and as such had to be "saved" by being brought into the Holy Church, at whatever cost.

For de Las Casas, the salvation of the Indians was always linked with the establishment of social justice proclaimed by the Gospel of Jesus Christ. De Las Casas saw the Indians not as infidels, but as poor, underprivileged people, oppressed and exploited, especially after they fell under the yoke of the white men. Not for nothing did he call the Indians "the scourged Christs of the Indies".[3] There is eloquent proof that the Indians protected by de Las Casas heard and accepted the Gospel he preached to them in these terms just as fervently as they rejected the Gospel as proclaimed by the monks who came with the soldiers, which amounted to no more than a disguised form of conquest, ill-treatment, slavery and the cruellest exploitation.

There is a letter from Bartolomé de Las Casas to the Emperor in which he says that, if the death and destruction of the Indians were the condition of their becoming Christians, "it would be better if they never became Christians at all".[4]

De Las Casas' belief that the Gospel proclaimed God's justice and that the Indians were not infidels, but poor, underprivileged people, subjected to the injustice of the conquistadores and colonizers, led not surprisingly to the so-called "Indian controversy" during which Bartolomé de Las Casas struggled hard against his colleague, the Dominican monk Juan Ginés de Sepúlveda. Basing his arguments on texts by Aristotle and St Thomas Aquinas, Sepúlveda defended the thesis that the enslavement of the Indians was legitimate, even if it involved war, and that the task of evangelizing "these vulgar, barbarian people, with their unnatural customs" was a special mission which God had entrusted to the conquistadores.

I mention this famous controversy because I believe that the subsequent task of proclaiming the Gospel to the Indians was oriented for more than 400 years by one or other of these two attitudes, with cultural and ideological variations imposed by changing times and customs. Either the American Indian receives Christianity as the proclamation of a kind of social justice which was never applied to him (except in a few contemporary attempts in some Latin American countries), which he then either accepts or rejects, or he rejects in his own way a preaching from which he expects nothing because it promises him nothing which could liberate him as a human being. I say "in his own way", because the Indian had and still has many ways of rejecting Christianity, akin to the special custom which allowed him to hide his idols under the altars of the saints or the Virgin, which, of course, he visits regularly. In the tableland region of Guatemala, I once witnessed a practice which is fairly common among the Indians who go to the Catholic Church on Sundays. After placing his offering of alcohol and flower petals before the image of a Catholic saint, an Indian began to curse the saint and beat with his fists on the glass screen which protected the image, while in his own language he reproached the saint because he had still not granted the rain so desperately needed in the countryside. I have also seen a procession of people, who had attended mass in apparent adoration, towards the middle of Sunday morning, making their way to a secluded place in the woods where they would worship their own idols.

Role of religion in alienation

The Indian's rejection of Christianity is not always a violent one. To suppose that it is would be to ignore the mentality of the Indians and their attitude towards a conqueror who is no longer religious. Passed on from father to son, the rejection of the white man takes many forms, including the religious one.

The marginalization of the Indians merges with the marginalization of the vast mass of poor in Latin America, and it began with the conquest. Any cultural form, any standard of values, any system of production, any ideological expression, any religious manifestation which in any way reproduces or intensifies the oppressor-oppressed relationship, meets with this response. It is not necessarily violent. But at the same time, it would be a mistake to suppose that this submissiveness was always present. From the beginning of the conquest, the indigenous peoples of America rebelled and fought against the conquistadores, just as the slaves did against their masters. Very little documentation has been preserved relating to these wars of resistance.[5] However, there is no shortage of documents concerning the Indians' submission, and it is these which help us to understand the powerful role played by religion in this process of alienation.

As Enrique Dussel so aptly points out, Latin America was established as a colonial Christendom, — a total and totalitarian system, whose religious, military, political, economic and social structure was juridically embodied in the *Compendium of Laws of the Indies*. Merely from observing the role played by the Indians in this collection of laws, it is easy to understand their rejection of Christianity as part of their rejection of the whole system. It was the Indian who paid the highest price for the Spaniards' imperial dream. The system which they established in America was merely the result of Spain's failure as an Empire in Europe itself, at the time of the Turkish invasions, the Protestant Reformation, the division of Germany as an outcome of the Lutheran revolt and the quarrels with France and England. The unity which they had lost in Europe, they sought to recover in the New World inhabited by Indians who would not be difficult to subdue. "What was established in Latin America", says José Míguez Bonino, "was not a Latin American church, but a Spanish church transplanted, together with its liturgy, buildings, laws, feasts and devotions." [6]

When the Indian saw his own gods who were powerless to defend him from the power and brutality of the conquistador being overthrown by the white man, he began to turn in upon himself. His response to Christianity then became a mixture of *submission and rejection*. If you travel today through those parts of Latin America which are inhabited by the millions of descendants of these races subdued by the Spanish, it is easy to see that the indigenous cultures subsist as a form of oppression, and that their ways of working, their customs and feasts, their dress, their way of defending their identity, their value systems and so on, are based on resignation, respect or fear of the authorities, and that they turn to the supernatural to justify and alleviate their pain, wretchedness and unfair treatment.

Today, proclamation is to the poor

The forms of popular religion which they cultivate can help us to realize that the preaching of the Gospel could find a fertile ground among these communities, provided that it spoke to them of the common needs of the poor and marginalized people of the continent, and showed them the way to achieve the liberation for which they long. In other words, today, it is not a question of preaching *to the Indians* or doing missionary work among them. Our task is to proclaim the Gospel *to the poor and the oppressed*.

A study of the various forms of popular religion which exist in Latin America,[7] especially among the indigenous communities, helps us to understand more clearly the hopes and fears of these people. Through the diversity of symbols and religious practices still used with bitter nostalgia for the myths and worship of the gods prior to the time of the conquest (for example, the system of relationships between God-saints-nature-work-society), we can discover the elements which might enable present-day missionaries and church ministers to undertake true evangelization. In many parts of Latin America, such efforts are being made with an honesty and vocational dedication which seem to imply a recognition of the tragic debt the Christian Church owes to the forebears of these suffering communities.

In saying this, of course, it is impossible to ignore the deep ambiguity of this kind of religious practice. The popular piety it expresses contains a strong element of alienation, inasmuch as it permits the continuation of forms of a servile mentality which help to reinforce oppression. However, at the same time, it links those who practise these forms of religion, or who administer them, with the daily lives of the people, their needs, sufferings and hopes.

For the Church and its ministers, the most difficult aspect of this situation is to make use of the continuity of these popular practices to transform the content of the religious consciousness they are designed to express. In other words, it is a question of releasing this consciousness, helping it to move towards forms of liberating praxis, a process in which pastoral action can play a vital role. This could be one of the many expressions of the new Church in the new situation of Latin America.

In this connection, Míguez Bonino has written: "The important thing is to understand the limited and transitory nature of this action and not to sacralize it in a new alienation of the religious conscience. In the final analysis, there cannot be a true process of liberation unless there is in and through it a new, liberated sense of solidarity. And this means overcoming an alienated, dehumanizing religiosity; it means the birth of a new consciousness of faith, of true *metanoia*. This conversion cannot be achieved through religious manipulation or magical transformations of the liturgy, but only by a readiness on the part of the churches to show their solidarity with the oppressed on the painful but joyous road of their struggle for liberation and, in that solidarity, to proclaim a word of encouragement, consolation, hope, invocation, which will indeed be a liberating and stimulating sign of the presence of the crucified, risen Lord who is to come among his people." [8]

In this sense, religious missions to the Indians, who are found in all parts of Latin America, bear an enormous responsibility. The Barbados Declaration: "For the Liberation of the Indian", devotes a whole chapter to this subject, and it speaks very frankly.[9] But it is not enough to make such declarations or even to shoulder such a responsibility. The whole Christian Church is faced with the challenge of the marginalization of more than two-thirds of the population of the continent, deprived not only of basic consumer goods, but also of work, security, health, education, housing, freedom and peace.

The Indians are part of this mass of marginalized people. They can no longer be considered pagans, and they have long since ceased to be barbarians. They are, quite simply and unfortunately, the poor. We can no longer talk of mission "to the pagans" or the "scourged Christs of the Indies". Today, the mission of the Church is to the dispossessed of the earth, the poor, the captive, those who hunger and thirst for justice.

Multinationals, the new conquistadores

Of course, there are still serious problems which relate specifically to the indigenous communities, and they continue to be exploited in new ways as they were in the past. In many parts of Latin America, the trucks, planes and rifles of the multinational companies have replaced the horses, armour and swords of the Spaniards and Portuguese. This is what is happening, for example, in vast areas of the Amazon, where the genocide of whole communities of Indians is taking place so that the new conquistadores from the multinational companies can take over the great mineral and ecological wealth of the region. Indeed, international protests have already been made against the evil work of some Christian missions which contribute to these enormous crimes by applying inexorable methods of sterilization to indigenous communities for unspecified reasons of public health.

At the same time, in Colombia, Peru, Ecuador, Venezuela, Paraguay and certain regions of Central America, indigenous groups which have been unwilling to submit to white penetration have been exterminated or moved to new territories which do not have sufficient natural resources for normal subsistence. Equally dramatic is the situation of the Indians in Bolivia and Peru who, to stay alive, are forced from the age of fifteen or under to go down to the tableland to work in the mines, most of them dying in the tunnels before they reach the age of 30. Or the vast legion of men, women and children of indigenous origin who each year swell the ranks of the migrants; because of the lack of work and poor health conditions in their natural environment, they are obliged to move to the huge, crowded, absurd cities of Latin America, ending up in the "*barrios de emergencia*" (shanty towns), with no security of employment, an easy prey to sickness, malnutrition, economic exploitation, prostitution, and so on.

Faced with such a situation, the Church's task of proclaiming the Gospel to the Indians no longer fits into the traditional mould. The new possibilities will be realized either through the mission of a Church consubstantial with the people, or not at all. The debate about ecclesiology is becoming more and more intense in Latin America. And it is a most welcome one, for it raises the possibility of Christian work through the only instrument able to bring the Gospel to the farthest corners and the most neglected people of the continent — the popular or people's church.

Up till now, there has been no evidence that men reject the Gospel when it speaks to them of the redeeming love of God and the need for social justice, when those who preach it witness to the truth of these claims through the example of their own lives and that of the Church. In the present history of Latin America, only the people's church can go out to meet the afflicted and poor. And these include the Indians. The "scourged Christs of the Indies" of whom Fray Bartolomé de Las Casas spoke have become part of a much larger number who cry more and more loudly for social justice.

NOTES

[1] For more precise and detailed information on the situation of America's indigenous communities today, see: *La Situación del Indígena en América del Sur* (various authors), produced by a symposium organized by the Ethnological Institute of the University of Bern, and sponsored by the Programme to Combat Racism and the Commission of the Churches on International Affairs of the World Council of Churches, held in Barbados. (Bilingual edition, Spanish/Portuguese, published by Editorial Tierra Nueva, Montevideo, 1972, 510 pp. An English edition has also been published in Geneva by the World Council of Churches: *The Situation of the Indian in South America*, 1972.)

Unfortunately, I am not aware of any complete work of this type which deals with the same problems in Central America, the Caribbean and certain parts of North America.

More comprehensive information concerning the process of the conquest and colonization carried out by the Spanish and Portuguese in all the American territories which it affected can be found in RICHARD KONETZKE's excellent book: *América Latina: La Epoca Colonial*. Madrid: Ed. Siglo XXI, 1974, 400 pp. The first version of this work was published in German: *Die Indianerkulturen Altamerikas und die spanisch-portugiesische Kolonialherrschaft*. Frankfurt-am-Main: Fischer Publishers, 1965.

[2] *La Situación del Indígena en América del Sur, op. cit.*, p. 28.

[3] FRAY BARTOLOMÉ DE LAS CASAS wrote: "I leave behind in the Indies Jesus Christ, our God, whipped, afflicted and crucified, not once, but a million times over," in *Historia de las Indias*, O.E., II, p. 356. Quoted by GUSTAVO GUTIERREZ in one of his most recent works: *Teología desde el Reverso de la Historia*. Lima: Ed. Cep, February 1977, 59 pp.

[4] FRAY BARTOLOMÉ DE LAS CASAS, in "Entre los Remedios" (1543), in *Obras Escogidas*. Madrid: BAE, 1958.

[5] I quote a few examples from the few documents available. There is evidence, for example, that the rebellion headed by Juan Santos Atahualpa in the Andean region towards the middle of the 18th century was inspired by a passion for justice which he found in the Gospel. (GUSTAVO GUTIERREZ: *Teología desde el Reverso de la Historia, op. cit.*) The complex history of the "*Cristeros*" in Mexico is also a good illustration. See MARÍA ISAURA PEREIRA DE QUEIROZ: *Historia y Etnología de los Movimientos Mesiánicos*. Mexico: Siglo XXI, 1969. Another good example is the rebellion of Tupac-Amaru. See BOLESLAO LEWIN: *Tupac-Amaru: Su Epoca, Su Lucha, Su Hado*. Buenos Aires: Ed. Siglo XX, 1973, 186 pp.

[6] José Míguez Bonino: "La Piedad Popular en América Latina", in *Cristianismo y Sociedad*, second series, No. 47. Buenos Aires: 1976.

[7] In Latin America, in recent years, a rich bibliography of books and magazines has been accumulating on this subject. See, for example, No. 47 of the magazine, *Cristianismo y Sociedad (op. cit.)*, devoted entirely to this theme. For further information, we recommend volumes 1, 2 and 3 of the *Bibliografía Teológica Comentada del Area Ibero-Americana*, published by the Protestant Institute of Advanced Theological Studies (ISEDET), Buenos Aires, April 1976 and December 1976. Comprehensive and up-to-date information on the subject can be found under the heading "Popular Religiosity".

[8] José Míguez Bonino: "La Piedad Popular en América Latina", *op. cit.*

[9] *La Situación del Indígena en América del Sur, op. cit.*, pp. 502-505.

9 • The Church and the Poor in Asian History

C. I. Itty

The title of this chapter, "The Church and the Poor in Asian History", can be misleading. Therefore, a word of explanation is appropriate. First of all, the period of Asian church history under discussion here is confined to the last three centuries, in other words the modern missionary era. Though the history of the Church in Asia is as old as the Christian Church itself, the period between the 17th and the 20th centuries is chosen because this volume is devoted to that period. Secondly, the discussion is limited to certain countries in Asia. Among them, the primary focus is on India because of the author's intimate knowledge of the area. Moreover, it is impossible to attempt a comprehensive review of church history of such a vast continent as Asia within the limited space of this chapter. Thirdly, though the title refers to the relationship between the Church and the poor, this chapter is equally about the relationship between the Church and the rich or dominating classes.

I. COLONIALISM, MISSIONS AND CHURCHES

With the exception of the churches related to the Syrian Christian Community in Kerala, South India, all the other churches in Asia came into being as a result of western missionary efforts since the 16th century. The period of missions in Asia coincided with the period of western domination. But it was more than a coincidence. Colonial powers and western missions complemented each other or even collaborated in promoting and maintaining western domination over Asian peoples over more than four centuries. When Vasco da Gama, pioneer, western navigator and explorer anchored his fleet off Calicut in May 1498, there were 20 canons on the deck and a flag above with painted cross. According to the Indian historian, K. M. Panikkar,[1] this picture which depicts the relationship between western military power and Christian missions, symbolized both the reality and the dominant image of the colonial period in Asia! However, the nature and intensity of this unholy alliance between colonialism and western missionary enterprises varied from time to time, and from country to country.

Mutual support

The Christian churches in western countries by and large supported their nations in their efforts at colonial domination. It was more so in the case of those countries where the relationship between Church and state was close. The Portuguese and Spanish governments received sanction and blessings from the church authorities for colonial expansion. According to the Papal bull promulgated in the 15th century, Portugal and Spain were given the right to sail the seas, conquer new lands and acquire riches, and were assigned the duty to "Christianize" the people of those lands, and to be financially responsible for the welfare of the churches and the religious institutions.[2] In the case of the British, the Anglican Church sent chaplains to accompany soldiers sent to protect British interests, but became involved in colonial expansion. Similarly, the Dutch Reformed Church sent chaplains along with their army in their conquests of Ceylon and Indonesia.

The different colonial powers gave varying degrees of support and protection to missionaries, especially those from their own countries. There again, the relationship between the Portuguese and Spanish colonial governments and the Catholic missions were the closest. The kings of Portugal were patrons of the new churches in their colonies in Asia. They appointed vicars and prelates to the dioceses. The churches depended on the civil authorities for financial support for the maintenance of clergy, construction of church buildings, religious institutions and even their running expenses.

Though the British East India company had chaplains to minister to their British employees, for a long time they were forbidden to do any sort of evangelism among the non-Christians. Only by the year 1698, when the charter of the company was renewed, a clause was added which permitted the chaplains to instruct the local inhabitants in the Anglican and Protestant faith. From then on, the company and later the British rulers provided a certain degree of support to missionary work. The only country in which the British did not permit missionary work was Malaysia due to an agreement entered into with the Muslim rulers. Similarly, missionaries were kept out of the island of Bali by the Dutch until the early part of this century.

In many instances, the support that the missions received from the colonial governments was more than normal state generosity. For example, in China, by the terms of the 1860 treaty forced upon her by France all properties belonging to the Catholic Church in the past centuries had to be restored, regardless of how many times the ownership had changed. In general, the Roman Catholic missions insisted upon their rights more openly and rigorously than the Protestants, although there were isolated cases where they also sought and used the political power of their home governments to further the obtaining of property for churches, Christian schools and residences.[3]

Collaboration in exploitation
There were instances, in several countries, of collaboration by missionaries with colonial powers in the domination and exploitation of the poor

masses. Perhaps it was in the Philippines that such exploitation was more manifest and blatant than in any other country. *Readings in Philippine History* by Horacio de la Costa [4] presents a vivid picture, based on historical documents, of the collaboration by Roman Catholic priests in colonial exploitation. For example, it was common practice in the early period of colonialism to force the dispersed villagers to vacate their lands and to resettle them in large communities. This practice facilitated the take over of lands by the Spaniards, the extortion of taxes and tributes from the peasants, as well as the political control of the people. The priests cooperated with the civil and military personnel in this process. In a few instances, the Church gained some of the lands for itself. The resettled communities were often forced to build churches and town halls. The priests found it easier to conduct their religious instruction and systematize their pacification programmes among the settled communities.

The friars (priests) also participated in extorting grain and services from the people without paying them and charged them exorbitant fees for their ministries. A letter of Charles II to the provincial superiors of the religious orders in the Philippines, dated 31 December 1677 points out: "He (Don Diego de Villatore, proctor general of Manila) adds, however, that while this province of Pampanga used to have a numerous native population, it now has less than eight thousand taxpayers. The reason for this decline is an abuse introduced by the governors of that colony, namely, the so called *bandalas* whereby they requisition from the province on credit twenty thousand *fanegas* (55½ litres) of rice each year, and some years thirty and forty thousand *fanegas*. Every man and woman is assigned to a certain quota which they are compelled to deliver by force. The wretch who cannot fill his quota because he had not planted any rice to begin with is cast into prison and his property impounded until he is able to make good his assessment. On top of that, they are importuned by the *alcaldes mayores*, police officers, clerks of court and parish priests of the said province who compel these miserable natives to support them *gratis* and without payment and take what they please from them by force and extortion, so that between them they have the towns filling some quota or other every week. The labour of many of the natives is taken up in this way, causing them great damage and losses, for they must pay besides, and they do pay promptly their taxes and voluntary contributions to the government." [5]

No doubt, the situation in the Philippines under the Spanish was an extreme case. Besides, the special relationship between the Church and the state in Spain facilitated the close collaboration of Catholic missionaries with the colonial governments. As a similar pattern of Church-state relationship existed in Portugal, the collaboration between the churches and colonial administration was also quite close in the Portuguese territories in Asia, such as Goa, East Timur, Macao and others. During the early period in Goa, for instance, the Christian population both foreign and indigenous, was allowed more rights and privileges than the non-Christians. Though elsewhere in Asia neither the churches nor the Christians gained as much material benefit from the colonial governments as those under the Spanish and Portuguese rule, nevertheless, it cannot be said that they gained nothing. For example, certain lands and real estate that the churches possessed were donated by the government or the ruling classes or bought cheaply with government help. It is also a well-known fact that Christians were a preferred section of the society for government jobs and other lucrative positions.

II. CHRISTIAN PARTICIPATION IN THE NATIONAL STRUGGLE FOR FREEDOM

This close alliance between colonialism and missions or churches is not the whole picture. There were people and movements within the churches as well as in the missions who raised their voices against colonialism and imperialism. A few examples are given below.

India

In India, the growing national consciousness against British rule found expression in the formation of the Indian National Congress in 1885. At that time, the leadership was in the hands of the educated middle class who were liberals in their political orientation. Their demand was not national independence, but greater political participation in the government, together with social and economic improvement. A number of Christians supported the Congress at that stage. "At the Madras meeting of the Congress in 1887, out of 607 delegates 35 were Christians. The Indian Christian community was also represented at the next four sessions of the Congress. The proportion of the Indian Christian delegates to the Congress sessions was much higher than their proportion in the population".[6] But by the turn of the century, Christian participation in the Congress sessions declined considerably due to several factors: the trend in the Congress to demand independence, radical tendencies in the nationalist movement; the growing opposition to and even suppression of the Congress by the British government; the fear that the interests of the Christian community might be seriously threatened by the dominant Hindu community if India attained independence; the missionary opposition to nationalism, and so on. So much so, by the time Mahatma Gandhi took the leadership of the Congress Party and launched the non-cooperation movements (1920-1923) and mass agitation, there was hardly any Christian participation. However, there were Indian Christian leaders like K. T. Paul, S. K. Dutta and V. S. Azariah who challenged the Christian community to recognize the legitimacy of the nationalist movement and to support the cause of Indian independence. According to K. T. Paul, the secretary of the Council of YMCAs of India, Christian participation in the national struggle for independence was a

God-given opportunity and a Christian duty. He wrote in 1911: "It would not only be a lamentable misapprehension of the spirit of Christ, but also a grievous neglect of a God-given opportunity, if it is not realized that Indian Christians have a tremendous duty in regard to the secular crisis in India".[7]

Most missionaries did not see it that way. They continued to be loyal supporters of British rule and were generally critical of the independence movement. One of the few who advocated an end to colonial rule was C. F. Andrews; he saw it as domination by the white race. He wrote: "Such dominance of one race over all others is by no means a sacred trust from God; it is rather a sordid commercial conquest and exploitation in which the 'white' race prejudice forms an important and integral part." [8] He asked if "independence which is every Englishman's birthright had made my own life free and fearless, what right have I to enslave others". Later in the 1930's, many Christians were convinced that the secular, socialist policies advocated by Jawaharlal Nehru offered the best hope for their community and nation. Some of them took a leading role in the 1940s, during the last stage of the independence movement.

China

In China, the nationalist struggle during the 19th century was against both the Manchu dynasty which ruled the country, and the various foreign powers who were competing with one another for territorial gains, economic exploitation and cultural influence. The first popular revolt happened in 1840 which was known as the T'ai P'ing rebellion.[9] A certain hakka by name of Hung H'siu-Ch'uan, on the basis of certain Protestant tracts, felt called to establish a heavenly kingdom and mobilized masses to revolt against the king and the foreigners. It was put down by the combined forces of the king and foreign powers. The second rebellion happened in 1899, known as the Boxer Revolution. It was specifically an anti-foreign upheaval, aimed at driving out the hated foreigners from the land and doing away with their political, economic and cultural invasion. It was missionaries who bore the brunt of the attack. In all, over 200 foreign missionaries were slaughtered. About 2,000 Chinese Protestants and about 30,000 Chinese Roman Catholics lost their lives.[10]

By the turn of the century, an organized political movement began to take shape. The Kuomintang or nationalist party was formed under the leadership of Sun Yat-Sen, a Protestant. There were other Christian leaders in the movement. However, when the communist party took the upper hand in the freedom movement, the nationalist party opposed it and the power struggle began. Most of the Christians gave their backing to the nationalists.

Korea

The Korean nationalist movement began with the formation of a restoration movement called "the independence association". It was founded by a Christian liberal and progressive minister, Dr Chae Pil Soh. Several other Christian liberals were members of it. The Independence Association broke up in 1899 when the concern of the nationalist movement became concentrated more towards social rather than political reform. At that time the Church opened its door to society. "She promoted a progressive attitude towards the nationalist movement through lectures, debates, training classes, night schools, dramatic performances and the like."[11] Since the Church took up social reform, it became a centre for the national independence movement and a new political climate was created. However, their concern was not as much political as social reform and character formation.

The independence uprising of 1 March 1919 was a significant event. Stimulated by students, leaders within the country organized a nation-wide independence uprising. Among the 33 leaders who signed the declaration of independence, 16 were Christian when only 3% of the population were Christians.[12] The uprising was suppressed by the Japanese government, and the national leaders were arrested. But, unhappily, after the end of 1920 when the Japanese oppression increased, the social activity of the Church became weak.

The Philippines

As mentioned before, no other society in Asia suffered as much from collusion of the Church with colonial powers as the people of the Philippines. At the same time, it is true that no other church in Asia played such a leading role in fighting against the same colonial powers. It was from within the same Catholic Church that the first voices of protest against colonialism were raised. It was as much against ecclesiastical colonialism as against political colonialism. Towards the end of the 19th century, under the leadership of a number of devout Catholic laymen and priests, a national movement for independence emerged. At the same time, a Catholic layman, Isabelo de los Reyes, took the lead in organizing workers. The labour movement joined forces with others in the fight for freedom.

Both the colonial powers and the Spanish hierarchy were badly shaken by the widespread unrest among the people and the growing demand for national independence. The ecclesiastical hierarchy and the political authorities tried their best to suppress the struggle and forbid Catholic priests and laymen from joining the movement. Such efforts produced two contrary results. On the political level, the United States of America made use of the occasion to overthrow the Spanish government and establish itself as the new colonial power. On the ecclesiastical level, a new Independent Church of the Philippines came into being in 1902. Fr Aglipay, who served as a priest with the freedom fighters, was consecrated bishop of the new church.[13] About half a million people belonging to the working classes left the Spanish-dominated Roman Catholic Church and joined the new Independent Church. The new church also took into its fold most of the nationalist laymen and priests of the time.

Other countries

Christian individuals and communities played a significant role in the struggle for independence in several other countries of Asia. A special mention must be made of Indonesia in this connection. Though the Christian population in Indonesia is not more than 5% of the total, a larger proportion of Christians are in leading positions in national life. One of the reasons for this is the role that Christians played in the national struggle for independence. (It should be mentioned, however, that many Christians in East Indonesia did not support the independence movement.) Throughout the history of the national movement, many Christians occupied positions of leadership. General Simatupang was a leader of the army which fought the Dutch. Dr J. Leimina and Dr A. M. Tambunan were the leading figures in the political wing of the nationalist movement.

III. THE CHURCHES' INVOLVEMENT IN SOCIAL SERVICE

Christian missions in Asia, as elsewhere, had from their very beginning a manifest concern for the poor and the oppressed. In the early stages of the Roman Catholic missions, their concern was mainly for new converts from the poor sectors of society. For example, Francis Xavier, the pioneer in Catholic missionary work in Asia, converted large sections of poor fishermen along the coastal regions of India and Ceylon. Soon after, the need was felt to provide such assistance as education and material help for the social and economic uplift of these people. Therefore, schools were started to provide education, including religious instruction. Similar efforts were initiated in all other places where Catholic missions spread.

The Protestant missions often followed a different path. Most of them initiated charitable work more as a form of service to the people who were mostly non-Christians. However, much of their efforts were meant as a preparation for preaching the Gospel. In later years, both the Roman Catholic churches and the Protestant churches developed their service programmes with all three objectives in view: that is, service to the people, service to Christian communities and a means of witness and evangelism. During the struggle for independence and after, the notion of the Christian contribution to nation-building was added as a fourth objective.

Education

The sphere of service in which most of the missions and churches have given the greatest attention is education. In the Philippines, where Christians were a majority, almost all the educational institutions and efforts were either controlled or influenced by churches. In other countries of Asia, where Christians remained a tiny minority, the Christian involvement in education was large and impressive. The objective was to help the poor move out of their world of ignorance and isolation into a more meaningful life in society, with a better standard of living. In India, the missions introduced the modern school system right from the beginning of their work in the early part of the 17th century. However, only after the arrival of the Protestant missions and expansion of Roman Catholic efforts during the 19th century did the educational efforts become a nation-wide programme, including university education. In the period before 1833, the bulk of Christian educational enterprises consisted of elementary education in Indian languages. Between 1833 and 1857, the emphasis was on secondary schools and colleges with English as the medium. During this period, a number of Christian colleges were established in different cities in India. Until the end of the 19th century, church-sponsored educational institutions dominated the scene. With the gradual expansion of educational efforts by the government and non-Christian agencies, the proportionate share of church-sponsored institutions began to decline considerably. However, the involvement of the churches continues to be significant both in quality and in quantity even today. At present, "the Christian community of India, numbering about 15 million, is responsible for the education of 3 million of India's children, more than half of whom are non-Christian ... If university education alone is taken, there are today 176 colleges (that is university-related institutions) in India with a total strength of 155,000 ... In fact, 1 out of 16 of the university students of India studies in a Christian college." [14]

The history of churches and missions in other countries of Asia presents very similar trends to those in India. Christian missions pioneered in introducing modern school systems in almost every Asian country. In a number of countries, university-level education was also initiated by the Christian churches. Their involvement in education is far more than the proportionate strength of the Christian population in the nation.

In Indonesia, for instance, the Protestant churches have about 3,700 schools, 12 institutions of higher education and 5 universities.[15] In Korea today, there are 11 Protestant colleges and universities, 81 high schools and innumerable middle and primary schools.[16] Even in China, before the period of the revolution, churches made a significant contribution in the educational field. For example, in 1940 there were 13 Christian universities and 200 middle schools run by Protestant churches and a much larger number of elementary schools.[17]

Health services

Another field in which missions rendered pioneering service is health services, more precisely, medical work. In fact, the modern system of medical services, based on western medicine and dispensed through clinics, hospitals, sanatoria and so on, was introduced into Asian countries through Christian missions. In contrast to education, the efforts in this field became large and significant only at a later period, that is, since 1870. Thereafter, by the establishment of Christian hospitals, medical and missionary training institutions, this form of missionary activity became prominent in countries such as India and China. The first Protestant missionary to Korea was a medical doctor, Dr Horace N. Allen. The missionary work which became so successful at a later stage with one of the largest Protestant communities in Asia had its origin in the medical services initiated by Dr Allen in 1884.

By the turn of the century, most countries in Asia, the governments and non-Christian private agencies had expanded their programmes of health care. Thus, the place of Christian medical institutions became proportionately less than before. However, they were still recognized as providing better services than state-run institutions. Besides, in the nursing profession and the training of nurses, Christians have continued to exercise a major role. In 1931, in China, 90% of the nurses were Christian.[18] In India, in 1940, it was estimated that a similar percentage of all nurses were Christian, and that 80% of these had been trained in Christian institutions.[19]

The most significant aspect of Christian medical work was and, to a great extent continues to be, that health care was made available to the neglected poor in the rural areas. Christians pioneered in this service, besides developing facilities for women who would not be treated by men.

Social welfare

The social work of the Christian missions, extended to other fields also, such as, orphanages, schools for the blind, deaf and dumb, mental hospitals, houses for widows and unwed mothers. In most of these, missionaries were the pioneers. In times of famine, which hit countries such as India and China often, the missions and churches rendered great service. For example, during the years between 1877 and 1900, when there was a severe famine in India, Christian churches organized major relief programmes. As a result, many people, mostly beneficiaries of relief work, became Christian. Both in India and in China, the biggest increase in the membership of the Christian churches occurred during and after periods of famine. Though this fact can be interpreted in different ways, the main point is that it reveals the active involvement of churches in caring for the poor and the destitute, and the impact it made on the local population.

Economic development

By and large, economic development is an area which the missions entered quite late and even with little resources and imagination. Only at the beginning of this century was any significant effort made in this field. When large sections of the poorest population joined the churches, the missionaries and church leaders were confronted with the necessity of improving the standard of living of those people. In response here and there, churches initiated programmes such as handicrafts, leather work, brick and tile making, and similar small-scale employment schemes. In some of the rural areas with majority Christian populations, efforts were made to improve agricultural production and to organize cooperatives and credit unions. In a few countries, such as, India, the Philippines and Korea, agricultural training institutions were also established. However, as indicated before, the involvement of the churches in this field continued to be very little when compared to their involvement in social service activities: education, health services and other welfare programmes.

Inadequacy of the welfare approach

Were the poor sectors of the population the main beneficiaries of these various social service efforts? In the case of famine relief, orphanages, institutions for the handicapped, etc., the poor were the main beneficiaries. The same could not be said of the educational and medical services. When a mission established a school or a hospital in a locality, it was meant to serve all the people in the area, irrespective of their economic and social backgrounds. But in actual practice, the rich and the middle class in the society made better and more use of these services than the poor. The poor people often lacked the awareness of the value of school education or western medicine and also the minimum economic means to make use of these services. Among the poor, those who were Christians benefited more than others, as the Christian institutions provided them with additional incentives and assistance.

How effective were these efforts in the fields of education, medical care and economic development in combatting social problems such as poverty, illiteracy, disease, underdevelopment etc? Very little research was done to make an assessment of the effectiveness of these approaches. Besides, the situation varies from country to country. Certain in-depth studies made in India indicate serious inadequacies, if not failures, of these institutional social service programmes to overcome long-range social problems. To illustrate, two case studies are worth mentioning.

One is a study of a Christian village called Bishrampur in central India.[20] The mission started their work there about 110 years ago. During the early period, the mission acquired 1,600 acres of land from the government and distributed it among the newly converted villagers. A school was established which was one of the first in the area. The mission also established a printing press and also a technical school which functioned for many years, before closing down. Several other initiatives such as poultry, new methods of farming and a bonefactory were undertaken during different periods. In spite of all these efforts involving large amounts of foreign resources and the dedicated services of many persons, today "the village represents a tragic picture of one of the most backward villages and consists of poverty-stricken people". Their standard of living is as bad as the poorest villages in the area.

The other study involved a socio-economic survey of the Christian community in a larger area called Malawa, including several villages and two cities, Indore and Mhow.[21] It indicates similar conclusions. In spite of the fact that the Christian communities in this area were the beneficiaries of Christian institutions and social service programmes during the last 100 years, the social and economic situation of village Christians is not better than that of other villagers in the area.

A team that examined the development project undertaken by the Roman Catholic Church in India in recent years made the following observation regarding the past efforts of the Church in the fields of education, health and welfare services. "These forms of action have most often developed according to a perspective which has been principally caritative and have integrated very little, or not at all, the dimensions of economic, social and political judgments and have acted very little, or not at all, on the causes of the situations within which these activities took place, but limiting for the people concerned, the most negative effects of these situations".[22]

The above-mentioned studies indicate that the social service programmes of the churches often failed to address the root causes of poverty, social deprivation and injustice. Paternalism of missions, lack of participation of the people, inadequate understanding of the systemic causes of poverty, and other such factors could have contributed to this failure.

IV. AGENTS OF SOCIAL CHANGE

From the very beginning of Christian missions, the churches in Asia had a deep concern for the most oppressed, depressed and marginalized sections of society. In almost every country, missionary efforts were focused on them. In the caste-ridden society of India, the low caste and the untouchables received major attention. In countries like Indonesia and Burma, missionary work was mainly among the minority groups. In a number of countries, much effort was made among the hill tribes, who had a marginal existence. The fact that the preponderant majority of the membership of Asian churches was drawn from such poor, oppressed and marginal groups is partly due to the attention of missionaries being deliberately concentrated among them, and partly to the special appeal and relevance of the Gospel in their situation.

Challenge to the caste system

T. V. Philip, an Indian church historian, writes: "The work of the Christian Church among the depressed classes of people is a glorious chapter in the history of Christianity in India. The stigma of untouchability that rested upon them for generations had condemned them to a semi-human existence. They were systematically exploited and kept down for centuries by caste people. For many who joined the Church, it represented an escape from the dehumanizing values and conditions of their existence. It was its concern for personal dignity and equality of persons which gave the Gospel relevance and appeal among the outcasts. With the liberation from various social and cultural limitations and with the educational facilities provided by the Church, the converts from outcast and underprivileged groups made a striking progress in their social and cultural life. This itself was enough justification for the work of the Church among these people, and was a contribution to the national life." [23] Besides, these efforts contributed a great deal to the awakening of the backward classes within the Hindu society as to their rights and privileges, to the creation of public consciousness of the evils of the age-old caste system, leading eventually to a constitutional and legal ban on discrimination based on caste. Untouchability was abolished in the constitution of India. (Its practice persists in some rural areas today, but illegally.)

Concern for the oppressed

Missionary work among the tribals in India had a similar effect. Most of them lived in relatively isolated areas, in the hilly regions all over the country. They, too, were victims of poverty, economic exploitation, forced labour and social discrimination. The efforts of the churches among them provided them with a new sense of dignity and a new consciousness about their legitimate place in society. In areas where the churches were active, the tribals succeeded in liberating themselves from the practice of forced labour, became owners of the land they were cultivating, organized cooperatives and credit unions and improved their educational, social and economic conditions.[24] Similar work was carried out by the churches among the tribals in Laos, Taiwan, Philippines and other countries in Asia.

In the Indonesian archipelago, the Javanese were numerically, culturally and economically the dominant majority. The successive stages of the religious influence of Hinduism, Buddhism and Islam were also focused on the people of Java. But Christian missions did not follow the same path. Instead, they concentrated their attention on the other islands, such as, Ambon, Celebes, Sumatra, Timur and Kalimantan. By doing so, the various communities in these islands were able to progress educationally, socially and economically and find their rightful place in the Indonesian nation as a whole.

Women have been another oppressed sector of Asian society. According to the traditional laws and customs of Hinduism, Islam and Confucianism, the women occupied an inferior place. Christianity challenged the perpetuation of this traditional status of women. One of the practical ways in which the churches presented this challenge was by opening up educational opportunities for women. In India, from about 1870, a large number of schools and colleges were established for women by the Protestant and Catholic churches in different parts of the country. Similar initiatives were taken in China, Korea, Japan, Sri Lanka, Burma and other countries. Many of the pioneers in the struggle for the emancipation of women in almost all countries of Asia were either Christians or women educated in Christian schools and colleges.

Revolutionary ferment

During the last three hundred years, the traditional Asian societal structures and values have been seriously challenged. The ancient hierarchical structures of society had been shaken. The feudal economic structures had been challenged. The traditional unity of culture and religion has been broken. Politics, law, education and many other realms of life are gradually being secularized. Concepts such as fundamental human rights, social justice, equality of citizens irrespective of their class, caste and creed, and rights of minorities in a pluralistic society are increasingly being accepted in societal structures and relationships. In this process of social transformation, the impact of western culture, science and technology, political and economic organization played the major role. However, the churches were an important contributing factor.[25] The Christian communities, through their Christian faith and values, their life and mission, made a significant contribution, in spite of their minority status. The churches also had an indirect role in bringing about reform and resurgence within the ancient religions of Asia, such as Hinduism, Buddhism, Confucianism and Islam.

V. CHALLENGE OF EVANGELICAL POVERTY

Rich churches in poor societies! This was a common comment on the church situation in most Asian countries. A number of factors had contributed to this general impression. The most important among them were the following: the connection of the churches with missions from rich western societies; the flow of foreign resources; the relatively high standard of living of missionaries and local church leaders; large numbers of paid employees on the payroll of the churches; and the growing size and number of Christian educational and welfare institutions.

Some of these factors were either inevitable or part of a natural course. It is understandable that the missionaries, coming from more prosperous societies, required a certain level of standard of living, which in their opinion was reasonable and necessary but which was seen by the generally poor Asian societies as rather luxurious. It was also natural that the missions transplanted the organizational structures and style of work that they were used to in their own societies. But what was normal in the West appeared strange and affluent in the Asian situation. In a similar way, it so happened that even the educational and welfare institutions with their buildings, equipment and employees became as much symbols of power as of Christian charity.

It was not merely the poverty of the society around that made this situation so anomalous; the fact that the majority of Christians belonged to the poorest sectors of society made the relatively expensive structures of the churches strange and unauthentic. The church members by and large had very little contribution to make and very little control over these institutions. Of course, many of them were beneficiaries. However, all of them felt a false sense of pride in belonging to an organization which projected signs of wealth, power and prestige.

This anomalous situation had the negative effect of preventing the poor people from recognizing or appreciating that dimension of the Gospel which questions undue reliance on worldly wealth and power. Besides, it proved to be a poor witness to the Hindus and Buddhists for whom voluntary poverty is a supreme virtue and a religious value. It is part of the fundamental beliefs of both Hinduism and Buddhism that in order to attain ultimate liberation or salvation from the law of Karma (law of retribution for one's acts in life) and the wheel of Punarjanmam (transmigration or rebirth) one must practise penance, asceticism and detachment from wealth, and worldly things and ways of life. Besides, the main communicators of the faith among Hindus are the Sadhus and among Buddhists the Bhikkus. Both these categories of people are those who have renounced wealth and material possessions, and lead a life of simplicity, asceticism and contemplation. They receive no salary; they live on food given freely by people. According to the census conducted in 1901, there were 1,142,157 Sadhus in India; in 1951 their number was estimated at 5-6 million.[26] The number of Buddhist monks in Sri Lanka, Thailand, Indochina, China, Japan, Korea, during the period of the missions was considerable.

Though by and large neither the missionaries nor the leaders of the young churches paid much attention to the factors mentioned above, there were a few exceptional initiatives, especially in the Indian churches.

Responses by charismatic individuals and groups

The first attempts in this direction were undertaken by the Jesuit missionary, Robert de Nobili, who arrived in Madurai, South India, in 1606. Realizing the need for communicating the Gospel through indigenous patterns of thought, values and ways of life, he lived the life of a Brahmin Sanyasi. He and his disciple, Father Vico, began a small ashram in the Hindu style and lived a simple life. Later on, he took to the life of a Sadhu, the wandering Hindu teacher. "With a band of devoted followers, de Nobili wandered all over South India from village to village, from city to city, teaching, comforting and baptizing. The wandering pilgrim commanded the respect of all who came in contact with him. Churches sprang up all over South India."[27] After about forty years of work, he retired to live in a mud hut near the shrine of St Thomas at Madras and died at the age of eighty. It was estimated that not less than 100,000 persons became Christian due to his work. His disciples, both missionaries and indigenous leaders, carried on the work of de Nobili and added more numerous converts to the Christian Church. But, later, with opposition from local non-Christian leaders, the conquest of the area by Muslim rulers, and the departure of Jesuit missionaries as a consequence of the suppression of the Jesuit order in Portugal in 1759, the noble work of de Nobili and the Madura mission declined and even collapsed.

Ever since, the challenge of evangelical poverty has been dormant in the Indian churches. It began to reappear as a serious issue only as late as the beginning of the present century. Even then, it was confined to a few attempts by certain charismatic individuals and movements.

Within the Protestant churches, among those who made significant witness through voluntary poverty, simple styles of life and indigenous modes of communication of faith, Narayan Vaman Tilak, B. C. Sircar and Sadhu Sunder Singh were notable examples. Tilak lived the life of a Sanyasi and communicated his faith through poems and lyrics in the Marathi language. Sircar practised yoga and set up a Christian shrine at Puri. Sunder Singh was the most famous of Christian Sanyasis. He travelled throughout India, went into Tibet, and witnessed to the Christian faith through his simple life and evangelical preaching. A great many non-Christians were brought to Christ. Besides, he challenged the Christian community to realize the value and power of evangelical poverty.

Among Roman Catholic individuals, special mention must be made of Peter Reddy and Sadhu Ittyavirah. Reddy left his teaching career in a Catholic college in South India and took to the life of a vagrant preacher and wandering beggar. He took his inspiration from the life of St Francis of Assisi. Sadhu Ittyavirah interrupted his course in the Jesuit college of Kurseong, left the Society and became an itinerant witness. He did so out of a deep conviction to follow the example of Christ "who became poor and helpless for our sake".[28]

The Missionaries of Charity, founded in 1949 by Mother Teresa of Calcutta, is perhaps the most significant response to the challenge of evangelical poverty. Members of the congregation take the vow to be poor, to love and serve the poorest of the poor. It is based on the belief that to "love the poor and to know the poor, they must be poor themselves". [29] Today, there are over 870 sisters and 180 novices belonging to the congregation, and its membership extends to several other countries. A parallel congregation of brothers started in 1963 and now counts 140 brothers and six priests. In many slums and villages of India, those belonging to this congregation are providing sacrifical service to the most needy, neglected and destitute. Another congregation dedicated to evangelical poverty is the one known as the Servants of the Poor.

Within the Protestant churches, the most important development was the Ashram movement. It began in the 1920's, out of the growing concern for indigenous expressions of Christian community life within the context of the poor villages of India. An ashram is the residential centre of a small community of individuals, in a few cases families, who are committed to simple living, prayer and service to the poor. More than twenty such ashrams came into being in various parts of India and Sri Lanka.

According to the tradition of the Syrian Orthodox Church, holy living is often associated with simplicity, piety and devotion. Throughout its history there were bishops, monks, priests and laymen who led such saintly lives. Metropolitans Mar Gregorios of Parumala, and Mar Gregorios of Pampady and Dr K. C. Chacko of Alwaye, are three memorable examples of recent times. Besides, the Church has a number of small communities including monasteries, convents and ashrams, which are committed to Christian witness, service of the poor and simplicity of life.

From what is stated above, it should not be concluded that the churches in India have finally taken up the challenge of evangelical poverty. Far from it. In fact, it has not yet become even a serious issue for consideration by the general membership and leaders of most of the churches in Asia.

However, there is an increasing recognition on the part of the churches of the necessity of evolving new patterns of service and new forms of church organization which will correspond to the social and economic realities and the cultural traditions of Asia. Two significant attempts, one in Japan and the other in China, are worth mentioning in this connection. The one in Japan was the Non-Church Movement, Mukyokai, initiated by Kanso Uchimura (1861-1930).[30] It was based on the conviction that the salaried ministers and the organized Church itself were unnecessary for the propagation and nurture of Christian faith. The other was a major initiative on the part of the churches in China during the period 1930-1950. It was called the "three-self" movement, aimed at enabling the churches to become self-governing, self-supporting, self-propagating.

CONCLUSION

From the brief historical account presented in this chapter, what conclusions can be drawn regarding the attitudes and approaches of the churches towards the poor and the oppressed? The role of the churches as organizations seemed to be ambiguous. The attitude of the ecclesiastical leaders appeared ambivalent. The cooperation of the early missionaries with the colonial governments, the tacit acceptance of colonialism by the leadership of the young churches or their silence in the face of colonial oppression, all these indicate a certain degree of alliance with the ruling powers and the dominating classes. The nature of the churches' organization, their ownership of expensive institutions, their investment in administration of foreign resources, the style of life of the missionaries and church leaders, and so on, contributed to the general impression that churches were associated with wealth, power and prestige. However, their impressive record of philanthropic activities in such fields as education, health care, social welfare and famine relief revealed the concern of the churches for service to the society. Their work among the low castes, the tribal communities, the marginalized and oppressed sectors of society, placed them on the side of the struggle of the poor and the oppressed for justice, dignity and freedom from poverty, illiteracy and social deprivation. Above all, the Gospel that was preached and the Christian values which were communicated through the Christian schools, colleges and other educational processes, provided inspiration, encouragement and hope for many poor people of Asia to initiate and sustain their struggle.

If by the term "churches" we mean the totality of their members or the Christian communities, then no doubt they belonged to the poor. As mentioned before, the large majority of the members of the Asian churches (except in Japan) were drawn from the poorer sectors of society, and they continued to remain poor. In this sense, the churches were and are poor. But those in a state of poverty cannot automatically be considered as being on the side of those who struggle against poverty, injustice and oppression. Most of the poor Christians, as in the rest of the society, were far from being conscientized for organized struggle. The dominant pietistic, theological outlook and even the philanthropic activities of the churches often contributed to a passive acceptance by the poor Christians of their plight.

However, within the Christian communities there were lay leaders and charismatic movements which challenged the churches to recognize the wholeness of the Gospel, the liberating power of Christ and to make a social option for the struggle of the poor and the oppressed, and this they continue to do.

In short, the attitudes and concern of the churches for the poor during the missionary era were ambiguous, if not contradictory. The question is, will it continue to be ambiguous? The plight of the poor majority of the Asian population is worsening day by day. The challenge that they pose is unambiguous. The social option that the Gospel presents is also unambiguous. What will be the response of the Church?

Only the future can tell.

NOTES

[1] K. M. PANIKKAR: *Asia and Western Dominance*. London: 1953.
[2] H. C. PERUMALIL C.M.I. and E. R. HAMBYE S.J. (eds): *Christianity in India*. Allepy, South India: 1972, p. 49.
[3] WILLIAM H. CLARK: *The Church in China*. New York: 1969, p. 34.
[4] HORACIO DE LA COSTA: *Readings in Philippine History*. Manila: 1965.

5 *Ibid.*, pp. 79-80.
6 H. C. PERUMALIL C.M.I. and E. R. HAMBYE S.J. (eds): *Christianity in India*, *op. cit.*, p. 278.
7 *Ibid.*, p. 282.
8 DAVID C. SCOTT (ed.): *Reflection*. Raipur, India: 1973, p. 35.
9 WILLIAM H. CLARK: *The Church in China*, *op. cit.*, p. 38.
10 *Ibid.*, pp. 42-43.
11 HAROLD S. HONG, WON YONG JI and CHUNG CHOON KIM (eds): *Korea Struggles for Christ*. Seoul: 1966, p. 40.
12 *The Korean Way*. Seoul: The Christian Literature Society of Korea. 1977, p. 74.
13 KENNETH SCOTT LATOURETTE: *A History of Christianity*. London: 1954, p. 1322.
14 MATHAI ZACHARIAH: *The Indian Church*. Madras: 1971, p. 85.
15 *Occasional Bulletin of Missionary Research*, Vol. I, No. 4, October 1977, p. 22.
16 HAROLD S. HONG, WON YONG JI and CHUNG CHOON KIM: *Korea Struggles for Christ*, *op. cit.*, p. 92.
17 WILLIAM H. CLARK: *The Church in China*, *op. cit.*, p. 85.
18 *Ibid.*
19 H. C. PERUMALIL C.M.I. and E. R. HAMBYE S.J. (eds): *Christianity in India*, *op. cit.*, p. 276.
20 *The Rural Life Program, Changing Patterns of Service*. Raipur: 1975.
21 K. P. POTHEN: *A Socio-Economic Survey of the Christian Community in Malawa*. Madras: 1975, p. 75.
22 FRANÇOIS HOUTART, GENEVIÈVE LEMERCINIER and MICHEL LEGRAND: *The Development Projects as a Social Practice of the Catholic Church in India*. Louvain, 1976, p. 35.
23 H. C. PERUMALIL C.M.I. and E. R. HAMBYE, S.J. (eds): *Christianity in India*, *op. cit.*, p. 271.
24 M. M. THOMAS AND RICHARD TAYLOR: *Tribal Awakening*. Bangalore: 1965.
25 M. M. THOMAS: *Towards a Theology of Contemporary Ecumenism*. Madras: 1978, p. 111.
26 JUSTINIAN CHERUPALLIKAT: *Witness Potential of Evangelical Poverty in India*. Switzerland: 1975, p. 143.
27 P. THOMAS: *Christians and Christianity in India and Pakistan*. London: 1954, pp. 71-72.
28 JUSTINIAN CHERUPALLIKAT: *Witness Potential of Evangelical Poverty in India*, *op. cit.*, p. 123.
29 *Ibid.*, p. 131.
30 STEPHEN NEILL AND HANS-RUEDI WEBER: *The Layman in Christian History*. London: 1963, p. 353.

10 · The Christian Mission and the African Peoples in the 19th Century

Sam M. Kobia

I. INTRODUCTION

European colonialism came to Africa at a very crucial stage of indigenous African development. We call it crucial because in the early and mid-19th century, African societies had come to the apparent limits of what is called Iron Age ways of life. This, coupled with long-distance trading that prevailed in many parts of Africa then, marked a period of transitional change to new indigenous forms of social organizations. While Africans were thus busy shaping their own history and destiny, the Europeans invaded and took over the history of Africa. Henceforth, Africa was enclosed as a vast tributary region of the international capitalist economic system. This historical process has been (especially of late) understood by some Africans and other scholars as underdeveloped Africa.[1]

In this historical process, we can identify two categories of actors: the invaded and the invaders. Africans are the invaded. The invaders are of two kinds: the missionaries and the colonialists. In this essay, we shall discuss mostly the Africans and the Christian mission. We shall attempt to analyse the relationship between the two. Our purpose is not so much to discuss the substance of the message preached by the missionaries as to understand the attitudes one had towards the other.

We have chosen to approach our subject within this framework because we cannot discuss adequately the Christian mission work in Africa in isolation from the historical context in which it took place.

This essay is brief and limited both in scope and context. In spatial terms, we shall consider what is normally referred to as Africa south of the Sahara, but also excluding what is modern Ethiopia. This is because Christianity in North Africa and Ethiopia dates back to the 1st century A.D. In fact, some scholars have shown that "Long before the start of Islam in the 7th century, Christianity was well established all over North Africa, Egypt, parts of Sudan and Ethiopia. It was a dynamic form of Christianity, producing great scholars and theologians like Tertullian, Origen, Clement of Alexandria and Augustine." [2]

However, African Christianity did not spread to other parts of Africa because, according to Mbiti, it was checked by Islam, paganism and political pressure. It managed to survive only in Ethiopia and Egypt "where Christianity has kept its identity both as universal faith and as an indigenous religion" (Mbiti). In terms of historical context, we shall confine ourselves to the epoch spanning from the mid-19th century to 1914.

The format we shall adopt is simple. After a brief description of the perspective from which this essay is written, we shall discuss the earliest encounter between the Africans and the missionaries. This is mainly the period prior to the 1880s, when the colonial administration was introduced in most of the African countries. Then we shall try to understand the effects colonialism had on the relationship between the missionaries and the Africans. Finally, we shall analyse the facts discussed and see how they fit into the mainstream of development during the historical epoch under consideration.

A lot has been written concerning the 19th-century work in Africa. It has been written either as part of the general history of European intervention in Africa or as church history in Africa. A great deal also has been written on the early missionary's attitude towards the African and his ways of life. But little is written on the African's view of the missionary and his work, and even less so written by Africans.

It is only in the 1950's that we have the first accounts by African scholars of what we can refer to as genuine African feelings towards the 19th-century missionaries. This was done by African novelists, outstanding among them Chinua Achebe,[3] Ngugi wa Thiongo[4] (formerly James Ngugi) and Tom Aluko.[5] Whereas their works are fictional, they nevertheless reveal the true African response to Christianity and colonialism. What they dramatize is traceable to a factual situation, since it is but written record of what was passed through oral medium. Such novels are the work that best captures the sensitivity, emotion and passion of the inner feelings of the Africans. Some of such Africans were those authors' grandparents who saw the first missionary who came into their village. That is what makes the novels a fertile resource ground for our understanding of the subject we are dealing with.

More recent work by Africans concerning this subject has been written by African historians, among them J. F. A. Ajayi[6] and A. J. Temu,[7] whose invaluable work we shall pay close attention to. In a sense, theirs is a historical analysis of the same situation dramatized by the kind of authors mentioned above.

II. MISSION WORK AND THE AFRICAN BEFORE 1885

The white man is very clever. He came quietly and peacefully with his religion. We were amused by his politeness and allowed him to stay. Now he has won our brothers, and our clan can no longer act like one. He has put a knife on the things that held us together and we have fallen apart.[8]

The above words articulate the sentiments expressed by the African elders after realizing how far the new religion (Christianity) had gone in terms of dividing the members of the same clan. And it is naked truth that henceforth things were never the same again for the Africans. Whereas that fact was lamentable, the cunningness with which the missionary approached the Africans was amusing to the latter.

Did the missionary use cunning or did the African misunderstand him? Had the missionary not posed as peaceful and polite, could the African have been less tolerant with him? Exactly how did the missionary manage to win some Africans over into accepting Christianity? Those are the major questions this section will try to answer.

The Church Missionary Society (CMS) pioneered the European Christian missionary work in Africa. CMS was founded in 1799 by among others the men who formed the Sierra Leone Company in 1791. This company was a commercial company owned by bankers and philanthropists whose major objective was to introduce commerce and Christianity in Sierra Leone. These same men participated in the campaigns to abolish slave trade since the economy of Europe, and also of the United States, had come to a stage where slave trade was no longer a profitable mode of production. As the campaigns to abolish slave trade gathered momentum, slaves were freed and some of them taken back to Africa. It is therefore natural that the CMS focused its interests on the freed slaves in Sierra Leone in the last decade of the 18th century. The freed slaves were among the first converts, but not necessarily converted by the CMS missionaries. Mbiti shows that before European missionaries came to West Africa, the freed slaves had already begun preaching Christianity to their own people. D. Abernethy shows that in West Africa ex-slaves introduced the missionaries (to the leaders) and were made part of the missionary movement.

The Bible and the plough

The concentration of the work of CMS in Sierra Leone was not only to make converts of ex-slaves, but also to train them as catechists, pastors and missionaries. These would then assume the role of cadres. The main philosophy that guided the mission work during this period was that of "the Bible and the plough". As propounded by men like Buxton, the mission was meant to create "an African middle class, thoroughly Christianized and made financially self-reliant by the production and export of cash crops. That middle class could then civilize Africa from within and do so far more efficiently than European missionaries, though the latter, of course, were needed initially to preach the Christian faith and to foster the spirit of entrepreneurship." [9] That concept is consistent with the CMS policy of self-supporting, self-propagating and self-governing native churches in Africa. Later in the essay, we shall show that with the introduction of colonialism both the concept and the policy were abandoned, either wholly or in part, in most of the countries in Africa.

Shortly after the CMS came to Sierra Leone, other missionary societies followed suit. In 1842, the Methodists were already in Nigeria to be followed in 1846 by the Church of Scotland. The Roman Catholics established a mission station in Lagos in 1867. The CMS was spreading rapidly all over West Africa. Its work began in Nigeria at almost the same time as that of the Methodists, and in 1857 Bishop Crowther established an Anglican mission at Onitsha.

Most of the evangelization at this period was done by the Africans. In 1864, the first African bishop, Crowther (an ex-slave) was consecrated Bishop of the Niger pastorate. He and his fellow African assistants preached the "good news" all over West Africa. By 1880, Crowther's mission had 11 stations and slightly over 1,000 Christian adherents in Southern Nigeria alone. (Abernethy)

Work among ex-slaves

CMS was also to pioneer in the missionary work along the coast of East Africa. Because of the success it had in West Africa, CMS expected similar results in East Africa where similar circumstances prevailed. However, it did not meet with such good fortune as in West Africa. Although in 1875 the CMS established a settlement for ex-slaves at Freetown on the east coast of what is now Kenya, the conversion of freed slaves was not an easy task. But a worse problem was posed by the Arabs who had already established an economy which flourished as a result of exploitation of slave labour. This fact was to be the source of constant conflicts between the Arabs and the missionaries: the former accusing the latter of harbouring fugitive slaves.

The mission work at Freetown, therefore, became static for a long time. But we cannot hold the above problem as the sole handicap to the expansion of Christianity on the east coast during this period. It appears as if, after three decades of missionary efforts in Mombasa area, John Rebman had converted but less than a dozen Africans. Hence, during a visit to the area in 1873, Sir Bartle Frere "censured Rebman for the rigidity he (Rebman) had adopted in spreading the Gospel there, and in particular for not adopting industrial training on the mission station as a means of spreading Christianity." [10]

The little evangelization that was done outside the settlement station was done by Bombay Africans,[11] who had been converted to Christianity. The CMS itself was "saved from local disaster" by the Imperial British East Africa Company in 1888. Actually, from the moment it came into the picture, the chartered company and the CMS collaborated in their work in many ways until the company relinquished its charter in 1895.

In other parts of Africa where there were no ex-slaves to give assistance, the work was a lot more difficult to manage. In most cases, there were either the chartered companies or individual white businessmen to help the Christian mission with finance or some other assistance.

In central Africa, the missionary work was pioneered by the Livingstone Inland Mission (LIM) in 1877. LIM was sponsored by the East London Institute for Home and Foreign Missions and the Baptist Mission. Three eminent businessmen provided the finance for the work that followed. However, the work was not an easy task. In 1887, after ten years of evangelization, the Baptists had baptized only 191 people. The Methodist Episcopal Church and other American missionary movements became numerous in the area after 1885. This is because the United States was the first to recognize the sovereignty of Leopold II over the Congo. Although the Holy Fathers had began their work in 1865, they restricted themselves to the coast until 1888 when they moved inland.

In the Southern part of Africa, what is now the Republic of South Africa had by this period been so much invaded that the Boers had even begun claiming parts of it as their home. So we shall deal mainly with the part north of South Africa. The London Mission went into Matebeleland in 1859. The Jesuit Fathers followed in 1879 after Khama refused them permission to settle at Shoshong which is South of Matebeleland. In Matebeleland, the leaders granted them permission to start industrial work, but not to preach.[12] With the coming of chartered rule, they were allowed to preach and build more stations. It appears as if the Anglicans too had been refused permission to settle, but this is not very clear. What is clear is that they began their work only after Matebeleland was under chartered rule, although they had been around for a dozen years.

The "good news" made no sense

How did the missionaries approach Africans when they went to a place for the first time? It seems that there was a pattern that was adopted by most of the missionaries. First, they sought the "chief" where one existed. In parts where there were no chiefs, they met the elders to seek permission to preach and eventually borrow a piece of land on which to build a church. Hardly ever were there cases where the missionaries did not seek permission from the leaders. Where missionaries attempted to travel inland (they had to begin their work on the coast), they needed to be under the guidance of the Africans. In many cases, they had to pay toll fees to pass through. This is because they were regarded as traders, since they had caravans like the latter.

In some cases, especially where there were established kingdoms, the missionaries gave the kings material incentives to be allowed to preach the Gospel. Where ruling was done by a council of elders, however, giving material incentives was not an advisable method of approach; it could not work. Some scholars of African history argue that in weaker societies the missionaries were regarded as a source of security. It is, however, difficult to conceive how one, two or even three white men could be regarded as having military prowess by a whole clan. At any rate, we find it a rather unacceptable argument with respect to the period we are dealing with in this section.

So we conclude that in the early period of their ventures the missionaries were able to survive only because of the generosity and friendship they got from the Africans.

How did the Africans respond to the Gospel? What seems to have been the most natural response to the "good news" is that it did not make sense to the Africans. It is impossible for a people who have a very strong view of the world to suddenly respond favourably to strange ideas about the world. Hence, the original missionary was usually subjected to all sorts of ridicules. Even as late as the 1950's, evening tales and jokes about the Africans' response to the white man's religion were told to children while waiting for the food to be ready. What prompted the Africans to hate the "good news" is that the preachers condemned the African ways of life and their gods.

The early missionaries did not regard African religions as religions. Hence the popular use of words like "paganism" and "heathenism" to describe African ways of life. What they did not understand is that while in Africa religion dominated all aspects in life, by the end of feudalism in Europe religion had ceased to dominate politics, medicine, dances, etc. This had been done through a process of secularization where life was dichotomized between the religious sphere and the secular sphere. (In Europe, this had happened so as to free various aspects of life from religious restraints in order to speed up development of capitalism.) It was easy for the missionaries, therefore, to condemn things like African dances, African ways of marriage, and many other aspects of life. These aspects of life were invariably linked with a religious world outlook. So, declaring them evil was to deprive the African of a vital part of himself, and this was by no means a comfortable thing for Africans to put up with.

The more the Gospel was preached, the more Africans became hostile towards the missionaries. When the missionaries built a church and won a few converts in "Umuofia" (Achebe's fictional name for one part of Nigeria), it was regarded as a source of great sorrow to the leaders of the clan. The winning of converts was seen as the undoing of clan solidarity. In Umuofia, the elders warned the youth who had begun to "fall victim" of the new religion: "You do not know what it is to speak with one voice. An abominable religion (Christianity) has settled among you. A man can now leave his father and his brother. He can curse the gods of his fathers and his ancestors, like a hunter's dog that suddenly goes mad and turns on his master." [13]

In other cases, the coming of the missionary was seen as a bad omen. In Taita, Kenya, in 1887, the absence of rain and the concomitant presence of famine was blamed on the two missionaries (Wray and Morris) who had established a station there. In spite of the fact that they organized famine relief, the missionaries were threatened with deportation. In return, they accused the Wataita of hypocrisy and ungratefulness (Temu). What the missionaries did not seem to understand is that Africans did not want them in their land, and so were quick at seizing the first opportunity, however weak, to create an excuse for getting rid of the unwelcome guests.

Instances of clashes between the Africans and the missionaries were very common during this period. Even African evangelists had problems because of preaching the white man's religion. But to a large extent, white missionaries were tolerated because they had African converts among them. By the 1860s and 1870s in Nigeria, African hostility became severe enough to provoke several incidents of general persecution of Christians in Benny, Nembe and Abeakuta (Abernethy).

In light of such problems, the early missionaries found it extremely difficult to convert African adults. Conversion of respected African adults was extremely rare and happened only where they wanted to take advantage of the missionary so as to enhance their own status or have material returns. Otherwise the early converts were children or those that were regarded as worthless, empty men. The priestess in "Umuofia" called them "the excrement of the clan, and the new faith was a mad dog that had come to eat it up". (Achebe).

The school and medicine drew converts

What made Christianity gain some roots in society and hold until colonialism came in full force is the school. The original response to the school was to reject it. This is because it too was associated with other aspects of European culture, most notably Christianity which had come to be regarded with suspicion.

Initially, people sacrificed the abandoned slaves and social outcasts to test the new institutions before sending their own children. Even among their own children they started by sending the weaker, the lazy, or the naughty ones. The presence of the social outcasts in particular in the school, and therefore also in the church (one never belonged to the school and not the church) made both institutions very unpopular with the rest of the society. To ensure constant attendance, the children were given things like sweets for themselves and salt to take back home. Through school, it was possible to shape the faith and world view of the youth who had not already solidified their traditional norms. In the schools, the first activity of the day was always a prayer and a sermon. It was also in the school that the children were introduced to their king, queen or emperor, as the case may be, and they had to pray for and bow down to their ruler.

On a more positive note, we must recognize that the early mission stations were mainly homes of ex-slaves and social outcasts. They gave refuge and a sense of belonging to those who otherwise could have lived a very hopeless and miserable life. The social outcasts could not help but embrace an institution which recognized him or her as a person worthy of respect. And so they made very good Christians.

However, we should not regard the missions station as Utopia even for the ex-slaves and social outcasts. For instance, Roland Oliver shows that in a Roman Catholic mission in Karema (on the shore of Lake Tanganyika) children did manual labour from 6.30 am to sundown with an intermittent break for religious instruction, a meal and a rest from 11.00 am to 2.30 pm. "Christian religion was a must for everybody who resided at the mission station." [14] In Freetown, the hardships were characterized by the cruelties, malpractices and indiscriminate punishment suffered by ex-slaves under the missionaries. In 1881, charges of flogging and imprisonment of the so-called Bombay Africans were brought against a missionary by the name of J. R. Streeter, who was responsible for the administration of the station. Temu argues that there is a probability that Bombay Africans were punished, although they were often innocent, so as "to silence them since they were the most articulate and politically conscious" among the Africans in the station. They were an educated class of Africans who knew that the administrator had no magisterial powers. A commission of inquiry set up to investigate the charges found them to be true. One of the investigators, a British official, best sums up the situation when he wrote: "Since I have been on the East Indian station, I have been the means of freeing several fugitive slaves on account of ill treatment by their masters, but none of them have been beaten as severely as the two men I saw at the mission." [15]

Introduction of western medicine has also been seen as another social benefit that persuaded Africans to become Christians. Health clinics were used as baits to fish Africans into the Christianity net. When W. E. Taylor, a missionary with medical training, established the first dispensary in Mombasa, Kenya, "those who came for treatment had to listen to a gospel lesson before being treated" (Temu). It is common knowledge in some parts of Africa that Roman Catholic clinics were not only used to induce Africans to become Christians, but also to proselytize Africans of Protestant persuasion to become Roman Catholic.

In concluding this section, we may say that the period under consideration was a source of frustration for the missionaries. However, in many instances the Africans, though with strong resentment of Christianity, were hospitable and friendly to the missionaries, especially when they learned the latter were also friendly and harmless.

III. EFFECTS OF COLONIALISM ON AFRICAN-MISSIONARY RELATIONS, 1885-1914

Gutiri Muthungu na Mubea
(Between a European colonialist and the priest there is no difference).
A Kikuyu saying

When the white man came, he had the Bible and we had the land; Now he has the land and we have the Bible.
A saying in Southern Africa

We have shown in the preceding section that the missionaries had a difficult time penetrating the African society with their new religion. In many situations, the mission lasted mainly because it was thought that it might turn out to be a good source of trade. Because of the numerous taxes and tolls that the missionaries had to pay to buy passing rights or stay among the African people, the missionaries quite often became impoverished. We note, for instance, that "in 1871, Wakefield was to cut short his journey to the Gala in Kauma Kaya because he could not pay the $100 which the elders demanded." [16] In general, the African hostility against the new faith began to mount in the 1870s. Accusations of the African converts as collaborators in "spoiling the land" became more numerous. In "Umuofia", the people's patience was growing thinner every new day. Traditionally, people never fought their brothers, but some elders reasoned out that that was because no white man had come to settle on their land. It was while Africans were planning strategies for driving out the missionaries that they learned: "the white man had not only brought a religion but a government which had built a place of judgment to protect the followers of their religion". (Achebe)

Under imperial protection

In 1885, Africa was partitioned in Berlin, Germany. With the establishment of the colonial rule, the missionaries became part of the establishment, and so inevitably did the Church. Colonial rule facilitated the penetration of the Church into new areas, and especially far in the interior which had been almost impenetrable up until then. Reciprocally, the Church spared no efforts in showing how Christian obedience to the colonial powers was the will of God, since the kings and emperors were divinely chosen. (But only the monarchs of the West were.) Henceforth, the missionary never depended on African hospitality or protection; permission to wander wherever he wished was given by fiat from the Governor's office, not in an African elder's *baraza*. In some instances, the missionaries collaborated in preparing the ground for the imperial invasion. Sir John Kirk, who was a British consul in Zanzibar, urged CMS to occupy Moshi in what is now Tanzania and "establish British influence at Kilimanjaro in order to set a prior claim for the British there" (Temu). Consequently, Bishop Hunnington cooperated with the consul in the plans for the British occupation of Moshi. In anticipation of imperial invasion in Uganda, the British government voted in 1892 £200,000 towards the pretext of a grant-in-aid to a survey for a railway between Mombasa and Lake Victoria in Kenya. But as Oliver shows, the radical editor of *Truth* luridly denounced the "spending of money and building railways in order to prevent missionaries from cutting each other's throats".[17] The cutting of throats refers to the battle of Mengo Uganda between the CMS and the White Fathers. The White Fathers accused Captain Lugard, head of IBEA Company in Uganda, of precipitating the war. All this was done to speed up the British occupation of Uganda so as to protect the company and the British missionaries there.

Our main concern here is to discuss the effects this historical period had on the relationship between the missionaries and the Africans. First let us look at the relationship between the missionaries and the ex-slaves.

Growth of racialist sentiments

In East Africa, the missionaries found the Bombay Africans indispensable in the mission work. They admitted that without the Africans' initiative the mission would have failed. Africans in fact opened missions in the immediate hinterland and they succeeded where the European missionaries had failed. Two noted African missionaries were George David and William Jones. George David succeeded where J. L. Krapf failed and William Jones was able to preach the Gospel in Taita where, for two years, Wray and Morris had laboured in vain. Price decided to send Jones, having been convinced that "W. Jones knows many of them well and is known and respected by them; ... if any one can bring these poor misguided people to their senses, it is him." [18]

Beginning with the mid-1880s, those Africans who had worked so hard began to experience a new attitude in the white missionaries. The missionaries began to accuse the Africans of laziness and immorality. Africans were regarded as "idle and slovenly in their habits and their women spending most of the time in gossiping ... and sleeping". (Temu)

The efforts made at discrediting the Africans at Freretown can be seen in several ways. Because the Africans were much more successful in the missionary work than the European missionaries, they kind of stole the show. This constituted a threat to the European missionary's position in the emerging church in Africa.

During this same period in West Africa, a bitter campaign was waged in particular against the very successful Niger Mission. The bishopric of Bishop Crowther was severely attacked, and Africans were accused of immorality (without any evidence to support the allegations). In the late 1880s, "a number of white missionaries were sent out to the Niger diocese

The Christian Mission and the African Peoples in the 19th Century 165

to make allegations that the whole diocese was rife with immorality and corruption, thus proving that the Africans were not fit to take responsible positions".[19] In the 1890s, things had gotten to such bad proportions that many Nigerians left European-controlled denominations to form their own movements. Among those who left was Bishop Crowther's son, who together with others formed Niger Delta Pastorate. (Abernethy.)

The reasons for the changed attitude of the missionaries cannot be explained merely by the jealousy of the European missionaries towards the Africans. Abernethy points out that "among other reasons, the chief one was that the early missionaries' optimistic beliefs about Africans' potential for religious leadership were replaced during the 1880s and 90s by a far more negative view of Africans in keeping with the racialist and jingoist sentiments that accompanied and helped to rationalize European imperialist expansion".[20] Temu agrees and elaborates further that "widely current in Great Britain at this time were the racist ideas of social Darwinism which proclaimed that Africans were inferior to the Anglo-Saxons".

So, from this time on, we see Africans confronting and being confronted by a missionary who was convinced of the inherent inferiority of those he had come to save. The effects this new situation had on the mission work were several. They could be seen as positive or negative, depending on who is looking at them.

Producing "black white men"

First let us consider the effect it had on schools. By this time, those Africans who had attended schools became wage earners as messengers or clerks. Their social status rose and they gained prestige. Hence, this became an incentive for parents to send their children to school. But what made the schools really popular is the fact that the Africans realized the only way to kick the white man out of his land was to dialogue with him. To dialogue effectively, it was necessary to learn the white man's language and therefore his education. So the increased enrollment at schools was a communal decision, since people still hoped it was possible to act as a clan. But the more the new rule made life individualistic, the more the decision to send a child to school became an individual parent's affair. With the introduction of monetary economy, and especially the poll tax that could only be paid in cash, going to school became almost necessary. Finally, having school education enhanced one's dignity and group prestige, since the schools manufactured an elitist bourgeoisie hopelessly alienated from the grassroots. So the hope people had placed on their schooled youth as vanguards who would champion the liberation of their land was shattered as the "educated" imbibed the white man's culture. They even came to earn the title of the "black white men".

Church leadership snatched away

What about the effects it had on the Church? The more the people went to school, the bigger the Church grew numerically. Every one who went to school had to become a Christian, however marginal. But the attitude the missionaries adopted had negative effects on the growth of the Church in Africa. Temu argues very convincingly (and we agree with him) that George David was not consecrated the first Bishop of East Africa in 1884 (or as it is commonly termed, did not become the first Samuel Crowther of East Africa), because by this time imperialism and the ideas of social Darwinism were at their peak, and the scramble for Africa had begun.[21] The church leadership in Africa was therefore snatched away from Africans until the 1950s. Hence the CMS's policy of self-supporting, self-propagating and self-governing native churches vanished with the advent of imperialism.

In other parts of Africa where there were no ex-slaves, the story was no different. In the Congo and in Southern Africa, the Church was almost like the spiritual department of imperialism. In 1888, King Leopold "made known to the Holy See (Pope Leo XIII) his wish that the evangelization of his Congo domain might be reserved for Belgian missionaries. Accordingly, on 11 May, 1888, the Pope created the vicariate apostolic of the Belgian Congo, a truly vast territory to be a single unit." [22] Since then, mission stations and churches mushroomed all over the place. After Cecil Rhodes took over in Matabeleland, he did not only dish out land to the Church, but he also gave it money. The Salvation Army was among the first to benefit from Cecil Rhodes' generosity. In 1891, it got 6,000 acres of land in the fertile Mazoe district. In the same year, "the Wesleyan Methodists entered the country with Rhodes' encouragement, receiving an offer from him on behalf of the Company of £100 per annum towards the support of a missionary".[23] The contributions to the missions were increased if the mission work expanded. The mission work (both for Church and school) for European and African was segregated. The African revolts that arose in 1894 and 1896 paralyzed the mission work for some time, reminding the missionaries that their lip-service to African interests was unwanted.

In 1925, the total area granted to the mission work was reported officially as 325,730 acres (Groves). To begin with, the missionaries justified their desire for large pieces of land by saying that the landless Africans could seek asylum on the mission land. However, when the so-called African reserves were later officially demarcated, the missions became landlords like everybody else. This made Groves comment (by quoting S. H. Harris: *The Chartered Millions*) that: "there would seem to have been little misgiving at the possible embarrassment, while offering the Christian faith, occasioned by holding large grants of land from an authority not generally regarded by the African peoples as entitled to make them." [24]

IV. CONCLUSIONS

In our concluding remarks, we shall attempt to analyse the variables, especially the indigenous variables, that caused the situation that we have discussed above. In so doing, our objective is to try and determine the relationship between the events in Africa and the general mainstream of international development during the period we are discussing.

We have shown earlier that the change in the missionaries' attitude towards Africans was prompted by at least three factors: (i) the remarkable success exhibited by Africans in their missionary work was a source of jealousy on the part of the European missionaries; (ii) the strong belief in social-Darwinism by Europeans; and (iii) the advent of imperialism in Africa. The first two have been discussed above and so we shall now concentrate more on the third.

Among those who were fighting for imperial extension in Africa "was the missionary interest of the CMS, supported by its home 'constituency' as well as by the ecclesiastical hierarchy of the established Church".[25] It was not the CMS alone that condoned imperialism in Africa, but the Church in general. The missionaries found their work necessary to save the African "heathens" from the terrors of hell, while they regarded imperialism as a benign intervention by Europe to save Africans from the evils of Islam and prevent Africans from butchering one another. The synthesis of the two efforts was to civilize Africa. (To put it rather crudely, most Africans now regard the idea of civilizing Africa as nothing but social chauvinism.) In this case, we argue that there was a very strong correlation between the cross and the flag.

It has been shown that the years between 1884 and 1900 mark the epoch of intensified colonial expansion of the European states. Similarly, it is the period which marks the zenith of missionary work in Africa. When Africans believe *Gutiri Muthungu na Mubea*, they argue that the ubiquitous work of the missionary and the colonialist in Africa was not just a happy coincidence. The two did not chance to meet in Africa, each one going about a mission unrelated to the other.

Now let us look at the imperial intervention that the Christian mission supported. What was its major interest in Africa? During this period, the economic development of Europe had come to a stage where it became necessary to seek raw materials and new markets elsewhere. Since the main purpose of business is to maximize profit, it made economic sense to look for new markets in places where capital is scarce, the price of land very low (if necessary free), labour is abundant and cheap (where necessary free) and raw materials are cheap to extract. Africa provided an ideal market for that purpose. Up to this time, Britain was ahead of all other European countries in economic development. But now its market was threatened by the growth of industrialization in America and the rest of

Europe, and so new markets in Africa were worthy of the expense of administration and development.[26]

The forefront imperialists gave us added information with regard to the invasion of Africa. Two of them are worth noting; Joseph Chamberlain advocated imperialism as a "true, wise and economical policy". In a more articulate manner, Cecil Rhodes summed up their view when he said:

> I was in the East End of London (working class quarter) yesterday and attended a meeting of the unemployed. I listened to the wild speeches, which were just a cry for bread, bread! and on my way home I pondered over the scene and I became more than ever convinced of the importance of imperialism ... My cherished idea is a solution for the social problem, i.e. in order to save the 40,000,000 inhabitants of the United Kingdom from a bloody civil war, we colonial statesmen must acquire new lands to settle the surplus population, to provide new markets for the goods produced in the factories and mines. An Empire, as I have always said, is a bread and butter question. If you want to avoid civil war, you must become imperialists.[27]

Cecil Rhodes says that he has *always said an Empire is a bread and butter question*. We choose to believe that the missionaries who supported imperialism had at one time or another heard Cecil Rhodes' testimony. In spite of everything, Cecil Rhodes seems to have had more missionary friends in Africa than any other imperialist. Actually, Cecil Rhodes never spared his efforts in pursuit of their imperialist goal until he found a home in Africa for so many of his countrymen that he had a whole country named after him. Significantly enough, that country (Rhodesia) is the last colony to become politically independent in Africa — we treat South Africa as a special case altogether.

Viewed from a politico-economic perspective, we see that at this stage of economic development at the international level the so-called free competition was succumbing to monopolization. Not long before this period, some British political leaders were opposed to colonial policy. But now, faced with especially American, German and Belgian competition in the world market, the politicians-cum-capitalists saw their salvation in monopolies and therefore in appropriating and colonizing those parts of the world not yet shared out by international capitalists. And hence the scramble for Africa.

In conclusion, we argue that in supporting imperialism, whether wittingly or unwittingly, the Christian missions objectively participated in the exploitation and subsequent underdevelopment of Africa.

Suggestions for further work

In Africa, the Church began as a home of ex-slaves, social outcasts and depressed people. In a word, it was the home of the poor. Is the

Church in Africa today a place where the wretched of the earth can feel at home? I tend to foster the conviction that the poor in Africa have not found a meaningful identity nor sufficient security in the Church in its present structures. Since it gained its roots on African soil, the Church, with an exception of some African independent church movements, has been identified and identifies comfortably with the African elite and the rich. A major question that needs to be further researched is: What are the social, economic and political factors that led to this phenomenon?

In order to identify and analyse those factors, it will be necessary to develop a framework that will help us to understand two basic things: first, the relationship between the Church and the status quo at any given historical period; and secondly, the objective relationship between the Church and the poor. If the framework adopted in our essay is applied to the period succeeding 1914, it will be possible to develop a colonial-neocolonial model which I believe will help us to understand the relationships between the Church and the status quo on the one hand, and the Church and the poor on the other. In fact, our essay is not complete as a means of understanding the Church and the African peoples without carrying it to the present time.

NOTES

[1] See especially the ideas and works of A. M. Babu, Samir Amin, Walter Rodney, Bosil Davidson and Colin Leys.

[2] J. S. MBITI: *African Religions and Philosophy*, p. 300. New York: Anchor Books, 1970.

[3] CHINUA ACHEBE: *Things Fall Apart*. Connecticut, USA: Fawcett Publishers, 1959.

[4] NGUGI WA THIONGO: *The River Between*. London: Heinman.

[5] TOM ALUKO: *One Man, One Wife*. London: Heinman.

[6] J. F. A. AJAYI: *Christian Missions in Nigeria 1841-1891: The Making of a New Elite*. London: 1965.

[7] A. J. TEMU: *British Protestant Missions*. London: Longman, 1972.

[8] CHINUA ACHEBE: *Things Fall Apart*, op. cit., p. 162.

[9] D. ABERNETHY: *The Political Dilemma of Popular Education: An African Case*, p. 28. Stanford University Press, 1969.

[10] J. F. A. AJAYI: *Christian Missions in Nigeria 1841-1891*, op. cit., p. 7.

[11] Liberated slaves kept in Bombay, India, prior to their repatriation to Africa.

[12] C. P. GROVES: *The Planting of Christianity in Africa*, Vol. III, p. 98. London: Lutterworth Press, 1955.

[13] CHINUA ACHEBE: *Things Fall Apart*, op. cit., p. 155.

[14] R. OLIVER: *The Mission Factor in East Africa*, p. 52. London: Longman, 1952.

[15] A. J. TEMU: *British Protestant Missions, op. cit.*, p. 19.

[16] *Ibid.*, p. 38.

[17] R. OLIVER: *The Mission Factor in East Africa, op. cit.*, p. 150.

[18] *Ibid.*, p. 70.

[19] *Ibid.*, p. 79.

[20] D. ABERNETHY: *The Political Dilemma of Popular Education: An African Case, op. cit.*, p. 50.

[21] A. J. TEMU: *British Protestant Missions, op. cit.*, p. 84.

[22] C. P. GROVES: *The Planting of Christianity in Africa, Vol. III, op. cit.*, p. 123.

[23] *Ibid.*, p. 101.

[24] *Ibid.*, p. 104.

[25] R. OLIVER: *The Mission Factor in East Africa, op. cit.*, p. 154.

[26] *Ibid.*, p. 162.

[27] See especially HOBSON: *Imperialism: A Study*. London: 1906; and V. I. LENIN: *Imperialism: The Highest Stage of Capitalism*, pp. 93-94.

Conclusion

Julio de Santa Ana

To conclude this volume, we focus attention on some of the thoughts which give unity and perspective to the essays assembled in the previous pages. In attempting such a synthesis, however, we must be careful to avoid facile generalizations. There is no one tidy and consistent "universal" conception which could embrace the period covered by these essays. On the contrary, each of the situations described has its distinctive features and no two of them are exactly similar. No completely coherent synthesis of these historical developments is possible. We have to accept the fact that there are contradictions between them, wide divergences due to the clash of different values, different cultures, contrasting systems, and so on. Nevertheless, if we seek a synthesis, we do so for two reasons. Firstly, because in all the situations dealt with in these essays, we encounter the fact of poverty, the presence of the poor, for different reasons and in different ways. We have here a universal phenomenon. Secondly, because this fact of poverty presents problems for the Christian community wherever it is found. We hardly need reminding [1] that Christians are led by the Gospel to see the poor as those in whom Jesus himself is present. This element in the Christian tradition is, therefore, relevant to all situations in which poor people are in some relationship to the churches. In the light of these two elements, an attempt to discern the main features of the various situations dealt with in this volume seems feasible. We emphasize, however, that such an attempt cannot lead to an interpretation which is universally valid. Account must always be taken of the distinctiveness of each individual situation.

It is also important to avoid the over-simplification of a one-sided approach to the problems considered in this period. An exclusively theological approach is just as inadequate as an analysis based exclusively on the social sciences. The Church is a reality on the social and historical level, and not only one which is radically determined by values preserved in the tradition of the people of God. Therefore, as the contributions to this volume show, a certain tension must be maintained between structures

---

Translated from Spanish by the Language Service, WCC.

and values, between the social sciences and theology. The approach must be an interdisciplinary one, taking into account both the historical and the religious aspects of the theme.

This is especially important, we believe, since the Church is one of the partners in the relationship under consideration. While it is impossible to reduce the Church to an institution, neither can it be reduced to the "community of believers". The Church forms part of the total human community and is subject to the same conditions. But it is also the "people of God", responding to living ideals, ethical demands, spiritual impulses, all of which constitute in varying ways the basis of Christian faith. It is essential, therefore, to respect the dynamic relation between the several elements, since these interpenetrate and interact in the concrete realities of everyday life. Moreover, other historical currents, other values, other cultures than those of the West, other structures of various kinds, have also played a part in the process which concerns us. This was the case, for example, with the cultures of Asia, of America "before Columbus", and of Africa, when they found themselves confronted with aggressive, colonialist, western nations which based their action on — among other things — a certain idea of the Christian faith. In a study of the problems of the relationship between the Church and the poor in the period covered by this volume, this interaction between different cultures cannot be reduced to either anthropology, theology, or sociology. All three aspects have to be taken into account and precedence given to none. This would seem to make a dialectical approach to the enquiry possible, one which most faithfully reflects the concrete realities where economics sometimes conditions ideologies, and sometimes ethical values, and demands determine material conditions.[2]

It should be remembered, therefore, that in the period studied in this volume the churches exercised an influence on the life of the western nations and on some of the peoples of the Middle East; to a lesser extent also on Asian, African and Amerindian communities. They were connected as institutions with the established civil authorities and occasionally even played a part in revolutionary proceedings.[3] They were profoundly shaken by the debate on the problem of slavery, and strongly affected by the different conflicts which marked the history of the 18th and 19th centuries. Finally (though this does not exhaust the list of factors influencing church institutions in this period), they failed (as André Biéler clearly shows in the present volume [4]) to take adequate account of the demands made on them by the development of new economic, social and political conditions in the life of the nations and to adjust their life and mission accordingly.

This picture of the churches would be incomplete if we failed to add that they are the clearest expression of the reality of the people of God in history. In spite of ambiguities and contradictions, the thought and action of the churches (or of believers, not excluding either Israel or other religious communities from the people of God) was connected with historical processes which helped to produce the events just mentioned. In this sense, the people of God is not divorced from the forces which have operated and which continue to operate in the midst of history to promote human liberation. Even if the institutional church opposed such currents, clearly certain groups did emerge within it, often despite its official leadership, and cooperated in varying degrees in bringing about certain social changes.[5]

Moreover, the contradictions we are thinking of here were not peculiar to church institutions and their hierarchies, but also appeared in the groups which accepted more liberating objectives. This does not invalidate their efforts, but it is a warning against misplaced glorification of them. For example, the call to unity which impels the action of the people of God frequently became a factor impinging on its historical efficacy. This happened, for instance, when Christians tried to act as mediators in social conflicts between different classes, on the basis of a particular interpretation of the ministry of reconciliation. In this case, the social action was powerfully motivated by an axiological, spiritual element. Yet at other times, it must be remembered, it was the spiritual factor which introduced a dynamic element into the social situation driving it forward towards new horizons, as, for example, in the case of the campaign against the slave trade in the early period of the industrial revolution.[6] That decision was a response to a vision of the unity which should govern the human family as a community of the children of God without discrimination or barriers. In this sense, it should be remembered that, according to the Christian tradition, it is the people of God which "pioneers the way" in history, impregnating it with a significance which it sometimes seems not to have at present, but which can become plain at some future time. But to be true, this affirmation must be implemented in practice. And this perhaps was the major problem facing Christians and churches in the period we are dealing with, for they frequently gave the impression of being conservative and even reactionary instead of being signs of the future, signs of hope.[7] The consequence was a divorce between the churches and the working classes, a divorce which still persists to this day, as can be seen from the very limited degree to which the poor participate in the life of the churches in our time. The problem is therefore not simply a historical, but a contemporary one, touching as it does the very nature of the Church, its essence and its mission.

From what has just been said, it is clear that in this volume we are not concerned with the past alone. Our concern is profoundly contemporary and topical. We are not seeking merely to explain what happened in the past, but to create conditions in which action is possible now to bridge the gulf which has opened up between the poor and the churches. For here, too, the social situation confronts Christians dramatically with the evangelical statement that the "new age" (the era of the coming of the Son of God which brings hope and new life) is announced to the poor.[8] The demonstrable estrangement between the poor and the Church (amply documented in the essays in this volume) presents the Christian communities with a clear obligation: namely, to mend their ways, to revise their programmes, to emphasize afresh the values attached to the life of the poor and the social reality of poverty and, in this way, to be in a position to embody in practice that new life which makes it possible "to preach good news to the poor".

The estrangement between the Church and the poor

The first symptom of this estrangement was the paternalistic, patronizing attitude of the churches to the existence of the poor and their unsatisfied needs. Not that the churches did not try to serve the poor. Indeed, they tried desperately to do so, initiating vast service programmes and creating the organization to implement them. As André Biéler and Nicolai Zabolotsky clearly show, however, the churches' effort did not in general go beyond works of charity. The result is well known. The poor were served, but the social reality of poverty and its underlying causes went practically unchanged. The service offered, mainly emotionally inspired, as John Kent indicates, while helping to mitigate the symptoms of poverty, did nothing in the majority of cases to eradicate poverty itself. Despite the insistence of the reformers of the 16th century that: "there should be no beggars among Christians",[9] it has to be admitted that the church welfare organizations were incapable of removing poverty and its causes, and did not know how to do so. The main reason for this was that they offered palliatives without, in most cases, making any attempt to attack the root causes.

Another factor, more psychological in character though with some social elements, must also be taken into account. A paternalistic attitude assumes a certain distance between the giver and the receiver of aid. There is no question of a relation of equals. However much love and compassion there may have been on the part of the churches in this relationship, therefore, it must have been an uncomfortable one for those on the receiving end, provoking responses which the would-be helpers of the poor sometimes simply could not understand. And so, instead of being resolved, the estrangement was aggravated. This situation was complicated still more by the consequences suffered by the western nations as a result of the historical processes initiated by the French Revolution. Jean Lacroix shows that, for society, it was equivalent to the death of the father, the end of established values, of tradition; the new classes (bourgeoisie and proletariat) took control of the course of western history. Remembering the paternalistic attitude of the churches towards the poor, the latter fulfilled their need for emancipation by turning against those who had formerly supported them by their charity, once a point had been reached in history when the poor could feel they had achieved maturity. Moreover, the "fraternity" which the liberal bourgeois ideology regarded as necessary for social existence demanded the abandonment of the traditional fount of authority, in this case the church.[10]

However, it has to be acknowledged that, in the period under review, church institutions made considerable efforts to base their relations with the poor on something deeper than a paternalism inspired by pity. The motive here was clearly derived from the Gospel. It was realized that Jesus described the poor as the "heirs of the Kingdom". Some mission stations in Africa, for example, as Sam Kobia points out, became veritable homes for the outcasts and ex-slaves who found in them a social basis and inspiration to support them in their efforts to overcome their social destitution and dependence. Unfortunately, this experience (which had its limitations, as Kobia also points out) was rather an exception, there being no evidence of its having been repeated or adapted very often in other parts of the world. In fact, although attention was given to these destitute members of society, this was done, as already mentioned, in a paternalistic way, in the form of compassionate charity, provoking the kind of reaction we have described.

This shows that, apart from a few isolated groups which realized what was happening, the churches failed to comprehend that the social changes created by the new methods of production were also leading to a qualitative transformation in the social position of the poor. On the one hand, there was the massive and terrible fact of poverty, with its appalling consequences for those affected by it. The practical programmes geared to individual rather than mass poverty were inevitably ineffective. Only slowly did some Christians realize that the response to the manifest social ills connected with mass poverty must be to urge government action and legislation for reform.[11] At the same time, new social classes emerged as a result of this massive incidence of poverty and destitution in the developing industrial revolution. These classes, generally called the "working classes", developed their own sub-culture to which, as John Kent points out in his essay on the churches and the trade union movement in England, little attention was paid until many years later. By then, the estrangement was already too deep.

Furthermore, and this is intimately related to the last point, the churches failed to appreciate the full extent of the changes attendant on the development of industry and the processes thus initiated which were transforming not only the economic situation, but also social, political and cultural life generally. There were a few isolated individuals and movements which drew attention to them, but their views were not heeded as they should have been. Nor did the changes brought about or speeded up by colonialization appear to have been sufficiently appreciated by the churches until long after they had taken firm hold. Despite the lack of response in the church institutions, these isolated voices persevered with their concern at the developing social problem, and sought to further their struggle on behalf of the underprivileged sections of society by allying themselves with forces which were not overtly Christian and were even openly hostile to the Church and to Christianity, which they regarded for the most part as mere auxiliaries of the rich ruling classes. Nicolai Zabolotsky speaks of "the liturgy after the liturgy",[12] that is, the organization of effective action in solidarity with and in aid of the poor outside the walls of the churches and their institutions. This led the working classes to draw a distinction between "the churches" (generally regarded as pillars of reactionary conservatism allied with the traditional ruling classes and increasingly also with the middle classes) and "some Christians" who diverged from the line taken by the churches on social issues. With these Christians, some dialogue was maintained by the working classes, but the latter continued to move further and further away from the churches.[13] Moreover, as John Kent and Günter Brakelmann both point out, even those Christians who were to some extent aware of the new social problem addressed their words and their actions more to the churches than to the working classes. Between them and the poor the same estrangement existed, though once more we must stress the impossibility of generalizations in this matter.

The lack of unanimity among these Christians themselves further complicated matters. While most of them concentrated on the churches, there were some whose commitment to the struggles of the masses and the poor was their dominant concern, and this often led to direct clashes between their views and those of the church institutions. Julio Barreiro mentions one example: Bartolomé de Las Casas, one of the first Christian missionaries in America, whose methods of evangelism and concern for the indigenous people were harshly criticized by the leading theologians of the day. The clash of opinion reflected a deepening contradiction between the social attitude of the ecclesiastical hierarchy and the deepest hopes and aspirations of the poor and the oppressed. This divergence of views, often sharpened to the point of confrontation and polemics, inevitably helped to bring about the divorce between the Church and the poor in the historical period under review.[14]

For the interdisciplinary approach we have adopted, recognition of the deepening estrangement between the churches and the poor raises a theological problem concerning the missionary work of the Church. From the fact that churches, charged with the vital mission of proclaiming the Gospel to all nations, were gradually becoming estranged from the poor, are we to conclude that in practice they had set limits to the announcement of God's love? The answer, of course, is "No". But the facts speak for themselves, compelling us to ask ourselves how social factors which have conditioned and limited the action of the churches in the course of history are to be overcome.[15] In other words, are God's love and liberating power really to apply to all? If so, the churches must fully embody that universal dimension of love and power, and not allow themselves to be hampered by a sort of social "predestination" which assumes that only those who are not poor can aspire to live the Christian life.

If we look at the statistics of poverty in the world today, it is clear that even the present situation of the churches is still influenced by the manifest rift which appeared between the churches and the poor, mainly at the time of western colonial expansion and the industrial revolution. The rich countries of the world, for example, are those with a long-established Christian tradition. Furthermore, in the poor countries, the richer sections of the population frequently include considerable groups of Christians. It may be pleaded, correctly, we believe, that as well as this, Christianity also manifestly contains a factor which impels the human groups which adhere to the Christian faith to try to overcome the forces which create poverty. We must also admit, however, that the existence of the poor today (and they are mostly not Christians, mostly people who have not been evangelized, mostly people who have been condemned to poverty as the result of the action of "Christian" nations in the past) raises serious questions about how the life and mission of the Church is conceived. Do not the poor directly confront us Christians and churches with an imperative need to reflect on our life in the past, to amend our ways, to redirect our steps, to try to carry out more effectively the mission God has entrusted to his Church? In other words, how is the Church to follow the direction pointed by Jesus, and thus to confirm the reality of the new age promised by God to the peoples of the earth when he declared that "the poor have good news preached to them"? In order to achieve this, it seems essential to end this divorce, to overcome this estrangement.

As a first step [16] in this direction, we shall try now, in the light of the contributions to this volume, firstly to tease out some of the specific questions which together make up the complex problem of the relationship between the poor and the churches, and secondly, to venture a preliminary comment on some of the theological aspects of this problem.

The nature of the divorce

It need hardly be said that this volume in no way calls in question the zeal, devotion and persistence of the churches in their missionary task. In the period in which all these changes took place, the churches undoubtedly displayed tremendous energy. This is evident from the missionary expansion of western Christianity, as well as from the various revivalist movements which reinvigorated the churches of the West during this period. Their spiritual inspiration is beyond question. What calls for comment, on the other hand, is the structural, institutional aspect of the problem which, as already noted, cannot be separated from the theological and ideological aspects.

When we try to define the divorce between the working classes and the churches, it is important to remember that, throughout the period of western colonial expansion with its resultant new global pattern and during the industrial revolution, the structures of the church institutions, with minor adjustments, continued to be those of a pre-industrial world, as André Biéler has shown. This has a real bearing on their inability to perceive the nature of the social structures which were coming into being in those years.

In the second place, as Günter Brakelmann makes clear in his chapter on the churches and social conflicts in 19th-century Germany (and the comment seems to apply to other western countries as well), the churches failed, from the institutional point of view at least, to grasp the many facets of the secularization process taking place in the years leading up to and following the French Revolution. The latter, together with the industrial revolution, unleashed a vast movement of change. The transition from traditional to urban industrial society in the West brought a profound change in life-style. The value of tradition was no longer accepted without question; indeed, change itself tended to become an institution. On the other hand, social behaviour which had been prescriptive in traditional society now became mainly a matter of choice. Instead of a society with only a few not very complex institutions (including the churches with their leading role), there was a society which was highly organized and with very complex institutions. In short, a homogeneous society became a pluralist one in which the prevailing social order could be questioned and challenged, as a result often of very painful and socially very costly experiences. The working class struggles of the 19th century and the early years of the present century are a good illustration of this.

Unfortunately, the churches were not sufficiently alert to accept this situation. The process of secularization which originated in the 13th century, although undoubtedly Christian in inspiration,[17] moved outside the church institutions and eventually took a direction which they found difficult to follow. As a result of this historical development, the workers, rural and industrial, came to the fore as historical protagonists, with a consequent development of secularized ideas and forms of life which the churches in the main refused to accept as they were taking shape. This, too, was basically a social decision. Instead of listening to the new classes, now the force moving history forwards, most of the church institutions opted for the past. It is as if they wished to arrest social change but then, in face of its inevitability, stood aside and remained isolated from important aspects of what was happening.

Thirdly, not as a direct consequence of this, but in dynamic interaction with it, Christian thought was gradually incorporated into the world-view of the dominant groups, who themselves had slowly been constructing their ideology on the basis of Christian ideas or even in convergence on these ideas. That is to say, while the church institutions were remote from the poor, the dominant sectors of society (unlike the working classes and the underprivileged) were adapting their thinking to Christian ideas or exploiting Christian ideas to their own ends, thereby helping to widen the gulf which had opened up between the poor and the Church.

It was in this context that Marxist ideas began to be adopted more and more by the most militant sections of the working classes. On the one hand, these ideas fitted the new situation which developed with the advance of the industrial revolution. In other words, the materialist thought of Marx and Engels seemed to fit the development of the economy and of society in the second half of the 19th century like a glove. This materialism made two assumptions: firstly, that human life is determined by modes of production. Social justice increases, therefore, as old forms corresponding to obsolete or obsolescent modes of production are abandoned and replaced by others which fit in with the inherent logic of the process; that is, by forms which are calculated to deal rationally with the fresh contradictions as they arise; for example, between a minority which owns the means of production and the majority which makes up the labour force. Obviously, the demands of the working classes were seen to be reflected in the Marxist analysis.

However, materialism also assumed an atheist position. It did so primarily on philosophical grounds peculiar to this school of thought. But it should also be remembered that atheism derived its militancy from opposition to the position of the churches which, as we have seen, were generally allied to those who defended vested interests and the status quo that went with them. The *Communist Manifesto*, in this sense, served not only to unite the working classes in the struggle to achieve their goals, but also to direct its militancy against the defenders of "law and order", including on the whole the church institutions.

Fourthly, as John Kent's chapter on the situation in England clearly illustrates, while some Christians tried indeed to put the radical case on behalf of the poor on the basis mainly of the sort of emotional grounds which usually appeal to the Christian conscience, the churches obviously gave *tacit* support to the political liberals while explicitly claiming to be "neutral". The only ones who managed to escape from the social "captivity" in which the churches were imprisoned were a few minority groups. But, as Kent also shows, even these addressed their exhortations and their activities to church opinion and met with no wider response among the sections of society they were wanting to defend.

Fifthly, among broad sections of the colonialized peoples, the participation of Christian missions in the colonialist enterprise (see the chapters by Itty, Barreiro and Kobia) aroused feelings of apprehension and alienation. This was intensified, in Africa and Latin America especially, by the racialist features of certain missionary methods which inflicted wounds which still persist today in the social memory of these peoples. In Africa, however, it has happily been offset to some extent by the way in which certain missionaries have immersed themselves in the indigenous cultures (something occasionally met with, though very rarely in Latin America in, for example, the work of Bartolomé de Las Casas and in the Jesuit missions in Uruguay), and also by the help given to the indigenous peoples through educational work.

The upshot of all this is that the gulf between the Church and the poor is still there today and goes deep. There *are* poor people in the churches, it is true; but the proportion is far fewer than in society as a whole. There *are* attempts to present the Gospel to the poor, to establish a Christian presence among the workers (for example, worker priests, or Christians who live in the slums of great cities or devote their lives to the cause of justice and human liberation). But these efforts do not represent a major current in the churches. The Pentecostal churches in certain parts of Latin America or Africa are described as "churches of the poor", but, as Christian Lalive d'Epinay's study of the Pentecostals in Chile makes very clear, these groups, although made up of poor people, do not really represent a "popular" mentality. Far from claiming their rights, they are actually seeking to climb the ladder in society, and for this purpose their assimilation of attitudes and values via their religious allegiance can be a useful tool.[18]

In view of all this, we are safe in saying, without claiming absolute validity for the statement, that the underprivileged sections of society have on the whole found no place in the churches and that these have not seriously tried to welcome them. The Salvation Army initially tried to do so, but its programmes have, on the whole, tended to conform gradually to the pattern prevailing in other Christian denominations, as André Biéler shows. The ultimate outcome is a vast, solid, structural *separation* between the poor and the churches.

"Structural" in what sense? The situation in which the churches find themselves is equivalent to a captivity in structures and institutions which are alien to the poor and to their sub-culture. As R. White points out in his chapter on the situation in the USA, when the churches claimed to be serving the poor, they depended on the contributions of the rich dominant classes of American society even for the organization of their work and service. This link with capital inevitably hindered their attempt to move nearer to the working classes which regarded the churches as institutions of the rich. The most they offered was a basis for efforts by those from the lowest levels of society to climb the social ladder. Their participation in the life of the Church was seen as an endorsement of efforts in this direction, making it possible for them to be accepted as socially respectable.

In our view, the problem transcends social analysis. Ultimately, it is a matter of the Church's *fidelity* to the essence of the Gospel that "the last will be first".[19] Among the signs of the messianic age is that "good news is preached to the poor", according to the well-known Lucan passage already quoted. There are in the Gospel other promises, too, of immense social significance; for example, in the beatitudes, which tell us that "the door will inherit the Kingdom" (Luke 6 : 20).[20] Fidelity to the Gospel compels the churches to ask themselves at least why there should be such a structural division separating them from the poor. When this question is answered, they can then begin to look for the remedy.

But consideration of the problem also includes consideration of the *catholicity* of the Church, its social and not only its geographical and cultural universality. Is the Church an institution for all social classes? Or are there classes which, representing the kind of sub-culture they represent, feel themselves *de facto* excluded from the churches because these are the sort of institutions they are? Really to affirm the catholicity of the Church in social terms will surely lead to a renewal in the Christian communities such that they will be able to become open towards those who at present are remote from them. Such openness may lend their message the credibility it at present lacks among the poor and in this way advance their missionary task. The underprivileged sections of society find it difficult to believe this message telling them that they, the "last", shall be "first", when those who bring this message obviously do not believe it themselves. This is why some speak of the "atheism" of believers, since it is often the "believers" who deny in practice the promises and tenets of Jesus Christ. The structural separation of the churches from the poor can be overcome only as they remain faithful to the Gospel and present themselves as truly universal, catholic institutions in this social dimension as well as in all others.

Problems requiring deeper reflection

A synthesis of the kind attempted in this final chapter cannot deal adequately with all aspects of the problems involved. I limit myself, therefore, to those which seem to me the most important.

First of all, there is the significance of the call of Christ through the poor for the Church today. Christ's call to us to follow him is a summons which claims the human being as a totality, and, once accepted, presupposes total and unconditional commitment to walk in the way which Jesus points out to us.[21]

Among other things, this means that, if need be, one has to be poor, to embrace the poverty experienced by our Lord and in this way to share the life and struggle of the poor. As St Basil rightly stressed in his own struggle for justice and the service of the poor, this is the way along which "it is possible to attain eternal life". Those who wish to be faithful to Jesus Christ cannot evade these requirements.

We must remember that, in the period covered by this book, a proletarianization of the workers in urban areas took place in the course of the industrial revolution. Drawn by new opportunities of work, they left their rural homes only to find themselves in many cases plunged into even greater poverty. As André Biéler points out, proletarianization means a state of alienation, social deprivation, personal degradation. It is, if you like, a condition in which the most tragic marks of human sin are displayed in the clearest possible light. None who wish to be faithful to Christ can fail to reflect on this. Nor can we ignore the transformation of the existing social order in the colonized regions consequent on the colonial enterprise, entailing the uprooting, exploitation and pauperization of the broad masses in the Third World. This is brought out very clearly in the contributions of Julio Barreiro, C. I. Itty and Sam Kobia to this volume.

When we heed these facts, we are stimulated to think and to take practical steps, always combining in dynamic interaction the concrete fact (the life of the poor, the existence of the poor) and the social fact (the form of poverty).[22]

That neither the existence of the poor nor the social fact of poverty can be attributed simply to natural causes or to personal conduct is obvious to anyone who examines the account given of them in the pages of this book. The fact is that poverty is in general the result of social injustice, of the exploitation of human beings by other human beings (we need only think of the way in which women and children were compelled to work during the last years of the 18th and the early years of the 19th century). Poverty is the result of economic growth of the kind which brings huge profits to some while offering others hardly even a bare subsistence. In other words, the existence of the poor and the social fact of poverty in the period in question cannot be explained simply in terms of individual behaviour, but also and chiefly by structural causes producing injustice, inequality, dependence and even destitution. In this context, therefore, the proclamation of the Gospel to the poor, the affirmation that they are heirs of the Kingdom of God, is inseparable from the effort to change the social conditions of the least favoured. That at least is how the awakened Christian conscience sees it. The proclamation of the good news must be rooted in practical action to secure a transformation of the structures which presuppose the existence of poverty and indeed tend inevitably to create poverty. The proclamation of the message of Jesus requires the Church to engage in action to promote justice at the social level (both institutional and structural)[23] and not simply at the level of the individual.

This unity between the concrete fact of the existence of the poor and the social fact of poverty, a unity which must constantly be heeded, seems to us also to require Christian communities to combine the demonstration of love with the struggle for justice. The practice of love leads us to seek to serve the poor, in whom Jesus Christ himself calls us to love and serve him in solidarity. But this still remains incomplete unless it is accompanied by militant action to promote justice at the level of the social structures and in accordance with the realities and the requirements of concrete social struggles.

This inseparable connection between the individual and the social, between the practice of love and the struggle for justice, between personal values and structural needs, also requires us to hold together in tension two sorts of action on these problems: action based on the decisions made by each individual in defining his or her own commitment to the struggle; and action which is necessarily pursued at the social level, in harmony with the individual type of action, but recognizing the autonomy of the secular and not falling into the trap which John Kent accurately defines as turning "political problems" into "theological issues".[24]

Secondly, this inseparable connection between the individual and the social leads us to the problem of the Church in relation to radical political and social changes. Pursuing our previous line of thought, it seems to us that, in certain circumstances, a charitable, critical and more or less reformist frame of mind is not enough. To bridge the gap between the churches and the poor, we have to some extent to accept their sub-culture, their world of values, their hopes, but also to engage in the social struggle to promote their cause,[25] establishing social justice in affirmation of our solidarity with the victims of the conditions which generate poverty. In opposition to such an attitude on the Church's part, of course, the argument is often advanced that the churches cannot become involved in action of this kind, because there is a radical incompatibility between religion and revolution. The atheism which usually accompanies popular movements is also adduced as a further ideological reason why the churches should maintain the gulf discussed in this chapter. It is also argued that the churches cannot approve the social disorder which frequently results from revolutionary action.

This view is a seriously-held position and deserves more attention than we can devote to it here. It will be discussed in the third volume of the present series on the Church and the poor. The first thing that needs to be said about it, however, is that in the stage of history we are now living through, the churches can be agents of revolution only in exceptional cases. It is true that they have been this in earlier times, but that was before the secularization process had burst upon the historical scene with the force that has characterized it in the last two centuries. The fact is that the only successful agents of revolution are those social forces which can sustain steady convictions in favour of social change and which organize themselves for effective struggle to that end. This is not the case with the churches today; as we have seen, they are estranged from the very sections of society on whose behalf the revolutionary forces are struggling. To pretend otherwise would be to indulge in pure fantasy. But, and this is the second thing to be said, this is not to suggest that the churches have *a priori* to adopt anti-revolutionary positions which would make them irrelevant for the people seeking social change. In other words, it is not necessary to assume automatically that the Church, by its very character, must always be a pillar of the establishment. This is the problem which Sam Kobia deals with. When the churches, on the basis of *a priori* definitions, adopt attitudes hostile to social change, this reflects a mental attitude which, according to John Kent, has shut them off from vast dynamic areas of society. Revolution is a political problem, at least when concrete conditions make it a practical possibility, and it cannot be defined without taking all its ramifications into account. To adopt an attitude to it on exclusively theological grounds is to fall into the error to which John Kent has drawn attention, and this is precisely what must be avoided.

Love of the poor, acceptance of the aims inspiring their struggle, these must obviously be measured by deeds. If the tension between individual commitment to the service of the poor and the decision to engage in the struggle for justice is maintained, this can very well lead in many cases to participation in profoundly radical and revolutionary social programmes on behalf of the Gospel. In such cases, the churches cannot adhere to an *a priori* opposition to revolution.

Thirdly, and in close connection with the last two points, we have to consider the nature and form of the Church when it tries to respond to Christ's presence in the poor. From historical experience, clearly only a minority responds in any adequate way. In many cases, the majority is indifferent, and in others is even hostile to the underprivileged sectors of society. André Biéler lays particular emphasis on this point, but it can also be seen in White's analysis of the rise and development of the "social gospel" in the USA, in Brakelmann's description of the situation in Germany, and Barreiro's account of Latin America. One possible theological interpretation of this appears in Biéler's essay: namely, to regard the conscious minority as the "faithful remnant" of the people of God, as in certain Old Testament passages. But it must be remembered that in the New Testament, the Church is thought of as a body, and indeed, as the body of Christ, in which a variety of ministries continues his service of love to human beings (1 Cor. 12; Rom. 12 : 4-8; Eph. 4 : 1-16; etc.). The body only functions properly when its members obey the directives of its head, that is, Jesus Christ. The problem is to know who is obeying the Lord's directives properly, the majority or the minority? Perhaps for the moment, the churches have simply to accept and face up to this internal division and facilitate free dialogue between holders of different views, so that they may grow together and make decisions which will correct errors and achieve greater fidelity to the Gospel.[26]

To follow this problem a little further: the problems arising from social injustice engendered by the industrial revolution and the colonialist expansion of the West undoubtedly produced rifts in the churches. People often evaded these problems by appealing to the need to witness to Christian unity on the basis not only of the image of the Church as the body of Christ, but also on the apostle Paul's words about the ministry of reconciliation committed to Christians. This ignored the fact that the unity of the body of Christ is for service, that the world may believe, and not for the abandonment of certain sections of society (least of all the underprivileged sections) which leaves them with no alternative but to reject the Gospel message. Furthermore, the doctrine of reconciliation was often appealed to without any heed to the basis of reconciliation in the cross of Christ. There can be no contact and peace between those who are at odds, unless they realize that they are subject to a process of judgment and radical transformation which has its prototype in the cross of Christ. This presupposes a substantial change in the situation, going far beyond the ambit of the Church and reaching with its influence right into society as a whole.

The problem of Christian unity cannot be separated from that of the unity of humankind. The unity in Christ is a unity of all, and fear of clashes within the Church cannot be allowed to prevent radical discussion of this connection. Because the unity in Christ is a unity of all, it demands decisions which are sometimes political, economic and social in character. The problem, then, is to define the criterion on which the decision is based. Is it the defence of institutional uniformity? Or is it, on the contrary, a decision in favour of the poor, the humiliated, an adoption of their aspirations for justice and freedom, an involvement in their struggles? Certainly, the two criteria are not mutually exclusive, though they are often presented as alternatives. It is appropriate, therefore, to choose the method of general dialogue, so that it is really the Church which accepts Christ's call through his poor.

Summing up

The problem of the relation between the poor and the churches constantly arises in our time. It seems to us important that it should be faced and that the inconsistencies and contradictions in our behaviour, which weaken the credibility of the churches' words and actions among the poor, should be overcome. From what has been said in this volume, certain lines of action emerge.

Firstly, the need to realize what the poor represent. From a theological standpoint, this means recognizing Christ's presence among them; by serving them, Jesus Christ is also served (Matt. 25 : 31-46). This not only means individual decisions, but also militant social action to achieve the aims for which the poor are struggling. It also means reviewing the churches' programmes and projects. Who are they intended to serve? Are they not actually paternalistic, reinforcing rather than helping to reduce the gap between the Church and the poor, even creating conditions which in the end lead the poor to reject ecclesiastical paternalism?

Secondly, a positive attitude towards the working classes and other poor sections of society means accepting them by creating opportunities for them to express themselves freely in the churches and providing scope for them to develop their talents. It means renouncing any attempt to control them or to "win them back"; instead we must stand solidly with them.[27]

Thirdly, and consequently, we need to restate in contemporary language just what a church of the people, or, to use the Latin American term, "a church sprung from the people",[28] can be. In some places, this church is beginning to emerge in the shape of the "base communities".[29] For the churches, this means reviewing their tacit alliances with the dominant groups in society, and with the rich. This is essential if they are to shake off the fetters which make them unreceptive to the claims and questions of the working classes. They must then reflect on ways and means of breaking out of this bourgeois captivity which keeps so many Christian communities estranged from the popular masses. On the other hand, they must also try to see more clearly how the Church's mission is related to the struggle for a justice which will put an end to poverty. As the Bangkok conference on "Salvation Today" declared: "Many Christians who for Christ's sake are involved in economic and political struggles against injustice and oppression ask themselves and the churches what it means today to be a Christian and a true Church. Without the salvation of the churches from their captivity in the interests of the dominating classes, races and nations, there can be no saving Church. Without liberation of the churches and Christians from their complicity with structural injustice and violence, there can be no liberating Church for mankind. Every church, all Christians, face the question of whether they serve Christ and his saving work alone, or at the same time also the powers of inhumanity. 'No man can serve two masters, God and Mammon' (Matt. 6 : 24). We must confess our misuse of the name of Christ by the accommodation of the churches to oppressive powers, by our self-interested apathy, lovelessness, and fear. We are seeking the true community of Christ which works and suffers for his Kingdom. We seek the charismatic Church which activates energies for salvation (I Cor. 12). We seek the church which initiates actions for liberation and supports the work of other liberating groups without calculating self-interest. We seek a Church which is the catalyst of God's saving work in the world, a Church which is not merely the refuge of the saved, but a community serving the world in the love of Christ." [30]

NOTES

[1] This was studied in my book, *Good News to the Poor*. Geneva: WCC, 1977. See also the abundant literature on the subject: MARIO MIEGGE: *I. Talenti Messi a Profito*. Urbino: Argalía, 1969; GUSTAVO GUTIÉRREZ: *Teología de la Liberación*. Lima: CEP, 1971 (English trans.: *Theology of Liberation*. London: 1976); *id.*, *Teología desde el Reverso de la Historia*. Lima: CEP, 1977; RONALD J. SIDER: *Rich Christians in an Age of Hunger*. Downers Grove, Illinois: Intervarsity Press, 1977; from a more technical and international point of view, but with a clear Christian tone, ALBERT TÉVOÉDJRÉ: *Pauvreté: Richesse des Peuples*. Paris: Editions Sociales, 1978.

[2] In this sense, we are trying to follow the method so often used with success by ROGER BASTIDE. Cf. especially *Les Religions Africaines au Brésil*. Paris: PUF, 1960.

[3] Events in 17th-century England are one example among many others.

[4] Cf. A. BIÉLER's chapter in the present volume.

[5] GUNTER BRAKELMANN shows this towards the end of his contribution to the present work.

[6] Cf. ALFRED N. WHITEHEAD: *Adventures of Ideas*. London: 1933. He refers to the role played by some Methodist communities in the campaign against the slave-trade and slavery.

[7] ANDRÉ BIÉLER brings out this fact very well by reference to the general support given by the churches to the schemes of the Holy Alliance for the maintenance of the status quo in Europe. JOHN KENT, GUNTER BRAKELMANN, NICOLAI ZABOLOTSKY AND MARIO MIEGGE also stress this characteristic of the Churches and Christians.

[8] Luke 7 : 18-22

[9] Cf. CARTER LINDBERG: "There Should be No Beggars among Christians: Karlstadt, Luther and the Origins of Protestant Poor Relief", in: *Church History*, No. 46, March 1977, pp. 313-334. Cf. also MARIO MIEGGE's chapter in the present volume, where he deals with "the new concept of charity and the impersonal regulation of social relations".

[10] Cf. JEAN LACROIX: *Dialectique de la Famille*.

[11] Cf. ANDRÉ BIÉLER's account of the second stage, when Christians realized the necessity for state legislative intervention imposed by the challenges of the social question in the 19th century.

[12] Cf. NICOLAI ZABOLOTSKY's chapter on the situation in Russia, section III.

[13] STEPHEN MAYOR: *The Churches and the Labour Movement*. London: Independent Press, 1967, p. 22: "In the great industrial centres, the working classes were already absent from the churches before 1850. In 1840, St Philip's, Sheffield, a "million" church, was the only Anglican church serving a parish said to contain 24,000 'labourers and mechanics', and until recently it had only one clergyman. It possessed 800 free seats, but far from being crowded, they were too often thinly tenanted."

[14] On this opposition between Bartolomé de Las Casas and the ecclesiastical institution, cf. the booklet of GUSTAVO GUTIÉRREZ: *Teología desde el Reverso de la Historia*, *op. cit.*, pp. 35-39, and especially p. 36: "For Las Casas, salvation —

the great concern of his whole life and the ultimate motive of his missionary work — is bound up with the establishment of social justice. Bartolomé regarded the connection as so profound that on two points at least it led him to reverse the order of problems traditionally envisaged by missionaries. Bartolomé de Las Casas pointed out in the first place that the Spaniards themselves were imperilling their own salvation by their treatment of the Indians. If they did not stop their robberies, looting and exploitation of the natives, they would indubitably be condemned, 'because it is impossible for anyone to be saved if he does not practise justice'. The salvation of the 'faithful', of those who claim to be Christians, is more in question than that of the 'unbelievers'. Secondly, Bartolomé had the prophetic depth to see the Indian more as a poor man, in the Gospel sense, than as an unbeliever, and for this reason he said in his letter to the emperor that if the death and destruction of the Indians were the condition for their becoming Christians, it would be better for them 'never to be Christians'. In other words, it was better to be 'an unbelieving Indian but alive' than 'a Christian Indian but dead'. A point of view which some would perhaps be quick to describe as materialist. But what strikes one is that, for Las Casas, salvation in Christ cannot ignore social justice."

[15] Cf. *Good News to the Poor*, op. cit., pp. 47-52, on the message of the Epistle of James on the subject, showing how the problem had already cropped up in New Testament times; those in the Christian community who practised "respect of persons" partiality incurred sharp criticism from the author of that epistle.

[16] The subject will be dealt with more fully in a third volume of this series, to be published as the findings of a working session which the Commission on the Churches' Participation in Development is to hold in September 1978 in Cyprus.

[17] Cf. PIERRE BURGELIN: "La Fin de l'Ere Constantinienne" in: *Foi et Vie*, 58, p. 8 ff.

[18] CHRISTIAN LALIVE D'EPINAY: *The Haven of the Masses*. UK: Lutterworth Press, 1969.

[19] HENRY MOTTU, in an excellent study on Joachim de Fiore, brings out how in the history of western thought these gospel sayings have nourished and sustained the hopes of groups claiming justification for their desire for social change. See *La Manifestation de l'Esprit selon Joachim de Flore*. Neuchâtel and Paris: Delachaux et Niestlé, 1977, pp. 259-264.

[20] Cf. *Good News to the Poor*, op. cit., pp. 14-18.

[21] *Ibid.*, chapter 3, pp. 23-35.

[22] The chapter of R. WHITE, JR. in this volume is very illuminating on this subject.

[23] In the course of the last few years, various ecumenical events have stressed this demand. For example, the Bangkok conference of the Commission on World Mission and Evangelism at the end of 1972 and the beginning of 1973 on "Salvation Today"; the December 1974 Montreux consultation organized by the Commission on the Churches' Participation in Development and the Commission on Inter-Church Aid, Refugee and World Service on "Justice and Development"; the WCC Fifth Assembly in Nairobi 1975, in particular the reports of Sections I, V and VI; the Valamo, Finland, consultation organized by the Orthodox churches in October 1977.

[24] Cf. JOHN KENT's criticism of F. D. Maurice's action.

[25] This was explicitly established at the WCC Fifth Assembly in Nairobi in the discussion regarding the continuation of the programmes of the churches' participation in development.

[26] Cf. A. BIÉLER in the present volume.

[27] An exemplary instance of this attitude was KARL BARTH's method as a pastor in Safenwil when he served in the organization of the workers' movement in this little town of the Argovia Canton of Switzerland. Cf. HELMUT GOLLWITZER: *Reich Gottes und Sozialismus bei Karl Barth*. Munich: Chr. Kaiser Verlag, 1972, pp. 8 ff.; and also GIORGIO BOUCHARD's introduction to the Italian edition of DANIEL CORNU's book, *Karl Barth et la Politique*. Turin: Claudiana, 1970.

[28] CARLOS MESTERS: *Una Iglesia que Nace del Pueblo*. Lima: Miec-Jeci, 1975.

[29] JETHER PEREIRA RAMALHO: "Basic Popular Communities in Brazil" in: *The Ecumenical Review*, Vol. 29, No. 4, October 1977, pp. 394-401.

[30] *Bangkok Assembly 1973: Minutes and Reports of the Assembly of the Commission on World Mission and Evangelism of the World Council of Churches*. Geneva: WCC, 1973, p. 89.

About the Authors

Dr Julio A. BARREIRO: lawyer, professor of Political Sciences. Author of several books and articles published in Latin America, USA and Europe. He is the editor of *Cristianismo y Sociedad*, the well known ecumenical magazine of Latin America. He is Uruguayan and a member of the Methodist Church.

Prof. Dr André BIELER: theologian and economist. He was pastor and chaplain of the student community in Geneva, where he also served as executive secretary of the Protestant Centre of Studies. He now teaches at the theological faculties of the universities of Geneva and Lausanne. Author of several books and articles, among them *La Pensée Economique de Calvin* (1961), *Le Développement Fou* (1973), etc. Swiss.

Prof. Dr Günter BRAKELMANN: theologian and historian, at present teaching at the University of Bochum. Previously, he was chaplain of Christian students in Siegen and also director of the Evangelical Academy in Berlin. Among his numerous books and articles, there is *Kirche, Sozialfrage und Sozialismus 1870-1914*. German.

Mr C. I. ITTY: psychologist and ecumenist. Engaged in the ecumenical movement, he has been working at the WCC since 1960. He was responsible for the department of Youth and Laity and at present he is director of the Commission on the Churches' Participation in Development. Author of many articles and essays. Member of the Syrian Orthodox Church. Indian.

Prof. Dr John H. S. KENT: professor of Theology at Bristol University, England. He has written widely on 19th-century religious history, and is publishing *Holding the Fort, Studies in Victorian Revivalism* (Epworth Press, London) in 1978. Methodist. British.

Mr Sam KOBIA: received his primary school and college education in Kenya. He then studied urban and community organization in the USA in 1972 and did graduate studies in City and Regional Planning at the MIT in Cambridge, Massachusetts, USA. At present, he is a member of the WCC staff in the sub-unit, Commission on World Mission and Evangelism. Kenyan.

Metropolitan George KHODR:	Metropolitan of Mount Lebanon (near Beirut) since 1970. He had previously been secretary general of the Orthodox Youth Movement in the Church of Antioch and editor of the magazine, *An Nour*. He studied law at St Joseph University in Beirut. Later, he took theological training at the Orthodox Institute of St Sergius, in Paris. A tireless worker for church renewal, Metropolitan Khodr is the author of a number of books on theology, church renewal, pastoral subjects and political issues, including the Palestine question. Member of the Holy Synod of the Greek Orthodox Patriarchate of Antioch. Lebanese.
Prof. Dr Mario MIEGGE:	of the Waldensian Church, undertook his University studies in Turin and Rome, where he acquired a doctorate in Philosophy. He now teaches at the University of Ferrara, where he is director of the Institute of Philosophy. Actively involved in trade-union activities, he collaborates in the formation programmes of the Italian workers' organization. He is engaged in the ecumenical movement both in his own country and at the international level. Author of *Il Protestante nella Storia* (1969), from which his contribution to this volume has been taken.
Dr Julio DE SANTA ANA:	editor of this book, was trained in theology, philosophy and sociology. He did post-graduate studies at the University of Strasbourg. Active member of the ecumenical movement in Latin America, he was secretary general of ISAL (Church and Society in Latin America) between 1969-1972. He was also director of the Department of Cultural Extension at the University of Montevideo. He has been a member of the Commission on the Churches' Participation in Development of the WCC since 1973. Author of various articles and books, among which *Good News to the Poor* (1977). Uruguayan.
Prof. Dr Ronald C. WHITE, Jr:	chaplain and associate professor of Religion, Whitworth College, Spokane, Washington, USA. B.A., University of California, Los Angeles; M. Div., Princeton Theological Seminary; M.A. and Ph.D., Princeton University; graduate study, Lincoln Theological College, England. Co-author, with C. Howard Hopkins, of *The Social Gospel, Religion and Reform in Changing America*. Presently working on a volume on the social gospel and racial reform. American.

Prof.
Nicolai A. ZABOLOTSKY:
of the Russian Orthodox Church, received theological training at the Theological Academy in Leningrad. He taught theology at the Saratov Seminary and at the Theological Academy in Leningrad. Master of Theology since 1969, he is also author of more than 80 articles published in the USSR and abroad. Since 1963, he has been involved in ecumenical studies at different levels. At present, he is a member of the WCC staff, working as study secretary of the Unit on Justice and Service. He is a citizen of the USSR.

Other Orbis books . . .

THE MEANING OF MISSION
José Comblin
"This very readable book has made me think, and I feel it will be useful for anyone dealing with their Christian role of mission and evangelism." *New Review of Books and Religion*
ISBN 0-88344-304-X CIP   Cloth $6.95

THE GOSPEL OF PEACE AND JUSTICE
Catholic Social Teaching Since Pope John
Presented by Joseph Gremillion
"Especially valuable as a resource. The book brings together 22 documents containing the developing social teaching of the church from *Mater et Magistra* to Pope Paul's 1975 *Peace Day Message on Reconciliation*. I watched the intellectual excitement of students who used Gremillion's book in a justice and peace course I taught last summer, as they discovered a body of teaching on the issues they had defined as relevant. To read Gremillion's overview and prospectus, a meaty introductory essay of some 140 pages, is to be guided through the sea of social teaching by a remarkably adept navigator."
National Catholic Reporter
"An authoritative guide and study aid for concerned Catholics and others." *Library Journal*
ISBN 0-88344-165-9   Cloth $15.95
ISBN 0-88344-166-7   Paper $8.95

THEOLOGY IN THE AMERICAS
Papers of the 1975 Detroit Conference
Edited by Sergio Torres and John Eagleson
"A pathbreaking book from and about a pathbreaking theological conference, *Theology in the Americas* makes a major contribution to ecumenical theology, Christian social ethics and liberation movements in dialogue." *Fellowship*
ISBN 0-88344-479-8 CIP   Cloth $12.95
ISBN 0-88344-476-3   Paper $5.95

THE CHURCH AND POWER IN BRAZIL
Charles Antoine

"This is a book which should serve as a basis of discussion and further study by all who are interested in the relationship of the Church to contemporary governments, and all who believe that the Church has a vital role to play in the quest for social justice." *Worldmission*

ISBN 0-88344-062-8 　　　　　　　　　　　　　　　　　　*Paper $4.95*

HISTORY AND THE THEOLOGY OF LIBERATION
Enrique Dussel

"The book is easy reading. It is a brilliant study of what may well be or should be the future course of theological methodology."
Religious Media Today

ISBN 0-88344-179-9 　　　　　　　　　　　　　　　　　　*Cloth $8.95*
ISBN 0-88344-180-2 　　　　　　　　　　　　　　　　　　*Paper $4.95*

DOM HELDER CAMARA
José de Broucker

"De Broucker, an internationally recognized journalist, develops a portrait, at once intimate, comprehensive and sympathetic, of the Archbishop of Olinda and Recife, Brazil, whose championship of political and economic justice for the hungry, unorganized masses of his country and all Latin America has aroused world attention."
America

ISBN 0-88344-099-7 　　　　　　　　　　　　　　　　　　*Cloth $6.95*

THE DESERT IS FERTILE
Dom Helder Camara

"Camara's brief essays and poems are arresting for their simplicity and depth of vision, and are encouraging because of the realistic yet quietly hopeful tone with which they argue for sustained action toward global justice." *Commonweal*

ISBN 0-88344-078-4 　　　　　　　　　　　　　　　　　　*Cloth $3.95*

MARX AND THE BIBLE
José Miranda

"An inescapable book which raises more questions than it answers, which will satisfy few of us, but will not let us rest easily again. It is an attempt to utilize the best tradition of Scripture scholarship to understand the text when it is set in a context of human need and misery."
Walter Brueggemann, in Interpretation

ISBN 0-88344-306-6	*Cloth $8.95*
ISBN 0-88344-307-4	*Paper $4.95*

BEING AND THE MESSIAH
The Message of Saint John
José Miranda

"This book could become the catalyst of a new debate on the Fourth Gospel. Johannine scholarship will hotly debate the 'terrifyingly revolutionary thesis that this world of contempt and oppression can be changed into a world of complete selflessness and unrestricted mutual assistance.' Cast in the framework of an analysis of contemporary philosophy, the volume will prove a classic of Latin American theology." *Frederick Herzog, Duke University Divinity School*

ISBN 0-88344-027-X CIP	*Cloth $8.95*
ISBN 0-88344-028-8	*Paper $4.95*

THE GOSPEL IN SOLENTINAME
Ernesto Cardenal

"Upon reading this book, I want to do so many things—burn all my other books which at best seem like hay, soggy with mildew. I now know who (not what) is the church and how to celebrate church in the eucharist. The dialogues are intense, profound, radical. *The Gospel in Solentiname* calls us home."
Carroll Stuhlmueller, National Catholic Reporter

ISBN 0-88344-168-3	*Vol. 1 Cloth $6.95*
ISBN 0-88344-170-5	*Vol. 1 Paper $4.95*
ISBN 0-88344-167-5	*Vol. 2 Cloth $6.95*

THEOLOGY FOR A NOMAD CHURCH
Hugo Assmann

"A new challenge to contemporary theology which attempts to show that the theology of liberation is not just a fad, but a new political dimension which touches every aspect of Christian existence."
Publishers Weekly

ISBN 0-88344-493-3 *Cloth $7.95*
ISBN 0-88344-494-1 *Paper $4.95*

FREEDOM MADE FLESH
The Mission of Christ and His Church
Ignacio Ellacuría

"Ellacuria's main thesis is that God's saving message and revelation are historical, that is, that the proclamation of the gospel message must possess the same historical character that revelation and salvation history do and that, for this reason, it must be carried out in history and in a historical way." *Cross and Crown*

ISBN 0-88344-140-3 *Cloth $8.95*
ISBN 0-88344-141-1 *Paper $4.95*

THE LIBERATION OF THEOLOGY
Juan Luis Segundo

"It is a remarkable book in terms of its boldness in confronting the shortcomings of the Christian tradition and in terms of the clarity of vision provided by the hermeneutic of liberation. Segundo writes with ease whether dealing with the sociological, theological, or political roots of liberation. His is a significant addition to the recent work of Cone, Alves, Moltmann, and Gutiérrez because it compels the movement to interrogate its own theological foundations. A necessary addition, in one of the more fruitful directions of contemporary theology, it is appropriate for graduate, undergraduate, or clerical readers." *Choice*

"The book makes for exciting reading and should not be missing in any theological library." *Library Journal*

ISBN 0-88344-285-X CIP *Cloth $10.95*
ISBN 0-88344-286-8 *Paper $6.95*

CHRISTIANS, POLITICS AND VIOLENT REVOLUTION

J.G. Davies

"Davies argues that violence and revolution are on the agenda the world presents to the Church and that consequently the Church must reflect on such problems. This is a first-rate presentation, with Davies examining the question from every conceivable angle."
National Catholic News Service
ISBN 0-88344-061-X   *Paper $4.95*

CHRISTIAN POLITICAL THEOLOGY A MARXIAN GUIDE

Joseph Petulla

"Petulla presents a fresh look at Marxian thought for the benefit of Catholic theologians in the light of the interest in this subject which was spurred by Vatican II, which saw the need for new relationships with men of all political positions." *Journal of Economic Literature*
ISBN 0-88344-060-1   *Paper $4.95*

THE NEW CREATION: MARXIST AND CHRISTIAN?

José María González-Ruiz

"A worthy book for lively discussion."
The New Review of Books and Religion
ISBN 0-88344-327-9 CIP   *Cloth $6.95*

CHRISTIANS AND SOCIALISM

Documentation of the Christians for Socialism Movement in Latin America

Edited by John Eagleson

"Compelling in its clear presentation of the issue of Christian commitment in a revolutionary world." *The Review of Books and Religion*
ISBN 0-88344-058-X   *Paper $4.95*

THE CHURCH AND THIRD WORLD REVOLUTION
Pierre Bigo

"Heavily documented, provocative yet reasonable, this is a testament, demanding but impressive." *Publishers Weekly*
ISBN 0-88344-071-7 CIP   Cloth $8.95
ISBN 0-88344-072-5   Paper $4.95

WHY IS THE THIRD WORLD POOR?
Piero Gheddo

"An excellent handbook on the Christian understanding of the development process. Gheddo looks at both the internal and external causes of underdevelopment and how Christians can involve themselves in helping the third world." *Provident Book Finder*
ISBN 0-88344-757-6   Paper $4.95

POLITICS AND SOCIETY IN THE THIRD WORLD
Jean-Yves Calvez

"This frank treatment of economic and cultural problems in developing nations suggests the need for constant multiple attacks on the many fronts that produce problems in the human situation."
The Christian Century
ISBN 0-88344-389-9   Cloth $6.95

A THEOLOGY OF LIBERATION
Gustavo Gutiérrez

"The movement's most influential text." *Time*

"The most complete presentation thus far available to English readers of the provocative theology emerging from the Latin American Church." *Theological Studies*

"North Americans as well as Latin Americans will find so many challenges and daring insights that they will, I suggest, rate this book one of the best of its kind ever written." *America*
ISBN 0-88344-477-1   Cloth $7.95
ISBN 0-88344-478-X   Paper $4.95